Christ in ancient America is a keystone to the Mormon faith. Dr. Bruce W. Warren's lifelong research, author Blaine Yorgason's talented writing style, and Harold Brown's scriptural background help bring the Book of Mormon alive as another witness of Jesus Christ.

V. Garth Norman, author of *Izapa Sculpture*
Director, Archaeological Research Consultants
Research Director of the Ancient America Foundation

This book presents rich archaeological and geographic evidences of Christ's Ministry to the people of Mesoamerica. It details many similarities now known about the life and culture of the Book of Mormon and the Old Testament peoples. I read these evidences with keen interest, and was intrigued by the wealth of new knowledge.

Edwin B. Morrell, PhD
Harvard University

It is my opinion that anyone interested in the title subject will enjoy and benefit from a careful reading of this book.

H. Smith Broadbent, PhD

I recommend a careful reading of this book. It makes a significant case that the Book of Mormon is an ancient record of historical importance, as well as being another testament of Jesus Christ.

H. Mark Nelson, PhD Harvard

Did Jesus appear to the people in the Western Hemisphere after his resurrection? The focus of this book is to present innumerable evidences to the incredible claim that Jesus did appear to the people of the Western Hemisphere. I recommend it to everyone as another witness for the divinity of Jesus Christ.

Darrell J. Stoddard

This must read book is additional evidence that the Lord has brought forth more new Book of Mormon enlightenment in the last two to three decades than in all previous years. Anyone who is serious about their Book of Mormon witness will want to read and use this book as a missionary tool.

Raymond C. Treat
President of Zarahemla Research Foundation

Blaine Yorgason's writing skills, Harold Brown's love of the Book of Mormon, and Bruce Warren's far-reaching knowledge of Mesoamerica combine to produce an inspiring and technically impressive book.

T. Michael Smith
Research Archaeologist, Ancient American Foundation

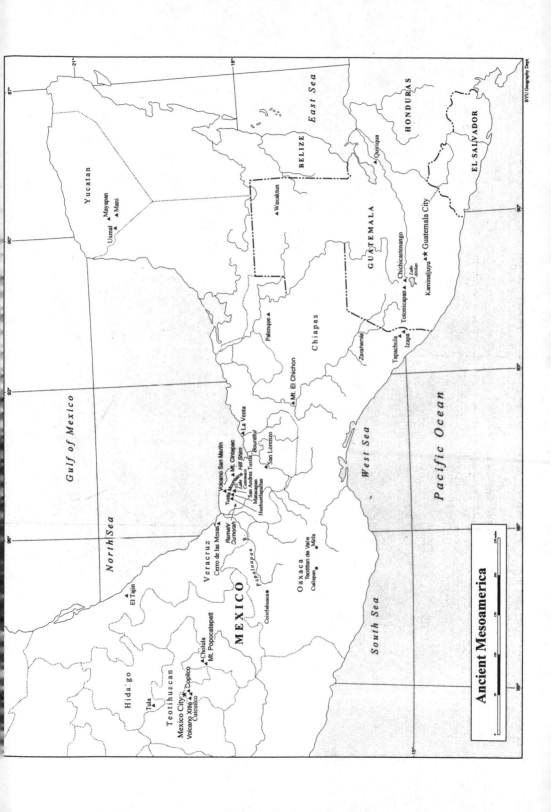

Ancient Mesoamerica

BYU Geography Dept.

Gulf of Mexico

North Sea

Pacific Ocean

West Sea

South Sea

East Sea

MEXICO

Yucatan

Hidalgo

Veracruz

Oaxaca

Chiapas

GUATEMALA

BELIZE

HONDURAS

EL SALVADOR

▲ El Tajín

▲ Uxmal ▲ Mayapan
▲ Mani

Tula ●
Teotihuacan ★
Mexico City ●
Volcano Xitle ▲ ★ Copilco
Cuicuilco ●
▲ Cholula
▲ Mt. Popocatepetl

Cerro de las Mesas ▲
Ramah/ ▲
Cumorah

Papaloapan

Coixtlahuaca ●

Teotitlan de Valle ●
Cuilapan ● ● Mitla

Volcano San Martín ▲
Tuxtla ▲ ▲ Mt. Cintepec
Catemaco ▲ ▲ Hill Shim
Lake ▲ *Bountiful*
San Andres Tuxtla ▲ La Venta
Matacapan ● ● San Lorenzo
Huehuetlapallan ●

▲ Palenque

▲ Mt. El Chichon

Zarahemla

Tapachula ▲
Izapa ●

Totonicapan ▲
Chichicastenango ▲
Lake ▲ Guatemala City
Atitlan
Kaminaljuyu ▲ ★

▲ Waxaktun

▲ Quirigua

87°
90°
93°
95°
97°
99°

21°
18°
15°

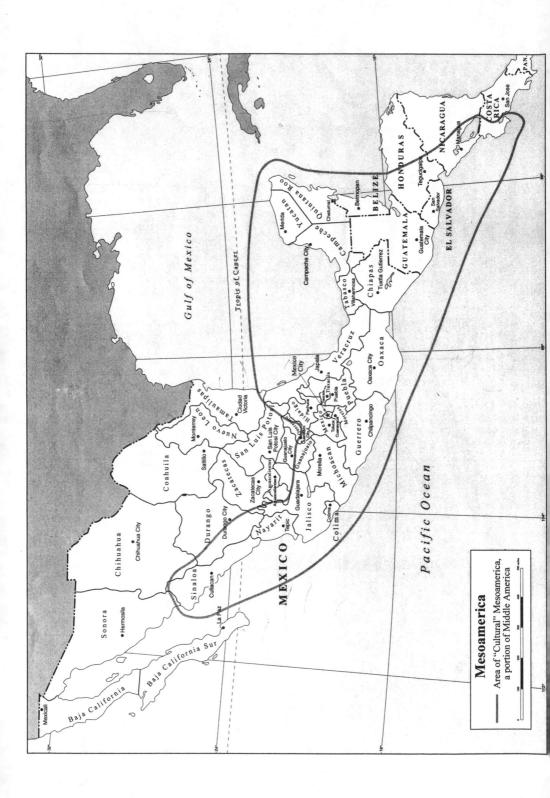

Mesoamerica

Area of "Cultural" Mesoamerica, a portion of Middle America

New Evidences of Christ in Ancient America

Blaine M. Yorgason
Bruce W. Warren · Harold Brown

BOOK OF
MORMON
RESEARCH
FOUNDATION

STRATFORD
BOOKS

Typeset and interior design by: TriQuest Books

ISBN: 0-929753-01-1

Copyright © 1999 Book of Mormon Research Foundation

Published by:

Book of Mormon Research Foundation

In association with:

Stratford Books, Inc.
Eastern States Office
4308 37th Road North
Arlington, Virginia 22207

Stratford Books, Inc.
Western States Office
P.O. Box 1371
Provo, Utah 84603-1371

First Printing: December, 1999
Second Printing: August, 2003
Third Printing: March, 2004

Printed in the United States of America

New
Evidences
of Christ in
Ancient
America

Author Bruce Warren at far right enroute to archaeological digs in Mexico, 1955.

THE MUSEUM AT TUXTLA, GUTIERREZ, CHAPAS, MEXICO WHERE THE ARTIFACTS ARE DISPLAYED IN 1962.

Co-Author Bruce Warren, Ph.D., and his associates on location. A dedicated archaeologist, Bruce lived for a period of eight years on or near the site while uncovering many artifacts, and learning more about the ancient inhabitants.

AT THE DIG IN CHIAPA DE CORZO IN 1956.

LATE CLASSIC STELA COMPACHE IN 700 A.D. NOTE THE STAR OF DAVID ON THE FIGURE'S EARSPOOL RING, AND THE BOATOHRTLIKE APPEARANCE OF THE HAT.

HAROLD BROWN'S FAMILY AND FRIENDS VISITNG XOCHICALCO, MORELOS, MEXICO

HAROLD BROWN STANDING BY STELA 67AT IZAPA, CHIAPAS, MEXICO.

TEMPLE OF QUETZALCOATL AT XOCHICALCO MORELOS, MEXICO

Table of Contents

INTRODUCTION

Although the New Testament paints a direct if brief picture of the birth, life, teachings, death, and resurrection of Jesus of Nazareth who is called the Christ, the Old Testament is also filled with prophetic references to him. These two books, combined as the Holy Bible, describe the first patriarchs of the human race and a particular portion of their posterity who are known today as the House of Israel—as they struggled to believe in and follow Christ's teachings.

Because Christ was considered by so many of these ancient people to be their God and Savior and because certain numbers of them actually knew him, much of their thinking and creative energy was devoted to him and his gospel. Today, we see evidences of this devotion in the forms of paintings, drawings, writings, architecture, sculpture, and other evidence spread throughout the Near East and portions of Asia and Africa. Because of these evidences, which, incidentally, are still coming to light, and because of the Holy Bible, which was kept as an official record, we call these ancient people Christians—or Christ-following people.

In 1841, John Lloyd Stephens published a book about his travels in Central America, Chiapas, and the Yucatan. His travels involved the geographic area known as Middle America or Mesoamerica. This geographic area consists of south and southeastern Mexico and also includes the countries of Guatemala, El Salvador, Honduras, Belize, and parts of Costa Rica and Nicaragua. The maps inside the front and back covers of this book show Mesoamerica. The major civilizations that occupied it and that we will be concerned with were the lowland and highland Maya, the Olmec culture along the Gulf Coast of Mexico, the Zapotec culture core in the Valley of Oaxaca, and the Valley of Mexico culture core.

But the name *Mesoamerica* involves more than this geographical definition. *Mesoamerica* also refers to the time period before the discovery of America by Columbus and before the conquest of Mexico. Therefore, the term *Mesoamerica* has direct reference to the great civilizations that flourished in Middle America during the pre-Columbus periods.

The great majority of the two American continents' archaeological sites that were in existence during the time period 2500 B.C. to A.D. 1500 are found in Mesoamerica. At the same time, only a small percentage of the archaeological sites dating to that time period are in North America.

It is also at these sites that the greatest preponderance of evidence is being found to show that these ancients were a Christ-knowing if not always a Christ-following people. Like those in the Old World, the peoples of the New World left behind evidences of their knowledge of Christ in the forms of paintings, drawings, writings, architecture, sculpture, and other cultural expressions. In other words, they too knew and worshiped the Lord Jesus Christ.

In this volume, we describe many such evidences from a variety of well-documented sources that confirm the ancients' knowledge of Christ and his mission of universal atonement, particularly as the evidences have been discovered in Mesoamerica. These new discoveries are startling and, as will be shown, are occurring at an ever-increasing rate.

Blaine M. Yorgason

PREFACE

Larry Ferguson, the son of the late Thomas Stuart Ferguson, has successfully brought together three unique scholars who manifest a deep interest in continuing the research regarding the historicity of the Book of Mormon started by Thomas in the 1940s.

As the project began to unfold, Harold Brown expressed an interest in coauthoring *New Evidences of Christ in Ancient America* with Bruce Warren. Larry was intrigued with this possibility for several reasons—especially because of Bruce's and Harold's love for the Book of Mormon and the Mexican people. Both men were convinced that the setting for events found in the Book of Mormon was in Mesoamerica rather than in upstate New York. The common thinking about and commitment to the Book of Mormon and its Mesoamerican setting among Thomas Ferguson, Harold Brown, and Bruce Warren set the stage for Larry's decision to team up Bruce and Harold on the project.

Once the manuscript was roughed out, Larry approached Blaine Yorgason with the request that he join Bruce and Harold as a third coauthor. Blaine, an award-winning author with twenty-five years of writing experience, was given the assignment to rewrite the manuscript by adding to, organizing and clarifying the work, and helping to make it more "reader friendly."

Harold Brown served as mission president of the Argentine Mission at the young age of thirty-two. His late and wonderful wife, Leanor, was also thirty-two years old when she began to serve as a mission mother to the returning soldiers of World War II who had accepted mission calls to Argentina.

The Browns soon found themselves living in Mexico City; and then, for the next thirty-five years, they played major roles in the development of the Church in Mexico and Central America. Harold served as the president of the first Spanish-speaking stake in the Church (in Mexico City), as the first temple president of the

Mexico City Temple, and as a regional representative for both Mexico and Central America. He was also instrumental in the early stages of Church education in Mexico. His rich background in and love for the gospel provide the spiritual impetus for his contributions to this book. Harold did his master's and doctoral work at Harvard's Littauer Center (School of Government).

Bruce Warren is a scholar's scholar. He earned a Ph.D. from the University of Arizona in archaeology and worked nine seasons with the New World Archaeological Foundation, a foundation started by Thomas Stuart Ferguson. Bruce is a meticulous researcher who has spent much of his professional career teaching courses in archaeology and the Book of Mormon at Brigham Young University. In the process, he has written countless papers and has served as president of the Society for Early Historical Archaeology and as president of the Ancient America Foundation. With Thomas Ferguson, Bruce coauthored *The Messiah in Ancient America*.

Bruce is proficient in interpreting the Maya and Mixtec codices. He is a man without guile, and his willingness to share his in-depth knowledge about the Mesoamerican culture is unparalleled. His contributions to this volume demonstrate his extensive grasp of the Preclassic Maya and the Olmec civilizations in relationship to the Book of Mormon. He carefully demonstrates his process of arriving at such dates as the visit of the Savior to the Nephites, the association of Quetzalcoatl with Christ, the names of Jaredite kings, and the destruction dates of the Nephites and the Jaredites. The evidences he presents contribute significantly to the historical authenticity of the Book of Mormon.

Best-selling author Blaine M. Yorgason, who holds an M.A. degree in history from Brigham Young University, is the author or coauthor of more than sixty published books, numerous essays, and nine video docudramas dealing with LDS Church history. Long a student of early American cultures, Blaine's novel *The Windwalker*, the story of an elderly Cheyenne warrior seeking meaning "atop the mountain of his years," was produced as an award-winning movie. His coauthored novel *Ride the Laughing Wind* is an imaginative and intriguing look at the Anasazi of the American Southwest during the eleventh and twelfth centuries A.D., and he has written three volumes of the series *Hearts Afire,* a historical/fictional account of the Navajos, Paihutes, Mormons, outlaws, and cattlemen of southeastern Utah during the late 1800s.

Charlie's Monument, Blaine's first novel, has been in print for twenty-five years; and his coauthored *Chester, I Love You* was filmed by Disney Productions as a made-for-television movie, *The Thanksgiving Promise*. *One Tattered Angel*, the touching biographical account of his family's experiences with their adopted daughter Charity, was awarded the Literary Award for Non-Fiction for 1997 by the American Family Institute, and the book also received the award for "Outstanding Book, Inspirational Category" by the LDS Independent Booksellers Association. For his cumulative work, which includes additional titles such as *Secrets, Spiritual Survival in the Last Days, Spiritual Progression in the Last Days, The Shadow Taker*, and *To Soar with the Eagle,* Blaine was presented Deseret Book Company's "Excellence in Writing Award."

My advice to readers is to read *New Evidences of Christ in Ancient America* for both its spiritual and technical flavor. Feel the love that Bruce, Harold, and Blaine express for the peoples of Mesoamerica. Let the Spirit confirm their testimonies of the gospel and of the Book of Mormon. And don't try to speed-read the chapters. Instead, dissect and analyze their contents as you expand your horizons about Jesus the Christ—the Messiah-Redeemer of Mesoamerica and of the world.

Joseph L. Allen, Ph.D.
Author of *Exploring the Lands of the Book of Mormon*

ACKNOWLEDGMENTS

As the authors of *New Evidences of Christ in Ancient America*, we thank our many friends and colleagues who have given us insights and encouragement about the manuscript. Without their spiritual and academic assistance, this project would not have reached fruition.

We especially thank four individuals who provided invaluable assistance in seeing the project through to its conclusion. We thank Ted D. Stoddard, professor of Management Communication in the Marriott School at Brigham Young University, for editing the manuscript. We thank Karyne Ferguson for her insights about shamanism and for her total support of the project. We thank Lee Nelson for the special support he has given to the book. And we thank Stephen Hales of Steven Hales Creative, Inc. for his work in designing the cover.

Above all, we thank Larry Ferguson for his dream and stamina in publishing and marketing the book.

Blaine M. Yorgason
Bruce W. Warren
Harold Brown

HOWARD W. HUNTER, AT THE FAR RIGHT, VISITS THE MAYAN TEMPLE OF INSCRIPTIONS AT PALENQUE, CHIAPAS, IN SOUTHERN MEXICO IN FEBRUARY, 1979. WILLAIM R. BRADFORD IS ON HIS IMMEDIATE RIGHT WITH OTHER FRIENDS, AND THOMAS S. FERGUSON IS AT THE FAR LEFT.

Chapter 1
THE PATRIARCHS AND THEIR REVEALED KNOWLEDGE OF CHRIST

The almost-universal belief or hope in a supreme being who exists beyond the sight or hearing of mortal man is in itself strong evidence not only of the existence of such a being but also of some degree of communication from that being to humans on this earth. Believers in the New Testament of the Hebrew Bible identify the source of this communication as "the light of Christ" or as "the true Light, which lighteth every man that cometh into the world" (John 1:9).

The boldest and most consistent confirmation of this enticing communication has come down through the ages from the patriarchs and Hebrew prophets—righteous men through whom that supreme being has revealed himself as a personal god in whose image and likeness all of us have been created and who has provided an infinite atonement so we might return to his presence. The first man to receive this information, of course, was Adam.

Adam and Eve and Revelation Concerning Christ

After Adam and Eve had separated themselves from the presence of God through an act of agency, the results of which are known as the fall, they could only "call upon the name of the Lord" but "[see] him not; for they were shut out from his presence." Nevertheless, after a period of time, the Lord began once again to communicate with them through a process called *divine revelation*, the sending forth, from heavenly realms, of pure, divine knowledge that always orients men and women toward God and his Beloved Son.

The record, which was compiled by Moses, states:

> And it came to pass that after I, the Lord God, had driven them out, that Adam began to till the earth, and to have dominion over all the beasts of the field, and to eat his

bread by the sweat of his brow, as I the Lord had commanded him. And Eve, also, his wife, did labor with him.

And Adam knew his wife, and she bare unto him sons and daughters, and they began to multiply and to replenish the earth.

And from that time forth, the sons and daughters of Adam began to divide two and two in the land, and to till the land, and to tend flocks, and they also begat sons and daughters. (Moses 5:1–3)

According to this account, three generations had been born since the fall of Adam and Eve and their entrance into a probationary state. But though shut out from God's presence, our first parents had not forgotten their divine creator. Moses' record continues:

And Adam and Eve, his wife, called upon the name of the Lord, and they heard the voice of the Lord from the way toward the Garden of Eden, speaking unto them, and they saw him not; for they were shut out from his presence.

And he gave unto them commandments, that they should worship the Lord their God, and should offer the firstlings of their flocks, for an offering unto the Lord. And Adam was obedient unto the commandments of the Lord.

And after many days an angel of the Lord appeared unto Adam, saying: Why dost thou offer sacrifices unto the Lord? And Adam said unto him: I know not, save the Lord commanded me.

And then the angel spake, saying: This thing is a similitude of the sacrifice of the Only Begotten of the Father, which is full of grace and truth.

Wherefore, thou shalt do all that thou doest in the name of the Son, and thou shalt repent and call upon God in the name of the Son forevermore.

And in that day the Holy Ghost fell upon Adam, which beareth record of the Father and the Son, saying: I am the Only Begotten of the Father from the beginning, henceforth and forever, that as thou hast fallen thou mayest be redeemed, and all mankind, even as many as will. (Moses 5:4–9)

Receiving this unparalleled communication concerning the life and sacrificial offering of the as-yet future Christ filled our first parents with unbounded joy, for now they knew they were not lost forever. As it is written:

> And in that day Adam blessed God and was filled, and began to prophesy concerning all the families of the earth, saying: Blessed be the name of God, for because of my transgression my eyes are opened, and in this life I shall have joy, and again in the flesh I shall see God.
>
> And Eve, his wife, heard all these things and was glad, saying: Were it not for our transgression we never should have had seed, and never should have known good and evil, and the joy of our redemption, and the eternal life which God giveth unto all the obedient.
>
> And Adam and Eve blessed the name of God, and they made all things known unto their sons and their daughters. (Moses 5:10–12)

Adam was taught not onlythe relationship of his sacrificial offerings to Christ's future redemption but also what he would have to do to receive the full benefits of that redemption: "This thing is a similitude of the sacrifice of the Only Begotten of the Father. . . . Wherefore, thou shalt do all that thou doest in the name of the Son, and thou shalt repent, and call upon God in the name of the Son forevermore. . . . That as thou hast fallen thou mayest be redeemed, and all mankind, even as many as will" (Moses 5:7–9).

Adam and Eve, now understanding that they offered sacrifices in anticipation of the great redemptive sacrifice to come, began teaching their children and endeavoring to build into their children's lives the appropriate teachings and practices that would enable all of them, through Christ's redemptive mission, to one day return to the presence of the Lord. However, their prerevelation children, responding to their agency and the influence of the adversary, "believed it not . . . and they loved Satan more than God" (Moses 5:13). Yet many chose righteousness, and through them continued the lineage of patriarchal prophets.

Revelation and the Patriarchs

Through such scriptures, we may follow the course of revealed knowledge of the Messiah-Redeemer down to Noah's time and then on through Noah's son Shem to Hebrew beginnings with Abraham—noting that all Hebrew prophets thereafter had revealed knowledge of the Messiah-Redeemer, whether in Asia Minor, in Palestine, or in the Americas. Peter confirms this important reality in these words: "But those things, which God before had shewed by the mouth of all his prophets, that Christ should suffer, he hath so fulfilled" (Acts 3:18).

Although this is not the place to examine the proclamations of all these ancient testifiers, a closer look at the words of a few of them will show that Christ's name and mission were thoroughly understood.

Enoch

For instance, Enoch, "the seventh from Adam, prophesied of Christ, saying, Behold, the Lord cometh with ten thousands of his saints" (Jude 1:14). And Enoch "saw the Lord, and he walked with him, and was before his face continually" (D&C 107:49). "And behold, Enoch saw the day of the coming of the Son of Man, even in the flesh; and his soul rejoiced, saying: The Righteous is lifted up, and the lamb is slain from the foundation of the world" (Moses 7:47).

Noah

Another example is the great Noah, of whom it is written: "And the Lord ordained Noah after his own order, and commanded him that he should go forth and declare his gospel unto the children of men, even as it was given unto Enoch. . . . And thus Noah found grace in the eyes of the Lord; for Noah was a just man, and perfect in his generation; and he walked with God, as did also his three sons, Shem, Ham and Japheth" (Moses 8:19).

The Tower of Babel

A short time thereafter, probably in the fourth generation of Noah's family, an event occurred that resulted in unique testimony about Christ and his future mission of atonement. Again according to the records of Moses, the descendants of Noah had gathered together on a plain in the land of Shinar. "And the whole earth was of one language, and of one speech. . . . And they said one to another, Go to, let us make brick, and burn them throughly. And they had brick for stone, and slime had they for mortar. And they said, Go to, let us build us a city and a tower, whose top may reach unto heaven" (Genesis 11:1–3).

Knowing as we do that there is only one divinely approved pathway back to the Lord's presence, which includes an "inner-man" course of faith in Christ, repentance of all sins, a broken heart filled with Godly sorrow for such sins, and a contrite or teachable spirit, we can understand why the Lord would not approve of a vainly imagined shortcut such as a brick tower.

In confirmation of this, Moses continues:

> And the Lord came down to see the city and the tower, which the children of men builded.
>
> And the Lord said, Behold, the people is one, and they have all one language; and this they begin to do: and now nothing will be restrained from them, which they have imagined to do.
>
> Go to, let us go down, and there confound their language, that they may not understand one another's speech.
>
> So the Lord scattered them abroad from thence upon the face of all the earth: and they left off to build the city.
>
> Therefore is the name of it called Babel; because the Lord did there confound the language of all the earth. (Genesis 11:5–9)

Ancient Gold Plates

Though we do not know who kept the records from which Moses, who lived approximately fifteen hundred years later, took the Pentateuch, we do know that there were those who dwelt on the plains of Shinar who kept records. Two of these were "a large and mighty man, and a man highly favored of the Lord" named Mahonri Moriancumr and his faithful brother Jared, who, as a record keeper of some note, recorded on thin plates of gold the experiences of the two families and a few others as they were being "scattered" by the hand of the Lord toward a new home. A part of this man's record, some two thousand years later, was included by a man named Moroni in a record of Hebrew prophets who dwelt in America, which record has now been translated and made available. (We will discuss this record at length in Chapter 2.)

Moroni writes:

> And now I, Moroni, proceed to give an account
> of those ancient inhabitants who were destroyed by the hand
> of the Lord upon the face of this north country.
>
> And I take mine account from the twenty and
> four plates . . . which is called the Book of Ether.
>
> And as I suppose that the first part of this record,
> which speaks concerning the creation of the world, and also
> of Adam, and an account from that time even to the great
> tower, and whatsoever things transpired among the children
> of men until that time, is had among the Jews—
>
> Therefore I do not write those things which
> transpired from the days of Adam until that time . . . but a
> part of the account I give, from the tower down until they
> were destroyed. (Ether 1:1–5)

A Lengthy Journey to the Sea

Moroni then details the successful efforts of Jared and his
brother to plead before the Lord that they retain their language,
that a few of their friends would also be allowed to retain their
language, and that the Lord, instead of simply scattering them,
would lead them and their friends to "a land which is choice above
all the earth. And if it so be, let us be faithful unto the Lord, that
we may receive it for our inheritance" (Ether 1:38).

According to the record, the Lord agreed to these things,
gave them instructions on how to prepare for their journey, and
then explained that he would meet them in a certain valley that
was northward of the plains of Shinar.

Moroni continues:

> And it came to pass that Jared and his brother,
> and their families, and also the friends of Jared and his
> brother and their families, went down into the valley which
> was northward, (and the name of the valley was Nimrod,
> being called after the mighty hunter). . . .
>
> And . . . the Lord came down and talked with the
> brother of Jared; and he was in a cloud, and the brother of
> Jared saw him not.
>
> And it came to pass that the Lord commanded
> them that they should go forth into the wilderness, yea, into
> that quarter where there never had man been. And it came

to pass that the Lord did go before them, and did talk with them as he stood in a cloud, and gave directions whither they should travel. (Ether 2:1–5)

For many years, this small band of people, whom Moroni's record calls *Jaredites*, traveled over mountains and deserts, building barges and crossing many waters, but never stopping until at last they came to "that great sea which divideth the lands. And as they came to the sea they pitched their tents; and they called the name of the place Moriancumer; and they dwelt in tents . . . upon the seashore for the space of four years" (Ether 2:13).

It was in the land of Moriancumer, at the end of those four years, that the Jaredites received additional knowledge concerning Christ and his future mission. The brother of Jared was chastened by the Lord for not calling upon the name of the Lord during those four years.

And the brother of Jared repented of the evil which he had done, and did call upon the name of the Lord for his brethren who were with him. And the Lord said unto him: I will forgive thee and thy brethren of their sins; but thou shalt not sin any more, for ye shall remember that my Spirit will not always strive with man; wherefore, if ye will sin until ye are fully ripe ye shall be cut off from the presence of the Lord. And these are my thoughts upon the land which I shall give you for your inheritance; for it shall be a land choice above all other lands. (Ether 2:15)

Revealed Knowledge of Jesus Christ

Following the Lord's instructions, the people once again built barges that were small, light upon the water, airtight like a dish unless a hole in the top or bottom was unstopped, and utterly without light. In these barges, they planned to launch themselves into the great sea. But Jared's brother was worried about the darkness in the barges, and so once again he knelt before the Lord, seeking instructions. This time, however, the Lord told him to come up with a plan of his own and present it before him.

And it came to pass that the brother of Jared, (now the number of the vessels which had been prepared was eight) went forth unto the mount, which they called the mount Shelem, because of its exceeding height, and did molten out of a rock sixteen small stones; and they were

white and clear, even as transparent glass; and he did carry
them in his hands upon the top of the mount, and cried
again unto the Lord. (Ether 3:1)

Moroni records at least a portion of this man's prayer, in
which, with fear and trembling, the brother of Jared praised God
and apologized again for his weaknesses. The brother of Jared
then declares:

And I know, O Lord, that thou hast all power,
and can do whatsoever thou wilt for the benefit of man;
therefore touch these stones, O Lord, with thy finger, and
prepare them that they may shine forth in darkness; and
they shall shine forth unto us in the vessels which we have
prepared, that we may have light while we shall cross the
sea. (Ether 3:4)

We do not know what the brother of Jared expected, but
certainly it wasn't what happened. According to Moroni:

When the brother of Jared had said these words,
behold, the Lord stretched forth his hand and touched the
stones one by one with his finger. And the veil was taken
from off the eyes of the brother of Jared, and he saw the
finger of the Lord; and it was as the finger of a man, like
unto flesh and blood; and the brother of Jared fell down
before the Lord, for he was struck with fear.

And the Lord . . . said unto him: Arise, why hast
thou fallen?

And he saith unto the Lord: I saw the finger of
the Lord, and I feared lest he should smite me; for I knew
not that the Lord had flesh and blood.

And the Lord said unto him: Because of thy faith
thou hast seen that I shall take upon me flesh and blood;
and never has man come before me with such exceeding
faith as thou hast; for were it not so ye could not have seen
my finger. Sawest thou more than this?

And he answered: Nay; Lord, show thyself
unto me.

And the Lord said unto him: Believest thou the
words which I shall speak?

And he answered: Yea, Lord, I know that thou
speakest the truth, for thou art a God of truth, and canst not lie.

And when he had said these words, behold, the Lord showed himself unto him, and said: Because thou knowest these things ye are redeemed from the fall; therefore ye are brought back into my presence; therefore I show myself unto you.

Behold, I am he who was prepared from the foundation of the world to redeem my people. Behold, I am Jesus Christ. . . . In me shall all mankind have life, and that eternally, even they who shall believe on my name; and they shall become my sons and my daughters.

And never have I showed myself unto man whom I have created, for never has man believed in me as thou hast. Seest thou that ye are created after mine own image? Yea, even all men were created in the beginning after mine own image.

Behold, this body, which ye now behold, is the body of my spirit; and man have I created after the body of my spirit; and even as I appear unto thee to be in the spirit will I appear unto my people in the flesh. (Ether 3:6–16)

And the Lord commanded the brother of Jared to go down out of the mount from the presence of the Lord, and write the things which he had seen; and they were forbidden to come unto the children of men until after that he should be lifted up upon the cross; and for this cause . . . [were their records kept], that they should not come unto the world until after Christ should show himself unto his people.

And after Christ truly had showed himself unto his people he commanded that they should be made manifest. (Ether 4:1–2)

Voyage to America

Filled with this amazing knowledge concerning the Lord Jesus Christ and his spirit form and role in the creation of mankind, Mahonri Moriancumer and the others embarked on their perilous voyage across the sea, "commending themselves unto the Lord their God." For 344 days, they were driven forth by furious winds, many times being buried in the depths of the sea and yet each time coming back onto the surface where they could obtain fresh air. And always they enjoyed the light from the stones the Lord had touched, and they "did thank and praise the Lord all the day long, and when the night came, they did not cease to praise the Lord" (Ether 6:9). And so finally the Lord brought them to their journey's end, and these nomads stepped forth onto the shore of their "choice land"—we believe somewhere along the Pacific coast of the state of Oaxaca, Mexico.

These Christ-following refugees from the unfinished tower on the plains of Shinar, known as the Jaredites, were now in Mesoamerica.

Chapter 2
JAREDITE CONNECTIONS WITH MESOAMERICA

The lineage history in the record or book of Ether, which was first translated and published in the nineteenth century, begins with Jared and proceeds through thirty generations to the prophet Ether. Twenty-three other family histories from the original Jaredite colonization, including Jared's prophet/brother Mahonri Moriancumer, are not available. It is Jared's lineage history that causes Moroni to refer to this original colony as the *Jaredites*.

As we read in the book of Ether, the Jaredites occupied territory in Mesoamerica or Middle America during a time period that began at about 2600 B.C. and lasted until shortly before the time of Christ. From the record, we must conclude that the Jaredites became a relatively advanced civilization that numbered in the millions. If this is so and if they had a knowledge of Jesus Christ and worshiped him as their God and Creator and if they reached an advanced-civilization stage in which they built major cites throughout their lands of occupation, we should be able today to find evidences of these things.

Ixtlilxochitl's Record

Mexican historians of the sixteenth and seventeenth centuries provide voluminous information of a Messiah who died for all mankind. These histories parallel the Bible and Jaredite accounts of Christ. Don Fernando de Alva Ixtlilxochitl (pronounced *Eesh-tleel-sho-cheet-l*), a native prince who lived near Mexico City, was one of the foremost of these historians.

Ixtlilxochitl was part Spanish on his mother's side but was descended from the pre-Conquest rulers of Texcoco, one of the three cities in the Aztec Triple Alliance. Therefore, he spoke Aztec. His mother owned the site of Teotihuacan, and it had been in the family since the beginning of the Late Postclassic period (the time span between A.D. 1250–1530). Perhaps for this reason, Ixtlilxochitl wished to link his ancestors back to Tula, probably Teotihuacan.

His history of Mexico is the earliest and most important
after European contact, incorporating as it does earlier
historical sources. He wrote *Relaciones* and the *Historia
Chichimeca*. The *Relaciones* consists of a multipart and
somewhat repetitious history of the Acolhua Chichimecs from
the time of Xolotl (thirteenth century A.D.) into that of
Nezahualcoyotl (his descendant and king of Texcoco) and up
through the Spanish conquest.

The *Historia Chichimeca*, also known as the *Historia
General de la Nueva Espana*, consists of ninety-five consecutive
chapters and treated Toltec, Acolhua, Chichimec, Tepanec, and
Tenochca history from the creation of the world up through the
Spanish conquest, but it was not finished. He apparently had access
to a large library of native records—he calls them paintings—for
he mentions several that have disappeared.

His manuscripts seem to have been completed between 1600
and 1625, for afterward they came into the hands of Siguenza y
Gongora (1645–1700, an antiquarian living in Mexico City) and
from him to the Jesuit College Library of San Pedro y San Pablo
in the Valley of Mexico.

Ixtlilxochitl's history was organized around the Four World
Age system—four time periods lasting 1,716 years each and
consisting of a Water Age, an Earth Age, a Wind Age, and a Fire
Age. (See Table 2–1, "Tultec Four-Solar Age System," that
follows.) Because the history is linked directly to the "Long Count"
calendar (a calendar system that counts days from a base date of
10 August 3114 B.C.) of the Maya, it is possible to assign dates to
Ixtlilxochitl's histories with considerable accuracy.

Thus, the Water Age, which begins with its creation in 4841
B.C., lasts until the great flood in 3126 B.C. Adam and Eve were
expelled from the Garden of Eden about 4783 B.C. After his brief
account of these events, Ixtlilxochitl introduces the second world
age:

> The Tultecas understood and knew of the creation of
> the world and how [God] created it, and the other things
> that are in it, such as plants, mountains, animals, etc., and,
> in the same manner they knew how God created a man and
> a woman from whom men descended and multiplied. . . .

And they say that the world was created in the year of the *ce Tecpatl,* and this epoch up to the *deluge* they called *Atonatiuh,* which means *age of the sun of water,* because the world was destroyed by the deluge; and it is found in the Tulteca histories that this age and first world, as they called it, lasted 1,716 years; that men were destroyed by very great storms and lightnings from heaven, and the whole world was without a thing remaining, and the highest mountains . . . were covered with water . . . and how men began to multiply from a few that escaped this destruction within a *Toptlipetlacalli,* which . . . means closed ark. . . .

And how afterwards men, multiplying made a very tall and strong *Zacualli,* which means the very high tower, in order to shelter themselves in it when the second world should be destroyed.

When things were at their best, their languages were changed and, not understanding each other, they went to different parts of the world, and the *Tultecas,* who were as many as seven companions and their wives, who understood their language among themselves, came to these parts, having first crossed large lands and seas, living in caves and undergoing great hardships, until they came to this land which they found good and fertile for their habitation.

And they say that they traveled for 104 years through different parts of the world until they arrived at *Huehue Tlapallan,* their country, which happened in *ce Tecpatl,* for it had been 520 years since the Deluge had taken place, which are five ages. (Hunter and Ferguson 1950, 21–22, 24–25)

Thus, the ancestral group called Tultecas, consisting of as many as seven men and their wives, left the Old World 416 years after the Deluge (2710 B.C.), traveled 104 years, and settled in southern Mexico at a place called *Huehuetlapallan* (2607 B.C.). There is general agreement among Mesoamerican scholars that this land of *Huehuetlapallan* is located in southern Veracruz. (Jimenez Moreno 1959, 1094)

The Four-Solar Age System

In the table that follows, Table 2–1, the "Tultec Four-Solar Age System," a chronology of Ixtlilxochitl's event sequences is presented.

Table 2–1
Tultec Four-Solar Age System

I. Water Sun:	Beginning of age to the flood: 1 Flint, 4841 B.C. to 1 Flint, 3126 B.C. Age destruction: 12.19.6.17.9 6 Muluk 17 Wo, Sunday, 6 October 3127 B.C.

II. Earth Sun:	Flood to earth destruction: 1Flint, 3126 B.C. to 1 Flint,1411 B.C. Age destruction: 4.6.6.7.15 4 Kaban 10 Kankin, Tuesday, 6 April 1412 B.C.
	    A. Zacualli episode: 1 Flint, 2710 B.C.
	    B. Arrival of seven Tulteca leaders to *Huehuetlapallan*: 1 Flint, 2607 B.C.

III. Wind Sun:	Earth destruction to wind destruction: Flint, 1411 B.C. to 1 Flint, A.D. 305 Age destruction: 8.13.7.16.2 4 Ik 5 Kankin, Sunday, 24 September A.D. 305
	    A.Quiname or Huixtoti migration: 1 Flint, 944 B.C., Ixtlil. Tomo 11:23, n.1. Astronomical convention at Huehuetlapallan at the end of the 9th calendar round of the Third or Wind Sun Age in which the concept of four Sun Ages was tied to the four natural elements (Veytia, Chapter 4). 5.10.1.11.19 6 Kawak 7 Ch'en, Tuesday, 2 September 944 B.C.
	    B. Huehuetlapallan conference: leap-year and equinox adjustment. 1 Flint, 7.9.12.8.19 6 Kawak 7 Ch'en, Sunday, 25 February 164 B.C.

IV. Fire Sun:	Wind destruction to fire destruction: 1 Flint, A.D. 305 to 1 Flint, A.D. 2019. Age Destruction:13.0.6.14.4 4 Kan 12 Mol, Saturday, 31 August A.D. 2019
	A. Tulteca flight from the area of Huehuetlapallan.1 Flint: A.D. 1136
	B. First king and queen at Tula. 7 Reed: A.D. 1155.

Equinoctial Precession: 25,740 year period in Mesoamerica, but modern astronomers say the period is 25,692 years.

Summer Solstice   Spring and Fall Equinoxes   Winter Solstice

One degree of a 360-degree circle equals 71.5 years in the equinoctial precession cycle. Twenty-four degrees of a solstice to equinox cycle equals 1,716 years. Fifteen 1,716-year periods equal the full equinoctial precession cycle of 25,740 years.

Jaredites in Mesoamerica

Moroni introduces us to the Jaredites by saying, "And now I, Moroni, proceed to give an account of those ancient inhabitants who were destroyed by the hand of the Lord upon the face of this north country"—a geographic area within Mesoamerica (Ether 1:1). The people Moroni alludes to left their original homeland about 2650 B.C. at the time of the confusion of the languages at the Tower of Babel. They knew about the Messiah-Redeemer, Jesus Christ; it was he who led them to Mesoamerica.

Ixtlilxochitl wrote in his history about a group of people who came from the great tower and were led to the land we know today as Mesoamerica. According to Ixtlilxochitl, they lived in an area in the northern parts of the land that are along the Gulf Coast of Mexico. (Allen 1989, 55)

Because of the remarkable similarities between Moroni's account of the Jaredites and the account of Ixtlilxochitl, we can easily assume that both accounts refer to the same people. In addition, the archaeological record verifies that the people known by the modern name of *Olmecs* are probably the same civilization referred to by Moroni and Ixtlilxochitl.

When it was first published, the Book of Ether gave a nineteenth-century suggestion that a major civilization—the Jaredites—rose and fell before other ancient American civilizations but overlapped geographically these other civilizations. In other words, the Book of Ether gives the first modern suggestion that the mother race of Mesoamerica was the Jaredites rather than the Maya as archaeologists had believed until about midway through the twentieth century.

In 1941, the Mexican Society of Anthropology sponsored a conference during which three archaeologists for the first time stated that a culture known as the Olmecs was the mother culture of Mexico (or of Mesoamerica). Since then, extensive archaeological and anthropological studies support, in general, the story of the Jaredite civilization in the Book of Ether.

According to Moroni's account of the Jaredites as contained in the book of Ether, the Jaredite civilization was destroyed, their last great battle taking place around the hill Ramah, which later was known to the Nephites as the hill Cumorah. Readers of the Book of Mormon have traditionally believed that every last Jaredite (Olmec) was killed as a result of that last battle.

However, after the last battle at the hill Ramah occurred, logic and archaeological evidence suggest that Jaredites (Olmecs) continued to inhabit Mesoamerican geographic areas other than the area surrounding the hill Ramah. An almost incidental comment about the continued existence of Jaredite people in the land southward is found in one verse in the Book of Mormon.

In the land of Nephi, king Limhi sent forty-three of his people to find the land of Zarahemla about 121 B.C. However, this group failed to find Zarahemla but did find evidence of the last battle of the Jaredites along with the twenty-four gold plates containing an account of the Jaredites.

King Limhi wanted the twenty-four gold plates to be translated, but no one among his people could accomplish that task. Later, after Ammon and his party from the land of Zarahemla located king Limhi and his subjects in the land of Nephi, Limhi said to Ammon:

> Knowest thou of any one that can translate? For I am desirous that these records should be translated into our language; for, perhaps, they will give us a knowledge **of a remnant of the people who have been destroyed**, from whence these records came; or, perhaps, they will give us a knowledge of this very people who have been destroyed; and I am desirous to know the cause of their destruction. (Mosiah 8:12; emphasis added)

Buried in this verse is a hint that Jaredites (Olmecs) were still living in the land southward long after the last Jaredite battle. "A remnant of the people who have been destroyed" suggests that some (a remnant) of the Jaredites (Olmecs) were still living long after the battle at the hill Ramah and were known to Limhi and his people who were living in the land of Nephi about 121 B.C.

We maintain that Jaredite (Olmec) people indeed continued to inhabit Mesoamerica after the last Jaredite battle at the hill Ramah. The archaeological record certainly supports that hypothesis. And the implications of this hypothesis are especially intriguing in connection with the Messiah-Redeemer. That is, all the various peoples alluded to in the Book of Mormon worshiped a supreme being. In connection with their worship, they all at one time knew about the Messiah-Redeemer and undoubtedly shared their knowledge and beliefs as they on various occasions interacted with each other. And both the Book of Mormon and archaeological records support the hypothesis that the Mesoamerican Messiah is Jesus Christ, the Redeemer-Messiah in both a premortal and a postmortal sense.

Jaredite-Olmec Connections

If the Jaredites were indeed the Olmec culture, as we believe they were, then our knowledge of the Olmec culture should also link the two cultures. To show that such is the case, we will use six personal names and three place names from the book of Ether to make a Jaredite/land northward connection with the cultural area of Mesoamerica. . The six personal names are *Kib*, *Shule*, *Akish*, *Com*, *Kish*, and *Shiblon*. The three place names are the hill *Shim*, the wilderness of *Akish*, and the land of *Heth*. Table 2–2 gives more detail on these nine names.

Table 2–2

Jaredite Names Used in Mesoamerica Today

Personal Names

Kib	Name of the sixth month in the Yucatec Maya calendar.
Shule	Name of the sixteenth day of the 260-day calendar in Yucatec.
Akish	Close parallel to the Quiche Maya *kaqix* (Caquix) of the *Popol Vuh*. The name combines kaq "red" and qix "feather" and means the scarlet macaw parrot. (Tedlock 1996, 237). (The *x* is pronounced as *sh* in English in Mesoamerican words and names.)
Com	Tzotzil Maya for "log stool" or "armadillo" (Laughlin 1975, 104).
Kish	Two meanings for this word are available: (1) "kix" in Yucatec and Chol Maya, meaning "spine," "thorn," and maybe "stingray spine" (Stross 1998, e-mail) and (2) "kix" in the Palenque hieroglyphs "feather" (Kelley 1965, 112, 114, Figures 23, 34, 49–53). The glyph at Palenque on the Tablet of the Cross is associated with the calendar name Nine Wind of Quetzalcoatl. Kelley's Figure 34 From Teotihuacan, Mexico, shows Quetzalcoatl with beard and feathers and emphasizes the serpent fangs. It could be that both the meanings are relevant, and that the feathers and fangs are both important.
Shiblon	The *Shib* or *Xib* part of the name is very common in Yucatec Maya—for example, Chak-Xib-Chak, Ek-Xib-Chak, Sak-Xib-Chak, Kan-Xib-Chak, etc.

Place Names

Hill Shim   In Yucatec Maya and other Mayan languages—for example, an ear of corn or kernels of corn is *ixim*. (Laughlin 1975, 419) In the Tuxtla Mountains of southern Veracruz, Mexico, one of the mountains is called *Cintepec* in the Aztec language. *Cintepec* means "corn hill." The Aztecs lived late in Mesoamerican history and were glossing earlier names with the equivalent in their own language. In Mayan languages, it would be *ixim* (as mentioned earlier, the *x* becomes *sh* in English).

Wilderness of Akish   As noted above, *Akish* is very similar to the Kiche Maya name *Kaqix* or *Caquix*. This name refers to the macaw parrot. The Tuxtla Mountains of southern Veracruz were glossed by the Aztecs as *Toztlan*, which means the place of the macaw parrots. The Aztec place name glyph also depicts a macaw parrot for these mountains (Covarrubias 1947, 26, n. 4).

Land of Heth   A land by the east sea mentioned early in the Jaredite account. The indirect hint for the location of this land centers on the meaning of the letter *Heth* in Hebrew. The letter *Heth* relates to the Big Dipper constellation and the number seven (Moran and Kelley 1969, 49, 81). The *Popol Vuh* account of Wukub Kaqix associates him with the Big Dipper, and his name means *seven macaw*. Could this tie the land of Heth to the Tuxtla Mountains region of southern Veracruz? Both the Big Dipper constellation and the macaw parrot are tied to *Wukub Kaqix*. Perhaps the land of Heth and the wilderness of Akish are adjacent to each other.

The personal name *Kish* gives us an especially intriguing connection between the Book of Mormon Jaredites and the Olmec culture.

In the Old Testament in about 1000 B.C., Saul's father was named *Kish* (1 Samuel 9:1). Interestingly, in the book of Ether, a Jaredite king, King Kish, lived about the same time. The book of Ether's account gives little information about King Kish other than his name. He was the son of a righteous king named Corom and the father of a righteous king named Lib (Ether 1:18–19; 10:17–19). Thus, King Kish was apparently one of the Jaredite monarchs.

Within the last twenty years, a new technique has been developed to translate Maya hieroglyphs. The process is a complex one that involves assigning sounds to as many of the glyphs as possible and then converting the sounds to the Maya language that is still spoken today by many native Mesoamericans.

Before the development of this method of translation, little more than dates could be deciphered from archaeological findings. With the new procedures, however, significant new information is now coming to light. For example, the name of the Jaredite king *Kish*, as well as his birthday, birthplace, and the day he ascended to the throne, may have been deciphered.

On the Tablet of the Cross at Palenque are found engravings that trace the genealogy of Kan Balam, the son of King Pacal who is buried in the great tomb there (Figure 2–1). Among the names of Kan Balam's royal ancestors is found what may be the full name of King Kish—U-Kish Kan, an ancient king of the Olmec culture.

Figure 2–1: The tomb lid of Pacal in the Temple of the Inscriptions at Palenque, Chiapas. (Courtesy of Merle Green.)

Kan means *serpent*. One of the meanings of *Kish* is *feathered*. Now that the Maya code is being deciphered, the name of U-Kish Kan has been translated as "he of the feathered serpent."

This symbolic connection between U-Kish Kan with the feathered serpent suggests a relationship to Jesus Christ, whom the Jaredites knew to be the Mesoamerican Messiah or the white god of Mesoamerica who is also known as "the feathered serpent."

This connection, in combination with the Old Testament account in which Moses lifted up the brazen serpent as a similitude of Christ, may indicate that the serpent motif as a representatio--n of Christ's condescension to earth was prominent in both Old and New World cultures.

U-Kish Kan was born on Wednesday, 8 March 993 B.C. In San Lorenzo Tenochtitlan in southern Mexico, an engraved stone known as Monument 47 depicts a king who has a serpent around his waist and who holds the head of the serpent in his hands. The serpent has feathers on its head. This monument is Olmec in style and dates to the beginning of the first millennium B.C. The monument's head is missing, but because of the dating and imagery of the monument, it could be a representation of Kan Balam's ancestor, U-Kish Kan, who took the throne on Wednesday, 25 March 967 B.C. (Figure 2–3). *Kish*, an Olmec and a Maya name, is prominent throughout the Jaredite history of the book of Ether. The component *Kish* is also evident in the compound names of two other Jaredite kings, Riplakish and Akish. Figure 2-2 shows the Tablet of the Cross at Palenque.

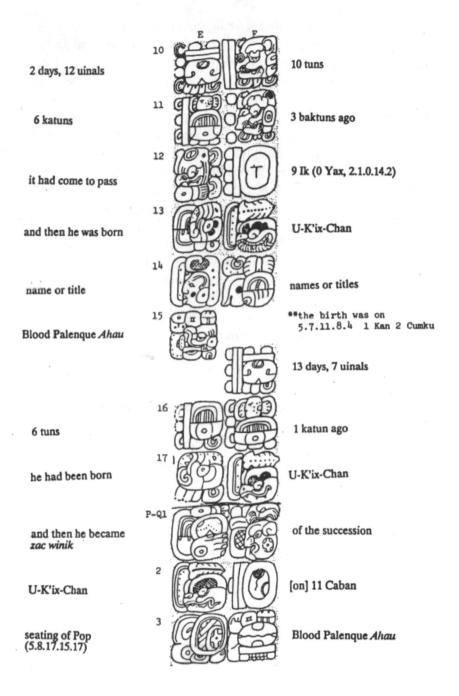

2 days, 12 uinals

6 katuns

it had come to pass

and then he was born

name or title

Blood Palenque *Ahau*

6 tuns

he had been born

and then he became
zac winik

U-K'ix-Chan

seating of Pop
(5.8.17.15.17)

10 tuns

3 baktuns ago

9 Ik (0 Yax, 2.1.0.14.2)

U-K'ix-Chan

names or titles

**the birth was on
5.7.11.8.4 1 Kan 2 Cumku

13 days, 7 uinals

1 katun ago

U-K'ix-Chan

of the succession

[on] 11 Caban

Blood Palenque *Ahau*

Figure 2–2: Palenque, Chiapas, Tablet of the Cross text referring to U-Kish Kan (formerly, Kan was read as Chan).

As can be seen, evidence continues to mount connecting the Jaredite culture with the Olmec culture. At the same time, information continues to surface suggesting that the Jaredite/Olmec culture knew about Jesus Christ as the Messiah-Redeemer—the Mesoamerican Messiah.

Jaredite Baggage

A shamanistic lunar zodiac calendar of 364 days was part of the cultural baggage brought by the Jaredite colony to ancient Mesoamerica. The book of Ether describes such baggage in this way: "Now the daughter of Jared was exceedingly fair. And it came to pass that she did talk with her father, and said unto him: Whereby hath my father so much sorrow? **Hath he not read the record which our fathers brought across the great deep? Behold, is there not an account concerning them of old, that they by their secret plans did obtain kingdoms and great glory?**" (Ether 8:9, emphasis added).

Though this account more particularly addresses records of secret societies or secret combinations, all of which were shamanistic or non-Christ in their views and philosophies, there can be little doubt that such records also contained shamanistic calendars.

Lunar Zodiac Calendars

Another calendar to be considered is the Lunar Zodiac calendar. A few years ago, David H. Kelley (1969, 143–94) analyzed the twenty-eight lunar mansions of some Old World lunar zodiac calendars that were widespread across Europe, the Near East, and northern and southern Asia. He concluded that the earliest evidence for this 364-day sidereal (measured by means of the stars) lunar calendar was from Semitic-speaking peoples of Mesopotamia early in the third millennium B.C. (Kelley 1969, 148–49).

Kelley also found such calendars in Mesoamerica. He learned that the Mesoamerican sidereal lunar calendar is composed of a year of 364 days grouped into fifty-two weeks of seven days and thirteen months of twenty-eight days. Each month had four, seven-day weeks. Each twenty-eight-day month represented two constellations in the nighttime sky. These thirteen constellations were observed in two different positions throughout the year: (1) the eastern sunrise horizon and (2) the western sunrise horizon (Table 2–3).

Table 2–3
Modified 364-day Sidereal Year

(365.2564 days to 364 days)^

Sunrise

Western horizon		Eastern horizon
12. Rattlesnake #2:	Pleiades	Libra: Quetzal #1+
1. Sea Turtle(*ac*)#3:	Orion	Scorpius:Scorpion (*sinaan*) #4
3. Muwan Owl #5:	Gemini	Sagittarius: Fishes #6*
5. Frog #8:	Regulus (Leo W.)	Capricornius: Vulture#7
7. Peccary #10:	Ursa Major (Leo E.)	Aquarius: Bat #9
9. Chak-Peccary #11	Crux	Pisces: Skeleton #12
11. Quetzal #1:	Libra	Aries: Jaguar #13
13. Scorpion (*sinaan*) #4:	Scorpius	Pleiades: Rattlesnake (*tzab*) #2-
2. Fishsnake #6:	Sagittarius	Orion: Sea Turtle (*ac*)#3
4. Vulture #7:	Capricornius	Gemini: Muwan Owl #5
6. Bat #9:	Aquarius	Regulus (Leo W.): Frog #8
8. Skeleton #12:	Pisces	Ursa Major (Leo E.): Peccary #10
10. Jaguar #13:	Aries	Crux: Chak-Peccary#11

^ The sidereal year is divided into 13 stations and each station is represented by a constellation.

\+ November 10 is the beginning of the calendar year of 364 days. Each month has 28 days divided into four, 7-day weeks.

* The vertical line connecting two constellations indicates that these two constellations are next to each other in the nighttime sky.

- The pleiades on the western horizon represents this constellation's mid-night zenith to western sunset descent. The eastern horizon represents the Pleiades in the process of helical rising.

The Sacred Almanac Calendar

Let us now return to the Sacred Almanac calendar. In ancient Mesoamerica, the Maya used thirteen numerical head glyphs in two different ways: (1) a number from 1–13 series for each sidereal lunar month of the year and (2) a number from 1–13 (a trecena) for thirteen special days in the 260-day ritual or Sacred Almanac calendar. This latter usage was as follows: 1 Kaban, 2 Etsnab, 3 Kawak, 4 Ahaw, 5 Imix, 6 Ik, 7 Akbal, 8 Kan, 9 Chicchan, 10 Kimi, 11 Manik, 12 Lamat, and 13 Muluk (Table 2–4). The other seven days of the twenty-day sacred calendar did not have a special head number reserved for them.

Table 2–4

The Trecenas of the 260-Day Ritual Calendar

		1	2	3	4	5	6	7	8	9	10	11	12	13	
Crocodile	1	1	8	2	9	3	10	4	11	5	12	6	13	7	Imix
Wind	2	2	9	3	10	4	11	5	12	6	13	7	1	8	Ik
Night	3	3	10	4	11	5	12	6	13	7	1	8	2	9	Akba
Iguana	4	4	11	5	12	6	13	7	1	8	2	9	3	10	Kan
Serpent	5	5	12	6	13	7	1	8	2	9	3	10	4	11	Chicc
Death	6	6	13	7	1	8	2	9	3	10	4	11	5	12	Kim
Deer	7	7	1	8	2	9	3	10	4	11	5	12	6	13	Mani
Rabbit	8	8	2	9	3	10	4	11	5	12	6	13	7	1	Lama
Rain	9	9	3	10	4	11	5	12	6	13	7	1	8	2	Mulu
Foot	10	10	4	11	5	12	6	13	7	1	8	2	9	3	Ok
Monkey	11	11	5	12	6	13	7	1	8	2	9	3	10	4	Chue
Tooth	12	12	6	13	7	1	8	2	9	3	10	4	11	5	Eb
Reed	13	13	7	1	8	2	9	3	10	4	11	5	12	6	Ben
Jaguar	14	1	8	2	9	3	10	4	11	5	12	6	13	7	Ix
Eagle	15	2	9	3	10	4	11	5	12	6	13	7	1	8	Men
Owl	16	3	10	4	11	5	12	6	13	7	1	8	2	9	Kib
Quake	17	4	11	5	12	6	13	7	1	8	2	9	3	10	Kaba
Flint	18	5	12	6	13	7	1	8	2	9	3	10	4	11	Etzna
Storm	19	6	13	7	1	8	2	9	3	10	4	11	5	12	Kawa
Lord	20	7	1	8	2	9	3	10	4	11	5	12	6	13	Ahav

The best single example of the 364-day calendar is located on pages 23–24 of the Maya *Codex Paris*. Recent research has dated this example beginning on Thursday, 10 November A.D. 755, or 9.16.10.04.08 12 Lamat 1 Muwan on Mesoamerican calendars (Bricker and Bricker 1992, 148–83). Twelve Lamat is likely the starting date because it is in the 168th position in the 260-day ritual calendar (Paxton 1992, 244, n. 11). (See Table 2-4.) The Maya manipulated the 364-day calendar by using multiples of 168 days or six 28-day months to involve both constellation positions at the sunrise eastern and western horizons.

If we use the *Codex Paris* example of the 364-day calendar, it is obvious that if we start with 12 Lamat, the following twelve months will start with the numbers 1, 3, 5, 7, 9, 11, 13, 2, 4, 6, 8, and 10 respectively. (See Table 2-3.) This is the result of systematically proceeding through the 260 days of the ritual calendar by units of twenty-eight days.

Because the 364-day calendar is 1.2422 days shorter than the true tropical year of 365.2422 days, the Maya needed to adjust this calendar periodically to keep it in line with the tropical year calendar. One way is to add twenty days every sixteen years by retaining the same day name (there are only twenty day names in this calendar) but changing the accompanying number for the day name. This procedure would take care of the needed sixteen days in sixteen vague years of 365 days plus four days for the leap-year adjustments. However, in other ways the Maya could have corrected this calendar.

As stated above, the 364-day calendar has a long history in the Old World (Moran and Kelley 1969; Graves 1957, 16; and Gruener 1987, 223–25, 300–2, and 318–21) and probably diffused to the New World early enough to be the parent calendar for later Mesoamerican calendars.

Vague Solar Year Calendar

However, those who have some acquaintance with Mesoamerican calendars know that the most widely used calendar was a Vague Solar year calendar, or one that was composed of 365 days with no allowance for regular leap-year adjustments. Recently (Edmonson 1988), a basic guide to Mesoamerican 365-day calendars has documented the earliest appearance of this calendar as the *Cuicuilco* calendar, which begins with the summer solstice date of Thursday, 21 June 739 B.C., or 6.00.09.08.01 6 Imix 4 Mol (Edmonson 1988, 115). Nearly a hundred known variants of the Vague Solar year calendar were apparently derived from this Cuicuilco calendar.

Nevertheless, the 364-day sidereal lunar calendar was probably earlier in Mesoamerica and continued in parallel usage throughout the history of Mesoamerican civilizations. For that reason, we believe that the first Jaredite calendar was most likely the 364-day sidereal lunar calendar. During the latter part of the Jaredite history, the Jaredites may have developed or been exposed to the other calendars that are typical of Mesoamerica.

Serpents

One of the fascinating episodes in Jaredite history is the account of poisonous serpents being a threat to their survival. Moroni writes as follows:

> And it came to pass [in the days of King Heth] that there began to be a great dearth upon the land, and the inhabitants began to be destroyed exceedingly fast because of the dearth, for there was no rain upon the face of the earth.
>
> And there came forth poisonous serpents also upon the face of the land, and did poison many people. And it came to pass that their flocks began to flee before the poisonous serpents, towards the land southward. . . .
>
> And it came to pass that there were many of them which did perish by the way; nevertheless, there were some which fled into the land southward.
>
> And it came to pass that the Lord did cause the serpents that they should pursue them no more, but that they should hedge up the way that the people could not pass, that whoso should attempt to pass might fall by the poisonous serpents. (Ether 9:30–33)

Seven kings later in Jaredite history, we are told that finally the plague of poisonous serpents was resolved:

> And it came to pass that Kish passed away also, and Lib reigned in his stead.
>
> And it came to pass that Lib also did that which was good in the sight of the Lord. And in the days of Lib the poisonous serpents were destroyed. Wherefore they did go into the land southward, to hunt food for the people of the

land, for the land was covered with animals of the forest.
And Lib also himself became a great hunter.

And they built a great city by the narrow neck of land,
by the place where the sea divides the land. (Ether 10:18–20)

Do we have any archaeological evidence from Jaredite times of a focus on serpents? We will consider such evidence from three Olmec archaeological sites in ancient Mesoamerica: Palenque, Chiapas, Mexico; San Lorenzo Tenochtitlan, southern Veracruz, Mexico; and La Venta, Tabasco, Mexico.

First, hieroglyphic writing on the Tablet of the Cross at Palenque speaks of an ancestral king mentioned earlier by the name of U-Kish Kan ("he of the feathered serpent" or "he of the serpent's fang"). (King Kish was born Wednesday, 8 March 993 B.C., 5.07.11.08.04 1 Kan 2 Kumku. He acceded to the throne Wednesday, 25 March 967 B.C., 5.08.17.15.17 11 Kaban 0 Pop [0 Pop is New Year's Day in the Tikal Calendar]). U-Kish Kan was considered the ancient divine founder of the Palenque dynasty of kings, even though he was not from Palenque originally (see Figure 2–1).

Second, as mentioned earlier, Monument 47 from San Lorenzo Tenochtitlan is a king who has a serpent around his waist and holds the head of the serpent in his hands (Figure 2–3). The serpent has feathers on its head (Figure 2–4). This monument is Olmec in style, and dates to the beginning of the first millennium B.C. The monument has the head missing, but the imagery of the monument equals that of U-Kish Kan from the much later Tablet of the Cross at Palenque. Could the San Lorenzo monument represent U-Kish Kan?

Figure 2–3: San Lorenzo, Veracruz, Monument 47, showing a decapitated serpent ruler.

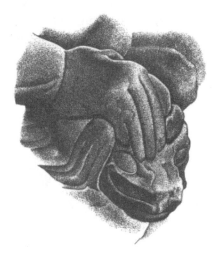

Figure 2–4: San Lorenzo Monument 47, showing a close view of the feathered serpent head.

Michael D. Coe and Richard A. Diehl comment on Monument 47 at San Lorenzo Tenochtitlan:

> The serpent with plumes or wings attached to the head or just behind the head is a motif which shows up at other Olmec sites: in Painting 2 in the Juxtlahuaca cave murals, in Painting I-C at Oxtotitlan (Grove 1970: fig. 12), and in Monument 19 at La Venta. Joralemon (1976) subsumes these creatures in his all-encompassing "dragon," God I, but it seems compelling to us that the plumed serpent must also be a manifestation of the god later known as Quetzalcoatl. . . . Apparently it has Olmec origins. (Coe and Diehl 1980, 356)

Third, the layout of the central part of the archaeological site of La Venta (Figure 2–5) represents a serpent focus: the large, volcanic-shaped mound representing the upturned head of a serpent, the ridges at the site of the serpent body, and the diamond-shaped tassels on two of the buried serpentine panels (Figure 2–6) representing the body design on a variety of rattlesnakes (Figure 2–7) and so forth. (Luckert 1976)

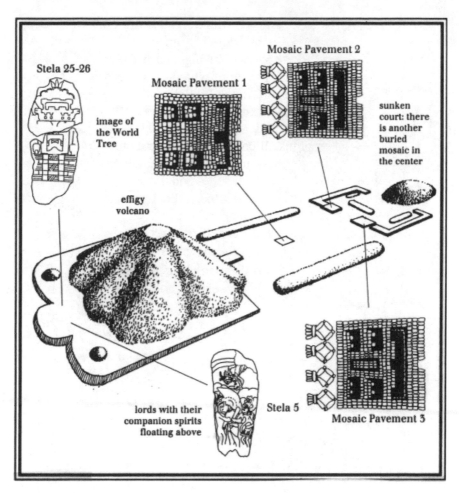

Figure 2–5: La Venta Complex A in Tabasco.

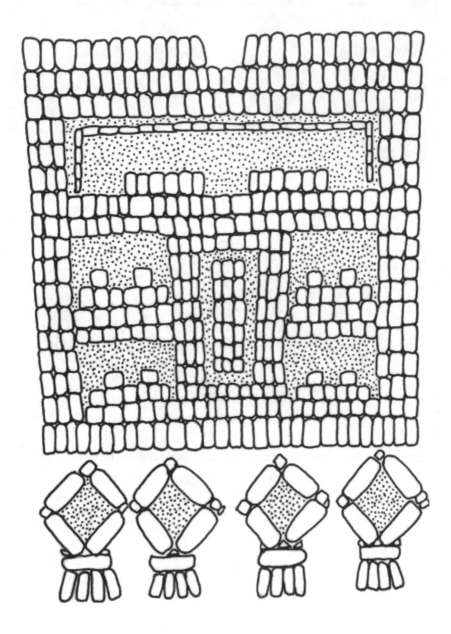

Figure 2–6: A La Venta serpent panel.

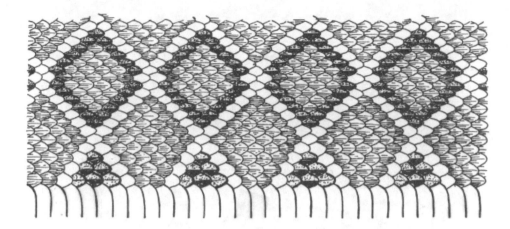

Figure 2–7: Diamond-shaped designs of a rattlesnake.

The implication is that the serpent for the Olmecs and/or the Jaredites became a symbol for the fertile earth and that corn or maize grows from its back or from the earth. By the way, we do have a good archaeological example, from the Olmec/Jaredite period, of the combination of fertilizing rain, corn plants, serpent mouth cave opening, and a human figure holding an Olmec serpent year bearer calendar unit on Monument 1 at Chalcatzingo, Morelos (Figure 2–8). There is also a much later Aztec monument that has rattles from a snake intertwined with corn cobs (Figure 2–9).

Figure 2–8: Chalcatzingo, Morelos, Monument 1, maize or corn symbolism in a ritual context.

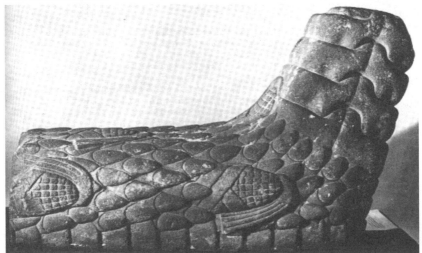

Figure 2–9: Aztec monument with rattlesnake combined with ears of corn.

A tentative hypothesis to explain the above information could be stated as follows: At least by the days of the Jaredite King Kish, a shamanistic cult that focused on the serpent was developing. Kish's son King Lib built a city in the narrow neck of land at La Venta, Tabasco, Mexico, that emphasized the serpent cult. Much later in time, the kings at Palenque, Chiapas, Mexico, were claiming divine kingship from this ancestral king, U-Kish Kan, who probably originally resided at San Lorenzo Tenochtitlan, Veracruz, Mexico. The imagery, dating, names, and locations all make sense. However, all hypotheses are designed to be tested, and so this hypothesis should be subjected to rigorous testing.

It is believed that the shamanistic creation story was enacted in archaeological features at the Olmec site of La Venta (Reilly 1989).

The Cult of the Divine Kings: Imitators of Christ

The cult of the Divine King with decapitation as part of its rituals was also part of the cultural baggage that was carried from the ancient Near East to ancient Mesoamerica. The decapitated Divine Kings won resurrection through torture and the shedding of their blood. In this manner, they believed they could resurrect themselves and so become their own Messiah-Redeemer. Thus, they were imitating the true Messiah-Redeemer and denying he was the only one who had the power and authority for the resurrection process.

By way of explanation, First Father, or, in resurrection, the corn deity of the Maya, is described by Douglas Gillette in the following manner:

> This Holy-First-Father-Decapitated-Dead-Creating-Thing is the singing ball of the Maya ballgame. It is the harvested and replanted "little skull" corn kernel [*ishim*] that made human life possible. It is the severed head on the Otherworldly platter and the bloody head on the tripod plate that powers the Cosmic resurrection. It is also the so-called Cauac and Waterlily Monsters—all manifestations of the ultimate, all-powerful, life-generation head of First Father. Not unlike the gruesome but redeeming image of the crucified Christ, this awesome Maya image is the closest the shamans and artists came to depicting the nameless Mystery of life-death from which all things arise, by which they are sustained, and into which they are drawn back,

only to be born again. The Holy Singing Skull Thing was their most profound image of the terrible and wonderful Power they experienced in every aspect of the cosmos. (Gillette 1997, 81)

First Father's head is sometimes shown as an ear of corn or a kernel of corn. Note the following statements concerning the shamanistic resurrection explanation:

We know that the ball of the sacred pitz [ballgame] carried a number of symbolic meanings for the Maya, one of which identified it with both the physical and spiritual sun. Like the maize kernel that created new life from its "decapitation" and "burial" in Xibalba [Underworld], the sun, through its decapitation sacrifice at the hands of Venus, also rose again to create and sustain all living things. In the end, the sun and the maize-kernel head of First Father/First Lord were one and the same Holy Thing. (Gillette 1997, 181)

The Cosmic Turtle Shell is the supernatural maize kernel that bursts open to allow the Resurrection Body to soar up from the realm of death into the world of Eternal life. (Gillette 1997, 198)

It is not surprising that First Lord goes to corn mountain to start repopulating the world after the chaos and darkness of the flood. Nor is it surprising that future divine kings stood on corn mountain to begin their dynastic reign. At the Maya site of Palenque, we see Kan Bahlum (Tablet of the Foliated Cross), in the dress of the Maize God, standing on the head of a deity (Figure 2–10). In the eyes of this deity are glyphs that say *Uitz nal*, or hill of corn. (Miller and Taube 1993, 130) For a more detailed analysis of this shamanistic view of resurrection, see Douglas Gillette's *The Shaman's Secret: The Lost Resurrection Teachings of the Ancient Maya* (1997).

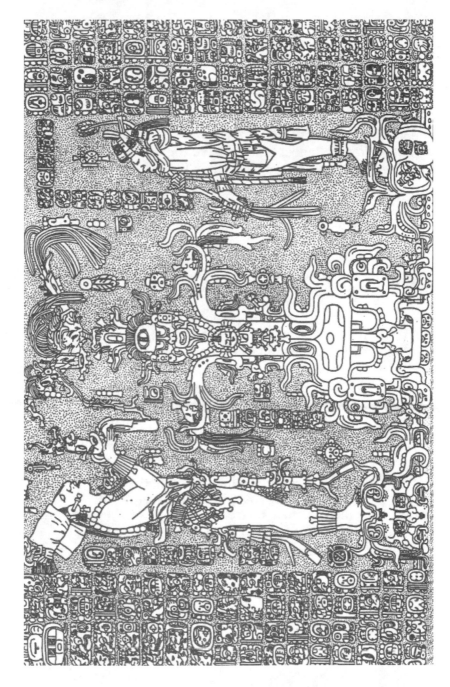

Figure 2-10: Tablet of the Foliated Cross showing Kan Bahlum in the dress of the Maize God and standing on the head of a deity.

Conclusion

In this chapter, we have seen how the Jaredite history ties their land northward to Mesoamerica through personal and place names. We have seen that the 364-day lunar calendar is key to the lunar zodiac and was probably brought to ancient Mesoamerica from the ancient Near East. The Jaredite story of the poisonous serpents is reflected in Olmec archaeology, especially at the sites of San Lorenzo Tenochtitlan, La Venta, and Palenque. Many elements of the shamanistic creation story and divine kingship concepts are noted at these archaeological sites. The Jaredite account of the origin of secret combinations or secret societies has several of the elements of the shamanistic divine kingship cult.

Finally, it is very clear that there are many similar elements between the shamanistic and divinely revealed accounts of creation and kingship, but the differences are profound and very important. The shamanistic traits are important for understanding the Jaredite history, but they also make a good case for the migration of the Jaredites from the ancient Near East.

The revealed creation story emphasizes God as the creator of the Cosmos and the role of prophets in communicating God's message through revelation. The shamanistic creation story stresses ecstatic trance hallucinations that highlight the deification of planets, constellations, and nature. God's revelations to the patriarchs underline the importance of free agency, whereas the shamanistic teachings are fatalistic in outlook. The patriarchs tell us that only the Messiah-Redeemer, Jesus the Christ, had the power and authority to resurrect humankind. The shamans tell us that people have the power to resurrect themselves if they are willing to be sacrificed or shed their own blood.

In all of the above, the evidence clearly indicates that the Olmec peoples of Mesoamerica are, in part, the Christ-following Jaredites of the book of Ether.

Notes to Chapter 2
Ancient American Writings

The knowledge of the existence—in earlier times—of the sacred books in ancient Mesoamerica was fairly widespread in Mexico and Central America when the first Europeans arrived after the discovery of America by Columbus.

Teoamoxtli

Ixtlilxochitl knew that such books had existed in Mesoamerica in very early times. He tells of the compilation of a divine book by one Huematzin, who lived in the twelfth century after Christ:

> And before going on I want to make an account of Huematzin the astrologer. . . . Before dying he (*Huematzin*) gathered together all the histories the Tultecas had, from the creation of the world up to that time [A.D. 1200] and had them pictured in a very large book, where were pictured all their persecutions and hardships, prosperities and good happenings, kings and lords, laws and good government of their ancestors, old sayings and good examples, temples, idols, sacrifices, rites and ceremonies that they had, astrology, philosophy, architecture, and the other arts, good as well as bad, and a resume of all things of science, knowledge, prosperous and adverse battles, and many other things; and he entitled this book calling it *Teoamoxtli,* which, well interpreted means *Various things of God and divine book*: the natives now call the Holy Scriptures *Teoamoxtli,* **because it is almost the same, principally in the persecutions and hardships of men**. (Hunter and Ferguson 1950, 337–38, emphasis added)

The "divine book" to which Ixtlilxochitl refers dealt with the creation of the world and the history of some of the New World colonizers. The complete consistency between Ixtlilxochitl's statement that these colonizers possessed histories and the story of the creation of the world and the declaration of the Catholic father Dionisio Jose Chonay is significant. In the preamble to the *Titulo de Totonicapan* account, which he translated from the Maya into Spanish in 1834, Chonay explains: "His said manuscript consists of thirty-one quarto pages; but the translation of the first pages is omitted because they are on the creation of the world, of

Adam, the early paradise in which Eve was deceived, not by a serpent, but by Lucifer himself, as an angel of light" (Recinos and Goetz 1953, 166–67).

Genesis creation data of the ancient colonizers were still in the possession of the Maya in Guatemala when the *Titulo de Totonicapan* account was written in 1554. Both Ixtlilxochitl and the Lords of Totonicapan credit the early colonizers with possession of the creation account. They therefore corroborate each other.

Huematzin lived in the twelfth and thirteenth centuries A.D. and was a great religious leader and prophet. Huematzin's divine book covered the period from the creation of the world up to his time—the twelfth century A.D. In that time period, Huematzin's book would encompass the personal New World appearance of the Messiah-Redeemer and should contain the details of Christ's appearance and ministry.

Popol Vuh

From the people of Chichicastenango in the beautiful highlands of Guatemala, neighbors of the nobles of Totonicapan, comes another independent testimony of a sacred book in ancient Mesoamerica. The Quiche-Maya were the most powerful nation of the Guatemalan highlands in immediate preconquest times and were a branch of the ancient Maya. Before the conquest, they painted the *Popol Vuh* in hieroglyphics. It was first transcribed in the Quiche language in the middle of the sixteenth century by highly literate Quiche-Maya natives (Tedlock 1985, 28, 59–61):

> This we shall write now [sixteenth-century alphabetic text] under the Law of God and Christianity; we shall bring it to light because now the hieroglyphic Popol Vuh, as it is called, cannot be seen any more, in which was clearly seen the coming from the other side of the sea and the narration of our obscurity, and our life was clearly seen. The original book, written long ago, existed, but its sight is hidden to the searcher and to the thinker. Great were the descriptions and the account of how all the sky and earth were formed; how it was formed and divided into four parts; how it was partitioned, and how the sky was divided; and the measuring cord was brought, and it was stretched in the sky and over the earth, on the four angles, on the four corners, as was

told by the Creator and the Maker, the Mother and the Father
of Life, of all created things, he who gives breath and
thought, she who gives birth to the children, he who watches
over the happiness of the people, the happiness of the human
race, the wise man, he who meditates on the goodness of all
that exists in the sky, on the earth, in the lakes and in the
sea. (Tedlock 1985, 71–72)

The same source makes another reference to the sacred book
of ancient Mesoamerica, the *Popul Vuh*:

Great lords and wonderful men were the marvelous
kings Gucumatz and Cotuha, the marvelous kings Quicab
and Cavizimah. They knew if there would be war, and
everything was clear before their eyes; they saw if there
would be death and hunger, if there would be strife. They
well knew that there was a place where it could be seen,
that there was a book which they called the Popol Vuh.
(Tedlock 1985, 219)

At the very end of the sixteenth-century *Popol Vuh,* the
author explains again that he had to write it because the original
sacred, ancient book had disappeared long ago. He was providing
the best substitution he could for the original. "And this was the
life of the Quiche, because no longer can be seen the book of the
Popol Vuh which the kings had in olden times, for it has
disappeared" (Recinos 1950, 234–35).

Shamanistic Calendars

The Early Olmec had shamanistic priests, but they had a
Four World Age system and a seven-day planetary week. Their
year was a 364-day year with mechanism to adjust periodically
for the "leap year."

However, details of the Long Count calendar included the
use of a 360-day year, a nine-day week, and a tradition of Five
World Ages.

Chapter 3
ANCIENT MESOAMERICAN RECORDS

The prophet-led Jaredites of ancient Mesoamerica wrote and preserved histories of the creation, their lineages, and their beliefs. Because they had carried certain records of the patriarchs (some of the Old Testament records) with them to Mesoamerica and had quoted them extensively in their own writings, we can expect to find in Mesoamerica widespread remnants of Old Testament knowledge in oral histories and traditions and in archaeological findings. Some of these ancient records have recently been discovered, and they shed light on the many fascinating parallels between the Old Testament and the cultures of Mesoamerica.

Titulo de Totonicapan

At eighty-two hundred feet above sea level, the Pan-American Highway passes through the ancient Guatemalan town of Totonicapan. In 1554, the leading native nobles of the town wrote a document that told the origin of their ancestors.

The original compilers signed it and certified its authenticity before the local Spanish magistrate. It was translated into Spanish in 1834 by Padre Dionisio Jose Chonay, a priest at Sacapulas, Guatemala. It was first published in 1885 in both Spanish and French. Its history and contents are a fascinating view of the sixteenth-century Quiche, the Indian people of Guatemala who were the descendants of the Maya.

Robert M. Carmack, an ethnohistorian from Albany University, describes his dramatic rediscovery of the original Totonicapan document whose whereabouts had been unknown for more than four hundred years:

> As part of our ethnological and archaeological survey [in the summer of 1973], we went to Totonicapan. We were primarily interested in locating the pre-Hispanic settlement of Totonicapan, which was unreported at that time. As I

had visited the community many previous times in search of ancient documents, we were well received by the native officials, who gave us their full collaboration. With the help of a guide assigned to us, we located the pre-Hispanic settlement. . . . More importantly, the indigenous alcalde was so excited about our work that he allowed me to do what I previously had been trying to do for 10 years; to personally examine the large stack of ancient titulos, which they kept in the alcadia. I was disappointed to find, however, that the original *Titulo de Totonicapan* was not one of the documents in their possession; even though I had previously been told that it was. In fact, the only document which seemed to refer to the pre-Hispanic cultures was the translation into Spanish of a tiny part of some document with which I was unacquainted. The document had been instigated as a land title by the parcialidad Yax, which I knew to be the most influential clan of the community.

It so happened that our guide was from the Yax parcialidad, and with his help, I was able to meet with the leaders of that group. I explained my interest in their history and culture, and showed them my book as an example of the kind of studies I made of ancient documents.

As we conversed in Quiche, I tried to communicate understanding of and interest in their clan organization. The approach worked because they soon sent for the keeper of the documents. Inside were several modern land titles and other legal documents, as well as a large, leather-bound ancient book, written in the Quiche language.

It did not take long to realize the importance of this book. I saw immediately that it contained the original Quiche text of the *Titulo de Totonicapan,* and other chronicles I had never seen before. As calmly as I could speak, for I was very excited, I asked permission to have the book copied. I offered several services in return: to make a typewritten copy of the documents and a translation of them into Spanish for their grandchildren; to provide them with their own photocopy of the documents, which were disintegrating; to donate money to their clan.

They agreed, and together we marched to the photocopying machine in the town center. They personally cut the binding holding the book together, and handed over and received in turn each page as it was copied. Unfortunately, the machine was not a very good one, and the pages became more faded as time went on (to my great anguish). Finally, after about three hours of photocopying, the work was completed. I took them all to dinner, and we parted. Later, as I returned to my *pension* [boarding house] with my precious treasure, I remember how paranoid I felt about losing the copies. I have since returned to Totonicapan to take photographs of certain parts of the documents, and to check my transcriptions with the original texts. The Yax have remained friendly and cooperative, and I have visited them several times since the 1973 discoveries. (Carmack 1981, 84–86)

The Yax book that Carmack photocopied has been translated and published in Spanish (Carmack and Mondlach, 1983). It actually contained six documents: a land title of the Yax Clan, three land titles for the Tamub clan, a document produced by the Ilocab clan, and the *Titulo de Totonicapan* itself. The document concludes: "Now on the 28th of September of 1554 we sign this attestation in which we have written that which by tradition our ancestors told us, who came from the other part of the sea, from Civan-Tulan, bordering on Babylonia" (Recinos and Goetz 1953, 194).

The first part of the text had never before been translated. It gave, in Carmack's words, "an account which is similar to that of the Old Testament, from the Creation to the Babylonia captivity. While it is true that this part of the narration follows the Bible much more closely than does the *Popol Vuh,* it nevertheless diverges in subtle and interesting ways" (Carmack 1981, 87). "The sixteen authors of the *Titulo* used biblical names and references (derived from the manuscript of the Dominican Friar Domingo de Vico titled *Theological Indorum* written in 1553) to describe their peoples' origins" (Carmack and Mondlach 1983, 13).

Popol Vuh

Significantly, the same group of sixteen nobles who wrote the *Titulo de Totonicapan* produced a second document, the famous *Popol Vuh*, about two to four years later. This work, the single most extensive account of Quiche history, does not use any biblical names, but it begins with the creation of heaven, earth, human beings, and animals; contains long sections of myths and legends; reports migrations, wars, settlements, and councils; and also gives the genealogies of the leaders. It was written in Santa Cruz Quiche, another important city in highland Guatemala, in Quiche about 1554–58. Although the location of the original manuscript is unknown, it was translated into Spanish by Fray Francisco Ximenez (1666–1729) in Chichicastenango about 1702.

The sacred book of the Quiche-Maya people of ancient Guatemala, the *Popol Vuh,* has been referred to as the "Genesis" of Central America. It was written in the Maya tongue from older records and traditions going back centuries before the time of Columbus. This ancient, sacred book has been translated into English by Dennis Tedlock. The lovely Maya creation account states in the preamble:

This is the beginning of the ancient word, here in this place called Quiche. Here we shall inscribe, we shall implant the Ancient Word, the potential and source for everything done in the citadel of Quiche, in the nation of the Quiche people. And here we shall take up the demonstration, revelation, and account of how things were put in shadow and brought to light . . . by the gods.

The account of the creation follows:

Now it still ripples, now it still murmurs, ripples, it still sighs, still hums, and it is empty under the sky. Here follow the first words, the first eloquence: There is not yet one person, one animal, bird, fish, crab, tree, rock, hollow, canyon, meadow, forest. Only the sky alone is there; the face of the earth is not clear. Only the sea alone is pooled under all the sky; there is nothing whatever gathered together. It is at rest; not a single thing stirs. It is held back, kept at rest under the sky.

And then came his word, he came here to the Sovereign Plumed Serpent, here in the blackness, in the early dawn. He spoke with the Sovereign Plumed Serpent, and they talked, then they thought, then they worried. They agreed with each other, they joined their words, their thoughts. Then it was clear, then they reached accord in the light, and then humanity was clear, when they conceived the growth, the generation of trees, of bushes, and the growth of life, of humankind, in the blackness, in the early dawn, all because of the Heart of Sky, named Hurricane.

And then the earth arose because of them, it was simply their word that brought it forth. For the forming of the earth they said, "Earth." It arose suddenly; just like a cloud, like a mist, now forming, unfolding. Then the mountains were separated from the water, all at once the great mountains came forth. By their genius alone, by their cutting edge alone they carried out the conception of the mountain-plain, whose face grew instant groves of cypress and pine. Such was the formation of the earth when it was brought forth by the Heart of the Sky, Heart of the Earth, as they are called, since they were the first to think of it. The sky was set apart, and the earth was set apart in the midst of the waters. Such was their plan when they thought, when they worried about the completion of their work. (Tedlock 1985, 72–75)

The *Popol Vuh* speaks of the knowledge found in the records and books of the early colonizers:

There is the original book and ancient writing, but he who reads and ponders it hides his face. It takes a long performance and account to complete the emergence of all the sky-earth: the fourfold siding, fourfold cornering, measuring, fourfold staking, halving the cord, stretching the cord in the sky, on the earth, the four sides, the four corners, as it is said, by the Maker, Modeler, mother-father of life, of humankind, giver of breath, giver of heart, bearer, upbringer in the light that lasts of those born in the light, begotten in the light; worrier, knower of everything, whatever there is: sky-earth, lake-sea. (Tedlock 1985, 71–72)

The *Popol Vuh* contains the Quiche-Maya version of the creation story as it survived down through the ages to the sixteenth century:

This is the account of how all was in suspense, all calm in silence; all motionless, still, and the expanse of the sky was empty. This is the first account, the first narrative. There was neither man, nor animal, birds, fishes, crabs, trees, stones, caves, ravines, grasses, nor forest; there was only the sky. The surface of the earth had not appeared.

There was only the calm sea and the great expanse of sky. There was nothing brought together, nothing which could make a noise, or tremble, or could make noise in the sky. There was nothing standing; only the calm water, the placid sea, alone and tranquil. Nothing existed.

There was only immobility and silence in the darkness, in the night. Only the Creator, the Maker, *Tepeu, Gucumatz* [the Fair God, Quetzalcoatl, the Messiah], the Forefathers, were in the water surrounded with light. They were hidden under green and blue feathers, and were therefore called Gucumatz.

By nature they were great sages and thinkers. In this manner the sky existed and also the Heart of Heaven, which is the name of God and thus He is called. Then came the word. *Tepeu* [God] and *Gucumatz* came together in the darkness, in the night, and *Tepeu* and Gucumatz talked together. They talked then, discussing and deliberating; they agreed, they united their words and their thoughts. Then while they meditated, it became clear to them that when Dawn would break, man must appear. Then they planned the creation, and the growth of the trees and the thickets and the birth of life and the creation of man. Thus it was arranged in the darkness and in the night by the Heart of Heaven who is called *Huracan.* The first is called *Caculha Huracan.* The second is *Chipi-Caculha.* The third is *Raxa-Caculha.* And these three are the Heart of Heaven [Godhead].

Then Tepeu and Gucumatz came together; then they conferred about life and light, what they would do so that there would be light and dawn, who it would be who would provide food and sustenance. Thus let it be done! Let the emptiness be filled! Let the water recede and make a void, let the earth appear and become solid; let it be done. Thus they spoke. Let there be light, let there be dawn in the sky and on the earth! There shall be neither glory nor grandeur in our creation and formation until the human being is made, man is formed. So they spoke.

Then the earth was created by them. So it was, in truth, that they created the earth. Earth! they said, and instantly it was made. Like the mist, like a cloud, and like a cloud of dust was, the creation, when the mountains appeared from the water; and instantly the mountains grew. Only by a miracle, only by magic art were the mountains and valleys formed; and instantly the groves of cypresses and pines put forth shoots together on the surface of the earth.

And thus *Gucumatz* was filled with joy, and exclaimed: "Your coming has been fruitful, Heart of Heaven; and you, *Huracan,* and you, *Chipi-Caculha, Raxa Caculha!*" "Our work, our creation shall be finished," they answered.

First, the earth was formed, the mountains and the valleys; the currents of water were divided, the rivulets were running freely between the hills, and the water was separated when the high mountains appeared. Thus was the earth created, when it was formed by the Heart of Heaven, the Heart of Earth, as they are called who first made it fruitful, when the sky was in suspense, and the earth was submerged in the water. So it was that they made perfect the work, when they did it after thinking and meditating upon it. (Goetz and Morley 1950, 57)

Lacandon Maya Traditions

A third Mayan source of related stories and legends has recently been reported for the Lacandon Maya Indians of Chiapas, located about 180 miles northwest of the Quiche Maya Indians of highland Guatemala. These Lacandon Maya number less than two hundred and live in a very remote area of southern Mexico. They had little European cultural influence until after World War II, so their stories and legends are relatively free of any European and Christian influences. These stories and legends are similar to those in the *Titulo de Totonicapan* and the *Popol Vuh.* They contain themes of the creation, the fall, and the crossing of the sea, but they have no biblical names or terminology. (Bruce 1976–1977, 173–208)

Apart from the Lacandon Maya traditions, these native records, produced by people who had grown up under Spanish rule but whose memories included preconquest legends, are a very important body of modern literature and history about Mesoamerica for modern researchers.

Although it would be natural for the Spanish priests to read biblical parallels into native legends of migration, redemption gods, creations, and ceremonies, they were still so impressed at what seemed to be Israelite and Near Eastern customs found among the Maya that they commented on the puzzle and stated that a knowledge of Near Eastern traditions existed in Central America long before the discovery of the New World by Columbus.

Father Juan de Torquemada

The second type of records we will consider consists of written accounts (*relaciones*) and histories (*historias*) left by sixteenth- and seventeenth-century Spanish priests who found themselves in the position of receiving and preserving native records. Many of these educated men produced their own versions of native histories. Father Torquemada was a seventeenth-century Spanish priest who lived in Mexico and who published in Spain a three-volume history. In it he recounts the legends of the Mesoamerican Indians about their own origins and relates:

> These Tultecs occupied these provinces [Mexico and Guatemala] as lords and proprietors of them. They say of them that they had knowledge of the creation of the world, and how the people of it were destroyed by the Deluge and many other things which they had in painting and in history. . . . And they also say that they had knowledge of how the world is to end again, by consummation, by fire. (Hunter and Ferguson 1950, 94)

He continues:

> They were a very wise people, and skilled in ship building, industries, and in working gold and silver, and they were very great artisans in whatsoever art [you might mention]; they were great lapidaries and they were skilled in delicate things, and in other industries for human sustenance; and in tilling and plowing land; and they were strong people noted for their good government and great industries and skills, and they were men of great capacity. When they arrived they were greatly esteemed and honored. (Hunter and Ferguson 1950, 131)

Torquemada continues his description by observing that the original colonizers wore "long robes of black linen, like Turks, the robes being like the cassocks of the clergy, open in front, and without capes, low-cut at the neck, and with short, wide sleeves which did not reach the elbow" (Hunter and Ferguson 1950, 318–19). This garb would have resembled the loose-fitting robes of the ancient Holy

Land. They also wore head coverings like short stocking caps and sandals, both of which were also articles of clothing in the ancient world.

Bishop Diego de Landa

Diego de Landa, the first bishop of Yucatan and a self-trained ethnologist, in 1556 also wrote a history of the Mayas, called the *Relacion de las Cosas de Yucatan*. He also believed the Maya claims of a transoceanic origin:

> Some of the old people of Yucatan say that they have heard from their ancestors that this land was occupied by a race of people who came from the East and whom God had delivered by opening twelve paths through the sea. If this were true, it necessarily follows that all the inhabitants of the Indies [the New World] are descendants of the Jews. (Tozzer, 1941, 16–17)

Bishop Landa also stated that the Maya of Yucatan believed "the world was destroyed by a deluge." The Maya word for flood is *haiyokocab,* meaning "water over the earth."

Bernardino de Sahagun

Bernardino de Sahagun, a Catholic priest who lived in the Valley of Mexico from 1529 to 1590, compiled Nahuatl texts and had native informants write histories. Sahagun's work has been called "one of the most comprehensive and important collections of material for the study of the culture, ethnology, and history of the Aztecs" (Gibson and Glass 1975, 360).

His history also describes a migration to the Valley of Mexico. He describes their immediate descendants as "white and of good and well-proportioned faces and good features. . . . These lived in good breeding, because the men wore good clothes and mantles; they [wore] shoes, jewels, and beads around the neck. They look at themselves in mirrors and their women put on painted and elegant skirts and blouses. They are polished and expert in everything" (Sahagun 1961, 10:188).

Sahagun was apparently convinced that the people whose history he recorded had an authentic Old World origin:

> They never ceased to have their learned men, or prophets. . . . Before their [the prophets'] departure they discourse as follows: "Know that our God commands you to remain here in these lands of which He makes you masters and gives you possession. He [God] returns to the

place whence He and we came but He will come back to visit you when it shall be time of the world to come to an end; in the meantime you will await Him in these lands, expectantly and possessing them and all contained in them, since for this [God's] purpose you came hither; remain therefore, for we go without God." (Sahagun 1950, 1:190)

The sixteenth-century Christian influence stemming from Spanish priests and converted native writers also had an impact on these documents. However, the reports from native and Catholic sources all agree that the concepts were possessed by the original colonizers many centuries before the coming of the Spanish priests. The ancients of Guatemala and Mexico did have some knowledge of the Old Testament and of their Old World roots.

Summary

The above information suggests that a knowledge of the ancient Israelite religious practices as found in the Old Testament did find its way into Mesoamerica. That knowledge remained intact because there were few forces present in Mesoamerica to diminish it. Most of the converts to Christianity in the Mediterranean world were Gentiles, and therefore Jewish tradition and customs were easily discarded. Jewish tradition was simply stronger in Mesoamerica, so Jewish rites were carried over into religious beliefs and practices in Mesoamerica.

Notes to Chapter 3
Mayan Baptismal Rites

Bishop Landa gives us the details of the ancient Maya baptismal rite—which is obviously a mixture of the ancient Hebrew purification rite and the Christian baptism taught by Mexico's Messiah. The indisputable parallels are clearly seen when quotations from Leviticus are paralleled with those from Bishop Landa's description of the Maya ceremony. However, the presence of so much of the Jewish purification rite in Mesoamerica does not suggest that all the Maya of the conquest days were of Israelite descent. Many Maya could qualify as Jews in appearance, but others look very much like Mongoloids. Certainly the Mongoloids had joined the ranks in Mesoamerica long before 600 B.C.

Hebrew Purification Rite

And the Lord spake unto Moses, saying,

This shall be the law of the leper in the day of his cleansing: He shalt be brought unto the priest (Leviticus14:1–2)

Maya Baptismal Rite

When there was anyone who wanted to have his child baptized, he went to the priest and gave him notice of his intention. . . . For three days before the festival, the fathers of the children and the officials fasted, abstaining from intercourse with their wives. On the appointed day all assembled at the house of the man who gave the feast, and brought with them all the children who were to be baptized. They were placed in the patio or court of the house, which they had swept and spread with fresh leaves (Tozzer 1941, 102–3).

Scapegoat

And he shall take the two goats and present them before the Lord at the door of the tabernacle of the congregation. . . .

And Aaron shall bring the goat upon which the Lord's lot fell, and offer him for a sin offering.

But the goat, on which the lot fell to be the scapegoat, shall be presented alive before the Lord, to make an atonement with him, and to let him go for a scapegoat into the wilderness (Leviticus 16:7, 9–10).

The Sprinkling or Anointing

As for the living bird, he shall take it, and the cedar wood, and the scarlet, and the hyssop, and shall dip them and the living bird in the blood of the bird that was killed over the running water:

And he shall sprinkle upon him that is to be cleansed from the leprosy seven times, and shall pronounce him clean, and shall let the living bird loose into the open field (Leviticus 14:6–7).

And the priest shall take some of the blood of the trespass offering, and the priest shall put it upon the tip of' the right ear of him that is to be cleansed, and upon the thumb of his right hand, and upon the great toe of' his right foot (Leviticus 14:14).

Linen Garb

He [the priest] shall put on the holy linen coat, and he shall have the linen breeches upon his flesh, and shall be girded with a linen girdle, and with the linen mitre shall he be attired: these are holy garments; therefore . shall he wash his flesh in water, and so put them on (Leviticus 16:4).

Scapegoat

And these censings being over, they took the brazier in which they made them, and the cord with which the *Chacs* had surrounded them, and they poured out a little wine into a vessel, and they gave the whole to an Indian to be carried out of town, enjoining upon him that he should not drink nor look behind him as he came back, and by this they said that the evil spirit had been driven away (Tozzer 1941, 104). (A close parallel in Hebrew rites is found in Numbers 5:17–18.)

The Sprinkling or Anointing

Then the principal whom the fathers of the children had chosen for this festival, rose, and armed with a bone, which the priest had given him, he went over to the boys and threatened to strike each one in turn on the forehead with the bone nine times. Then he wet it in a vessel of a certain water which he carried in his hand, and anointed them on their foreheads and the features of their faces, as well as the spaces between the fingers and toes of all of them, without speaking a word. They made this water from certain flowers and of cacao pounded and dissolved in virgin water, which they called that brought from the hollows of the trees or of the rocks of the forest (Tozzer 1941, 105).

Linen Garb

After this anointment, the priests arose and took off from their heads the white linen which had been put upon them, as well as others [white linens] which linen had hanging from their shoulders (Tozzer 1941, 105–6).

Chapter 4
DIVINE REVELATION TO THE HEBREW PROPHETS

Even though the prophet-led Jaredites had been led by the Lord toward their "choice land" in Mesoamerica after the Lord had "scattered" them, we must not suppose that there were no other Christ-following prophets leading other groups in other directions. Though records for all these groups have not been discovered, we know that one such group established the ancient city of Salem (Jeru-Salem or Jeru-Shiloam). We also know that a righteous king named Melchizedek, who both knew of and worshiped Christ, established peace in that city.

Melchizedek, ca. 2000 B.C.

Moses recorded:

And Melchizedek lifted up his voice and blessed Abram.

Now Melchizedek was a man of faith, who wrought righteousness; and when a child he feared God, and stopped the mouths of lions, and quenched the violence of fire.

And thus, having been approved of God, he was ordained an high priest after the order of the covenant which God made with Enoch,

It being after the order of the Son of God; which order came, not by man, nor the will of man; neither by father nor mother; neither by beginning of days nor end of years; but of God;

And it was delivered unto men by the calling of his own voice, according to his own will, unto as many as believed on his name.

For God having sworn unto Enoch and unto his seed with an oath by himself; that every one being ordained after this order and calling should have power, by faith, to break mountains, to divide the seas, to dry up waters, to turn them out of their course;

To put at defiance the armies of nations, to divide the earth, to break every band, to stand in the presence of God; to do all things according to his will, according to his command, subdue principalities and powers; and this by the will of the Son of God which was before the foundation of the world.

And men having this faith, coming up unto this order of God, were translated and taken up into heaven.

And now, Melchizedek was a priest of this order; therefore he obtained peace in Salem, and was called the Prince of peace.

And his people wrought righteousness, and obtained heaven, and sought for the city of Enoch which God had before taken, separating it from the earth, having reserved it unto the latter days, or the end of the world;

And hath said, and sworn with an oath, that the heavens and the earth should come together; and the sons of God should be tried so as by fire.

And this Melchizedek, having thus established righteousness, was called the king of heaven by his people, or, in other words, the King of peace.

And he lifted up his voice, and he blessed Abram, being the high priest, and the keeper of the storehouse of God;

Him whom God had appointed to receive tithes for the poor (JST, Genesis 14:25–38)

Of Melchizedek, Paul also writes:

For this Melchizedec, king of Salem, priest of the most high God, who met Abraham returning from the slaughter of the kings, and blessed him;

To whom also Abraham gave a tenth part of all; first being by interpretation King of righteousness, and after that also King of Salem, which is, King of peace; . . .

[He was] made like unto the Son of God; [and] abideth a priest continually.

Now consider how great this man was, unto whom even the patriarch Abraham gave the tenth of the spoils (Hebrews 7:1–4)

Obviously, Melchizedek and his people were followers of the premortal Lord Jesus Christ, though no record of them is found in any current versions of the Old Testament. One day it is to be hoped that the records from which Moses and Paul were evidently reading, as they made their own writings, will become available to us.

Abraham, ca. 2000 B.C.

Abraham, who lived long years after the dispersion of the people at Babel as well as the founding of Salem, nevertheless desired the great spirituality displayed by his prophetic fathers. He writes of this desire and the way it was granted:

> And, finding there was greater happiness and peace and rest for me, I sought for the blessings of the fathers, and the right whereunto I should be ordained to administer the same; having been myself a follower of righteousness, desiring also to be one who possessed great knowledge, and to be a greater follower of righteousness, and to possess a greater knowledge, and to be a father of many nations, a prince of peace, and desiring to receive instructions, and to keep the commandments of God, I became a rightful heir, a High Priest, holding the right belonging to the fathers.
>
> It was conferred upon me from the fathers; it came down from the fathers, from the beginning of time, yea, even from the beginning, or before the foundation of the earth, down to the present time, even the right of the firstborn, or the first man, who is Adam, or first father, through the fathers unto me. . . .
>
> Behold, I lifted up my voice unto the Lord my God, and the Lord hearkened and heard, and he filled me with the vision of the Almighty, and the angel of his presence stood by me. . . .
>
> And his voice was unto me: Abraham, Abraham, behold, my name is Jehovah, and I have heard thee. . . .
>
> Behold, I will lead thee by my hand, and I will take thee, to put upon thee my name, even the Priesthood of thy father, and my power shall be over thee.
>
> As it was with Noah so shall it be with thee; but through thy ministry my name shall be known in the earth forever, for I am thy God (Abraham 1:2–3,15–16,18–19)

Thus, Abraham, who was apparently both tutored and ordained by the great high priest Melchizedek, both saw and spoke with Jehovah, the premortal Lord Jesus Christ. Later, after having opened a vision to Abraham concerning his premortal life and foreordination, God closed that vision and gave Abraham additional knowledge of the coming Messiah-Redeemer: "And the Lord said: Whom shall I send? And one answered like unto the Son of Man: Here am I, send me" (Abraham 3:27).

Isaac, ca. 1800 B.C.

Isaac blessed his son Jacob with the blessings of Abraham (Genesis 28:3–4), which blessings were confirmed upon Isaac by the Lord: "And, behold, the Lord stood above [the altar], and said, I am the Lord God of Abraham thy father, and the God of Isaac; the land whereon thou liest, to thee will I give it, and to thy seed; And thy seed shall be as the dust of the earth . . . and in thee and in thy seed shall all the families of the earth be blessed" (Genesis 28:13–14).

Joseph, ca. 1750 B.C.

Abraham's revealed knowledge of the coming Messiah-Redeemer would certainly have been passed on to Jacob and his sons as the foremost of the blessings of Abraham, Isaac, and Jacob. Of Jacob's son Joseph, it is written:

> And Joseph said unto his brethren, I die, and go unto my fathers; and I go down to my grave with joy. The God of my father Jacob be with you . . . for the Lord hath visited me, and I have obtained a promise of the Lord, that out of the fruits of my loins, the Lord God will raise up a righteous branch out of my loins; and unto thee, whom my father Jacob hath named Israel, a prophet; (not the Messiah who is called Shiloh;) and this prophet shall deliver my people out of Egypt in the days of thy bondage.
>
> And it shall come to pass that they shall be scattered again; and a branch shall be broken off, and shall be carried into a far country; nevertheless they shall be remembered in the covenants of the Lord, when the Messiah cometh; for he shall be made manifest unto them in the latter days, in the Spirit of power; and shall bring them out of darkness into light (JST, Genesis 50:24–25)

Moses, ca. 1500 B.C.

Moses, the great record keeper and prophet of whom Joseph who was sold into Egypt had prophesied, was given a powerful witness of the coming of the Lord and Savior Jesus Christ—the Messiah Joseph had also referred to. "And [Moses] saw God face to face, and he talked with him, and the glory of God was upon Moses; therefore Moses could endure his presence. . . . And [God said,] I have a work for thee, Moses, my son; and thou art in the similitude of mine Only Begotten; and mine Only Begotten is and shall be the Savior, for he is full of grace and truth" (Moses 1:2, 6).

Moses not only obtained his own personal witness of the reality of the Lord Jesus Christ but also learned that through righteousness and obedience to priesthood principles and ordinances, as revealed to the fathers, others could also obtain the same blessing. "Therefore, in the ordinances thereof, the power of godliness is manifest," the Lord declared. "And without the ordinances thereof, and the authority of the priesthood, the power of godliness is not manifest unto men in the flesh; For without this no man can see the face of God, even the Father, and live" (D&C 84:20–22).

How thrilled Moses must have been to understand this! Not only he but also all the children of Israel who had followed him into the wilderness could, through fervently laying hold upon the gospel of Christ, be brought to know God, to stand in his presence, and eventually even to see his face. What more could a prophet ever hope for the people he had been called to lead?

And so the scripture continues: "Now [these things] Moses plainly taught to the children of Israel in the wilderness, and sought diligently to sanctify his people that they might behold the face of God" (D&C 84:23).

In one such teaching moment, Moses was commanded to use a symbol foreshadowing the redemption of Christ: "And the Lord said unto Moses, Make thee a fiery serpent, and set it upon a pole: and it shall come to pass . . . that if a serpent had bitten any man, when he beheld the serpent of brass, he lived" (Numbers 21:8–9). John confirmed this symbolism as foreshadowing the redemption when he wrote: "And as Moses lifted up the serpent in the wilderness, even so must the Son of man be lifted up, that whosoever believeth in him should not perish, but have everlasting life" (John 3:14–15).

Despite Moses' desires and diligence, however, the children of Israel "hardened their hearts and could not endure [God's] presence; therefore, the Lord in his wrath, for his anger was kindled against them, swore that they should not enter into his rest while in the wilderness, which rest is the fulness of his glory. Therefore, he took Moses out of their midst, and the Holy Priesthood also" (D&C 84:24–25).

As we ponder the incredible difficulties through which the House of Israel has passed since Moses was taken from them, perhaps they will provide thought-provoking lessons for us modern-day seekers after Christ.

Job, date unknown, before 600 B.C.

The rejoicing of Job over the future redemption of mankind is an ever-moving testimony: "For I know that my redeemer liveth, and that he shall stand at the latter day upon the earth: And though after my skin worms destroy this body, yet in my flesh shall I see God: Whom I shall see for myself, and mine eyes shall behold, and not another; though my reins be consumed within me" (Job 19:25–27).

Hosea, ca. 780 B.C.

The Lord revealed to Hosea: "Yet I am the Lord thy God from the land of Egypt, and thou shalt know no god but me: for there is no saviour beside me. . . . I will ransom them from the power of the grave; I will redeem them from death" (Hosea 13:4, 14).

Amos, ca 760 B.C.

Although the prophet Amos, in his very brief writing, alludes to the redemption only indirectly as he speaks of the latter-day gathering, he assures us that "Surely the Lord God will do nothing, but he revealeth his secret unto his servants the prophets" (Amos 3:7). Concerning the gathering, the book of Amos ends as follows:

> And I will bring again the captivity of my people of Israel, and they shall build the waste cities, and inhabit them; and they shall plant vineyards, and drink the wine thereof; they shall also make gardens, and eat the fruit of them.
>
> And I will plant them upon their land, and they shall no more be pulled up out of their land which I have given them, saith the Lord thy God (Amos 9:14–15)

It is, of course, the resurrected Lord who will bring about the gathering in the latter days; so Amos, as well as other prophets who speak of the gathering, also had a spiritual witness of the redemption.

Isaiah, ca. 740 B.C.

Isaiah, the prophet of the dispersion and gathering of Israel and of the coming of the Redeemer of Israel, laments:

> Who hath believed our report? and to whom is the arm of the Lord revealed?
>
> For he shall grow up before him as a tender plant, and as a root out of a dry ground; he hath no form nor comliness; and when we shall see him, there is no beauty that we should desire him.
>
> He is despised and rejected of men; a man of sorrows, and acquainted with grief: and we hid as it were our faces from him; he was despised, and we esteemed him not.
>
> Surely he hath borne our griefs, and carried our sorrows: yet we did esteem him stricken, smitten of God, and afflicted.
>
> But he was wounded for our transgressions, he was bruised for our iniquities: the chastisement of our peace was upon him; and with his stripes we are healed (Isaiah 53:1–5)

Speaking in the name of the Lord, Isaiah and most of the Hebrew prophets affirm their revealed knowledge of the redemption and of the sacred symbols of that redemption. As to rejoicing over the redemption, Isaiah invites all heaven and earth to rejoice: "Sing, O ye heavens; for the Lord hath done it: shout, ye lower parts of the earth: break forth into singing, ye mountains, O forest, and every tree therein: for the Lord hath redeemed Jacob, and glorified himself in Israel" (Isaiah 44:23).

Isaiah also foresaw the birth, the life, and the death of the Messiah-Redeemer as prophesied in the following chapters and verses: 7:14; 9:6; 40:3; 42:7; 50:6; 53:5; 59:20; and 61:1–3.

Micah, ca. 725 B.C.

Micah saw the Messiah-Redeemer coming out of Bethlehem: "But thou, Bethlehem Ephratah, though thou be little among the thousands of Judah, yet out of thee shall he come forth unto me that is to be ruler in Israel; whose going forth have been from old, from everlasting" (Micah 5:2).

Jeremiah, ca. 627 B.C.

Jeremiah continued with Isaiah's great concern over the dispersion and gathering of Israel and twice inserted his revealed knowledge of the Messiah-Redeemer, referring to him as the King, the Lord, and the Branch (Jeremiah 23:5–6; 33:15–16).

Zechariah, ca. 520 B.C.

Zechariah speaks messianically: "Is not this a branch plucked out of the fire?" (Zechariah 3:2). And "Thus speaketh the Lord of hosts, saying, Behold the man whose name is The BRANCH" (Zechariah 6:12). This prophet then speaks of the "rejoicing" so repeatedly linked with revelations concerning the Messiah-Redeemer: "Rejoice greatly,. . . O daughter of Jerusalem: behold, thy King cometh unto thee; he is just, and having salvation; lowly, and riding upon an ass, and upon a colt the foal of an ass" (Zechariah 9:9). "And one shall say unto him, What are these wounds in thine hands? Then he shall answer, Those with which I was wounded in the house of my friends" (Zechariah 13:6).

Malachi, ca. 435 B.C.

Old Testament revelations to Hebrew prophets concerning the Messiah-Redeemer end with "The burden of the word of the Lord to Israel by Malachi. I have loved you, saith the Lord. Yet ye say, Wherein hast thou loved us?" (Malachi 1:1). Some four centuries without the word of God to living prophets follow this questioning: "Wherein hast thou loved us?" Malachi gives the reasons. In Malachi 1, the Jews despised the Lord by offering polluted bread upon the altar and by sacrificing animals with blemishes; in Malachi 2, the priests are reproved for not keeping their covenants and teaching the people; and in the next chapter, Malachi continues: "Even from the days of your fathers ye are gone away from mine ordinances, and have not kept them. Return unto me and I will return unto you, saith the Lord of hosts. But ye said, Wherein shall we return? . . . In tithes and offerings" (Malachi 3:7–8).

We quote Malachi 4 in its entirety, thus having this last of the Old Testament Hebrew prophets announce a "coming" and a "second coming" of the Messiah-Redeemer:

> For behold, the day cometh, that shall burn as an oven; and all the proud, yea, and all that do wickedly, shall be stubble: and the day that cometh shall burn them up, saith the Lord of Hosts, that it shall leave them neither root nor branch.
>
> But unto you that fear my name shall the Sun of righteousness arise with healing in his wings; and ye shall go forth, and grow up as calves of the stall. And ye shall tread down the wicked; for they shall be ashes under the

soles of your feet in the day that I shall do this, saith the Lord of hosts. Remember ye the law of Moses my servant, which I commanded unto him in Horeb for all Israel, with the statutes and judgments.

Behold, I will send you Elijah the prophet before the coming of the great and dreadful day of the Lord: And he shall turn the heart of the fathers to the children, and the heart of the children to their fathers, lest I come and smite the earth with a curse (Malachi 4)

From the above information, it should be obvious that God was continually revealing his Beloved Son, as well as his divinely appointed mission as the Messiah-Redeemer, to all his servants the prophets— no matter in what land they lived.

Notes to Chapter 4

Since we mentioned that all the Hebrew prophets had revealed knowledge of the redemption, but not wishing to tire the reader, we have included in this chapter some of the most outstanding witnesses of those prophets. For those who wish to review all the testimonies in the Old Testament, they follow below.

Indications of revelation to Old Testament patriarchal and Hebrew prophets concerning the redemption are in some cases specific and in others indirect. We list below these patriarchs and prophets in the order of their appearance in the record, noting that some were taught about specific revelations that may have been confirmed to them individually and that others were told by the Lord to warn the people their sacrifices were not acceptable as a "similitude of the sacrifice of the Only Begotten of the Father," while still others rejoiced in the "salvation of the Lord."

Warnings by these prophets to Israel that the full blessings of the redemption would come to covenant Israel only through the "gathering" and the "second coming" in the latter days if they, in their time, persisted in practices of idolatry, improper sacrifices, and other abominations are indications of revealed knowledge of the redemption. Such warnings came from all the "minor prophets" in their brief writings.

Of the patriarchs, **Seth, Enos, Cainan, Mahalaleel, Jared, Enoch, Methuselah**, and **Lamech** all lived with Adam as their patriarchal head; and Adam and Eve "made all things known unto their sons and their daughters." We have previously cited revelations to **Enoch, Noah, Shem**, and **Abraham**, with Abraham reconfirming his patriarchal or priesthood rights (including that of a revelator) as having come down to him from the fathers:

I became a rightful heir, a High Priest, holding the right belonging to the fathers.

It was conferred upon me from the fathers; it came down from the fathers, from the beginning of time, yea, even from the beginning, or before the foundation of the earth, down to the present time, even the right of the firstborn, or the first man, who is Adam, or first father, through the fathers unto me (Abraham 1:2–3)

Continuing on with revelations to the prophets concerning the Messiah-Redeemer, we go from Abraham to **Isaac** to **Jacob** and then to **Joseph**, all previously referred to, and then to **Moses**, whose symbolic serpent of brass upon a pole foreshadowed the redemption. It is through Moses that we have the account of Adam's knowledge of the meaning of blood sacrifice, which leaves no doubt as to Moses' revealed knowledge of the redemption.

Joshua's position as a revelator was confirmed in these words: "Now after the death of Moses the servant of the Lord it came to pass, that the Lord spake unto Joshua" (Joshua 1:1). "And the Lord said unto Joshua, This day will I begin to magnify thee in the sight of all Israel, that they may know that, as I was with Moses, so I will be with thee" (Joshua 3:7). "Then Joshua built an altar unto the Lord God of Israel in Mount Ebal . . . and they offered thereon burnt offerings unto the Lord, and sacrificed peace offerings" (Joshua 8:30–31).

"And **Samuel** grew, and the Lord was with him. . . . Samuel was established to be a prophet of the Lord" (1 Samuel 3:19–20).

And Saul said, Bring hither a burnt offering to me, and peace offerings. And he offered the burnt offering. . . .

And Samuel said, What hast thou done. . . . And Samuel said to Saul, Thou hast done foolishly: Thou hast not kept the commandment of the Lord thy God, which he commanded thee: for now would the Lord have established thy kingdom upon Israel for ever.

But now thy kingdom shall not continue (1 Samuel 13:9, 11, 13–14).

The book of **Nathan** the prophet (1 Chronicles 29:29) is lost, so we do not have the testimony of this Hebrew prophet concerning the redemption.

Elijah the prophet (New Testament Elias) was taken into heaven without tasting death (2 Kings 2:11) to fill a special mission with the premortal Messiah-Redeemer before the resurrection (Matthew 17:3) and to fulfill a special mission in the latter days, as prophesied by Malachi (Malachi 4:5–6) and as confirmed in latter-day revelation (D&C 110:13–16).

Elisha, on whom Elijah's mantle fell, was a prophet of many revelations and many miracles: "His miracles form the chief part of his recorded work. These were for the most part acts of kindness and mercy" (LDS Bible Dictionary, 664). As Elisha was counseling a king of Israel, the symbol of the redemption was properly practiced: "And it came to pass in the morning, when the meat offering was offered, that, behold, there came water by the way of Edom, and the country was filled with water" (2 Kings 3:20).

Job's testimony of and rejoicings over the Messiah-Redeemer will be cited later, as will **Isaiah's** extensive witnessing and **Jeremiah's** references to "the branch."

Ezekiel was identified as a prophet when the word of the Lord came to him (divine revelation): "The word of the Lord came expressly unto Ezekiel the priest, the son of Buzi, in the land of the Chaldeans by the river Chebar; and the hand of the Lord was there upon him" (Ezekiel 1:3). Israel was called to order through Ezekiel because of the impropriety of their sacrifices as a symbol of the redemption:

> Therefore, son of man, speak unto the house of Israel, and say unto them, Thus sayeth the Lord God; Yet in this your fathers have blasphemed me, in that they have committed a trespass against me. . . .
>
> And they offered there their sacrifices, and there they presented the provocation of their offering: there also they made their sweet savour, and poured out there their drink offerings (Ezekiel 20:27–28)

Ezekiel's revealed knowledge of the redemption is further evidenced through the Lord's prophesying of the latter-day gathering of Israel through him: "I will even gather you from the people, and assemble you out of the countries where ye have been scattered, and I will give you the land of Israel. . . . And I will give them one heart, and I will put a new spirit within you; and I will take the stony heart out of their flesh, and will give them an heart of flesh" (Ezekiel 11:17, 19).

Daniel was a prophet with revealed knowledge: "Then was the secret revealed unto Daniel in a night vision. Then Daniel blessed the God of heaven" (Daniel 2:19). "And in the days of these kings shall the God of heaven set up a kingdom, which shall never be destroyed: and the kingdom shall not be left to other people, but it shall break in pieces and consume all these kingdoms, and it shall stand forever" (Daniel 2:44). "The keys of the kingdom of God are committed unto man on the earth, and from thence shall the gospel roll forth unto the ends of the earth, as the stone which is cut out of the mountain without hands shall roll forth, until it has filled the whole earth" (D&C 65:2).

Hosea's testimony of the Savior will be cited later.

Joel reminds Israel of the second coming of Christ: "Alas for the day! for the day of the Lord is at hand, and as a destruction from the Almighty shall it come" (Joel 1:15).

> Blow ye the trumpet in Zion, and sound an alarm in my holy mountain: let all the inhabitants of the land tremble: for the day of the Lord cometh, for it is nigh at hand. . . .
>
> And ye shall know that I am in the midst of Israel, and that I am the Lord your God, and none else: and my people shall never be ashamed.
>
> And it shall come to pass afterward, that I will pour out my spirit upon all flesh; and your sons and your daughters shall prophesy, your old men shall dream dreams, your young men shall see visions:
>
> And also upon the servants and upon the handmaids in those days will I pour out my spirit.
>
> And I will shew wonders in the heavens and in the earth, blood and fire, and pillars of smoke.
>
> The sun shall be turned into darkness and the moon into blood, before the great and terrible day of the Lord come.
>
> And it shall come to pass, that whosoever shall call on the name of the Lord shall be delivered; for in mount Zion and in Jerusalem shall be deliverance, as the Lord hath said, and in the remnant whom the Lord shall call (Joel 2:1, 27–32)

Amos will be cited as a witness that all prophets are revelators and that Israel will be gathered in the latter days.

Obadiah, in his very brief prophecy on the downfall of Edom, says about the gathering of Israel: "But upon mount Zion shall be deliverance, and there shall be holiness; and the house of Jacob shall possess their possessions. . . . And saviours shall come upon mount Zion to judge the mount of Esau; and the kingdom shall be the Lord's" (Obadiah 1:17, 21).

Jonah, the son of Amittai the prophet, spoke "the word of the Lord God of Israel" (2 Kings 14:25), and "the word of the Lord came unto Jonah . . . saying, Arise, go to Nineveh, that great city, and cry against it, for their wickedness is come up before me" (Jonah 1:2).

Then certain of the scribes and of the Pharisees
answered . . . and said unto them,

An evil and adulterous generation seeketh after a sign;
and there shall no sign be given to it, but the sign of the
prophet Jonas:

For as Jonas was three days and three nights in the
whale's belly; so shall the Son of man be three days and
three nights in the heart of the earth (Matthew 12:38–40)

Micah's vision of the Messiah-Redeemer coming out of
Bethlehem will be cited later.

Nahum says: "The mountains quake at him and the hills
melt, and the earth is burned at his presence, yea, the world, and all
that dwell therein. . . . Behold upon the mountains the feet of him
that bringeth good tidings, that publisheth peace" (Nahum 1:5, 15).

For whosoever shall call upon the name of the Lord
shall be saved.

How then shall they call on him in whom they have
not believed? and how shall they believe in him of whom
they have not heard? and how shall they hear without a
preacher?

And how shall they preach, except they be sent? as it
is written, How beautiful are the feet of them that preach
the gospel of peace, and bring glad tidings of good things!
(Romans 10:13–15)

Habakkuk spoke of the second coming of Christ in these words:
"For the earth shall be filled with the knowledge of the glory of the
Lord, as the waters cover the sea" (Habakkuk 2:14).

On the second coming, **Zephaniah** also spoke of the Lord's
promise:

For then will I turn to the people a pure language,
that they may all call upon the name of the Lord, to serve
him with one consent. . . .

Sing, O daughter of Zion; shout O Israel; be glad and
rejoice with all the heart, O daughter of Jerusalem. . . .

The Lord thy God in the midst of thee is mighty; he
will save, he will rejoice over thee with joy; he will rest in
his love, he will joy over thee with singing (Zephaniah 3:9, 14, 17)

Haggai spoke messianically:

> According to the word that I covenanted with you when ye came out of Egypt, so my spirit remaineth among you: fear ye not.
>
> For thus saith the Lord of hosts; Yet once, it is a little while, and I will shake the heavens, and the earth, and the sea, and the dry land;
>
> And I will shake all nations, and the desire of all nations shall come: and I will fill this house with glory, saith the lord of hosts.
>
> The silver is mine, and the gold is mine, saith the Lord of hosts.
>
> The glory of this latter house shall be greater than of the former, saith the Lord of hosts: and in this place will I give peace, saith the Lord of hosts (Haggai 2:5–9)

Zachariah and **Malachi** ended the witnesses and prophecies of the Old Testament, as we pointed out earlier.

Chapter 5
A SECOND EMIGRATION TO MESOAMERICA

Before Malachi's time, in about 601 B.C. and during the reign of the Jewish king Zedekiah as well as the prophetic tenure of Jeremiah, representatives of three Hebrew families departed from the land of Jerusalem. Fleeing into the Arabian Peninsula, the faithful band of approximately twenty people carried with them precious "records . . . engraven upon plates of brass" that contained the treasured writings of the first patriarchs as well as previous Hebrew prophets. These people slowly worked their way southward along the borders of the Red Sea. After eight difficult years in the Arabian wilderness (covering over three thousand miles), they arrived, probably, in what we now call Oman.

There, as he had done with the Jaredites some two thousand years before, the Lord directed these Hebrews to build some sort of ship and set forth upon the sea, carrying with them all sorts of provisions. After a lengthy and difficult voyage, they arrived in what they termed the Promised Land (interesting that the Jaredites called it a "choice land")—most likely landing on the Pacific coast somewhere near the Chiapas-Guatemalen border of Mesoamerica.

Over time, this small group of Hebrews became a community and then, because of internal dissension between the brothers and their families, two. Both of these flourished and grew into a huge civilization that lasted, relatively intact, for a thousand years. After that, many were destroyed in a great civil war, and the rest disintegrated into numerous "bands" and "nations." These continued to flourish in one form or another until the arrival of the Spaniards in the sixteenth century.

It is not surprising, therefore, to find, in the writings of early Mesoamerican and Spanish historians, references to this second group of emigrants from the Near East.

Titulo de Totonicapan

The sixteen authors of the *Titulo* de *Totonicapan*, which we mentioned earlier, write:

> The three wise men, the Nahuales, the chiefs and leaders of three great peoples and of others who joined them, called U Mamae [the ancients], extending their sight over the four parts of the world and over all that is beneath the sky, and finding no obstacle, came from the other part of the ocean, from where the sun rises, from a place called [in Mayan] Pa Tulan, Pa Civan.
>
> The principal chiefs were four. . . . Together these tribes came from the other part of the sea, from the East, from Pa Tulan, Pa Civan. These, then, were the three nations of Quiches, and they came from where the sun rises, descendants of Israel, of the same language and same customs.
>
> When they left Pa Tulan, Pa Civan, the first leader was Balam-Quitze, by unanimous vote, and then the great father Nacxit [God] gave them a present called Giron-Gagal. When they arrived at the edge of the sea, Balam-Quitze touched it [the sacred director] with his staff and at once a passage opened, which then closed up again, for thus the great God wished it to be done, because they were the sons of Abraham and Jacob. (Recinos and Goetz 1953, 169–70)

Ixtlilxochitl

Ixtlilxochitl, whom we met in Chapter 2, relates an important council of the colony's intellectual leaders that, in our calendar system, took place in 164 B.C.:

> All the land of this New World being in peace, all the Tulteca wisemen, the astrologers as well as men of other arts, got together in Huehuetlapallan, seat of the kingdom, where they discussed many things, happenings and calamities that they had, and movements of the heavens since the creation of the world, as well as many other things which, because their histories were burned [by Spaniards], have not been able to be known nor understood more than what has here been written. Among other things, they added the leap year in order to make the solar year agree with the equinox, and many other curiosities, as will be seen in their tables and rules for their years, months, weeks, and days,

signs, and planets, according as they understood them, and many other curiosities. (Hunter and Ferguson 1950, 147)

Thus, by 97 B.C., the descendants of the original Mesoamerican colonizers had become a real kingdom, with enough differentiation of labor to support a leisure class of learned artisans and scholars. They had an important capital city, "Ancient Place of the Red"—Huehue meaning "ancient" and Tlapallan meaning "place of the red."

Ixtlilxochitl describes their kings as "high of stature, and white, and bearded like the Spaniards." He also reports that as late as the tenth century A.D., white, blond children were born to the descendants of these early Tultecas.

Gaspar Antonio Chi

Gaspar Antonio Chi was born in Yucatan, Central America, in 1531. His mother was a Maya princess and his father a Maya nobleman of the Xiu family. For a number of years, he served as royal interpreter to the Spanish governors of Yucatan. He had a knowledge of Maya, Nahuatl (Mexican), Spanish, and Latin languages. Chi provided Bishop Landa with much of the data for Landa's book. And Chi supplied the Spanish civil authorities with material they needed for the purpose of replying to a questionnaire sent to them by the Spanish crown in 1579. The crown wanted to know, among other things, something about the ancient inhabitants.

The original questionnaires and answers turned up in the archives of the Indies in Seville, Spain, during the latter part of the nineteenth century. In them, we have the truth concerning the ancient colonizers as the Spanish authorities of the time accepted it:

> They had letters. Each letter was a syllable, and with them they were understood. And they had a year consisting of three hundred and sixty-five days. They had knowledge of a Creator of all things, of the creation of the sky and of the earth, and of the fall of Lucifer, and of the creation of man, and of the immortality of the soul, and of Heaven and Hell, and of the general Flood.

> Those who anciently came to people this land of Yucatan . . . were very simple in their worship and did not worship idols or make any sacrifice. It is said that the first settlers of Chichen Itza were not idolaters. For a thousand years they did not worship idols, because the lords of

Chichen Itza and their subjects wished it to be said that they were not idolaters. (Jakeman 1952, 95–102)

The date of the arrival of the colonizers at Chichen Itza is fixed at about the time of Christ's death and resurrection. If they did not have idolatry for "a thousand years," it must have been introduced about A.D. 1000. That leaves over five hundred years for religious beliefs and traditions to decay and change before the coming of the Spaniards.

Ancient Religious Records

Like the Jaredites, at least one segment of these Near East emigrants were wonderful record keepers. Those records that have been found and translated were kept mostly by prophets, and so they frequently write of their religion, particularly as it pertained to Jesus Christ and his mission of redemption.

Lehi

The first leader of these people was a Hebrew prophet by the name of Lehi, who besides having read the witnesses recorded in his precious brass records (most of the Old Testament), had earlier obtained for himself a knowledge of the Messiah-Redeemer. Lehi's son, Nephi, records this event, which occurred before Lehi had ever led his family and others into the wilderness. The record states:

> Wherefore it came to pass that my father, Lehi, as he went forth prayed unto the Lord, yea, even with all his heart, in behalf of his people.
>
> And it came to pass as he prayed unto the Lord, there came a pillar of fire and dwelt upon a rock before him; and he saw and heard much; and because of the things which he saw and heard he did quake and tremble exceedingly.
>
> And it came to pass that he returned to his own house at Jerusalem; and he cast himself upon his bed, being overcome with the Spirit and the things which he had seen.
>
> And being thus overcome with the Spirit, he was carried away in a vision, even that he saw the heavens open, and he thought he saw God sitting upon his throne, surrounded with numberless concourses of angels in the attitude of singing and praising their God.
>
> And it came to pass that he saw One descending out of the midst of heaven, and he beheld that his luster was above that of the sun at noon-day.

> And he also saw twelve others following him, and
> their brightness did exceed that of the stars in the firmament.
>
> And they came down and went forth upon the face of
> the earth. (1 Nephi 1:5–11)

Concerning his father's vision of this glorious being, Nephi
continues:

> After my father had made an end of speaking the words
> of his dream, and also of exhorting [us] to all diligence, he
> spake to [us] concerning the Jews. . . .
>
> Yea, even six hundred years from the time that my
> father left Jerusalem, a prophet would the Lord God raise
> up among the Jews—even a Messiah, or, in other words, a
> Savior of the world.
>
> And he also spake concerning the prophets, how great
> a number had testified of these things, concerning this
> Messiah, of whom he had spoken, or this Redeemer of the
> world.
>
> Wherefore, all mankind were in a lost and in a fallen
> state, and ever would be save they should rely on this
> Redeemer. (1 Nephi 10:2, 4–6)

Some years later, as Lehi blessed his children before his death,
he testified once again of this Messiah: "Wherefore, redemption
cometh in and through the Holy Messiah; for he is full of grace
and truth. Behold, he offereth himself a sacrifice for sin, to answer
the ends of the law, unto all those who have a broken heart and a
contrite spirit; and unto none else can the ends of the law be
answered" (2 Nephi 2:6–7).

Nephi

Nephi, one of Lehi's six sons and the one who forged plates
of gold so he might keep a record of his own people, desired to
see the things his father had seen. Accordingly, he went before the
Lord and obtained the same vision. He then relates:

> And it came to pass that I saw the heavens open; and
> an angel came down and stood before me. . . .
>
> And he said unto me: Behold, the virgin whom thou
> seest is the mother of the Son of God, after the manner
> of the flesh. . . .
>
> And I looked and beheld the virgin again, bearing a
> child in her arms. . . .

And I looked, and I beheld the Son of God going forth among the children of men; and I saw many fall down at his feet and worship him. . . .

And I looked and beheld the Redeemer of the world, of whom my father had spoken; and I also beheld the prophet who should prepare the way before him. And the Lamb of God went forth and was baptized of him; and after he was baptized, I beheld the heavens open, and the Holy Ghost come down out of heaven and abide upon him in the form of a dove.

And I beheld that he went forth ministering unto the people, in power and great glory; and the multitudes were gathered together to hear him; and I beheld that they cast him out from among them. . . .

And I beheld the Lamb of God going forth among the children of men. And I beheld multitudes of people who were sick, and who were afflicted with all manner of diseases, and with devils and unclean spirits; and the angel spake and showed all these things unto me. And they were healed by the power of the Lamb of God; and the devils and the unclean spirits were cast out. . . .

And I looked and beheld the Lamb of God, that he was taken by the people; yea, the Son of the everlasting God was judged of the world. . . .

And I, Nephi, saw that he was lifted up upon the cross and slain for the sins of the world. (1 Nephi 11:14–33)

Of great interest was what Nephi was shown regarding events that would occur in their newly obtained land of promise at a time immediately following Christ's crucifixion. He wrote:

And it came to pass that I saw a mist of darkness on the face of the land of promise; and I saw lightnings, and I heard thunderings, and earthquakes, and all manner of tumultuous noises; and I saw the earth and the rocks, that they rent; and I saw mountains tumbling into pieces; and I saw the plains of the earth, that they were broken up; and I saw many cities that they were sunk. . . .

And I saw the heavens open, and the Lamb of God descending out of heaven; and he came down and showed himself unto [this people]. (1 Nephi 12:4, 6)

Benjamin

About 124 B.C., some three hundred years after Malachi had prophesied to the Jews in Palestine and nearly five hundred years after Nephi had spoken the above, a Mesoamerican prophet-king named Benjamin awakened his whole nation to the reality and blessings of Christ and his atonement:

> And the things which I shall tell you are made known unto me by an angel from God. . . .
>
> For behold, the time cometh, and is not far distant, that with power, the Lord Omnipotent who reigneth, who was, and is from all eternity to all eternity, shall come down from heaven among the children of men, and shall dwell in a tabernacle of clay, and shall go forth amongst men, working mighty miracles, such as healing the sick, raising the dead, causing the lame to walk, the blind to receive their sight, and the deaf to hear, and curing all manner of diseases.
>
> And he shall cast out devils, or the evil spirits which dwell in the hearts of the children of men.
>
> And lo, he shall suffer temptations, and pain of body, hunger, thirst, and fatigue, even more than man can suffer, except it be unto death; for behold, blood cometh from every pore, so great shall be his anguish for the wickedness and the abominations of his people.
>
> And he shall be called Jesus Christ, the Son of God, the Father of heaven and earth, the Creator of all things from the beginning; and his mother shall be called Mary.
>
> And lo, he cometh unto his own, that salvation might come unto the children of men even through faith on his name; and even after all this they shall consider him a man, and say that he hath a devil, and shall scourge him, and shall crucify him.
>
> And he shall rise the third day from the dead; and behold, he standeth to judge the world; and behold, all these things are done that a righteous judgment might come upon the children of men. . . .
>
> And the Lord God hath sent his holy prophets among all the children of men, to declare these things to every kindred, nation, and tongue, that thereby whosoever should believe that Christ should come, the same might receive

remission of their sins, and rejoice with exceedingly great joy, even as though he had already come among them. (Mosiah 3:2, 5–10, 13)

Samuel the Lamanite

In about 6 B.C., a prophet by the name of Samuel, who was called by the people a Lamanite, told of signs that would occur in Mesoamerica at the birth of Christ and also at his death, thus echoing the nearly six-hundred-year-old words of Nephi. Samuel declared:

Behold, I give unto you a sign; for five years more cometh, and behold, then cometh the Son of God to redeem all those who shall believe on his name.

And behold, this will I give unto you for a sign at the time of his coming; for behold, there shall be great lights in heaven, insomuch that in the night before he cometh there shall be no darkness, insomuch that it shall appear unto man as if it was day.

Therefore, there shall be one day and a night and a day, as if it were one day and there were no night; and this shall be unto you for a sign; for ye shall know of the rising of the sun and also of its setting; therefore they shall know of a surety that there shall be two days and a night; nevertheless the night shall not be darkened; and it shall be the night before he is born.

And behold, there shall a new star arise, such an one as ye never have beheld; and this also shall be a sign unto you. (Helaman 14:2–5)

And behold, again, another sign I give unto you, yea, a sign of his death. . . .

Behold, in that day that he shall suffer death the sun shall be darkened and refuse to give his light unto you; and also the moon and the stars; and there shall be no light upon the face of this land, even from the time that he shall suffer death, for the space of three days, to the time that he shall rise again from the dead.

Yea, at the time that he shall yield up the ghost there shall be thunderings and lightnings for the space of many hours, and the earth shall shake and tremble; and the rocks which are upon the face of this earth, which are both above the earth and beneath, which ye know at this time are solid, or the more part of it is one solid mass, shall be broken up;

Yea, they shall be rent in twain, and shall ever after be found in seams and in cracks, and in broken fragments upon the face of the whole earth, yea, both above the earth and beneath.

And behold, there shall be great tempests, and there shall be many mountains laid low, like unto a valley, and there shall be many places which are now called valleys which shall become mountains, whose height is great.

And many highways shall be broken up, and many cities shall become desolate. (Helaman 14:14, 20–24)

Christ to Come to America

We mentioned above the prophecies of Nephi, one of the sons of the leader of this band of immigrants to Mesoamerica. One of the most intriguing of these prophecies is the following: "**And I saw the heavens open, and the Lamb of God descending out of heaven; and he came down and showed himself unto [this people]**" (1 Nephi 12:6, emphasis added).

In other words, following the birth, death, resurrection, and ascension of Jesus of Nazareth in Palestine, Nephi and others of the Mesoamerican prophets firmly believed that this same Christ would descend out of heaven to show himself to their Mesoamerican descendants.

Other Sheep of Another Fold

Jesus of Nazareth also contemplated this visit, which he knew he would make after laying down his life and then taking it up again. Before he identified himself to the Jews in Palestine as the Son of God, he said:

I am the good shepherd, and know my sheep, and am known of mine.

As the Father knoweth me, even so know I the Father: and I lay down my life for the sheep.

And other sheep I have, which are not of this fold: them also I must bring, and they shall hear my voice; and there shall be one fold, and one shepherd.

Therefore doth my Father love me, because I lay down my life, that I might take it again.

No man taketh it from me, but I lay it down of myself. I have power to lay it down, and I have power to take it

again. This commandment have I received of my Father.
(John 10:14–18, emphasis added)

Although we may not know the identities of all the "other
sheep" to which Christ was making reference, we have already
given overwhelming evidence that there was a great, intelligent
population of Hebrew peoples in the Americas—people who knew
of the premortal Christ by way of revelation, who worshiped him,
who expected him to appear to them following his death and
resurrection, and who would obviously qualify to become
recipients of the Lord's promise.

Moreover, there is ample evidence that at least certain
Palestinian individuals had an understanding of these
Mesoamerican peoples. Religious scholar and philosopher Hugh
Nibley has written about the very "interesting hint" dropped
by Origen:

> Clement, the disciple of the Apostles, recalls those
> whom the Greeks designate as *antichthonians* [dwellers on
> the other side of the earth], and other parts of the earth's
> sphere [or circuit] which cannot be reached by anyone from
> our regions, and from which none of the inhabitants dwelling
> there is able to get to us; he calls these areas "worlds" when
> he says: "The Ocean is not to be crossed by men, but those
> worlds which lie on the other side of it are governed by the
> same ordinances [*lit.* dispositions] of a guiding and directing
> God as these."

Nibley continues:

> Here is a clear statement that the *earliest* Christians
> taught that there were people living on the other side of the
> world who enjoyed the guidance of God in complete isolation
> from the rest of the world. Origen knows of mysterious
> knowledge that was had among the leaders of the Primitive
> Church but was neither divulged by them to the general
> public nor passed on to the general membership, and this
> includes the assurance that there were people living on the
> other side of the world who enjoyed the same divine guidance
> as themselves in a state of complete isolation. (Nibley, *An
> Approach to the Book of Mormon*, 1988, 326)

This knowledge of the existence of "other sheep" was an
important reality also confirmed by Peter as he came to understand
the universality of Christ's ministry and redemption: "Of a truth I

perceive that God is no respecter of persons: But in every nation he that feareth him, and worketh righteousness, is accepted with him" (Acts 10:34–35). Further confirmation of this universality followed as the resurrected Messiah-Redeemer charged his apostles: "Go ye into all the world, and preach the gospel to every creature" (Mark 16:15). Unfortunately, as Origen quoted Clement as stating: "The Ocean is not to be crossed by men." Therefore, those apostles had no access to such other sheep as we have described who were living in Mesoamerica.

They Shall Hear My Voice

Who would go to them, then? The only one who could would be the resurrected Lord himself, who would thus fulfill not only Nephi's but also his own prophecy: "And other sheep I have, which are not of this fold: them also I must bring, **and they shall hear my voice**; and there shall be one fold, and one shepherd" (John 10:16, emphasis added).

Chapter 6
ANOTHER WITNESS FOR CHRIST

Very early in the history of Lehi's Mesoamerican colony of transplanted Hebrews, dissension arose. Two of his six sons turned against the ways of Christ and those of the other four brothers. The leader of the dissenters was called Laman; hence, his followers ever after were called *Lamanites*. The leader of the group who chose to believe in Christ was Nephi; and ever after those who endeavored to choose righteousness were called *Nephites*.

But even this picture is not entirely accurate, for over the next six hundred years, frequent, even great, strife arose within each of the two groups—the wicked often going so far as to slay the righteous. And, of course, regular conflict and terrible war occurred between the Nephites and the Lamanites themselves. As the six hundredth year from Lehi's departure out of Palestine approached—the year that Christ was to be born as prophesied—the record from Mesoamerica details an interesting sort of internal division among the Nephites.

Death If the Signs Are Not Given

According to the record:

It was six hundred years from the time that Lehi left Jerusalem. . . .

And . . . the prophecies of the prophets began to be fulfilled more fully; for there began to be greater signs and greater miracles wrought among the people.

But there were some who began to say that the time was past for the words to be fulfilled, which were spoken by Samuel, the Lamanite.

And they began to rejoice over their brethren, saying: Behold the time is past, and the words of Samuel are not fulfilled; therefore, your joy and your faith concerning this thing hath been vain.

And it came to pass that they did make a great uproar throughout the land; and the people who believed

began to be very sorrowful, lest by any means those things
which had been spoken might not come to pass.

But behold, they did watch steadfastly for that
day and that night and that day which should be as one day
as if there were no night, that they might know that their
faith had not been vain. (3 Nephi 1:1–8)

The unbelievers were unrelenting in their persecution—and even
went so far as to set aside a day where all the believers would be put
to death unless the sign should be given. Naturally, great consternation
arose among the believers, but as the eve before they were to be put
to death approached.

Behold, at the going down of the sun there was
no darkness; and the people began to be astonished because
there was no darkness when the night came.

And there were many, who had not believed the
words of the prophets, who fell to the earth and became as
if they were dead, for they knew that the great plan of
destruction which they had laid for those who believed in
the words of the prophets had been frustrated; for the sign
which had been given was already at hand.

And they began to know that the Son of God
must shortly appear; yea . . . all the people upon the face
of the whole earth from the west to the east, both in the
land north and in the land south, were so exceedingly
astonished that they fell to the earth. . . .

And they began to fear because of their iniquity
and their unbelief. (3 Nephi 1:15–18).

So the sign was given. In all that night, there was no darkness,
but all was "as light as though it was mid-day." Yet in the morning the
sun arose just as it always had, and "a new star did appear." Therefore,
the people "knew that it was the day that the Lord should be born" (3
Nephi 1:19–21).

People Are Human

One might suppose that after seeing such signs, everyone would
have been converted. And though indeed a wave of repentance and
conversion took place, the record states that "from this time forth
there began to be lyings sent forth among the people, by Satan, to
harden their hearts, to the intent that they might not believe in those
signs and wonders which they had seen" (3 Nephi 1:22).

The Mesoamerican record does not contain a great deal of information about the next third of a century. What we do know is that, because of the signs they had seen, most of the Nephites returned to the Lord. Time has a way of diminishing memory, however; and by the time thirty years had passed away, most of the Nephites once again chose wickedness and ignored the words of the prophets.

According to the record:

> The people began to be distinguished by ranks, according to their riches and their chances for learning, yea, some were ignorant because of their poverty, and others did receive great learning because of their riches.
>
> Some were lifted up in pride, and others were exceedingly humble; some did return railing for railing, while others would receive railing and persecution and all manner of afflictions, and would not turn and revile again, but were humble and penitent before God.
>
> And thus there became a great inequality in all the land, insomuch that the church began to be broken up; yea, insomuch that in the thirtieth year the church was broken up in all the land save it were among a few of the Lamanites who were converted unto the true faith; and they would not depart from it, for they were firm, and steadfast, and immovable, willing with all diligence to keep the commandments of the Lord.
>
> Now the cause of this iniquity of the people was this—Satan had great power, unto the stirring up of the people to do all manner of iniquity, and to the puffing them up with pride, tempting them to seek for power, and authority, and riches, and the vain things of the world.
>
> And thus Satan did lead away the hearts of the people to do all manner of iniquity; therefore they had enjoyed peace but a few years. (3 Nephi 6:12–16)

By the end of the thirty-third year after Christ's birth, this wickedness had grown so great that the central government of the Nephites was utterly dissolved; and the people separated into bands and tribes. Unfortunately, "they did not sin ignorantly, for they knew the will of God concerning them, for it had been taught unto them; therefore they did wilfully rebel against God . . . and had turned from their righteousness, like the dog to his vomit, or like the sow to her wallowing in the mire" (3 Nephi 6:18, 7:8).

The Sign of Christ's Death

Now events began to transpire that were to culminate in the most glorious, sublime occurrence in perhaps all of recorded history. According to the Mesoamerican record of these transplanted Hebrews:

In the thirty and fourth year, in the first month, on the fourth day of the month, there arose a great storm, such an one as never had been known in all the land.

And there was also a great and terrible tempest; and there was terrible thunder, insomuch that it did shake the whole earth as if it was about to divide asunder.

And there were exceedingly sharp lightnings, such as never had been known in all the land. (3 Nephi 8:5–7)

The record goes on to delineate an amazing amount of physical destruction this great storm wrought upon the face of the land. Many cities were burned; others sank into the sea; and still others were demolished or swallowed up by the earth—until "the whole face of the land was changed" by the destruction.

Obviously, a terrible destruction also took place among the people. Untold thousands were slain by the fires, lightning, and earthquakes, and "there were some who were carried away in the whirlwind; and whither they went no man knoweth, save they know that they were carried away" (3 Nephi 8:16).

Nephi's Prophecy

In Chapter 5, we mentioned several Mesoamerican prophets who had spoken futuristically of this land. One of these was a man named Nephi, who lived more than five hundred years before the cataclysmic events we have just described. Consider with us once again his prophetic utterance:

I saw a mist of darkness on the face of the land of promise; and I saw lightnings, and I heard thunderings, and earthquakes, and all manner of tumultuous noises; and I saw the earth and the rocks, that they rent; and I saw mountains tumbling into pieces; and I saw the plains of the earth, that they were broken up; and I saw many cities that they were sunk. (1 Nephi 12:4)

Three Hours of Storm; Three Days of Darkness

This storm was so savage and violent that "the whole earth became deformed." Interestingly, it was not a lengthy storm but one that lasted for only about three hours.

And . . . there was thick darkness upon all the face of the land, insomuch that the inhabitants thereof who had not fallen could feel the vapor of darkness;

And there could be no light, because of the darkness, neither candles, neither torches; neither could there be fire kindled with their fine and exceedingly dry wood, so that there could not be any light at all;

And there was not any light seen, neither fire, nor glimmer, neither the sun, nor the moon, nor the stars, for so great were the mists of darkness which were upon the face of the land. And it came to pass that it did last for the space of three days that there was no light seen; and there was great mourning and howling and weeping among all the people continually; yea, great were the groanings of the people, because of the darkness and the great destruction which had come upon them. (3 Nephi 8:20–22)

Interestingly, Jesus was nailed to the cross at the third hour of the Jewish day and died six hours later at the ninth hour. At the sixth hour, three hours before his death, darkness fell over the land of Palestine and continued during the three hours immediately preceding his death. Earthquakes occurred and rocks were rent. Concerning these phenomena, one of the early Christian writers of the Old World states:

And it was the third hour, and they crucified him. . . .

And when the sixth hour was come, there was darkness over the whole land until the ninth hour.

And at the ninth hour Jesus cried with a loud voice, Eloi, Eloi, lama sabachthani? which is, being interpreted, My God, my God, why hast thou forsaken me?
. . .

And Jesus cried with a loud voice, and gave up the ghost.

And the veil of the temple was rent in twain from the top to the bottom.

And when the centurion, which stood over against him, saw that he so cried out, and gave up the ghost, he said, Truly this man was the Son of God. (Mark 15:25, 33–34, 37–39)

Matthew adds: "Now from the sixth hour there was darkness over all the land unto the ninth hour . . . and the earth did quake, and the rocks rent" (Matthew 27:45, 51).

And Luke inserts a final detail that corroborates the Mesoamerican account: "And the sun was darkened" (Luke 23:45).

A Voice from the Heavens

It is difficult to imagine how terrifying such an experience as the one in Mesoamerica would be. The loss of homes, cities, and loved ones would by itself be horrible enough. But then to compound it with a darkness so thick that no light in any form could be seen would make the whole experience almost unendurable. But the survivors were not left alone. The record declares:

> There was a voice heard among all the inhabitants of the earth, upon all the face of this land, crying:
>
> Wo, wo, wo unto this people; wo unto the inhabitants of the whole earth except they shall repent; for the devil laugheth, and his angels rejoice, because of the slain of the fair sons and daughters of my people; and it is because of their iniquity and abominations that they are fallen. . . .
>
> And many great destructions have I caused to come upon this land, and upon this people, because of their wickedness and their abominations.
>
> O all ye that are spared because ye were more righteous than they, will ye not now return unto me, and repent of your sins, and be converted, that I may heal you?
>
> Yea, verily I say unto you, if ye will come unto me ye shall have eternal life. Behold, mine arm of mercy is extended towards you, and whosoever will come, him will I receive; and blessed are those who come unto me. (3 Nephi 9:1–2, 12–14)

What thoughts must have filled the frenzied, terrified minds of these people! All could hear the voice; all could understand it. Nevertheless, in case any might have questioned the identity of the voice's author, the voice continued:

> Behold, I am Jesus Christ the Son of God. I created the heavens and the earth, and all things that in them are. I was with the Father from the beginning. I am in

the Father, and the Father in me; and in me hath the Father glorified his name.

I came unto my own, and my own received me not. And the scriptures concerning my coming are fulfilled.

And as many as have received me, to them have I given to become the sons of God; and even so will I to as many as shall believe on my name, for behold, by me redemption cometh. . . .

I am the light and the life of the world. I am Alpha and Omega, the beginning and the end. . . .

Behold, I have come unto the world to bring redemption unto the world, to save the world from sin.

Therefore, whoso repenteth and cometh unto me as a little child, him will I receive, for of such is the kingdom of God. Behold, for such I have laid down my life, and have taken it up again; therefore repent, and come unto me ye ends of the earth, and be saved. (3 Nephi 9:15–18, 21–22)

The Voice Speaks Again

The hearing of this voice must have overwhelmied the survivors of the great storm and destruction. In fact, according to the record, they were so astonished by it that "they did cease lamenting and howling for the loss of their kindred which had been slain; therefore there was silence in all the land for the space of many hours" (3 Nephi 10:2).

Then the voice came again—this time identifying them and reminding them that the speaker had always been their God and always would be, if they would follow him:

O ye people of these great cities which have fallen, who are descendants of Jacob, yea, who are of the house of Israel, how oft have I gathered you as a hen gathereth her chickens under her wings, and have nourished you. . . .

O ye house of Israel whom I have spared, how oft will I gather you as a hen gathereth her chickens under her wings, if ye will repent and return unto me with full purpose of heart.

But if not, O house of Israel, the places of your dwellings shall become desolate until the time of the fulfilling of the covenant to your fathers. (3 Nephi 10:4, 6–7)

For the rest of the three days of darkness, caused undoubtedly by the massive volcanic eruptions that occurred and that caused the other catastrophes, the people once again sent up a weeping and a howling because of their terrible losses. But then at last

> The darkness dispersed from off the face of the land, and the earth did cease to tremble, and the rocks did cease to rend, and the dreadful groanings did cease, and all the tumultuous noises did pass away.
>
> And the earth did cleave together again, that it stood; and the mourning, and the weeping, and the wailing of the people who were spared alive did cease; and their mourning was turned into joy, and their lamentations into the praise and thanksgiving unto the Lord Jesus Christ, their Redeemer.
>
> And thus far were the scriptures fulfilled which had been spoken by the prophets. (3 Nephi 10:9–11)

Nearly a Year Passes By

We should remember that the storm and three days of darkness occurred "in the thirty and fourth year, in the first month, on the fourth day of the month" (3 Nephi 8:5). Though the record is silent about what the people did after the darkness had dispersed, we can assume they did their best to put their lives back together and try to understand all they had been through. Certainly their religious beliefs and understanding had been affected, for when the record takes up again "in the ending of the thirty and fourth year," (3 Nephi 10:18) it tells us that a crowd of twenty-five hundred of them had assembled "round about the temple which was in the land Bountiful." Thus, nearly a year had passed by, and still the people "were marveling and wondering one with another, and were showing one to another the great and marvelous change which had taken place. And they were also conversing about this Jesus Christ, of whom the sign had been given concerning his death" (3 Nephi 11:1–2).

A Most Glorious Appearance

The record states that while the twenty-five hundred people were "conversing one with another" round about the temple,

> They heard a voice as if it came out of heaven; and they cast their eyes round about, for they understood not the voice which they heard; and it was not a harsh voice, neither was it a loud voice; nevertheless, and

notwithstanding it being a small voice it did pierce them that did hear to the center, insomuch that there was no part of their frame that it did not cause to quake; yea, it did pierce them to the very soul, and did cause their hearts to burn.

And it came to pass that again they heard the voice, and they understood it not.

And again the third time they did hear the voice, and did open their ears to hear it; and their eyes were towards the sound thereof; and they did look steadfastly towards heaven, from whence the sound came.

And behold, the third time they did understand the voice which they heard; and it said unto them:

Behold my Beloved Son, in whom I am well pleased, in whom I have glorified my name—hear ye him.

And it came to pass, as they understood they cast their eyes up again towards heaven; and behold, they saw a Man descending out of heaven; and he was clothed in a white robe; and he came down and stood in the midst of them; and the eyes of the whole multitude were turned upon him, and they durst not open their mouths, even one to another, and wist not what it meant, for they thought it was an angel that had appeared unto them.

And it came to pass that he stretched forth his hand and spake unto the people, saying:

Behold, I am Jesus Christ, whom the prophets testified shall come into the world.

And behold, I am the light and the life of the world; and I have drunk out of that bitter cup which the Father hath given me, and have glorified the Father in taking upon me the sins of the world, in the which I have suffered the will of the Father in all things from the beginning. (3 Nephi 11:3–11)

More than five hundred years earlier, the great Nephi had also prophesied: "And I saw the heavens open, and the Lamb of God descending out of heaven; and he came down and showed himself unto [this people]" (1 Nephi 12:6). Abruptly, this prophecy was fulfilled.

And it came to pass that when Jesus had spoken these words the whole multitude fell to the earth; for they remembered that it had been prophesied among them that

Christ should show himself unto them after his ascension into heaven. (3 Nephi 11:3–12)

They Felt with Their Hands

Such an appearance, literally by God our Creator, is beyond human comprehension. Who can begin to guess the emotions that filled the hearts of these twenty-five hundred people as they gazed upon him? Who can imagine their feelings as they listened to the actual sound of his voice, bearing divine witness to them of his mission of mercy in their behalf? It is no wonder that every one of them fell to the earth.

But to more perfectly establish this witness, Christ knew that seeing and hearing would not be enough. The record continues:

And it came to pass that the Lord spake unto them saying: Arise and come forth unto me, that ye may thrust your hands into my side, and also that ye may feel the prints of the nails in my hands and in my feet, that ye may know that I am the God of Israel, and the God of the whole earth, and have been slain for the sins of the world. (3 Nephi 11:14)

And so, wonder of all wonders,

The multitude went forth, and thrust their hands into his side, and did feel the prints of the nails in his hands and in his feet; and this they did do, going forth one by one until they had all gone forth, and did see with their eyes and did feel with their hands, and did know of a surety and did bear record, that it was he, of whom it was written by the prophets, that should come.

And when they had all gone forth and had witnessed for themselves, they did cry out with one accord, saying:

Hosanna! Blessed be the name of the Most High God! And they did fall down at the feet of Jesus, and did worship him. (3 Nephi 11:15–17)

The True Meaning of Easter

Every year all of Christendom celebrates Easter, doing it in commemoration of Christ's resurrection, wherein he took up his dead body from the darkness of the tomb. We read in the New Testament of the two Marys who, in their grief, had gone to more properly embalm the body of their crucified Lord. To their surprise and wonder, however, they found that morning an already opened tomb, empty save for a glorious, angelic being.

> And the angel answered and said unto the women, Fear not ye: for I know that ye seek Jesus, which was crucified.
>
> He is not here: for he is risen, as he said. Come, see the place where the Lord lay.
>
> And go quickly, and tell his disciples that he is risen from the dead. . . .
>
> And as they went to tell his disciples, behold, Jesus met them, saying, All hail. And they came and held him by the feet, and worshipped him. (Matthew 28:5–7, 9)

In wonder, we may all ponder this momentous and miraculous event—this resurrection of Christ the Lord from the dead—as we seek to understand. The two Marys had held Jesus by the feet—not the feet of a spirit but those of a physical, tangible being, resurrected or raised up from the dead by the power of God, his mortal body made immortal and eternal. In continuing witness of this event, that same day in the evening the apostles had gathered together in a private room to discuss Jesus' appearance to the two women and to other disciples who had been on their way to Emmaus. Next, we read:

> And as they thus spake, Jesus himself stood in the midst of them, and saith unto them, Peace be unto you.
>
> But they were terrified and affrighted, and supposed that they had seen a spirit.
>
> And he said unto them, Why are ye troubled? and why do thoughts arise in your hearts?
>
> Behold my hands and my feet, that it is I myself: handle me, and see; for a spirit hath not flesh and bones, as ye see me have.
>
> And when he had thus spoken, he shewed them his hands and his feet. (Luke 24:36–40)

Again, lest they (or we) be confused or doubt that the resurrected Lord had taken up his physical body of flesh and bones in an immortal state, the scripture continues:

> And while they yet believed not for joy, and wondered, he said unto them, Have ye here any meat? And they gave him a piece of a broiled fish, and of an honeycomb. And he took it, and did eat before them. (Luke 24:41–43)

Later, Peter testified of these things before the world, again reiterating that Jesus had eaten with him and the other apostles (see Acts 10:39–41).

Now twenty-five hundred people in Mesoamerica had received that same glorious witness and knew for themselves about the truthfulness of the prophecies concerning the Messiah-Redeemer.

The Eye Hath Never Seen

On three consecutive days during the month of March, A.D. 34, the resurrected Jesus Christ visited and taught and blessed the people of Mesoamerica, showing them he was indeed Jehovah, the God of their fathers Adam, Noah, Enoch, Abraham, Isaac, Jacob, Moses, Lehi, and Nephi—and allowing them to bask in the light and love of his divine presence. Moreover, the record states that after those three days, "he did show himself unto them oft, and did break bread oft, and bless it, and give it unto them" (3 Nephi 26:13).

We cannot possibly imagine what overwhelming and life-changing experiences those visits were for the people, and the feasibility of their adequately describing what they were seeing, hearing, and feeling is also beyond the realm of possibility. In fact, as the record informs us:

> The eye hath never seen, neither hath the ear heard, before, so great and marvelous things as we saw and heard Jesus speak. . .
>
> And no tongue can speak, neither can there be written by any man, neither can the hearts of men conceive so great and marvelous things as we both saw and heard Jesus speak; and no one can conceive of the joy which filled our souls at the time we heard him pray for us unto the Father. (3 Nephi 17:16–17)

And concerning one of Christ's prayers to the Father:

> Tongue cannot speak the words which he prayed, neither can be written by man the words which he prayed.
>
> And the multitude did hear and do bear record; and their hearts were open and they did understand in their hearts the words which he prayed.
>
> Nevertheless, so great and marvelous were the words which he prayed that they cannot be written, neither can they be uttered by man. (3 Nephi 19:32–34)

Neither Contentions nor Disputations

Though we do not know many particulars about the Lord's visits to the people, the record is quite clear regarding the results. Within two years:

> The people were all converted unto the Lord, upon all the face of the land, both Nephites and Lamanites, and there were no contentions and disputations among them, and every man did deal justly one with another.
>
> And they had all things common among them; therefore there were not rich and poor, bond and free, but they were all made free, and partakers of the heavenly gift. (4 Nephi 1:2–3)

Significantly, under these conditions, the people were developing great spiritual strength—obtaining and using for themselves the marvelous power of the resurrected Lord.

> And there were great and marvelous works wrought by the disciples of Jesus, insomuch that they did heal the sick, and raise the dead, and cause the lame to walk, and the blind to receive their sight, and the deaf to hear; and all manner of miracles did they work among the children of men; and in nothing did they work miracles save it were in the name of Jesus. (4 Nephi 1:5)

In fact, life grew so amazingly peaceful and prosperous that the historians or record keepers, used to the typical affairs of mankind, found themselves hard pressed to know what to say.

> And thus did the thirty and eighth year pass away, and also the thirty and ninth, and forty and first, and the forty and second, yea, even until forty and nine years had passed away, and also the fifty and first, and the fifty and second; yea, and even until fifty and nine years had passed away.
>
> And the Lord did prosper them exceedingly in the land . . .
>
> And the people . . . did wax strong, and did multiply exceedingly fast, and became an exceedingly fair and delightsome people.
>
> And they were married, and given in marriage, and were blessed according to the multitude of the promises which the Lord had made unto them. (4 Nephi 1:6–7, 10–11)

Nevertheless, the descriptions those historians did leave give us a rare glimpse into what life will one day be like for those who are fortunate enough to live under Christ's millennial reign:

And it came to pass that there was no contention in the land, because of the love of God which did dwell in the hearts of the people.

And there were no envyings, nor strifes, nor tumults, nor whoredoms, nor lyings, nor murders, nor any manner of lasciviousness; and surely there could not be a happier people among all the people who had been created by the hand of God.

There were no robbers, nor murderers, neither were there Lamanites, nor any manner of -ites; but they were in one, the children of Christ, and heirs to the kingdom of God.

And how blessed were they! For the Lord did bless them in all their doings; yea, even they were blessed and prospered until an hundred and ten years had passed away; and the first generation from Christ had passed away, and there was no contention in all the land. (4 Nephi 1:15–18)

Though such a blissful state of affairs may seem impossible to us today, none of us have experienced such intimate contact with our God—the Lord God of Israel, our Messiah-Redeemer. Neither can we imagine, as we muddle our way through our worldly, often sinful lives, that Christ quite literally has the power to rid our hearts of such baseness and to lift us until we experience the same sort of joy these ancient Mesoamericans wrote of.

A Falling Away

Unfortunately, this state of joy did not last, even for them. Gradually, a generation arose who did not know Jesus. By A.D. 194, "a small part of the people . . . had revolted from the church and taken upon them the name of Lamanites; therefore there began to be Lamanites again in the land" (4 Nephi 1:20).

By A.D. 200, this revolt was spreading, and it is interesting to note why. According to the record:

The people had multiplied, insomuch that they were spread upon all the face of the land, and . . . they had become exceedingly rich, because of their prosperity in Christ.

And now, in this two hundred and first year there began to be among them those who were lifted up in pride, such as the wearing of costly apparel, and all manner of fine pearls, and of the fine things of the world.

And from that time forth they did have their goods and their substance no more common among them. (4 Nephi 1:23–25)

Pride was the issue, and seeking after the vain things of the world was the vehicle in which these people began driving themselves toward destruction.

And they began to be divided into classes; and they began to build up churches unto themselves to get gain, and began to deny the true church of Christ.

And it came to pass that when two hundred and ten years had passed away there were many churches in the land; yea, there were many churches which professed to know the Christ, and yet they did deny the more parts of his gospel, insomuch that they did receive all manner of wickedness, and did administer that which was sacred unto him to whom it had been forbidden because of unworthiness.

And this church did multiply exceedingly because of iniquity, and because of the power of Satan who did get hold upon their hearts.

And again, there was another church which denied the Christ; and they did persecute the true church of Christ, because of their humility and their belief in Christ; and they did despise them because of the many miracles which were wrought among them. (4 Nephi 1:26–29)

Worse, now the spirit of murder began to manifest itself:

Therefore they did exercise power and authority over the disciples of Jesus . . . and they did cast them into prison; but by the power of the word of God, which was in them, the prisons were rent in twain, and they went forth doing mighty miracles among them.

Nevertheless, and notwithstanding all these miracles, the people did harden their hearts, and did seek to kill them, even as the Jews at Jerusalem sought to kill Jesus, according to his word. . . .

And thus they did dwindle in unbelief and
wickedness, from year to year, even until two hundred and
thirty years had passed away. . . .

[But those who rejected the gospel] did not
dwindle in unbelief, but they did wilfully rebel against the
gospel of Christ; and they did teach their children that they
should not believe. (4 Nephi 1:30–31, 34, 38)

The Records Preserved

By A.D. 300, almost all of these Mesoamerican Hebrews, both
the Nephites and the Lamanites, had grown exceedingly wicked
together. This gross wickedness increased until, in A.D. 320, the keeper
of the sacred records, a man by the name of Ammaron,

. . . being constrained by the Holy Ghost, did hide up
the records which were sacred—yea, even all the sacred
records which had been handed down from generation to
generation, which were sacred—even until the three
hundred and twentieth year from the coming of Christ.

And he did hide them up unto the Lord that they
might come again unto the remnant of the house of Jacob
according to the prophecies and the promises of the Lord.
And thus is the end of the record of Ammaron. (4 Nephi
1:48–49)

Ammaron then located a youth of about ten years of age, who
he could see was of a sober disposition and quick to observe, and
said to him:

When ye are about twenty and four years old I
would that ye should remember the things that ye have
observed concerning this people; and when ye are of that
age go to the land Antum, unto a hill which shall be called
Shim; and there have I deposited unto the Lord all the
sacred engravings concerning this people. And behold, ye
shall take the plates of Nephi unto yourself, and the
remainder shall ye leave in the place where they are; and
ye shall engrave on the plates of Nephi all the things that
ye have observed concerning this people. (Mormon 1:3)

Doing as he was told, this Christ-following Mesoamerican
prophet and historian, whose name was Mormon, obtained the records
and then made an abridgement of them that he could carry with him,
all the time being called upon to witness the terrible wickedness and

wars of his people. He knew they were destroying themselves, and yet even though he served on at least two occasions as the commander of all the Nephite armies, he was powerless to do anything but record the awful fate that approached.

The Final Battle

In A.D. 385, a now elderly Mormon led his people into what would prove to be the final battle of this Nephite civilization, a civilization that had by then survived almost a thousand years. In his eyewitness report, Mormon records:

> And it came to pass that my people, with their wives and their children, did now behold the armies of the Lamanites marching towards them; and with that awful fear of death which fills the breasts of all the wicked, did they await to receive them.
>
> And . . . they came to battle against us, and every soul was filled with terror because of the greatness of their numbers.
>
> And it came to pass that they did fall upon my people with the sword, and with the bow, and with the arrow, and with the ax, and with all manner of weapons of war.
>
> And . . . my men were hewn down, yea, even my ten thousand who were with me, and I fell wounded in the midst; and they passed by me that they did not put an end to my life.
>
> And when they had gone through and hewn down all my people save it were twenty and four of us (among whom was my son Moroni) and we having survived the dead of our people, did behold on the morrow, when the Lamanites had returned unto their camps, from the top of the hill Cumorah, the ten thousand of my people who were hewn down, being led in the front by me.
>
> And we also beheld the ten thousand of my people who were led by my son Moroni.
>
> And behold, the ten thousand of Gidgiddonah had fallen, and he also in the midst.
>
> And Lamah had fallen with his ten thousand; and Gilgal had fallen with his ten thousand, and Limhah had fallen with his ten thousand; and Jeneum had fallen with his ten thousand; and Camenihah, and Moronihah, and

Antionum, and Shiblom, and Shem, and Josh, had fallen with their ten thousand each.

And . . . there were ten more who did fall by the sword, with their ten thousand each; yea, even all my people, save it were those twenty and four who were with me, and also a few who had escaped into the south countries, and a few who had deserted over unto the Lamanites, had fallen; and their flesh, and bones, and blood lay upon the face of the earth, being left by the hands of those who slew them to molder upon the land, and to crumble and to return to their mother earth.

And my soul was rent with anguish, because of the slain of my people, and I cried:

O ye fair ones, how could ye have departed from the ways of the Lord: O ye fair ones, how could ye have rejected that Jesus, who stood with open arms to receive you!

Behold, if ye had not done this, ye would not have fallen. But behold, ye are fallen, and I mourn your loss. (Mormon 6:7–18)

Some time afterward, Mormon's son Moroni, who was the sole Nephite survivor of the great last battle and therefore the last to keep the record, quietly buried them in a stone box beneath a boulder on the side of a hill in upstate New York. With that, this ancient Hebrew record was completed. Two great civilizations had now passed away from the face of Mesoamerica—first the Jaredites and now the Nephites. The stillness of their ruins is today a solemn reminder of what happens when a nation forgets God.

A Modern Translation

For more than fourteen long centuries, this ancient record, inscribed on thin gold plates so it would withstand the ravages of time and the elements, lay undisturbed, awaiting the time when the work of God would once again roll forth. No treasure hunters were allowed to find the record, and no archaeologists were led, through their scientific methods, to its resting place. "For," as Moroni recorded anciently, "none can have power to bring it to light save it be given him of God; for God wills that it shall be done with an eye single to his glory, or the welfare of the ancient and long dispersed covenant people of the Lord" (Mormon 8:15).

In 1827, the record was finally brought forth by the power of God and placed in the hands of a young man named Joseph Smith, whom the Lord had raised up for that very purpose. "And blessed be he that shall bring this thing to light; for it shall be brought out of darkness unto light, according to the word of God; yea, it shall be brought out of the earth, and it shall shine forth out of darkness, and come unto the knowledge of the people; and it shall be done by the power of God" (Mormon 8:16).

Laboriously, the youthful Joseph Smith worked to translate the ancient language inscribed on the gold plates, using the gifts God had given him for that very purpose. Finally, in 1829, the translation was completed, and in 1830 this ancient record was published for the first time and was appropriately titled after the great prophet who had abridged the work and witnessed the awful destruction of his people—the Book of Mormon.

Two Witnesses

During his mortal ministry, Jesus taught his disciples the importance of multiple witnesses: "But if he will not hear [thee, then] take with thee one or two more, that in the mouth of two or three witnesses every word may be established" (Matthew 18:16).

Now Christ had reiterated this true doctrine by establishing multiple witnesses to his own infinite atonement. In Palestine, he conquered death by laying down his body and then taking it up again, and many in that area of the world were made witnesses to it. Next, in Mesoamerica, he established even more witnesses to the glorious reality of the resurrection, descending out of the sky and appearing in actual Godly, bodily form to these transplanted members of the House of Israel.

One in the Lord's Hand

In about 601 B.C., the Lord warned the prophet Lehi that he "should take his family and depart into the wilderness" (1 Nephi 2:2). Lehi obeyed and fled from Jerusalem before its pending destruction. The armies of Babylonia, under Nebuchadnezzar, marched into Jerusalem in 587 B.C. Zedekiah, king of Judah, was taken captive. His sons were killed before his eyes, and then his eyes were put out. The leadership of Israel was marched off in captivity to Babylonia (2 Kings 24:17; 2 Chronicles 36).

Following this great destruction of Jerusalem, Ezekiel the prophet went to the Lord and inquired concerning the destiny of fallen Israel. The Lord told Ezekiel that captive and scattered Israel was like a valley of dry bones—desolate and without hope. But the Lord went on to promise Ezekiel that the people of Israel ultimately would be gathered back to their own land. The Lord also assured Ezekiel that with the gathering to the homeland, the Lord would again be the God of Israel. Ezekiel was told further that even the heathen would come to know that he, the Lord, sanctified Israel. The Lord promised not only to eventually gather Israel back from among the nations and restore the people to their own land but also to breathe his Spirit back into Israel.

Through the prophet Ezekiel, the Lord then uttered an interesting pronouncemen:

> Moreover, thou son of man, take thee one stick, and write upon it, For Judah, and for the children of Israel his companions: then take another stick, and write upon it, For Joseph, the stick of Ephraim, and for all the house of Israel his companions:
> And join them one to another into one stick; and they shall become one in thine hand. . . .
> Say unto [those who ask what is meant], Thus saith the Lord GOD; Behold, I will take the stick of Joseph, which is in the hand of Ephraim, and the tribes of Israel his fellows, and will put them with him, even with the stick of Judah, and make them one stick, and they shall be one in mine hand. (Ezekiel 37:16–17, 19)

In 1953, M. E. L. Mallowan discovered two sets of wax-coated writing tablets at the bottom of a well at the archaeological site of Nimrud in Iraq. The phrase *is le'u shinpiri* was inscribed on the cover-board. *Is le'u* means "wooden tablet" and *shin piri* "ivory." The Hebrew word in Ezekiel 37 that is translated as *stick* or *wood* is *'es*, which means wood or board. Mallowan's writing board, dated to 707 B.C., provides an important confirmation that the two "sticks" in Ezekiel 37 refer to two written records. (Meservy 1978, 26)

Though the debate is still open whether Ezekiel's "sticks" were tally boards or scrolls of leather or parchment rolled about a stick like the Torah, the issue matters little.

The symbolism is the same and the reference in each instance is to a book, a divine record, a volume of holy scripture kept by the respective peoples. One record is to flow from the Kingdom of Judah, composed in that day of Judah, Benjamin, and those of such other tribal lineages as dwelt in that kingdom. The stick of Judah is the Bible. The other stick, the stick of Joseph in the hands of Ephraim . . . was [to be] kept by the house of Joseph, of whom the Nephites were a branch . . . [and] is symbolical of the Book of Mormon. This record Moroni, the last of the Nephite prophets, who holds "the keys of the record of the stick of Ephraim" (D&C 27:5), brought . . . to light in modern times. (McConkie 1985, 454–55)

But were the Nephites of Mesoamerica actually related to Joseph and his son Ephraim? The Joseph in the phrase "stick of Joseph" that Ezekiel referred to was the Joseph in the Old Testament. He received the coat of many colors from his father, Jacob, and then his jealous brothers sold him into slavery in Egypt. He became a high official in Egypt and was patriarchal father of one of the Twelve Tribes of Israel. He lived about 1,750 years before Christ and about 400 years before Moses.

Joseph's father Jacob, whose name was changed by God to Israel, blessed each of his sons as the head of one of the Twelve Tribes of Israel. When it was Joseph's turn, Jacob gave him a special and more lengthy blessing than the others:

Joseph is a fruitful bough, even a fruitful bough by a well; whose branches run over the wall:

The archers have sorely grieved him, and shot at him, and hated him:

But his bow abode in strength, and the arms of his hands were made strong by the hands of the mighty God of Jacob; (from thence is the shepherd, the stone of Israel:)

Even by the God of thy father, who shall help thee; and by the Almighty, who shall bless thee with blessings of heaven above, blessings of the deep that lieth under, blessings of the breasts, and of the womb.

The blessings of thy father have prevailed above the blessings of my progenitors unto the utmost bound of the everlasting hills: they shall be on the head of Joseph, and on the crown of the head of him that was separate from his brethren. (Genesis 49:22–26)

This special blessing on Joseph and his sons, Ephraim and Manasseh, who each became head of a tribe of Israel, was repeated and enlarged upon some 240 years later by Moses as he finished his ministry as the prophet of Israel:

> And of Joseph he said, Blessed of the Lord be his land, for the precious things of heaven, for the dew, and for the deep that coucheth beneath,
>
> And for the precious fruits brought forth by the sun, and for the precious things put forth by the moon,
>
> And for the chief things of the ancient mountains, and for the precious things of the lasting hills,
>
> And for the precious things of the earth and fulness thereof, and for the good will of him that dwelt in the bush: let the blessing come upon the head of Joseph, and upon the top of the head of him that was separated from his brethren.
>
> His glory is like the firstling of his bullock, and his horns are like the horns of unicorns: with them he shall push the people together to the ends of the earth: and they are the ten thousands of Ephraim, and they are the thousands of Manasseh. (Deuteronomy 33:13–17)

The statement that Joseph is a "fruitful bough" means that he would have numerous descendants. That his branches would "run over the wall" appears to mean that his descendants would migrate beyond the borders and boundaries of Palestine. The blessings that Israel pronounced upon Joseph are to be greater than those received by Israel's forebears and are to reach to "the utmost bound of the everlasting hills: they shall be on the head of Joseph."

Interestingly, the American continent is the only place in the world where the mountains run continuously the length of the continent. They emerge from the sea in Alaska and run as if *everlastingly* until they enter the sea at the southern tip of South America.

There is nothing to suggest that Joseph himself wrote a scroll or a book. The "stick of Joseph" was written by his descendants who went "over the wall" and beyond the vineyard unto the "utmost bound of the everlasting hills." It was written by the ancients of the New World who claimed to be descendants of Jacob.

Scientist and theologian James E. Talmage has written:

> Plainly the record of Judah, which we recognize
> as the Holy Bible, was to be supplemented by the record
> of Joseph; and the bringing forth of the latter was to be
> effected by the direct exercise of Divine power, for the
> Lord said "I will take the stick of Joseph"; and of the two
> He averred "they shall be one in mine hand," even as the
> prototypes had become one in the hand of Ezekiel.
> (Talmage 1919, 142)

And what did the Lord mean when he said that "they shall be
one in mine hand?" Again, "Both records, the one from Judah and the
one from Joseph, are for the benefit and blessing of all the house of
Israel. And these records shall be one in the Lord's hands because
they testify of the same Christ, teach the same gospel, breathe the
same spirit, and come from the same source" (McConkie 1985, 455).

Other than Jesus of Nazareth, the people of the world need not
look forward any more for a Messiah. There is but one Messiah—the
one spoken of by the prophets of Israel, by the apostles of the early
Church, and by the historians of ancient Mesoamerica. His resurrection
in the Old World redeemed men and women from the chains of death.
His New World appearance in Mesoamerica prepared a second
witness of the resurrection and of the fact that Jesus is the Christ, the
Son of the Living God.

Mormon's Testimony

In witness of this fact, Mormon bore fervent testimony, saying:

> And now, behold, I would speak somewhat unto
> the remnant of this people who [may be] spared. . . .
>
> Know ye that ye are of the house of Israel.
>
> Know ye that ye must come unto repentance, or
> ye cannot be saved. . . .
>
> Know ye that ye must come to the knowledge
> of your fathers, and repent of all your sins and iniquities,
> and believe in Jesus Christ, that he is the Son of God, and
> that he was slain by the Jews, and by the power of the
> Father he hath risen again, whereby he hath gained the
> victory over the grave; and also in him is the sting of death
> swallowed up.
>
> And he bringeth to pass the resurrection of the
> dead, whereby man must be raised to stand before his
> judgment-seat.

> And he hath brought to pass the redemption of
> the world, whereby he that is found guiltless before him at
> the judgment day hath it given unto him to dwell in the
> presence of God in his kingdom, to sing ceaseless praises
> with the choirs above, unto the Father, and unto the Son,
> and unto the Holy Ghost, which are one God, in a state of
> happiness which hath no end. (Mormon 7:1–3, 5–7)

The Ancient Record

Concerning the purpose of the record he had kept and abridged before handing it to his son Moroni at the time of Mormon's own death, Mormon declared with finality: "Therefore I, Mormon, do write the things which have been commanded me of the Lord" (3 Nephi 26:12). Some time thereafter, Moroni wrote these words that serve as part of the preface to the Book of Mormon:

> Written by way of commandment, and also by
> the spirit of prophecy and of revelation—Written and sealed
> up, and hid up unto the Lord, that they might not be
> destroyed—To come forth by the gift and power of God
> unto the interpretation thereof. . . . The interpretation thereof
> by the gift of God . . . to show unto the remnant of the
> House of Israel what great things the Lord has done for
> their fathers; and that they may know the covenants of the
> Lord, that they are not cast off forever—And also to the
> convincing of the Jew and Gentile that Jesus is the Christ,
> the eternal God, manifesting himself unto all nations.
> (Preface, Book of Mormon)

A Final Witness

Finally, Moroni, who was the last to record on the plates before he buried them in a "stone box" on the hill in upstate New York, speaks as if from the dust, instructing us:

> And when ye shall receive these things, I would
> exhort you that ye would ask God, the Eternal Father, in
> the name of Christ, if these things are not true; and if ye
> shall ask with a sincere heart, with real intent, having faith
> in Christ, he will manifest the truth of it unto you, by the
> power of the Holy Ghost.
> And by the power of the Holy Ghost ye may
> know the truth of all things. (Moroni 10:4–5)

And now, I would commend you to seek this Jesus of whom the prophets and apostles have written, that the grace of God the Father, and also the Lord Jesus Christ, and the Holy Ghost, which beareth record of them, may be and abide in you forever. Amen. (Ether 12:41)

That such can quite literally be the case, we have no doubt.

Chapter 7
MESOAMERICA: THE LAND OF THE BOOK OF MORMON

Since Joseph Smith first translated and published the Book of Mormon in 1830, many different land areas have been proposed as the places where the various parts of the account took place. The contents of these various geographical models need to be evaluated in light of current knowledge available from ancient America.

One of these models, which we support, holds that the records of both the Nephites and the Jaredites describe cultures and civilizations that were born, flourished, and died in Middle America or Mesoamerica. This geographic area consists of south and southeastern Mexico and also includes the countries of Guatemala, El Salvador, Honduras, Belize, and parts of Costa Rica and Nicaragua. The maps inside the front and back covers of this book show Mesoamerica.

As was pointed out in the "Introduction," however, there is more to this definition. Mesoamerica also refers to the time period before the discovery of America by Columbus and before the conquest of Mexico. Therefore, the term *Mesoamerica* has direct reference to the great civilizations that flourished in Middle America during the pre-Columbus periods (Allen 1989, 4). These were the lowland and highland Maya, the Olmec culture along the Gulf Coast of Mexico, the Zapotec culture core in the Valley of Oaxaca, and the Valley of Mexico culture core.

Three Questions

A brief evaluation of this and other geographical models will focus on three important questions. First, what type of society is described in the Book of Mormon? Second, is there justification in limiting the historical events and geographical locations of the Book of Mormon to Mesoamerica? And third, to what extent can we apply an analytical sociocultural model to the Book of Mormon in Mesoamerica?

Rather than describe and evaluate societal types such as "hunters and gatherers of wild natural resources," "simple farmers," and so forth, we propose as a working hypothesis that the Book of Mormon peoples developed into a civilizational level of societal development. And just what is a civilization? K.C. Chang writes: "I would refer to civilization, archaeologically recognized, as the cultural manifestation of these contrastive pairs of societal opposites: class-class, urban-nonurban, and state-state. In other words, economic stratification, urbanization, and interstate relations are three of civilization's necessary societal determinants" (Chang 1980, 365–66).

What Type of Society?

Does the text of the Book of Mormon satisfy Chang's definition of a society? As indicated by the following references, we believe it does.

1. **Civilization**: Alma 51:22; Moroni 9:11–12
2. **Classes/inequalities**: Mosiah 29:32; Alma 4:12, 15; 3 Nephi 7:10–14; 4 Nephi 1:26
3. **Cities**: Jaredites—Ether 9:23; Nephites—Alma 8:7; 50:1; 62:32: Helaman 3:9; 4:9, 16; 8:6; 3 Nephi 6:7; 8:8–10, 14–15; 9:3; 4 Nephi 1:7–9; Mormon 8:7
4. **Kingdom, nation, governor**: Jaredites—Ether 1:43; 7:20; Nephites—Mosiah 29:6–9; Alma 2:16; 9:20; 50:39; 61:1; 3 Nephi 1:1

Based upon these and other references, there is little doubt that the peoples of all three Book of Mormon colonies—the Jaredites, the people of Lehi, and the people of Mulek—developed high and extremely diverse and stratified societies.

Justification for Placing Main Book of Mormon Lands in Mesoamerica

If the Jaredites, the Nephites, and the Lamanites in the course of their history developed into a civilizational type of society, then their lands and cities must have been located in an area of ancient America that today has ruins representing a civilizational level of development. In answer to the second question posed above, these ruins most certainly do exist.

The accumulated information from archaeology, anthropology, and history over the past 150 years for deciphering the past of ancient America is voluminous. A summary analysis of this information indicates that two geographical areas of ancient America reached the civilizational level of society before the coming of Columbus and other European explorers: Mesoamerica and the Andean region of South America.

Book of Mormon Geographical Information

Internal analysis of the Book of Mormon text characterizes the major features of Book of Mormon lands as including a "land northward" connected to a "land southward" by "a small neck of land" (Alma 22:32); the lands of Nephi and Zarahemla in the land southward being "nearly surrounded by water" (Alma 22:32); the land of Zarahemla and Nephi separated "by a narrow strip of wilderness, which ran from the sea east even to the sea west" (Alma 22:27); this "narrow strip of wilderness" contained "the head of the river Sidon" (Alma 22:27); "and it came to pass that they [Nephites] did multiply and spread, and did go forth from the land southward to the land northward, and did spread insomuch that they began to cover the face of the whole earth, from the sea south to the sea north, from the sea west to the sea east" (Helaman 3:8).

The Andean Region

The Andean region of South America does not have any of the above features. Andean civilization developed from the Pacific Ocean on the west to the west flanks of the Andean Mountains on the east, and from southern Ecuador on the north to central Chile on the south. The Andean region lacks the surrounding seas, writing systems (dating to the Book of Mormon period), and appropriate topographical patterns mentioned in the Book of Mormon, and the region has no surviving written traditions. Further, Andean civilizational development did not begin with an agricultural economy like that of the Jaredites (Ether 6:13) and Nephites (1 Nephi 18:23–24) but with a maritime economy. Irrigation agriculture as a subsistence base came later.

The Mesoamerican Region

On the other hand, the Mesoamerican region contains all the major geographical features required by the text of the Book of Mormon. In addition, travel distances in the Book of Mormon are recorded in days of foot travel when on land. The example of Alma the Elder's leading a group of about "four hundred and fifty souls" from the Waters of Mormon in the land of Nephi to their eventual settlement in the land of Zarahemla took 21 days. (Mosiah

18:35; 23:3; 24:20, 25) Alma's group included children and animals, so the journey probably involved a distance of between 250 and 300 miles—or 11 to 13 miles per day if they traveled every day, a good day's journey for such a diverse group. This information strongly suggests that the land southward in the Book of Mormon was a relatively small area.

Even the Jaredite land northward appears to be a relatively small area. For example, in a time of extreme drought, cattle in search of water and feed wandered from the land of Moron in the western highlands of the land northward "towards the land southward, which was called by the Nephites Zarahemla" (Ether 9:31). When we ask the question "How far would cattle wander in extreme drought conditions?" the answer would be as follows: "Not very far—certainly not in excess of a hundred or so miles."

The Andean civilization from north to south covered about twenty-five hundred miles, as compared to the Mesoamerican civilization from northwest to southeast, covering about a thousand miles. On the basis of distances required by the Book of Mormon, we logically choose Mesoamerica as the region best fulfilling the distance requirements.

Language Traditions

Other important differences between the Mesoamerican and Andean civilization regions include the lack of written traditions in the Andean region as contrasted with surviving written traditions from Mesoamerica. Additionally, the major language families of the Mesoamerican and Andean regions are not related to each other.

Missing Data

Available information concerning the Mesoamerican and Andean civilizations pinpoints Mesoamerica as the region where the three colonies of the Book of Mormon account landed and settled. However, if we conclude that Mesoamerica is indeed the homeland for the peoples mentioned in the Book of Mormon, then we must also acknowledge that the histories of the people who settled in North or South America are not recorded in the Book of Mormon.

The Book of Ether account of the Jaredite people states that the original colony consisted of twenty-four families (Ether 6:14–16). However, we have the abridged record of the family lineage of just one of these—Jared. We know nothing of the other twenty-three family histories.

The main body of information in the rest of the Book of Mormon refers to the lineage or tribe of Nephi. However, seven tribes evolved from the Lehi colony (Jacob 1:13), six of which the abridged record mostly ignores.

Another colony mentioned is one called the people of Mulek (Mosiah 25:2) or the Mulekites, though the Book of Mormon contains so little information on them that we do not even know if they came in one ship or several ships. If we had an abridgement of the records of all these neglected lineages and tribes, we would possibly find that some of them may have settled in North and South America.

Interesting Possibilities

At present, we have sufficient information to set up a working hypothesis for locating part of the Jaredites in southern Veracruz and western Tabasco (see Table 2–2 with Jaredite names of individuals and places). Highland Guatemala has sufficient information to hypothesize that this was the ancient land of Nephi (see Sorenson 1985, 1988, and Allen 1989). Other interesting prospects for locating Book of Mormon lands are the Valley of Guatemala, the Oaxaca Valley, and the Tuxtla Mountains of southern Veracruz.

Bruce Warren has written:

Two stelae are significant to Book of Mormon geography studies. A recent book by Munro S. Edmonson dates the first one, Stela 10, at Kaminaljuyu, Guatemala, in three separate calenders, at 10 November 147 B.C. [Julian calendar]. Kaminaljuyu is an archaeological site located on the western edge of Guatemala City in the Valley of Guatemala. Stela 10 at this site is really a royal throne with hieroglyphic writing that cannot be read at the present time, [though] the throne does depict a person who is dead by fire and a second figure of a king ascending to a throne. This monument has parallels to an episode in Mosiah chapter 19 which describes the death by fire of King Noah and the ascension to the throne of his son Limhi (this episode is dated about 145 B.C. according to the date at the bottom of the page of Chapter 19). The implications of this monument for the Book of Mormon is that Kaminaljuyu could be the city of Nephi.

Edmonson dates Stela 13 at Monte Alban in the Oaxaca Valley at 563 B.C. following Alfonso Caso or 251 B.C. based on Edmonson's own research. The stela shows the capture of a king at Monte Alban by a foreign Olmec ruler from the lowlands of Veracruz. This event could parallel the capture of King Coriantumr in the land of Moron. (Ether 14:6). However, until the choice between the two different dates can be resolved, Stela 13 cannot contribute to the question of whether the Jaredites destroyed themselves at the coming of the Mulekites in the sixth century B.C. or at the time of King Zarahemla in the third century B.C. (Warren 1990, 135)

An Analytical Sociocultural Model

The third question posed above relates to historical or cultural geography as applied to models of Book of Mormon geography. J. E. Spencer and William L. Thomas Jr. state that "cultural geography is concerned with the systems of human technologies and cultural practices as these are developed in particular regions of the earth through time by human populations conceived as cultural groups" (Spencer and Thomas 1969, 4). In other words, cultural geography deals with population, environment, technology, and social organization. Figure 7–1 shows a way to integrate these issues in a single model.

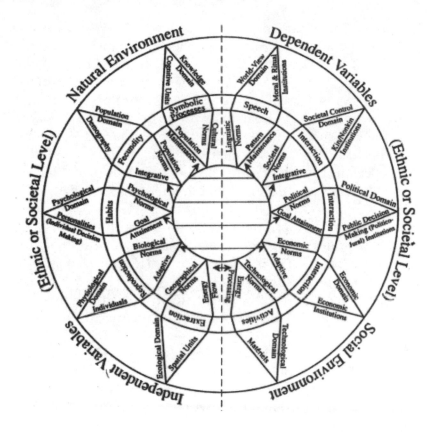

Figure 7–1. Warren's analytical sociocultural model. This figure has the independent variables for the Mesoamerican region on the left-hand side of the model, which would be the controls for explaining the information applicable to the dependent variables on the right-hand side of the model.

Archaeology can supply important data for the technological and economic domains of the sociocultural model but limited information for the political, societal control, and world view domains. Many other scientific disciplines will be needed to help in these latter domains. The bottom-line control for all these analytical domains will be information that can be gleaned from the Book of Mormon.

A few scholars have already begun these sociocultural types of research on the Book of Mormon, but we are very much in a pioneering stage of inquiry. The time has come for everyone to get more serious about the historical claims of the Book of Mormon.

Joseph Smith's Opinion

It may come as a surprise that Joseph Smith, who translated the ancient records of the Nephites and published them as the Book of Mormon, expressed an opinion as to where Book of Mormon lands were located. As was pointed out in the "Introduction," in 1841, just eleven years after the Book of Mormon was published, John Lloyd Stephens published a book about his travels in Central America, Chiapas, and the Yucatan.

Speaking of Stephens' travels and book, Joseph Smith says, "Mr. Stephens' great development of antiquities are made bare to the eyes of all the people by reading the history of the Nephites in the Book of Mormon. **They lived about the narrow neck of land, which now embraces Central America, with the cities that can be found**" (*Times and Seasons*, 3:915, emphasis added).

Men Across the Ocean

Despite what we know scientifically concerning the high cultural civilizations that existed in Mesoamerica, the question must still be asked, "How did they get there?" In spite of the fact that the Book of Mormon describes barges (Ether 2:6, 16–17) and a ship (1 Nephi 18:1–4), is it really practical to believe that a colony of settlers, let alone three separate and distinct colonies, actually arrived in ancient Mesoamerica using such conveyances? We believe that it is.

The absence in ancient Alaska, Canada, and the United States of the many cultural and religious elements common to the Near East and Mesoamerica indicates that ancient Americans were not all brought over the land bridge connecting Siberia and Alaska. Atomic energy dating by radiocarbon places the beginnings of complex society in Mesoamerica at 2500 B.C., with no primitive underpinnings to indicate that all the elements did not develop independently, step by step. In other words, this highly complex and civilized culture was not there, and then it was.

The only plausible explanation is the one given by the early histories of Mesoamerica—that some of the people came by assorted types of boats to the central part of the New World. But how could people have made it across the ocean hundreds, even thousands, of years before Columbus?

Rafts, Boats, Ships

In 1950, Thor Heyerdahl, a Norwegian explorer, focused the world's attention on his balsa raft with its square sail as he crossed the South Pacific from Peru to the Tuamotu Islands. His historic voyage is recounted in his *American Indians in the Pacific: The Theory Behind the Kon-Tiki Expedition.*

A young German graduate of the medical school at the University of Hamburg, Dr. Hannes Lindemann, has twice crossed the Atlantic in simple crafts. In 1955, he used a twenty-four-foot dugout canoe. In the fall of 1956, he used a seventeen-foot rubberized canvas craft on a collapsible wooden frame with an outrigger made from an inner tube (Lindemann 1957).

On 21 September 1958, DeVere Baker, an American shipbuilder, drifted into the Hawaiian Islands on his raft *Lehi* after bobbing twenty-one hundred miles for sixty-nine days across the Pacific from Redondo Beach, California. Also in 1958, a sixty-six-year-old Frenchman, Eric de Bisschop, made it from South America to the South Sea island of Manikiki, only to be killed when his raft broke up on a reef.

Two additional scholars summarize other contemporary transoceanic voyages:

> Merrien lists 120 modern intentional *solo and two-man* long voyages. Among these are a 17-day voyage from the Cape Verde Islands to Martinique by a pair of Estonians in a 29-foot sloop; a 30-day Atlantic crossing in a 24-foot 8-inch sailing craft by a toeless, fingerless sailor; William Verity's 68-day passage from Florida to Ireland in a home-built, 12-foot sloop; a sail-less, oar-propelled crossing by two men from New York to the Scilly Islands in 55 days in a dory 17 feet, 8 inches long; a solo, 93-day crossing from Japan to San Francisco in a 19-foot sloop; a 68-day raft drift from California to Hawaii; a solo voyage in a converted Indian dugout canoe (bottom length, 3 feet) from Vancouver directly to the Cook Islands, a journey of some 5,500 miles in 56 days, followed by an ultimate landing in England; a solo, 162-day journey in a 19.5 foot schooner 6,500 miles from San Francisco to Australian waters without a single port of call; the solo, three-year, 46,000-mile, round-the-world voyage of Joshua Slocum in the *Spray* (36 feet 9

inches); the round-the-world journey of Vito Dumas in a 32-foot ketch, a journey that included a direct 7,200-mile run in the Roaring Forties from the Cape of Good Hope to New Zealand, on to Valparaiso, Chile (5,400 miles in 72 days), and then around the Horn; sixty-six-year-old Francis Chichester's 28,500-mile, one-stop circumnavigation via Cape Horn in a 54-foot ketch; the voyages of Eric de Bisschop—including one with a single companion from Hawaii to Cannes in 264 sailing days in a double canoe, one by bamboo sailing raft some 5,000 miles into the southeastern Pacific from Tahiti, and one by raft from Peru 5,500 miles to Rakahanga; the 7,450-mile pontoon raft journey from Peru to Samoa by seventy-year-old William Willis (1965), who eventually sailed 3,000 additional miles to Australia, though suffering an abdominal hernia, a fractured sacrum, and partial paralysis; four other raft journeys from Peru, with safe landings ranging from the Galapagos to Australia; a journey by three Americans in an old Polynesian outrigger from Oahu to San Francisco; a trip down the Amazon and on to Miami by an eighteen-year-old in a leaky, 19-foot dugout fitted with sails, including a run of over 850 miles on the Atlantic; a solo, 72-day crossing of the Atlantic in a 17-foot canvas foldboat; an island-hopping expedition by a sixteen-year-old in a 24-foot sloop from California to South Africa, including a 2,300-mile run under jury-rig due to a dismasting; and a solo voyage in a 6-foot sailboat from Casablanca to Florida in 84 days. . . . Even transatlantic races for loners have now been established. (Jett 1974, 17-19)

Edwin Doran Jr., investigating transpacific voyages, mentions the following:

Of sixty cases of inadvertent drifts of Japanese junks into the Pacific, at least a half dozen reached the coast of America between Sitka and the Columbia River and another half dozen were wrecked on the Mexican coast or encountered just offshore. Survivors of such drift voyages were not uncommon, and Japanese slaves were held by Salmon Indians of the northwest coast of America when they first were visited by Whites. Drift voyages between Asia and America not only are clearly possible but actually have occurred repeatedly in historic time. In view of the ability of rafts to sail close-hauled against the wind in remarkable effective fashion, a phenomenon noted repeatedly and with great surprise by early Western mariners who encountered rafts off the coast of Ecuador and Peru, an even greater feasibility for early transpacific raft voyages can be inferred. There appears to be no question that rafts could have crossed the Pacific, repeatedly and in appreciable number. (Doran 1974, 133–35)

These intrepid, modern sailors were duplicating ancient voyages, incomplete records of which have survived in fragmentary reports. The sailors of Crete during the first and second millennia B.C. traveled from the Mediterranean Sea to Britain and back. About 950 B.C.,

> King Solomon made a navy of ships in Ezion-geber [an Israelite port off the northeast corner of the Red Sea], which is beside Eloth, on the shore of the Red Sea, in the land of Edom. And Hiram [king of Tyre in Phoenicia] sent in the navy his servants, shipmen that had knowledge of the sea, with the servants of Solomon. And they came to Ophir, and fetched from thence gold, four hundred and twenty talents, brought it to king Solomon (1 Kings 9:26–28). Also, between 608–594 B.C., Necho II of Egypt sent out an expedition that went around Africa. (Herodotus 1942, 306; Warren and Ferguson 1987, 210)

Thus, both in modern and ancient times, transoceanic voyages are clearly possible. In fact, the feat was not unique. America has long been a melting pot for many peoples and many cultures. Ancient times were no exception. There are many indications that other groups came to Mesoamerica anciently. The cultural pattern is a giant jig-saw of complexity. Each group of colonizers brought its own piece of the puzzle—to be fitted in with the indigenous population.

Other Immigrants

The essays of Stephen C. Jett and Edwin Doran Jr., dealing with documented transoceanic voyages in historic times, have already been mentioned. However, Meggers, Evans, and Estrada (1965) take voyages a step further in establishing probable Japanese colonization of a South American site. The Valdivia culture of Ecuador, which dates back to nearly 3000 B.C., produced ceramics that have close parallels with Jomon pottery from ancient Japan, which dates before 3000 B.C. Reporting records from historic times of Japanese fishermen caught in storms and landing on the coast of Ecuador, the authors hypothesize a probable Japanese origin for the Valdivia culture.

Recent important works investigating possible Southeast Asian sources of influence upon Mesoamerica include "The Trans-Pacific Origin of Mesoamerican Civilization: The Preliminary Review of the Evidence and Its Theoretical Implications" by Betty Meggers of the Smithsonian Institution. This paper focuses on the Shang Dynasty of China and the Olmec civilization of Mesoamerica, maps their territories, and analyzes parallel symbols, artifacts, and monuments. Her conclusion is that a fairly strong case can be made for some type of transpacific contact between the two.

Chinese archaeologist Paul Shao, who did his graduate work in America and is now a resident of the United States, has published *Chinese Influence in Pre-Classic Mesoamerican Art* and *The Origin of Ancient American Culture,* a full-length treatment of Chinese influences in Mesoamerican civilizations. His interest, initially triggered by a visit to Mesoamerican sites where he was greatly excited by the similarities he saw between Chinese and Mesoamerican monuments and artifacts, has not lessened after several years of concentrated work on the topic.

David H. Kelley, an anthropologist emeritus from the University of Calgary, found several distinctive features of the Maya Long Count calendar that paralleled features of the Hindu calendar of northern India. For example, certain plant, animal, and deity names have artistic similarities. Both use a Four World Age system with associated colors. The base date in both systems is a cataclysmic flood in the distant past. According to Kelley, the Hindu calendar dates from 3102 B.C., associated with the mass planetary conjunction at the time of the flood. A mass planetary conjunction occurs when the five visible planets—Venus, Mercury, Mars, Jupiter, and Saturn—appear on the eastern horizon on the same evening. This event occurs approximately every 179–180 years. The Maya Long Count system theoretically begins in 3114 B.C. and is associated with the destruction of the earth by flooding. Both systems at one point switched from a seven-day to a nine-day week, and both added two eclipse deities to bring the seven deities of the seven days up to nine deities for the nine-day week.

The Long Count calendar was an innovation in the Late Olmec period of ancient Mesoamerica and we believe an introduction from foreigners who arrived by ships from the east— according to several Mesoamerican legends.

The seven-day week was associated with the same planetary bodies in both systems. Perhaps not coincidentally, our own seven-day week uses the same planets in the same order: sun (Sunday), moon (Monday), Mars (Tuesday), Mercury (Wednesday), Jupiter (Thursday), Venus (Friday), and Saturn (Saturday). This particular order of days was first set among the Greeks during the Hellenistic period, who imported them into the Indus Valley and West Pakistan as part of Alexander the Great's wars of conquest between 331– 323 B.C. Thus, Kelley also argues that it is possible to date the departure of the Hindu migrants from this area to the Maya of Mesoamerica as no earlier than the first century B.C. (Kelley 1974, 135–44).

The research of Shao and Kelley suggests that other Old World colonists may have come to Mesoamerica during the Book of Mormon time period. If so, they could have had an impact on the Book of Mormon peoples. Two recent publications are significant in the evaluation of possible voyages and migrations to the New World: Nigel Davies' *Voyages to the New World* and Irving Rouse's *Migrations in Prehistory: Inferring Population Movement from Cultural Remains.*

John L. Sorenson's 1971 essay "The Significance of an Apparent Relationship Between the Ancient Near East and Mesoamerica" is also important. He presents a table of over a hundred cultural features shared by both Mesoamerica and the Near East (water confined beneath the temple, zero concept, and navel-of-the-world concept). (See the notes at the end of Chapter 13 for additional shared cultural features.)

Long-distance trading is another interesting area of research. Robert Chadwick compared the strong parallels between cultures dating from about 500 B.C. at Tlatilco, in the Valley of Mexico, Monte Negro, in Oaxaca, and Paracas, on the south coast of Peru.

In a separate presentation, Chadwick cites Ezekiel's lamentation for the seaport of Tyre, "a merchant of the people for many isles," which includes an enumeration of more than thirty cities or countries included in its merchandising network. He then concludes: "Although we can't say definitely that Ezekiel's chapter 27 description of long-distance trading and the 'prospector' colonies' intrusions in the New World at Tlatilco, Monte Negro, and Paracas refer to the same event, it seems likely this may be the case" (Chadwick 1974, 10).

In summary, transoceanic voyages in very simple crafts were possible in ancient times and have been replicated in our own century. The numerous cultural and religious parallels between the biblical and Book of Mormon cultures indicate that emigrants from several Old World cultures, including the Near East, have come to Mesoamerica. It seems probable that some of the colonizers were descendants of one of the tribes or branches of the family of Jacob or Israel.

Sometime shortly after 600 B.C., the Mesoamerican Hebrew prophet Nephi wrote: "For I came out from Jerusalem, and mine eyes hath beheld the things of the Jews, and I know that the Jews do understand the things of the prophets, and there is none other people that understand the things which were spoken unto the Jews like unto them, save it be that they are taught after the manner of the things of the Jews" (2 Nephi 25:5).

Chapter 8
EVIDENCES OF CHRIST'S VISIT TO MESOAMERICA

If the claims of the Hebrew prophets of Mesoamerica are true—that the resurrected Christ actually did visit his "sheep" in their land—we can expect to find numerous evidences of this supernal event almost everywhere we turn. As it turns out, such is most definitely the case. Though the evidence is at times diluted or distorted, much important information exists even today about the "Fair God" who visited Mesoamerica and who was known most generally as the deity *Quetzalcoatl*.

Quetzalcoatl

The fair god of ancient Mexico and Central America was known by many symbolic names. But in central Mexico, the most common symbolic name for him was *Quetzalcoatl*. The name is derived from two Nahuatl/Aztec language words: *quetzal*, the name of a nearly extinct beautiful bird with long, undulating green tail feathers (the word also means "precious"), and *coatl*, meaning "serpent" or "twin." In Guatemala, this ancient god was commonly called *Gucumatz*—a Quiche Maya term identical in meaning to the Aztec name *Quetzalcoatl*. Both the quetzal bird and the serpent appear as art motifs associated with Quetzalcoatl. Several sixteenth-century documents written by both native and Catholic priest-historians contain word-pictures of this figure.

A belief in Quetzalcoatl's divine power as creator and in his second coming was general throughout the ancient Mesoamerican world (central and southern Mexico and northern Central America). It was clear to the ancients of Mexico and Central America that this Messiah-Redeemer, who had been cocreator of the world, had appeared on earth in the flesh and was to return. In his antemortal existence, it was he, and not the Father, who had appeared to Abraham and Jacob and the other prophets and patriarchs of Israel. Table 8–1 presents the reference material to six variant developments or versions of this deity.

Table 8–1
Variant Versions of Quetzalcoatl, The Feathered Serpent

1. **Human figure wearing the Wind God Mask**
   Calendar date: 9 Ik 15 Keh (1 Reed Year: Texcoco).
   Astronomical identity: Venus, Evening Star. (Schlak 1983,
   Chapter 8)
   Traits: conical hat, bearded, shell jewelry, creative role,
   wind, patron of the day and the trecena 1 Jaguar.
   Chronology:
   Early Preclassic
      Birth or rebirth of 9 Ik 15 Keh (Palenque,
      Chiapas [Tablet of the Cross] Saturday, 18 October
      2360 B.C.)
   Postclassic (A.D. 900–1525)
      Selden Roll, p. 1
      Vienna, pp. 49d, 48c, 47b, 36, 35, 32, 30,
      29, 25, 24, and 10
      B*orgia*, pp. 9, 16, 20, 29, 30, 36, 38, 40, 41, 45,
      51, 55, 56, 72, and 73
      Nuttall, pp. 18, 38, 46, and 65c
2. **Rattlesnake with feathers on its body**
   Calendar date: 9 Ik 15 Xul (1 Reed year: Tepexic).
   Astronomical identity: Mercury, inferior conjunction.
   (Kelley 1980, S18)
   Name: Nine Wind Quetzalcoatl.
   Traits: rattlesnake with feathers, bearded, patron of the
   day reed and the trecenas 1 Deer and 1 Dog.
   Chronology:
   Proto-Preclassic (prior to 2500 B.C.)
      Projected date: Sunday, 10 December 3072 B.C.
   Middle Preclassic (1200–250 B.C.)
      San Lorenzo, Veracruz, Monument 47 (Coe and
      Diehl 1980, 356) with a parallel with the first
      divine king of the Palenque, Chiapas, dynasty by
      the name of *U-Kish Kan.* (Schele and Freidel 1990, 247)
      U-Kish Kan was born Wednesday, 8 March 993 B.C.
         La Venta, Tabasco, Monument 19. (Drucker,
      Heizer, and Squire 1959, 198) This monument has

a rattlesnake, two quetzal birds, and a priest carved on its surface. The projected date for Monument 19 is Sunday, 1 April 525 B.C.

Chalcatzingo, Morelos, Monument 1 (Kubler 1962, 127) has serpent elements and two quetzal birds.

Monte Alban, Oaxaca, from the first period at the site had a jar with a mask of a serpent (Caso and Bernal 1952, 147). The suggested date for the jar is Wednesday, 20 March 473 B.C. The 20th of March is the spring equinox in that particular year.

Late Classic (A.D. 650–950)

Cacaxtla, Tlaxcala, murals have a feathered serpent and a 9 Ik calendar date.

A stone palma from Veracruz depicts a human head, bicephalic serpents, two quetzal birds as hands, and a conch shell. (Miller and Taube 1993, 141)

Early Postclassic (A.D. 950–1250)

Xochicalco, Morelos, Temple of Quetzalcoatl (Kubler 1962, 71–72) has a date of 1 April A.D. 983. A special episode in *Codex Borgia*, pages 35–44, involves "strip-eyes" Quetzalcoatl, who is probably a priest of the deity. This same priest is illustrated in the *Codex Bodley*, pp. 39–40, *Codex Nuttall*, page 16, and the *Selden Roll*, page 2.

Chichen Itza, Yucatan, Temple of Kukulcan has a bearded priest of Quetzalcoatl or Kukulcan carved on one of the door lintels. The date of 6 April is significant to the shadowing effects along one of the stairways facing the causeway leading to the sacred well or cenote.

Codex Magliabecchiano has Quetzalcoatl with a wind-jewel on his chest. The date is probably Saturday, 21 March A.D. 1035. This date falls on the spring equinox.

3. **Flint-helmeted human figure**

Calendar date: 9 Ik 5 Mol (10 House year: Tepexic)
Astronomical Identity: Venus, Evening Star (?).

Traits: Flint Helmet, birth from a stone, jeweled temple, and 5 Mol is New Year's Day in the Izapa calendar.
Chronology:

Middle Preclassic (1200–250 B.C.)

Projected date: Wednesday, 26 April 503 B.C., seventeen years after the beginning of the Izapa calendar.

Early Postclassic (A.D. 950–1250)

Codex Vienna page 49b celebrates the birth of 9 Ix from a large flint blade on Saturday, 27 April A.D. 1005.

Texupan, Oaxaca, shows the temple of Nine Wine Helmet. (*Nuttall*, pp. 15, 17, 18, 19a, 20c, and 21b and *Codex Borgia*, pp. 32–33)

Zaachila, Oaxaca (?) located at flint-covered White Mountain has another temple of Nine Wind Flint Helmet. (*Nuttall*, pp. 19b and 21b)

Two other temples of Nine Wind Flint Helmet at Cholula, Puebla (*Nuttall*, p. 22) and Tilantongo, Oaxaca (*Nuttall*, p. 46) have the dates of Tuesday, 19 June A.D. 987 and Friday, 27 April A.D. 992 respectively.

4. Divine born Man-God

Calendar date: 1 Ben 6 Mak (1 Reed year: Tilantongo calendar).

Astronomical identity: Pleiades.

Name: Ce Acatl Topiltzin Quetzalcoatl (Our prince One Reed feathered serpent).

Traits: Virgin birth and red crosses on cloak.

Late Preclassic (250 B.C.–A.D. 200)

First Divine Birth: Thursday, 6 April 1 B.C. (This date is also the New Year's Day of the late San Andres Istacostoc, Chiapas [San Andres Larrainzar] calendar. See Edmondson 1988, Figure 3, p. 6.)

Early Postclassic (A.D. 950–1250)

Second Divine Birth: Thursday, 29 July A.D. 1039. This individual's actual birth was six days earlier on the 360th day of the year (Friday, 23 July A.D. 1039 on 8

Manik 0 Mak). Thus, the second ritual divine birth (1 Reed) was on New Year's Day as required.

Two carvings of One Reed Quetzalcoatl are from the Tula, Hidalgo area. One rock carving is on the Cerro de la Malinche, and the other is on a stone box at Ixtapantongo (Covarrubias 1957, 267).

The late temple of Quetzalcoatl at Cholula, Puebla, was built about 16 July A.D. 1091.

The deity Tlahuizpantecuhtli as the feathered serpent with calendar name of 1 Reed is known from Chichen Itza, Yucatan. (Miller and Taube 1993, 166)

A late Quetzalcoatl's journey to the east, his cremation then becomes the "morning star" or Tlahuizcalpantecuhtli (the Lord of the place of dawn).

Late Postclassic (A.D. 1250–1525)

Tenochtitlan, Mexico, the Temple of Quetzalcoatl was rebuilt and dedicated on Sunday, 7 April A.D. 1507 (1 Ben 6 Mak). Historical data on the year 1507 are provided by Brundage 1972, 242–43, 337.

Early Sixteenth Century A.D.

Quetzalcoatl with a cloak that has red crosses and associated with a 1 Reed date is found in the *Codex Telleriano-Remensis*. (Miller and Taube 1993, 167)

5. **Priest-king with insignia of royalty**
   Calendar date: 1 Ben 1 Sip (1 Reed year, Tepexic).
   Astronomical identity: Mercury, superior conjunction.
   (Kelley 1980, S18)
   Name: Ce Acatl Nacxitl Quetzalcoatl
   Traits: blue interlocked step-fret design, bearded, and patron of the trecena 1 Ik.
   Chronology:
   Early Classic (A.D. 150–450)
   Teotihuacan, Mexico, Temple of Quetzalcoatl dedicated as early as 7 August A.D. 152. (Millon 1973, 55)
   Tikal, Guatemala, the fourth century A.D. rule "Blue-Green Knot" was buried with a mask honoring the creator god Quetzalcoatl. (Coggins 1987)

Early Postclassic (A.D. 950–1250)
Birth of Meconetzin Nacxitl Quetzalcoatl of Tula,
Hidalgo, on Friday, 20 November A.D. 1191. (1 Ben 1
Sip). El Tajin, Veracruz, has a carving of Nacxitl on a
ball court.
Late Postclassic (1250–1525 AD.)
Aztec and Texcocan rulers wore blue-knotted capes
with interlocked step-fret designs. (Anawalt 1990, 291–307)

6. Tlaloc-Quetzalcoatl/Chak-Kukulcan: War Serpent
Calendar date: 4 Ik 15 Chen (1 Reed year, Tepexic).
Astronomical identity: Mercury, superior conjunction.
(Kelley 1980, S18)
Traits: goggle-style eyes and feathered-serpent designs,
patron of the day 4 Ik and the trecena 1 Kawak.
Chronology:
Early Classic (A.D. 150–450)
Teotihuacan, Mexico, Temple of Tlaloc-
Quetzalcoatl (some scholars now see the Tlaloc deity as
Xiuhtecuhtli the fire serpent and connected with
warfare on the empire level).
Teotihuacan, Mexico, Temple of Atetelco (Kelley
1980, S11) with a possible date of 13 November A.D.
307.
Early Postclassic (A.D. 950–1250)
Borgia, p. 67, a Central Mexican example of this
deity.
Chichen Itza, Mexico, gold mask of Tlaloc with a
feathered rattlesnake above the Tlaloc eyes. (Kelley
1980, S10)
The first three variants have an astronomical tie to the planets
Venus or Mercury. All three of these variant Quetzalcoatls have a
9 Wind birth date in the ritual or 260-day calendar. All three are
heavenly deities and are involved in the creation. Likewise, all
three deity variants have mythological and projected dates going
back into the first to third millenniums B.C.
Quetzalcoatl Variant 4, the Man-God variant, has a projected
birth date at 1 B.C. and archaeological and codical evidence from
the Postclassic period of Mesoamerica (ca. A.D. 900–1525). This
variant is the one we are most concerned about in this book.

The fifth Quetzalcoatl variant (royal priest-king) begins about the middle of the first century A.D. at Teotihuacan. More than one royal priest-king is involved in Classic and Postclassic Mesoamerica (ca. A.D. 150–1525). This Quetzalcoatl variant is a departure or elaboration on the Man-God variant.

Finally, the sixth Quetzalcoatl/Tlaloc variant, or "war serpent," dating from the second century A.D. to the Spanish conquest, is still a further departure fromm and elaboration on earlier Quetzalcoatl traditions.

We need to start distinguishing among these variant Quetzalcoatls to avoid some horrifying and brutal aspects of some of the variants. Further, much research will be required to clarify the development of Quetzalcoatl as a deity, particularly in sorting out the priests who took his name at various time periods.

The earliest illustrations of Nine Wind Quetzalcoatl as an ancestral culture hero show his birth and subsequent ritual activities in the third millennium B.C. (Figures 8–1, 8–2, and 8–3). A sixth century B.C. Olmec monument at La Venta, Tabasco, Mexico, shows the graphic symbolism of the "feathered serpent" (Figure 8–4). Around 500 B.C., shell earplug pendants from Burial 74 at Chiapa de Corzo (Figure 8–5) depict the "feathered serpent." Also in Chiapa de Corzo in Tomb 1, dating to the time of Christ, was found a carved bone with the symbolism of the "feathered serpent" (Figure 8–6). The *Codex Nuttall* depicts a death and resurrection scene in the tenth century A.D. connected with a Quetzalcoatl calendar date. Two *Codex Vienna* scenes deal with a tenth century A.D. priest of Quetzalcoatl (Figures 8–7 and 8–8). The famous Toltec priest-king from Tula, Hidalgo, fled eastward to Yucatan, where he is shown at Chichen Itza (Figures 8–9 and 8–10) as Kukulcan (Maya name for Quetzalcoatl) in the tenth century A.D. The Toltecs, in the tenth century A.D. and later, show a shift toward idolatry, with Quetzalcoatl appearing for the first time in a mask (Figure 8–11). Some of the Aztecs, in the thirteenth century A.D. and later, painted him in their codices as a monster (Figure 8–12).

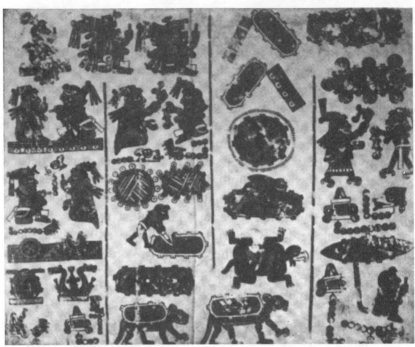

FIGURE 8–1: BIRTH OF NINE WIND QUETZALCOATL, THE CULTURE HERO, FROM PAGE 49, LOWER-RIGHT CORNER OF CODEX VIENNA IN 1005 A.D. THIS MIXTEC CODEX OR SCREENFOLD BOOK WAS PAINTED ABOUT A.D. 1350.

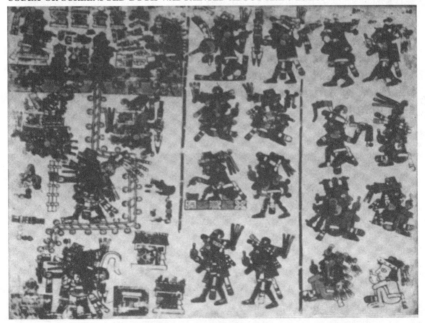

FIGURE 8–2: THE CULTURE HERO, NINE WIND QUETZALCOATL, RECEIVING HIS DIVINE INSIGNIAS. (CODEX VIENNA, PAGE 48) NINE WIND IS SHOWN THREE TIMES IN THE LEFT-HAND COLUMN.

FIGURE 8–3: THE SKY AND WATER SYMBOLS BEING LIFTED OFF THE EARTH BY THE CULTURE HERO NINE WIND QUETZALCOATL SHOWN IN THE UPPER-LEFT-HAND CORNER. (CODEX VIENNA, PAGE 47)

FIGURE 8–4: LARGE FEATHERED SERPENT WITH PRIEST AND BUCKET CARVED ON MONUMENT 19 AT THE OLMEC SITE OF LA VENTA, TABASCO, MEXICO (SIXTH CENTURY B.C.). (PHOTO BY DANIEL BATES. COURTESY DAVID A. PALMER AND THE SOCIETY FOR EARLY HISTORIC ARCHAEOLOGY.)

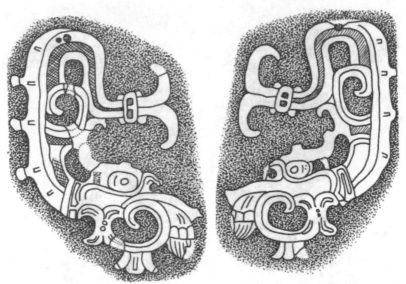

FIGURE 8–5: SHELL EARPLUG PENDANTS IN THE SHAPE OF THE FEATHERED SERPENT FROM BURIAL 74 AT CHIAPA DE CORZO, CHIAPAS, MEXICO (FIFTH CENTURY B.C.).

FIGURE 8–6: DRAWING OF BONE 3 FROM TOMB 1 AT CHIAPA DE CORZO (FIRST CENTURY B.C.)

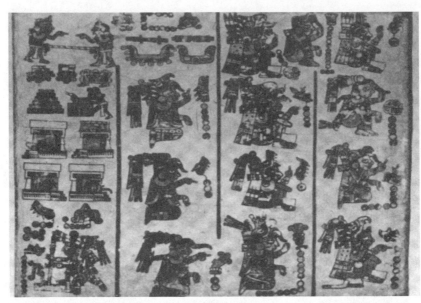

FIGURE 8–7: ELEVENTH CENTURY A.D. PRIEST/SCRIBE OF QUETZALCOATL (HUEMATZIN?), LOWER-LEFT CORNER, PERFORMING A "FIRE-DRILLING" RITUAL. (CODEX VIENNA, PAGE 32)

FIGURE 8–8: QUETZALCOATL (HUEMATZIN?) ASSOCIATED WITH THE "SWEAT HOUSES" OF SEVERAL COMMUNITIES IN SOUTHERN MEXICO IN THE ELEVENTH CENTURY A.D. SHOWN IN THE LOWER RIGHT CORNER. (CODEX VIENNA, PAGE 31)

FIGURE 8–9: THE BEARDED CE ACATL QUETZALCOATL OR KUKULCAN FROM THE DOORWAY OF THE EL CASTILLO/KUKULCAN TEMPLE AT CHICHEN ITZA, YUCATAN, MEXICO (TENTH CENTURY A.D.).

FIGURE 8–10: THE TEMPLE OF EL CASTILLO/KUKULCAN AT CHICHEN ITZA, YUCATAN, MEXICO, DATING FROM THE TENTH CENTURY A.D.

FIGURE 8–11: THE UPPER-RIGHT-HAND FIGURE FROM PAGE 46 OF THE MIXTEC CODEX NUTTALL DEPICTING THE GOD QUETZALCOATL WITH THE "WIND MASK" IN THE ELEVENTH CENTURY A.D. THE CODEX NUTTALL WAS PAINTED ABOUT A.D. 1350.

FIGURE 8–12: THE GOD QUETZALCOATL BACK TO BACK WITH THE DEATH GOD. THIS SCENE IS FROM THE CODEX BORGIA FROM CHOLULA, PUEBLA, MEXICO. THE CODEX BORGIA WAS PAINTED IN PREHISTORIC TIMES (LATE POSTCLASSIC) AND IS NOW LOCATED IN THE VATICAN LIBRARY.

Returning now to our search for information on the Man-God variant of Quetzalcoatl (see Variant 4, Table 8–1), we can begin with a tradition from Oaxaca, Mexico. Juan de Cordoba, a Spanish friar in Oaxaca, recorded the following account just a few years after the coming of Cortes. As part of a discussion of one of the day signs in the ritual calendar of ancient Mesoamerica, he describes the eighteenth one, a flint blade that is sometimes called the solar beam. This passage has recently been translated into English in Tony Shearer's *Beneath the Moon and Under the Sun*, which introduces it with this commentary: "Here is one of the strangest glyphs among the twenty. It is, if investigated, one of the best clues for superior beings reaching us from another planet."

Cordoba's account then follows:

Among the oldest glyphs, this one comes to earth from another planet. The tenochs [a term that refers to the Aztecs] thought it came from the sun. Earlier uses of it suggest that it came from the northern sky, perhaps from the northeastern sky, and could be seen in broad daylight; so the story goes.

A story was told to the Spaniards shortly after the conquest in Oaxaca. . . . On the day we call Tecpatl [the Aztec name for the day sign flint knife] a great light came from the northeastern sky. It glowed for four days in the sky, then lowered itself to the rock; the rock can still be seen at Tenochtitlan [*sic* Teotitlan] de Valle in Oaxaca. From the light there came a great, very powerful being, who stood on the very top of the rock and glowed like the sun in the sky. There he stood for all to see, shining day and night. Then he spoke, his voice was like thunder, booming across the valley. Our old men and women, the astronomers and astrologists, could understand him and he could understand them. He (the solar beam) told us how to pray and fixed for us days of fast and days of feasting. He then balanced the "Book of Days" (sacred calendar) and left vowing that he would always watch down upon us his beloved people. (Shearer 1975, 71–72)

As may be remembered, Cordoba's account of a heavenly visitor mostly parallels the Book of Mormon account:

They cast their eyes up again towards heaven; and behold, they saw a Man descending out of heaven; and he was clothed in a white robe; and he came down and stood in the midst of them. . . . And it came to pass that he stretched forth his hand and spake unto the people, saying: Behold, I am Jesus Christ, whom the prophets testified shall come into the world (3 Nephi 11:8–10).

Don Hernando Cortes: A Mistaken Identity

When Cortes landed on the east coast of Mexico in 1519, the inhabitants of the land thought he was their benevolent, personal God, Quetzalcoatl, who had appeared to their ancestors centuries before Columbus and had promised to return. Like Cortes, Quetzalcoatl had been bearded and white skinned, and he was associated with the cross.

An American scholar of the last century, Daniel Brinton, states that "whenever the personal appearance of this hero-God is described, it is, strangely, enough, represented to be that of one of the white race, a man of fair complexion, with long flowing beard, with abundant hair, and clothed in ample and loose robes" (Brinton 1868).

Brinton reports that when messengers from the Gulf of Mexico brought descriptions of the bearded, white-skinned Cortes to Montezuma (or, more correctly, Moctezuma), the emperor said, "This truly is the *Quetzalcoatl we* expected, he who lived with us of old in Tula" (Brinton 1868).

Therefore, Quetzalcoatl was, in the understanding of Moctezuma, an anthropomorphic god in the image of a bearded white man, whose return had been predicted anciently. In confirmation of this, Bernardino Sahagun, a Spanish priest, wrote: "In the year 1519, when the Captain, Don Hernando Cortes, came [to Mexico] . . . they thought that Quetzalcoatl had come" (Sahagun 1954, 8:21).

Any confusion was only temporary. The ruthless and murderous conduct of the Spanish conqueror convinced the Aztecs that Cortes was not their ancient god and lord returned. Cortes executed six thousand Aztecs in Cholula alone.

A Physical Description of Quetzalcoatl

Juan de Torquemada, a Catholic priest born about 1564, arrived in Mexico from Spain early in the seventeenth century and describes Quetzalcoatl as a:

> white man, large of body, wide of forehead, large eyes, long and black hair, large and round beard. . . . They held him in great esteem . . . and in spiritual and ecclesiastical matters this *Quetzalcoatl* was supreme, a great priest. . . . They say about this God, Quetzalcoatl, that while living in this mortal life, he dressed in long clothes down to his feet, though modestly, with a cloak on top, scattered with red crosses. He was perfect in moral virtues and they say that He is alive and He is to return. (Torquemada 1943, 2:48, 52) (See Figure 8–13.)

FIGURE 8–13: QUETZALCOATL WEARING HIS CLOAK WITH RED CROSSES. FROM CODEX TELLERIANO-REMENSIS IN LORD KINGSBOROUGH'S ANTIQUITIES OF MEXICO, VOLUME 2.

Quetzalcoatl Taught Christian Virtues

Hubert H. Bancroft, the prolific nineteenth-century historian of western America and Mexico, admits that Quetzalcoatl taught Christian virtues. In his five-volume work, *Native Races,* he summarizes the teachings of Quetzalcoatl, who exhorted the people "to practice brotherly love and other Christian virtues, introducing a milder and better form of religion" (Bancroft 1883–86, 5:23–24).

The Padre Torquemada wrote of Mexico's Messiah-Redeemer:

> He never wanted nor permitted sacrifices of blood of dead men, nor of animals, but only of bread and roses and flowers and perfumes and other smells. He very efficiently prohibited and forbade wars, robberies, and deaths and other harm they inflicted on each other. They say that whenever they mentioned deaths or wars or other evils in front of Him, He would turn his head and stop His ears in order not to see or hear them. Also, in Him is praised the fact that He was very chaste and very honest, and very moderate in many other things.
>
> This God was held in such reverence and devotion, and so revered with vows and pilgrimages in all these kingdoms, on account of His prerogatives, that even the very enemies of the City of Cholula would promise to come in pilgrimage to fulfill their covenants and devotions, and they came secure [in safety], and the lords of the other provinces or cities had their chapels, oratories, and their idols and images, and only this one, among all the Gods, was called in that city "Lord par excellence"; so that when they took an oath or said, "By our Lord," it was understood they referred to Quetzalcoatl, and not to any other god, although there were many others who were very esteemed gods. All of this was because of the great love they had for Him and continued to have for Him for the reasons mentioned.
>
> Also, it is true that the lordship of Quetzalcoatl was gentle, and he asked of them in service but light things as distinguished from painful things, and He taught them those things which were virtuous, prohibiting them those things which were evil, noxious and harmful, teaching them also to hate evil things. . . . For this reason it seems that the Indians who made and make human sacrifices were not following the will [of Quetzalcoatl]. . . . And among other doctrines He gave them, was to tell them that the inhabitants of the city of Cholula were to hold as certain that in future times there were to come by sea, from whence the sun rises,

some white men, with beards like His, and that they were His brothers. Thus, these Indians always expected that they immediately called them "son of Gods" and "brothers of Quetzalcoatl," although after knowing them [the Spaniards] and experiencing their deeds, they did not hold them as heavenly, because the slaughter the Spaniards perpetrated in that city [Cholula] was outstanding [no other like it up to that time in the Indies nor, perhaps, in other parts of the world].

This [Quetzalcoatl] was the God of the Wind, and His temple was round and very sumptuous. . . . The Indians applied the name to Quetzalcoatl, on account of His gentleness and tenderness toward everybody, not wanting the harsh and disagreeable things that others esteemed and prized. . . . These said Tultecs were good men and friends of virtue. They did not tell lies, and their way of speaking and greeting each other was "Sir" and "Sir, brother" . . . and "Sir, older brother" and "Sir, younger brother." Their speech, instead of swearing, was "It is true," "thus it is," "it is ascertained," and "yes" for yea, and "no" for nay. (Torquemada 1943, 2:50–51)

A God of Great Virtues

With respect to the teachings of the New World Messiah-Redeemer, the learned Ixtlilxochitl wrote:

And when they were in the height of their power [in the twelfth century A.D.], there arrived in this land a man whom they called Quetzalcoatl and others Huemac on account of his great virtues, considering him as just, saintly [holy], and good, teaching them by deeds and words the path of virtue and forbidding them their vices and sins, giving laws and good doctrine. And in order to refrain them from their pleasures and dishonesties, he instituted [established] fasting for them and [He was] the first who worshiped and placed the cross which they called *Quiahuiteotlchicahualizteotl* and others *Tonacaquahuitl,* which means: God of rains and of health and tree of sustenance or of life. (Hunter and Ferguson 1950, 203)

Quetzalcoatl, the Messiah-Redeemer of Mexico, is thus identified with the tree of life.

Baptism

One of the most persistent doctrines of the Christian tradition is baptism, which, as it turns out, was practiced throughout Mesoamerica. Diane E. Wirth states, "Somehow, the religion of Jesus Christ, or Quetzalcoatl as he was known to these early Americans, was kept alive" (Wirth 1986, 147). Wirth then associates Quetzalcoatl with baptism, among other Christian-like traits. (Wirth 1986, 147) Incidentally, her book *A Challenge to the Critics: Scholarly Evidences of the Book of Mormon* has a fine discussion of Quetzalcoatl in the fourteenth chapter.

Likewise, Bishop Diego de Landa, who arrived in Yucatan on the heels of Cortes before the smoke of battle had cleared was surprised to learn that baptism had been practiced, as a "rebirth," for many centuries before the time of Columbus, and baptisms were performed in the name of the Messiah-Redeemer or Fair God (Tozzer 1941, 102).

Frans Blom, a pioneer Mesoamerican archaeologist, explorer, map maker, and author, and his wife operated a museum and retreat for scholars in the picturesque town of San Cristobal de las Casas on the Pan-American Highway in southernmost Mexico. In his book *The Conquest of Yucatan,* Blom says that the ancient Mayan baptismal rite "was in some ways more elaborate than Christian baptism, but contained the same fundamental ideas" (Blom 1936, 79).

M. Wells Jakeman translated the writings of the learned Antonio Chi of sixteenth-century Yucatan. Chi wrote that his preconquest Mayan ancestors

> baptized in this manner; the chief priest of the idols took water and he threw certain flowers, and he said some words over it, and moistened a stick and brought it with him to the forehead and eyes and over the face of [the child], saying three times, "ah, ah, ah," which appears to signify and mean "revive" or "recover." And they could not marry or be priests unless they were baptized, and if any died without baptism, they held that he had to have more punishments in hell than the baptized. (Jakeman 1952, 103)

The use of the terms "revive" and "recover" in the ceremony, as set out by Antonio Chi, is further corroboration of the point that the baptismal rite of the Maya symbolized being "born again," "a new birth," or a regeneration, exactly as was the case with the Old World rite.

From Mexico's central mesa comes an entirely independent account concerning baptism. Whereas the accounts of Diego de Landa and Antonio Chi come from Yucatan, Padre Sahagun wrote in central Mexico. Sahagun states that the following words were in the baptismal ceremony after the child was washed with water: "Evil, wheresoever thou art, be gone, depart—for the child *lives anew* and *is born* again—once more it is purified" (Sahagun 1969, 6:202, emphasis added).

In both the Old and New Worlds, the baptismal rite symbolized being born again or spiritual rebirth. The Maya term for the ceremony, *caput sihil*, means "to be born anew." The meaning of this Maya term is confirmed from the central-mesa account of Sahagun. This "rebirth" in water was one of two requisites to the attainment of "glory" of the kingdom of God in Mesoamerica. Bishop Landa said that by baptism and by "a well-ordered life," the Maya hoped to attain the kingdom.

In the Cholula-Puebla region of Mexico, the Tlaxcalans baptized infants by immersing and bathing them in a sacred spring. Among the Zapotec at Mexico's narrow neck of land, Tehuantepec, both the mother and the child were washed in a stream.

Thus, a knowledge of baptism—a special symbol of the cleansing, rebirth, and regeneration of the individual—was widespread in Mesoamerica. Tomas Lopez Medel, in a document written in 1612 concerning Mesoamerica, also mentions the ancient baptismal rite:

> There was also practiced and used among the Yucatecan Indians a certain kind of baptism which although it was not obligatory nor general among all, was held in repute. . . . And when they had already attained to six or seven years, the time when they were to be baptized was discussed with the priest, and the day . . . appointed. By this and other similar ceremonies which had been observed in the Yucatecan Indians and in others, some of our Spaniards have taken occasion to persuade themselves and

believe that in times past some of the apostles or a successor
to them passed over to the West Indies and that ultimately
those Indians were preached to. (Tozzer 1941, 226)

Crucifixion

Crucifixion was a method of capital punishment in ancient
Mexico, as it was in ancient Palestine. The "refinement" of leg
breaking as part of crucifixion procedure was practiced in both
lands. Viscount Kingsborough, in his monumental nine-volume
work *Antiquities of Mexico,* states: "The Mexicans were
accustomed to break the legs of a crucified person on one of their
most solemn festivals, and to leave him to die upon the cross.
This curious fact is stated by Motolinia in the tenth chapter of the
first part of his unedited treatise concerning the idolatry of the
Indians of New Spain" (Kingsborough 1841–48, 6:16).

Kingsborough's books, published between 1830 and 1848,
include reproductions of most of the Aztec and Maya hieroglyphic
and pictographic books written in Mexico before the discovery
by Columbus. These books survived destruction at the hands of
the Spaniards. With respect to certain of the ancient Aztec paintings
preserved by Kingsborough in Volume 2 of *Antiquities of Mexico,*
he explains:

> It is extremely singular that several Mexican paintings
> should represent Quetzalcoatl with his side pierced with a
> spear and water flowing from the wound. . . . The paintings
> which represent Quetzalcoatl pierced with a spear and water
> issuing from the wound, occur at the sixty-first page of the
> Borgian manuscript [Kingsborough's Volume 6] and at the
> ninth page of the Mexican painting preserved in the Library
> of the Institute at Bologna. (Ferguson 1958:138)

After careful study and review of the evidence available in
his lifetime, Lord Kingsborough was of the firm conviction that
Quetzalcoatl was identical with Jesus of Nazareth and that he
appeared to the ancient inhabitants of Mexico. In Volume 8,
Kingsborough says: "In the tenth page of the manuscript of
Bologna . . . in the lower compartment of the page is a mysterious
image of the Sun transfixed by a spear—symbolic, it is supposed,
of Quetzalcoatl, who, like the Hebrew Messiah, was typified by
the Sun" (Kingsborough 1841–48, 8:21).

In the same volume, he also says: "A slip of tiger skin was fastened by the Mexicans to the miter of Quetzalcoatl. . . . The Mexicans named Quetzalcoatl "Light," and believed that light was created before the sun. It hence appears that the tradition in the Pentateuch that light was created before the sun, was known in various parts of the New World very remote from each other" (Kingsborough 1841–48, 8:34).

Referring to another of the manuscripts of the Aztecs, Kingsborough notes: "The seventy-fifth page of the Borgian manuscript [reproduced by Kingsborough] is very remarkable for the representation which it contains of Quetzalcoatl in the attitude of a crucified person, with the impressions of the nails visible in his hands and feet" (Ferguson 1958, 139).

Killed and Lashed, with a Crown of Thorns

In 1541, Francisco Hernandez arrived in Yucatan as chaplain to the Spanish governor, Montejo II. He was one of the first Catholic priests to reach Mesoamerica and was a brilliant and honorable man. Four years later, in 1545, Bartolome de Las Casas, benevolent friend of the natives, took his post as second bishop of Chiapas (which included Yucatan). By then, Francisco Hernandez had learned the Maya language. He was able to serve efficiently as an aide to Las Casas. The latter sent Francisco Hernandez to the interior to preach to the native Maya. About a year later, Francisco Hernandez wrote to Las Casas concerning the religious beliefs of the Maya of the interior. Las Casas reported the entire matter. He was strongly of the opinion that Christianity and the crucifixion of the Messiah-Redeemer were known in the region many centuries before the coming of the Spaniards to the region.

With respect to Mexico's Messiah, Las Casas wrote:

> After a certain number of months (I believe it was one year) he [Francisco Hernandez] wrote me that on his trip he had met a principal lord or chief, and that on inquiring of him concerning his faith, and the ancient belief all over his realm, he answered him that they knew and believed in God who was in Heaven; that God was the Father, the Son, and the Holy Ghost. That the Father is called by them *Itzamna* and that he created man and all things. The Son's name was Bacab, who was born from a maiden who had ever remained a virgin, whose name was *Chiribirias,* and

who is in heaven with God. The Holy Ghost they called *Echuac*. They say *Itzamna* means "the Great Father.". . . About Bacab, who is the Son, they say that he was killed and lashed and a crown of thorns put on him, and that he was placed on a timber with his arms stretched out. They did not understand that he was nailed, but rather they thought he had been tied, and there he died. And he was dead for three days, and on the third day he came to life and went up to heaven, and that he is there with his Father. And after this, then came *Echvah* who is the Holy Spirit, and filled the earth to overflowing with all the things that were needed.

Asked also how they had knowledge of these things, he answered that the lords (chiefs) taught it to their children, and that this doctrine descended from generation to generation. They affirmed that in ancient times twenty men came to this land, and their leader was called Cozas, and that the leaders commanded the people to confess and fast. For this reason, some [of the Maya] fasted on the day that corresponds to Friday since they say that Bacab [the Son of God] had died on that day. (Las Casas 1875–76, 1:426–27)

After ending his quotation from the letter of Francisco Hernandez, Bishop Las Casas went on to comment, "If these things are true, it seems that our holy faith was known in that land. . . . Finally, these are secrets that only God knows" (Las Casas 1875–76, 1:Chapter 123).

Notes to Chapter 8

Names of the Mesoamerican God

Goetz and Morley add the following observation: "The great civilizer was worshiped as a divinity by the ancient Mexicans, who gave him different names. They called him *Ehecatl*, or God of the Wind; *Yolcuat,* or the Rattle Snake; *Quetzalcoatl,* or Serpent Covered with Green Feathers." The last meaning corresponds also to the Maya name *Kukulcan* and to the Quiche name *Gucumatz* (Goetz and Morley 1950, 189, n. 10).

Still another Guatemalan name for this god was *Nacxit Quetzalcoatl*, mentioned several times in the *Cronica Mexicana* of Alvarado Tezozomoc as the founder of the throne on which the Aztec emperors sat during their coronation ceremonies. (Goetz and Morley 1950, 209, n. 5)

Names of the Messiah-Redeemer

About fifty of the Israelite-Jewish names of the Messiah-Redeemer were applied to the New World Messiah-Redeemer. In Mesoamerica, as in the Near East, he was the God of the Sky and Earth, God of Abraham and Jacob, Great Lord, Yohualli, Sovereign Lord, Father of Life, God of Rains, Lord of the Green Earth, Creator, Son of God, and the Wonderful King. The virgin-born and crucified Man-God, Itzamna-Quetzalcoatl, was symbolized by the cross, the serpent, the quetzal bird, the tree of life, fire, the hand, the shepherd's staff, Venus the Morning Star, and other appropriate reminders of the Creator of Life—God. These symbols precede the earthly ministry of Jesus by many centuries, going back to "the beginning."

In the following list, the Old World names are all from the Old and New Testaments. The New World names are taken from the earliest and most reliable sixteenth-century Mesoamerica documentary sources. The letter in parentheses following each New World name for the Messiah-Redeemer is the key to the source in each instance. The following designations are used:

- (H) Francisco Hernandez
- (I) Ixtlilxochitl
- (M) Maya Chronicles
- (C) Juan de Cordoba
- (P) *Popol Vuh*
- (S) Sahagun

(T)   *Titulo de Totonicapan*

The names are grouped into obvious classifications.

Old World Names from the Bible	New World Names from Mesoamerican Sources
Almighty	Conqueror (P)
Author of Eternal Salvation	Author of that which surrounds the heavens and the earth (T)
Creator	Creator and Maker (P)
Counselor	Wiseman (P) (I)
Everlasting Father	Grandfather (P) (I)
Father	Father (T)
Father of Heaven and Earth	Great Father (H)
Lord God of thy Fathers	God of the Sky and Earth (P)
	Heart of the Sky and Earth (P)
	Spirit of Heaven (P)
	Heart of Heaven (P)
God	God (I) (P)
Great Lord	Great Lord (P)
Great Spirit	Great God (T)
Heavenly Father	Spirit of Heaven (P)
Judge (Righteous Judge) (Eternal Judge)	The Only Judge (P)
King of Kings	Sovereign Lord (T) (P)
King of all the Earth	King (M)
King of Heaven	Monarch (M)
	Majesty (P)
Lamb of God	Tapir of the Dawn (P)
Light and Life of World	Light of the Sons (P)
	Splendor of the Lightning (P)
	Lord of the Eye of the Sun (M)
	Sun-Lord of the Day (M)
	Father of Life (P)
Lord	Lord (T) (M)
Lord God	Lord God (P)
Lord of Heaven and Earth	Lord of Heaven and Earth (I)
Lord of the Vineyard	God of Maize (P)
Lord of the Harvest	Planting God (P)
Lord God of Hosts	God of Rains (I) (P) (M)
God of the Hills	Lord of the Green Earth (P)

Maker	Maker (P)
	Former (P)
	Builder (P)
Master	Giant Master (P)
Master of the Vineyard	Master of All Things (I)
	Master Magician (P)
	God of Rain (P)
Son of God	Son of God (H)
Son of Elohim	Son of Hunab Ku (M)
Supreme Creator God	Supreme Creator God (M)
The Only Lord God	The Only God (P)
The Word	The Word (P)
Wonderful	Wonderful King (P)
True and Living God	True and Living God (C)

Attributes

The Messiah-Redeemer in Mesoamerica controlled certain fields of human experience and possessed certain powers in the natural world. The same powers were possessed by the Messiah-Redeemer of the Bible. The following list is one of attributes or powers common to the Messiah-Redeemer of both the Bible and Mesoamerica. The attributes or powers suggest that he was one and the same divine Lord and God of all mankind.

Creator and Lord of Nature
Lord of Heaven and Earth
Lord of Life
King, Prince, Monarch
Great High Priest
God of the Sky
Great Judge of Mankind
Lord of the Winds
Lord of Wisdom
God of Health
God of Rain and Agriculture
God of Fertility
Lord of the Resurrection
Lord of Light

Symbols

The same symbols for the Messiah-Redeemer in Mesoamerica are also found in the Near East. They are symbols of the ancient Lord of Mexico and Guatemala as well as for the ancient Israelites and early Christians. The following symbols for

Old World Symbols	New World Symbols
Sun (symbol of light)	Sun (symbol of light)
Cross (symbol of the crucifixion and of the Messiah of Life)	Cross (symbol of the crucified God of Life—Quetzalcoatl)
Brazen Serpent (symbol of the river, of the sky, and water source of life—and of Israel's Messiah)	Feathered Serpent (symbol of the river, of the sky, and water—source of life)
Tree of Life (symbol of the word of God—the way to happiness, law, order, and peace; opposite of death and evil)	Tree of Life (symbol of the word of God—the way to happiness, law, order, and peace; opposite of death and evil)
Bird (as in winged disk-symbol of the highest God—the Messiah—God of life)	Quetzal bird (and its long serpent-like tail feathers, symbol of the highest God—The Messiah—God of life)
Fire (symbol of the mysterious power of God)	Fire (symbol of the mysterious power of God)
Hand (symbol of the powerful hand of God)	Hand (symbol of Itzamna—"he of the powerful hand")
Lion (symbol of the mysterious vitalism or life-force of God)	Jaguar (symbol of the mysterious vitalism or life-force of God)
Calf (or bull) (symbol of the mysterious vitalism or life-force of God)	Tapir (symbol of the mysterious vitalism or life-force of God)
Tall Staff (symbol of the divine royalty, majesty, power, and priesthood of God)	Tall Staff (symbol of the divine royalty, majesty, power, and priesthood of God)
Morning Star (symbol of the Messiah as the light of the world)	Morning Star (symbol of the Messiah as the light of the world)
All-Seeing Eye (symbol of the all-knowing Lord and God)	Divine Eye (symbol of the all-knowing Lord and God)

the Messiah-Redeemer are common to both the Old World and the New World.

Baptism

Sahagun gives a full account of the baptismal ceremony as it was conducted by the late Toltec-Aztec people of conquest days in the central-mesa region of Mexico as follows:

> Concerning the baptism of the child, and all the ceremonies that were made of it, and of naming the child and the feast of the children, etc.

> At the time of baptizing the child they prepared the necessary things for the baptism. They made a little shield, a small bow and four small arrows, one arrow pointing to the east, one to the west, one to the south and the other to the north. . . . They also made food *of molli,* a dish with beans and toasted corn.

> And after having prepared everything that was necessary for the baptism, then all the relatives of the child, both old men and old women, would get together. Then they would call the midwife, who was the one who would baptize the child that she helped to deliver. All would get together very early, before the sun was up, and when the sun was up, when it was somewhat high, the midwife called for a new pottery tub, filled with water. Then she would take the child in both hands and those who were present would take all the things that were ready for the baptism and place them in the middle of the patio of the house. To baptize the child the midwife would face the east and then she would begin to perform the ceremony by saying: "Oh eagle! Oh tiger! Oh brave, brave man—my grandchild— you have arrived in this world. Your father and mother, the great lord and the great lady have sent you. You were reared and engendered in your house, which is the place of the supreme Gods of the great Lord and the great Lady that are above the nine heavens; *Quetzalcoatl,* who art everywhere, have mercy on our son."

> After saying this she would then give him a taste of water, placing her wet fingers in its mouth, saying: "Take this [baptismal water], for upon it thou hast to live, to wax strong, and flourish—by it we obtain all necessary things— receive it." Then touching the child on the breast with her

moistened fingers, she says: "Take the celestial water, try here the very pure water that washes and cleanses your heart—that takes away all uncleanliness—receive it. May it purify and cleanse your heart."

After this, she would put water on its head and say: "Oh my son, my grandchild receive and take the water of the Lord of the world, which is our life—it is to help our body to grow vigorous—it is to wash, to cleanse. I pray that this celestial light-blue water enter into your body and remain there. I beg that it destroy and deliver you from all evil and any adverse thing that was given you before the beginning of the world, because all of us are left in its care, because it is our mother *Chalchiuhtlicue* [Our Lady of the Turquoise Sky]."

After this, she would wash the entire body of the child and would say: "Evil, wheresoever thou art, be gone, depart—for the child *lives anew and is born again*—once more it is purified—again our mother *Chalchiuhtlicue* forms it and engenders it again."

Then lifting up the little one toward Heaven, she would say: "Behold, Oh Lord, your child, that you have sent to this place of sorrow, affliction and anguish which is this world. Give it, lord, your gifts and your inspirations, for thou art the great God, and also with thee [is] the great goddess." (Sahagun Book 6, Chapters 32, 37)

And It Came to Pass

The phrase "and it came to pass" occurs frequently throughout the Book of Mormon. It has a fascinating parallel in Mayan hieroglyphs. J. Eric Thompson, probably the leading Maya scholar until his death in the early 1970s, discussed what he called posterior and anterior date indicators in Classic Maya hieroglyphs. He discovered that the posterior date indicators meant "to count forward to" and the anterior date indicators meant "to count backward to." When he presented these opinions in 1950, he did not know of an equivalent phrase in contemporary Yucatec or other Mayan dialects (Thompson 1950, 162–64).

Proto-Cholan is now considered to be the main Mayan dialect used in the Classic period hieroglyphs. In 1984, David Stuart gave a Proto-Cholan reading of *uht* as "to finish, come to pass" or Chontal *ut* with the same meaning (Warren 1988, 4–5). Schele, a professor of anthropology at the University of Texas, considered one of the leading scholars of ancient Maya hieroglyphs, also translated this Maya hieroglyph as "then it came to pass" (Schele 1982, 21–25).

Some posterior phrases from the Maya hieroglyphs are "count forward to," "count until," "until it came to pass," "then it came to pass," etc. Schele also lists some phrases for the anterior indicators as "count back to," "count since," "since it had come to pass," etc. A couple of hieroglyphic examples of this usage can be found on the Palace Tablets at Palenque, Chiapas, Mexico (Schele 1982, 68–69).

In 1982, Schele illustrated with Maya glyphs and verbal descriptions four types of directional count indicators: posterior date indicators, posterior event indicators, anterior date indicators, and anterior event indicators (Schele 1982, 22).

Many examples of several types of these directional count indicators can be found in the Book of Mormon. For example:

• **Posterior Date Indicator**: "And it came to pass that thus passed away the ninety and fifth years also" (3 Nephi 2:1).

• **Posterior Event Indicator**: "And it came to pass that the people began to wax strong in wickedness and abominations." (3 Nephi 2:3)

• **Posterior Date and Event Indicator**: "And it came to pass in the thirteenth year there began to be wars and contentions throughout the land" (3 Nephi 2:11).

• **Anterior Date Indicator**: "And thus did pass away the ninety and sixth year" (3 Nephi 2:4).

• **Anterior Event Indicator**: "And it had come to pass, yea, all things, every whit, according to the words of the prophets" (3 Nephi 1:20).

• **Combined Anterior Date and Event Indicator**: "And six hundred and nine years had passed away since Lehi left Jerusalem" (3 Nephi 2:6).

The combined forms of directional count indicators in the Book of Mormon have not yet been detected in hieroglyphic studies. Perhaps Mesoamerican linguists should be encouraged to search for similar phrases in Mayan dialects and other Mesoamerican Indian languages. Pursuing such an investigation might lead to some startling discoveries.

New Year Rituals

According to the Christian scriptures, God the Father has remained somewhat aloof from the world and has left direct and close contact with inhabitants of the world to the Son, who is the Messiah-Redeemer. That is interesting because in Yucatan, the Messiah-Redeemer was known as *Itzamna*, the Son.

Itzamna was invoked by the Maya in their New Year rituals. It is significant that the ancient New Year ritual of southern Mexico was virtually identical to the ancient New Year ritual of the Israelites. The New Year's festival, widespread throughout Bible lands, is described in detail by Henri Frankfort in *Kingship and the Gods*. The Mesoamerican New Year festival is described by Bishop Landa in his monumental work written in 1566 and published by Professor Tozzer at Harvard University in 1941 (see his book *Relaciones de las Cosas de Yucatan*, 133ff.).

In both regions, the ceremony was a festive celebration of a new beginning in the annual cycle. In both regions, the renewal of life for the current year was involved. Jewish, Babylonian, and Maya traditions also connected the New Year festival with the creation of the world. There was an appeal to God for a new period of agricultural fruitfulness. It was a time of atonement and purification in the Old World, and Landa tells us it was a time of fasting, abstinence, and atonement to the Maya (Tozzer 1941, 152).

A part of the festival in both Bible lands and Mesoamerica was a victory banquet. The Jewish Talmud (Finkelstein 1949, 63) states that "destinies" are determined at the beginning of the new year. "The books are opened" at the new year. The destiny of society for the ensuing year was determined at the festivals in both Israel and Mesoamerica. Landa tells us the gods were asked by the Maya to supply remedies for any calamities they feared might come during the year, and the priest would give predictions for the year.

The worship of the Messiah-Redeemer of ancient Mexico and Guatemala was in harmony with worship of God in ancient Israel.

Chapter 9
DATING THE EVENTS IN CHRIST'S LIFE

As we discuss further the appearance of Christ/Quetzalcoatl in Mesoamerica, we will first consider the dating of the events of his life from his birth to his appearance to the Nephites.

The Date of Christ's Birth

Most scholars date the birth of Jesus Christ somewhere between the years 6–4 B.C. The Jewish historian Josephus considered Herod the Great's death to be about 5–4 B.C., and this event has been the deciding factor for these scholars. Because Jesus was born while Herod was still alive, the birth must be dated no later than 4 B.C.

In 3 Nephi 1:1, we are told that "it was six hundred years from the time that Lehi left Jerusalem" to the beginning of the year in which the sign was given for the birth of Christ. Currently, the accepted date for Lehi's departure from Jerusalem is 597 B.C. Obviously, only 593 years are involved from 597 to 4 B.C. This amount of time falls short of six hundred years by seven years.

One suggested solution to this apparent discrepancy in dating is that the Nephites used a *tun* year of 360 days as found in the famous "Long Count" calendar of ancient Mesoamerica. Six hundred *tun* years equals 591 1/3 years. However, Alma 48:2, 21 and 49:1 indicate that the Nephite calendar consisted of twelve months of thirty days, which, if five days are added at the end of the year, would equal a vague solar year of 365 days.

Another difficulty with this solution to our dating problems is that the *tun* or 360-day year requires a nine-day week both in the Near East and in Mesoamerica. There is no reason to believe, as long as they were observing the Mosaic Law, that the Nephites had substituted their seven-day week for a nine-day week.

In looking at the Jewish historian Josephus, other scholars have pointed out that he has not always been correct in his writings;

and from additional information, they have put the Messiah-Redeemer's birth in 1 B.C. (Hoehner 1977; Pratt 1985; Pratt 1994).
6 April 1 B.C.

The Mixtec Indians of Oaxaca in southern Mexico are noted for their beautifully painted screen-folds. Two of these screen-folds are the *Codex Vienna* and the *Codex Nuttall*. Both were painted in the fourteenth century A.D., about 150 years before Cortes came to Mesoamerica in 1519. Page 4 of the *Codex Nuttall* shows two deities in death bundles (Figure 9–1). Their descent into the underworld and then their emergence from the underworld are also depicted. Scenes of death and resurrection are not unknown in other Mesoamerican codices.

FIGURE 9–1: A DEATH AND RESURRECTION SCENE FROM THE CODEX NUTTALL, PAGE 4, DATING TO A.D. 1018. THE CENTRAL COLUMN SHOWS TWO DEAD GODS IN DEATH BUNDLES, AND THE LEFT COLUMN SHOWS THE SAME TWO GODS RESURRECTED.

The *Codex Nuttall* is one of two codices sent by Cortes in 1519 back to Charles V of Spain. It was sent from Veracruz before Cortes marched into Mexico on the only ship Cortes did not scuttle off the coast of Veracruz.

On page 4 of the *Codex Nuttall*, there is a date of 6 Rabbit, which Jill Leslie Furst determined from her studies of the *Codex*

Vienna is a Quetzalcoatl date. This 6 Rabbit year was probably A.D. 1018. The codex depicts two deities in death bundles. One deity is Four Earthquake (whose face appears in the center of the Aztec calendar stone); the other is Seven Flower. Four Earthquake is a calendar date of a deity representing a descent into the underworld and death and destruction. The other deity, Seven Flower, represents an ascent and rebirth or resurrection out of the underworld, like the sun or Venus in the east.

Seven Flower is associated with the sunrise or the rise of the planet Venus as the morning star. Birth and rebirth are also symbolic of Seven Flower. So what is shown in the codex are two deities symbolizing death and resurrection. The patron deity directing the ritual is the deity Quetzalcoatl (the god of life and resurrection).

The god Quetzalcoatl is assumed to have been born on a day 1 Reed in the ritual 260-day calendar and in a year 1 Reed in the vague year calendar of 365 days. Following our hypothesis that the Mesoamerican deity Quetzalcoatl is a parallel to the Jewish Messiah and the Christian deity Jesus the Christ, we will accept the conclusions of two scholars who have recently examined the dating of the Messiah's birth. John C. Lefgren's book *April Sixth* places the Messiah's birth in Bethlehem on Thursday, 6 April, in 1 B.C. according to the Gregorian calendar. John P. Pratt, who holds a Ph.D. in astronomy, has recently reached the same conclusion for the birth of the Messiah. (Pratt 1985, 75).

The Long Count Calendar

In 1987, Dennis O. Clawson was examining the Olmec-Maya Long Count calendar of Mesoamerica to see how the date of 6 April 1 B.C. would be recorded. To his delight, the Long Count date was Thursday, 6 April 1 B.C., 7.17.17.17.13 1 Ben 6 Mak. Two intriguing and surprising aspects of this date involve the Calendar Round (1 Ben 6 Mak) portion of the date. First, 1 Ben in Yucatec Maya is equivalent to 1 Acatl (which means Reed) in the Central Mexican calendars of Mesoamerica. The birthday of the Man-God aspects of the deity Quetzalcoatl is 1 Ben or 1 Acatl. Quetzalcoatl was the bearded God of life, rebirth, resurrection, and creation. Second, the 6 Mak portion is the New Year's Day of a Mixtec calendar (Kelley 1989, 69). It is likely that the

Calendar Round 1 Ben 6 Mak marks the origin of one of the Mixtec calendars on Thursday, 6 April 1 B.C.

According to the record of 3 Nephi 2:7–8: "And nine years had passed away from the time when the sign was given, which was spoken of by the prophets, that Christ would come into the world. Now the Nephites began to reckon their time from this period when the sign was given, or from the coming of Christ; therefore, nine years had passed away." In other words, the Nephites had now developed a new calendar, which had as its New Year the date of Christ's birth!

Two scholars, with no awareness of a possible connection of Christ's April 6 birth date, have independently determined that a Mixtec calendar had its point of origin on the Calendar Round date of 1 Ben 6 Mac—Thursday, April 6, 1 B.C. (Edmonson 1988; Snow 1986 in Kelley 1989, 69) It seems likely that the Mixtec and Nephite calendars are one and the same.

If our hypothesis is correct that the Messiah-Redeemer and Quetzalcoatl are the same deity, then Quetzalcoatl's birth in the year 1 Reed and on the day 1 Reed would have occurred on Thursday, 6 April, 1 B.C. in Mesoamerica. In the Olmec-Maya Long Count calendar of Mesoamerica, this date would be 7.17.17.17.13 1 Reed 6 Mak or 7.17.17.17.13 1 Ben 6 Mak (Clawson 1989, 1).

The Date of Christ's Death

In 3 Nephi 8:5, the record states: "And it came to pass in the thirty and fourth year, in the first month on the fourth day of the month, there arose a great storm, such an one as never had been known in all the land." Again, this account would be according to the new Nephite calendar.

Both Lefgren and Pratt calculate 12,049 days from the birth of the Messiah-Redeemer to his death. They also calculate 12,051 days from the birth of the Messiah-Redeemer to his resurrection (Lefgren 1980, 52, 59 and Pratt, personal communication).

Ixtlilxochitl, working from records that preceded the coming of the Spaniards, describes and dates to the time of the crucifixion events as they occurred in southern Mexico. The darkness and the quaking and the rending of rocks at the very time of the crucifixion are described:

It was 166 years since they had adjusted their years and times with the equinox, and 270 since the ancient ones had been destroyed, when the Sun and the Moon eclipsed, and the earth trembled, and the rocks broke, and many other things and signs took place. . . . This happened in the year of ce Calli, which, adjusting this count with ours, comes to be at the same time when Christ our Lord suffered, and they say it happened during the first days of the year. These and many other things the Tultecs comprehended, from the creation of the world up to our times. As I have said, in order to avoid prolixity all things they knew are not set out according as they appear in their histories and pictures, especially the original, I mean all the things which can be found in pictures and history, for everything is abridgment (contraction) in comparison with the histories that the first archbishop of Mexico ordered burned. (Hunter and Ferguson 1950, 190)

We point out that Ixtlilxochitl was careful to state that this data came from the ancient histories of Mexico and that had not the archbishop destroyed many of the histories, more details would be available. He was not robbing the Christian scriptures brought to Mexico by the Spaniards, but was accusing the Spaniards of robbing the Mexicans of their ancient records. Furthermore, the writings of Ixtlilxochitl, the elders of Totonicapan, and the native reports recorded by the Spanish padres contain so many elements completely unique and foreign to the Spaniards as to leave little room for the argument that the native writers were "borrowing" from the scriptures brought by the Spaniards at the time of the conquest.

The historical implications of this information are that this new Nephite calendar would have as its New Year's Day that portion of the Calendar Round noted above, which would be 6 Mak. Table 9–1 demonstrates that from Thursday, 6 April 1 B.C. to Friday, 4 April A.D. 8 is nine years. Continuing, Tuesday, 28 March A.D. 33 (Long Count date of 7.19.12.08.02 8 Ik 5 Mak) is exactly thirty-three complete years from 6 April 1 B.C. and is the last day of the Mixtec calendar year, with New Year's Day of the thirty-fourth year of the Mixtec calendar being on Tuesday, 29 March A.D. 33 (Long Count date of 7.19.11.07.18 8 Etsnab 6

Mak). The fourth day of this new year would fall on Friday, 1
April A.D. 33 (7.19.11.08.01 11 Imix 9 Mak)!

Put another way, the Messiah-Redeemer's death would be
12,049 days later than his birth and would have occurred on Friday,
1 April, A.D. 33. The resurrection of the Messiah would have
occurred two days later (12,051 days from his birth) on Sunday, 3
April, A.D. 33 (Judean calendar date 16 Nisan and Olmec-Maya
Long Count date of 7.19.11.08.03 13 Akbal 11 Mak).

Table 9–1
New Nephite Calendar (3 Nephi 2:6–8)

Number	Long Count Code	Day	Day/Month	Year
1	**7.17.17.17.13 1 Ben 6 Mak**	**Thursday**	**6 April**	**1 B.C.**
2	7.17.18.17.18 2 Etznab 6 Mak	Friday	6 April	1 A.D.
3	7.18.00.00.03 3 Akbal 6 Mak	Saturday	6 April	2 A.D.
4	7.18.01.00.08 4 Lamat 6 Mak	Sunday	6 April	3 A.D.
5	7.18.02.00.13 5 Ben 6 Mak	Monday	5 April	4 A.D.
6	7.18.03.00.18 6 Etznab 6 Mak	Tuesday	5 April	5 A.D.
7	7.18.04.01.03 7 Akbal 6 Mak	Wednesday	5 April	6 A.D.
8	7.18.05.01.08 8 Lamat 6 Mak	Thursday	5 April	7 A.D.
9	**7.18.06.01.13 9 Ben 6 Mak**	**Friday**	**4 April**	**8 A.D.**
10	7.18.07.01.18 10 Etznab 6 Mak	Saturday	4 April	9 A.D.
11	7.18.08.02.03 11 Akbal 6 Mak	Sunday	4 April	10 A.D.
12	7.18.09.02.08 12 Lamat 6 Mak	Monday	4 April	11 A.D.
13	7.18.10.02.13 13 Ben 6 Mak	Tuesday	3 April	12 A.D.
14	7.18.11.02.18 1 Etznab 6 Mak	Wednesday	3 April	13 A.D.
15	7.18.12.03.03 2 Akbal 6 Mak	Thursday	3 April	14 A.D.

16	7.18.13.03.08 3 Lamat 6 Mak	Friday	3 April	15 A.D.
17	7.18.14.03.13 4 Ben 6 Mak	Saturday	2 April	16 A.D.
18	7.18.15.03.18 5 Etznab 6 Mak	Sunday	2 April	17 A.D.
19	7.18.16.04.03 6 Akbal 6 Mak	Monday	2 April	18 A.D.
20	7.18.17.04.08 7 Lamat 6 Mak	Tuesday	2 April	19 A.D.
21	7.18.18.04.13 8 Ben 6 Mak	Wednesday	1 April	20 A.D.
22	7.18.19.04.03 9 Etznab 6 Mak	Thursday	1 April	21 A.D.
23	7.19.00.05.03 10 Akbal 6 Mak	Friday	1 April	22 A.D.
24	7.19.01.05.08 11 Lamat 6 Mak	Saturday	1 April	23 A.D.
25	7.19.02.05.13 12 Ben 6 Mak	Sunday	31 March	24 A.D.
26	7.19.03.05.18 13 Etznab 6 Mak	Monday	31 March	25 A.D.
27	7.19.04.06.03 1 Akbal 6 Mak	Tuesday	31 March	26 A.D.
28	7.19.05.06.08 2 Lamat 6 Mak	Wednesday	31 March	27 A.D.
29	7.19.06.06.13 3 Ben 6 Mak	Thursday	30 March	28 A.D.
30	7.19.07.06.18 4 Etznab 6 Mak	Friday	30 March	29 A.D.
31	7.19.08.07.03 5 Akbal 6 Mak	Saturday	30 March	30 A.D.
32	7.19.09.07.08 6 Lamat 6 Mak	Sunday	30 March	31 A.D.
33	7.19.10.07.13 7 Ben 6 Mak	Monday	29 March	32 A.D.
34	**7.19.11.07.18 8 Etznab 6 Mak**	**Tuesday**	**29 March**	**33 A.D.**
a	7.19.11.07.19 9 Kawak 7 Mak	Wednesday	30 March	33 A.D.
b	7.19.11.08.00 10 Ahua 8 Mak	Thursday	31 March	33 A.D.
c	**7.19.11.08.01 11 Imix 9 Mak**	**Friday**	**1 April**	**33 A.D.**
d	7.19.11.08.02 12 Ik 10 Mak	Saturday	2 April	33 A.D.
e	**7.19.11.08.03 13 Akbal 11 Mak**	**Sunday**	**3 April**	**33 A.D.**
New Nephite Year				
35	7.19.12.08.03 9 Akbal 6 Mak	Wednesday	29 March	34 A.D.
36	7.19.13.08.08 10 Lamat 6 Mak	Thursday	29 March	35 A.D.
37	7.19.14.08.13 11 Ben 6 Mak	Friday	28 March	36 A.D.
38	7.19.15.08.18 12 Etznab 6 Mak	Saturday	28 March	37 A.D.
39	7.19.16.09.03 13 Akbal 6 Mak	Sunday	28 March	38 A.D.
40	7.19.17.09.08 1 Lamat 6 Mak	Monday	28 March	39 A.D.
41	7.19.18.09.13 2 Ben 6 Mak	Tuesday	27 March	40 A.D.
42	7.19.19.09.18 3 Etznab 6 Mak	Wednesday	27 March	41 A.D.
43	8.00.00.10.03 4 Akbal 6 Mak	Thursday	27 March	42 A.D.

Another striking thing about the Mesoamerican date of 6 April 1 B.C. is that this Calendar Round combination can occur only on 6 April once every 1,507 years. Interestingly, the Aztecs rebuilt their temple to Quetzalcoatl in A.D. 1507 (Cartwright 1972, 337).

Two different events recorded in the reign of Tiberius Caesar (A.D.14–37), emperor of Rome, support the birth of Christ as being in the year 1 B.C. First, Luke 3:1–3 reports that John the Baptist was preaching and baptizing "in the fifteenth year of the rein of Tiberius Caesar." This was at the same time John baptized

Second, "Everyone has once read, for it comes up many times in literature, of that pilot in the reign of Tiberius, who, as he was sailing along in the Aegean on a quiet evening, heard a loud voice announcing that Great Pan was dead. . . . The myth has been understood as telling of the death of Christ in the 19th year of Tiberius" (de Santillana and von Dechend 1969, 275). The nineteenth year of Tiberius would be A.D. 33, the year of Christ's death and resurrection if his birth was in 1 B.C. (see Table 9–2).

Table 9–2
Zeroing in on Christ's Birth and Death Dates
Christ's Appearance to the Nephites

Christ's 15 of Nisan Birthday Possibilities				Christ's 14 of Nisan Death Date Possibilities			
Tuesday	15	April	10 B.C.				
Saturday	3	April	9 B.C.				
Thursday	24	March	8 B.C.				
Tuesday	11	April	7 B.C.				
Saturday	31	March	6 B.C.	Monday	27	March	28 A.D.
Thursday	20	March	5 B.C.	Saturday	14	April	29 A.D.
Thursday	9	April	4 B.C.	Wednesday	3	April	30 A.D.
Sunday	28	March	3 B.C.	Monday	24	March	31 A.D.
Thursday	17	March	2 B.C.	Monday	12	April	32 A.D.
Thursday	**6**	**April**	**1 B.C.**	**Friday**	**1**	**April**	**33 A.D.**
Tuesday	27	March	1 A.D.	Monday	20	March	34 A.D.

Dating the appearance of the resurrected Messiah-Redeemer to the Nephites begins with 3 Nephi 10:18–19 pointing to "the ending of the thirty and fourth year," when Christ "did truly manifest himself unto them." In other words, there was nearly a between the signs of Christ's of Christ's death in Jerusalem and his appearance in Mesoamerica. In 3 Nephi 11:1, we learn that there was "a great multitude gathered together, of the people of Nephi, round about the temple which was in the land Bountiful." This is where Christ first descended out of heaven to visit the Nephites.

Earlier, we quoted the Spanish friar Juan de Cordova as stating:

> On the day we call Tecpatl [the Aztec name for the day sign flint knife] a great light came from the northeastern sky. It glowed for four days in the sky, then lowered itself to the rock; the rock can still be seen at Tenochtitlan (Teotitlan) de Valle in Oaxaca. From the light there came a great, very

powerful being, who stood on the very top of the rock and glowed like the sun in the sky. There he stood for all to see, shining day and night. Then he spoke, his voice was like thunder, booming across the valley. (Shearer 1975, 72)

What information we have to work with from these two sources is as follows: (1) Christ's appearance in the land of Bountiful was in the ending of the thirty-fourth Nephite year, or A.D. 33 in our Gregorian calendar; (2) the Nephites were gathered in a great multitude at the temple in Bountiful; (3) the great Being of Light in the Oaxacan story first appears in the northeastern sky on a day Flint in the ritual calendar; and (4) this great Being of Light remains glowing in the northeastern sky for four days and then descends as a personage of light to the people.

When we combine the above information, we are probably dealing with two separate events in two separate locations that help to date each other—Bountiful (the southern Gulf Coast of Tabasco) and Oaxaca, Mexico (the land of Desolation). We tend to think of Christ's visit to the Nephites as a single event at Bountiful, but we cannot rule out the possibility that Christ might have visited and ministered to some of his "other sheep" in Mesoamerica at the same time. In fact, after his initial three-day mission, the Book of Mormon declares that "he did show himself unto them oft" (3 Nephi 26:13). We should not suppose that all of these later visits were confined to the land Bountiful.

At Least Two Visits

The place of the heavenly visitation in Oaxaca is still known today as *Teotitlan* (which Shearer mistakenly translated as Tenochtitlan) de Valle. The name *Teotitlan* preserves the actual sacred place of this visitation, because in Nahuatl *Teo* means god, and *titlan* means "to send a messenger" (Karttunen 1983), just as Christ was literally the messenger of God (3 Nephi 16:3).

A sacred hill near Cholula in Mexico is similarly named *Teteolatitla*. The *Te* prefix is a human designator, so the name means "a place where a human god messenger came." It is of interest that the ruling god of Cholula at the great temple of that city was Quetzalcoat. (Torquemada 2:50).

The Book of Mormon is silent on Jesus' later visits, but the Mesoamerican record is not: "He [Quetzalcoatl] having preached

. . . in the majority of the cities of the Ulmecas and Xicalancas and in particular in that of Cholula, . . . returned through the same part from whence he had come, which was by the orient [east] disappearing through Coatzalcoalco" (Ixtlilxochitl, translation in Hunter and Ferguson 1950:218; Quetzalcoatl's departure, in Kingsborough 1848).

(We note here that this historical tradition is of the Toltec priest king Topiltzin Quetzalcoatl and not the original Quetzalcoatl god. But when the parallels to the Book of Mormon are drawn, we cannot help but suspect that this history was being written in the historical framework of the Quetzalcoatl-Christ.)

According to Warren and Norman:

> The cities of the Ulmecas and Xicalancas are in the southern Gulf Coast of Tabasco (which means *abundance* [Scholes and Roys 1948]), the eastern coastal territory of the narrow neck of land—the southern Gulf Coastal region of the Isthmus of Tehuantepec. Coatzalcoalcos, located on the, lies east southeast from Cholula, Puebla, while approximately midway on line between the two in the Tehuacan valley is a site named Teotitlan del Camino, meaning "the road of God's messenger." Tehuacan valley is the primary communication route between Puebla and the southern Gulf Coast. If Cholula was one of the places that Quetzalcoatl-Christ visited, according to Ixtlilxochitl and implied by the hill named Teteolatitla noted above, then Teotitlan del Camino may have been named for the direction if not the only valley pass road that Christ would have traveled overland from Cholula to the east of Coatzalcoalcos, where he returned to the land of Tabasco-Bountiful "from whence he had come." Thus, according to Ixtlilxochitl, Topiltzin's final departure would have been from Bountiful where Christ's ministry had begun and was centered. (Warren and Norman 1995)

The Dates of Christ's Appearances in Mesoamerica

In the ritual calendar, from the day Flint (Tecpatl or Etsnab) to the day Crocodile (Imix) would be four days, and the following day would be Ik or Wind, a day associated with Quetzalcoatl. Thus, the light appeared in the sky above Oaxaca on the day Flint and remained visible until it descended and Christ stepped out of it four days later on the day Imix. Also, the four days in the Oaxaca tradition relating to Christ's visitation, from March 24 to his appearance on March 27, fall in the Passover week of the year A.D. 34, which began on Tuesday 21 March (15 Nisan and the Spring Equinox) and ended seven days later on Monday 27 March (21 Nisan). (See Table 9-3.)

Accordingly, we believe Christ appeared to the Nephites in Bountiful on the sixth day of Passover, 6 Ahau 3 Mak, Sunday, March 26 A.D. 34, which was the Passover sabbath birthday of his resurrection the year before. He then appeared in Oaxaca during the early part of the next day, 7 Imix 4 Mak, before returning to Bountiful. The third day of Christ's visit on 8 Ik 5 Mak, Tuesday 28 March, was the last day of the Nephite-Maya Long Count, 34th year. Thus, Christ would have completed his three-day ministry at the exact end of the 34th Nephite year as is implied in 3 Nephi 10:18 19.

It is also significant that the Mayan day Ik, the last day of the year, means wind, breath and life, and is a day associated with Quetzalcoatl. Ik takes the Nahuatl name from Eecatl-Quetzalcoatl for his wind-rain-life god aspect. (Warren and Norman 1995)

Table 9–3
Calendar Correlations

Gregorian	Judean	Long Count	Ritual	Solar Year
Thu 6 Apr 1 BC	15 Nisan	7.17.17.17.13	1 Ben	6 Mak
Fri 1 Apr 33 AD	14 Nisan	7.19.11.08.01	11 Imix	9 Mak
Sat 2 Apr 33 AD	15 Nisan	7.19.11.08.02	12 Ik	10 Mak
Sun 3 Apr 33 AD	16 Nisan	7.19.11.08.03	13 Akbal	11 Mak
Tue 21 Mar 34 AD	15 Nisan	7.19.12.07.15	1 Men	18 Keh
Wed 22 Mar 34 AD	16 Nisan	7.19.12.07.16	2 Kib	19 Keh
Thu 23 Mar 34 AD	17 Nisan	7.19.12.07.17	3 Kaban	0 Mak
Fri 24 Mar 34 AD	18 Nisan	7.19.12.07.18	4 Etsnab	1 Mak
Sat 25 Mar 34 AD	19 Nisan	7.19.12.07.19	5 Kawak	2 Mak

Sun 26 Mar 34 AD	20 Nisan	7.19.12.08.00	6 Ahaw	3 Mak
Mon 27 Mar 34 AD	**21 Nisan**	**7.19.12.08.01**	**7 Imix**	**4 Mak**
Tue 28 Mar 34 AD	22 Nisan	7.19.12.08.02	8 Ik	5 Mak

Wed 29 Mar 34 AD	23 Nisan	7.19.12.08.03	9 Akbal	6 Mak

Feast of the Passover

As we have shown, the appearance of the resurrected Christ in Mesoamerica as recorded in the Book of Mormon occurred nearly a year after the crucifixion and ascension of Jesus of Nazareth in the Old World. The prophet Moroni, the last writer of the Book of Mormon, declared that "it was by faith that Christ showed himself unto our fathers, after he had risen from the dead; and he showed not himself unto them until after they had faith in him; wherefore, it must needs be that some had faith in him, for he showed himself not unto the world" (Ether 12:7). The exercising of faith for these people, apparently, was not instantaneous.

The Nephites were still following the Mosaic Law until Christ's appearance to them, and then they changed to the Law of the Gospel of Jesus Christ. This situation explains why the Nephites were gathered together in a great multitude. Because the Law of Moses was still in effect, they had apparently exercised their faith by gathering for the week of Passover feast. In the wake of the terrible destruction they had endured only a year before, we can see why their attendance was quite literally an act of faith.

In the year A.D. 34, the Passover began on Tuesday, 21 March (15th of Nisan and the Spring Equinox—see Table 9–3), and ended seven days later on Monday, 27 March or 21st of Nisan. We believe that Christ appeared on the sixth day of Passover, 6 Ahau 3 Mak, Sunday, 26 March A.D. 34, which was the Passover Sabbath birthday of his resurrection the year before. Was this to notify the Nephites of the end of the Mosaic Law and to inaugurate Sunday Sabbath observance as well as all the other elements of the Law of the Gospel?

The Writings of Siguenza

One of the foremost experts on ancient Mexican history was Don Carlos de Siguenza y Gongora (1645–1700). On the basis of his lifelong study of ancient Mexican historical sources, Siguenza felt Quetzalcoatl appeared in Mexico shortly after the crucifixion. In coded or disguised language, he tells us that Quetzalcoatl was the resurrected Messiah-Redeemer of the Bible. Siguenza believed that the Olmecs (people of the rubber land of southern Veracruz and western Tabasco who were part of the Jaredite civilization) had come to Mexico from the Near East. He did not contend that all of the ancestry of the Indians came from the Near East, however. His book dealt only with Mesoamerica.

The very title of what Siguenza considered to be his lifetime work—*Phoenix of the West*—suggests that he believed the resurrected Jesus of Nazareth was the Fair God of the western hemisphere. *Phoenix* is a term from Egyptian mythology. A phoenix was a beautiful, lone bird that lived in the Arabian desert for five hundred or six hundred years and then consumed itself in fire, rising resurrected from the ashes to start another long life. It is used as a symbol of immortality. It was a subtle pseudonym for the resurrected Messiah-Redeemer of ancient Mexico and Central America.

Siguenza pretended to give the Apostle Thomas credit for establishing Christianity in Mesoamerica "in the days of the apostles." But Jesus was referring to himself when he said, "And other sheep I have, which are not of this fold: them also I must bring, and they shall hear my voice: and there shall be one fold and one shepherd" (John 10:16). It was Jesus the Christ who was resurrected to immortality in the days of the apostles. It was he who appeared in Mesoamerica as a resurrected being.

Because of their Christian background, it would have been difficult for Siguenza's Spanish associates to conclude that Christ himself had appeared in Mesoamerica following the crucifixion. Besides, such an idea would not have been tolerated in the days of the Spanish Inquisition. So Siguenza and others granted that power to one of Christ's apostles—St. Thomas (Lafaye 1976).

Siguenza believed that *Phoenix of the West* would throw further light on the work of God. He must have known Quetzalcoatl was the true shepherd. He apparently could not declare it openly, so he disguised his beliefs within the symbol of the phoenix. Siguenza obtained most of his data from the royal Ixtlilxochitl family of the Valley of Mexico. Ixtlilxochitl, it is recalled, reported darkness, earthquakes, and a breaking of rocks in Mexico at the very time of the crucifixion of Jesus in the Old World.

Cholula of the Ulmecas

Ixtlilxochitl dates the appearance of Quetzalcoatl in Mexico in a more general way: "He [Quetzalcoatl] having preached the said things in the majority of the cities of the Ulmecas (Olmecs) and Xicalancas and in particular in that Cholula, where he most visited" (Hunter and Ferguson 1958, 218).

Thus, when Ixtlilxochitl states that Quetzalcoatl visited Cholula of the "Ulmecas" or Olmecs, he is dating the ministry of the Fair God to an early era many centuries before Aztec times. A whole series of Olmec communities were flourishing in Mesoamerica in the days of Jesus, Cholula among them, and stone cities remain to prove it.

As previously mentioned, archaeologists working in Mesoamerica generally refer to the Olmec era as being included in the Early and Middle Preclassic periods (2500 B.C.–250 B.C.). Thus, the Olmec era reached backward many centuries before 600 B.C. and lasted until shortly before the coming of Christ.

Incense Burning and Idolatry Abandoned

John L. Sorenson, in a paper entitled "A Chronological Ordering of the Mesoamerican Pre-Classic," published in 1955 by the Middle American Research Institute at Tulane University, New Orleans, dates to about A.D. 50 the cultural remains known as Santa Clara (Guatemala), Chicanel (Guatemala), and Monte Alban II (Oaxaca, Mexico), observing:

> What now appears to be one of the most unprecedented religious events in Mesoamerica's long history can be detected in the late pre-Classic [time of Christ] in connection with indications of sharp, sudden change and other aspects of culture. The modification is evidenced most clearly by the widespread abandonment of the time-honored figurine cult. This drastic step occurred simultaneously over a wide area according to our studies . . . [and] this innovation can be seen to originate abruptly. As Borhegyi has already tentatively pointed out, the figurine hiatus [a gap or break] corresponds in time to the abandonment of the long-traditional incense-burner forms of highland Guatemala (three-pronged burners, scored covers and rim-head vessels), and presumably, the particular rituals [associated with] those forms. . . .

These suggestions of severity, austerity, or elegance in esthetics of the period might well be interpreted as appropriate indications of the puritanical religious spirit [of early and undefiled Christianity] which alone could account for the giving up of an old, established folk feature like figurines. (Sorenson 1955, 53, 57)

Thus, shortly following the crucifixion of Jesus in the Old World, there occurred in Mesoamerica an abandonment of incense burning and idolatry—exactly as ordered by Jesus of Nazareth. Jesus said, in the Old World, with respect to the Israelite practices of incense burning and burnt offerings: "Think not that I am come to destroy the law, or the prophets: I am not come to destroy, but to fulfill" (Matthew 5:17).

The abandonment of figurine-cult practices and the burning of incense and their replacement with "indications of the puritanical religious spirit which alone could account for the giving up of an old established folk feature like figurines" took place simultaneously with the New World appearance and ministry of the Messiah-Redeemer. Says Sorenson, "Santa Clara, Chicanel, Monte Alban II, Early Ticoman and contemporaries we place about A.D. 50" (Sorenson 1959, 60). This is rather close to A.D. 30, the date given by the original eyewitness record for the New World appearance of the Light and Life of the World.

Feathered Serpent Religion

Further help on dating the appearance of the Messiah-Redeemer in Mexico comes from the Mexican scholar Jose Diaz-Bolio. In his book *La Serpiente Emplumada* (The Feathered Serpent), he states that the original Quetzalcoatl appeared in Olmec times. (Diaz-Bolio 1965, 71) And he rightly says that the "cult" can be traced back—entirely through the Old-Empire Maya period and to Olmec times (Diaz-Bolio 1965, 155). As has already been indicated, the serpent symbol of the Messiah-Redeemer accompanied to Mesoamerica the Israelite colonizers of the sixth century B.C. The symbol dates to the time of Moses and Abraham and far beyond to the dawn of religion in the fourth millennium B.C. Diaz-Bolio also states that the time of Quetzalcoatl coincides with the end of the third age of the world of Mexican cosmogony (Diaz-Bolio 1965, 131), which is placed at the very time of the crucifixion of Christ, according to Ixtlilxochitl.

The Eleventh Century Quetzalcoatl Vs. the First

One of Diaz Bolio's primary themes is that we must distinguish the original Quetzalcoatl from the eleventh-century Mexican hero who also bore the symbolic name of Quetzalcoatl. This eleventh-century person, Topiltzin Quetzalcoatl, was a king and descendant of earlier Toltecs. He adopted the symbolic "bird-serpent" name of the Messiah-Redeemer as his own—just as many Mexicans today bear the name *Jesus*. But Topiltzin Quetzalcoatl followed the original Quetzalcoatl by almost a thousand years. The matter has been clarified to the pointthat very few now confuse the two personages.

Lecomte H. de Charencey, in his book *Les Cites Votanides*, expresses his view that the first Quetzalcoatl appeared in southern Mexico to the serpent-men in A.D. 68 (de Charencey 1985, 57). If Jesus appeared in Mexico shortly after the crucifixion, Charencey is off in his dating by only 38 years.

Ixtlilxochitl and Siguenza date the appearance of the Messiah-Redeemer to the days of the apostles and the time of the crucifixion. He appeared in the days of the Zapotecs—whose culture dates to the time of Christ by radiocarbon determinations. The appearance of the Messiah-Redeemer in Mesoamerica was accompanied by an abrupt termination of idolatry—which reflects itself in archaeological sites by the absence of figurines shortly following the time of Christ.

Notes to Chapter 9

An Alternative Date for the Birth of Christ

An alternative date for the birth of the Savior can be argued from the following information.

Nephi, the Book of Mormon prophet who left Jerusalem with his father Lehi in the "commencement of the first year of the reign of Zedekiah, king of Judah" (1 Nephi 1:1), wrote, "[Christ] cometh, according to the words of the angel, in six hundred years from the time my father left Jerusalem" (1 Nephi 19: 8). Thus, we can ascertain the true date of Christ's birth if we can determine the date of the first year of the reign of Zedekiah. This birth was to have been six hundred years after Lehi left Jerusalem.

Biblical scholars have lately completed the translation and publication of the Babylonian tablets for the years 626 B.C. through 556 B.C. These records suggest that Nebuchadnezzar, king of Babylon, captured Jerusalem on 16 March 597 B.C. King Jehoiachin of Judah went down with the fall of Jerusalem, his reign ending on the day of Jerusalem's capture. Zedekiah was appointed by Nebuchadnezzar to succeed Jehoiachin. "Zedekiah's first regnal year began the following month, April 597 B.C." (Freedman XII, 100). Because Lehi departed from Jerusalem "in the commencement of the first year of the reign of Zedekiah, king of Judah" (1 Nephi 1:4), we may assume he left by December 597 B.C.

Six hundred years following the departure of Lehi from Jerusalem, a Book of Mormon historian recorded:

It was six hundred years from the time that Lehi left Jerusalem. . . .

[In the commencement of the next year,] there was no darkness in all that night, but it was as light as though it was mid-day. And it came to pass that the sun did rise in the morning again, according to its proper order; and they knew [in Mesoamerica] that it was the day that the Lord should be born, because of the sign which had been given. (3 Nephi 1:1, 19)

If Lehi and his companions left Jerusalem in 587 B.C. and if six hundred years later the Savior was born in Bethlehem, then the Savior's birth should be in A.D. 2 or 3. However, the Savior was born while Herod the Great was still alive. Herod died in about 4

B.C., according to skimpy evidence from the Jewish historian Josephus. At first glance, the Book of Mormon appears to contain an error when it states that six hundred years are involved from the first year of King Zedekiah to the birth of Christ.

Jay H. Huber in his article "Lehi's 600-Year Prophecy and the Birth of Christ" demonstrates that the Nephite years could have been 360 days in length and not 365.2423 days or less. Huber initiated his research from a suggestion from Dr. John L. Sorenson that a Nephite year could have been a *tun* year in the Olmec-Maya Long Count calendar. A *tun* year consists of 360 days. Huber concludes that the Savior was probably born on 11 April 4 B.C. (Huber 1982).

According to the Nephite record, the Nephites used the birth of Christ as a new and additional zero point from which to count the years in ancient Mesoamerica. If so, it was only one of many calendar systems in Mesoamerica at the time (see Edmonson 1988 for more details). But one of Edmonson's discovered calendars does have a New Year's date on the day 6 Mak, which fits with the Book of Mormon requirements (Edmonson 1988, 129, 183, 261): "And nine years had passed away from the time when the sign was given, which was spoken by the prophets, that Christ should come into the world. Now the Nephites began to reckon their time from this period when the sign was given, or from the coming of Christ; therefore, nine years had passed away" (3 Nephi 2:7–8).

The authors ascribe to the point of view that the birth of Christ took place in 1 B.C.

The Birth Tree

The *Codex Vienna* depicts a "birth tree" from which many deities were born. Nine Wind Quetzalcoatl is the deity supervising this process. The dates associated with this "birth tree" are A.D. 982 and A.D. 985. The events are part of the ritual establishing the Fifth World Age in ancient Mesoamerica. The codex also shows the birth tree as a goddess with the calendar name of Nine Reed (Figure 9–2). She is giving birth to approximately fifty-one deities. As mentioned above, the deity Quetzalcoatl is supervising this "birth tree" episode.

The *Codex Gomez de Orozco* from northern Oaxaca, Mexico, shows a picture of the footsteps of the deity Quetzalcoatl descending from the heavens (Figure 9–3) in the year A.D. 982.

Apparently, once the death and resurrection of the Messiah-Redeemer, or Mesoamerica's Quetzalcoatl, were completed in the

FIGURE 9–2: BIRTH TREE AT APOALA (CERRO DE LAS MESAS IN SOUTH CENTRAL VERACRUZ) ABOUT A.D. 982, FROM THE CODEX VIENNA, PAGE 37.

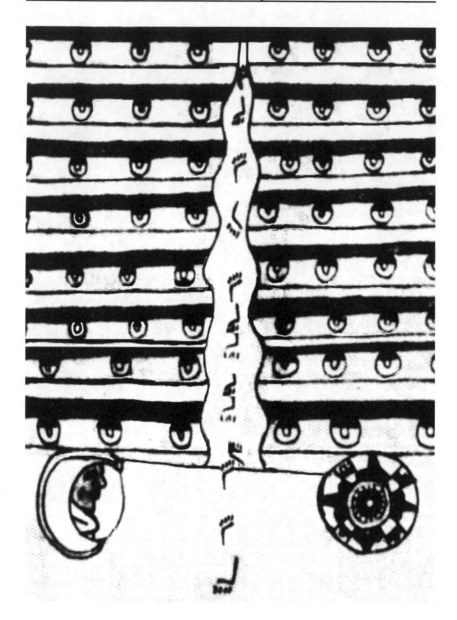

FIGURE 9–3: RESTORED SCENE IS PAGE 1 OF THE CODEX OF A DESCENT OF QUETZALCOATL FROM THE HEAVENS IN THE TENTH CENTURY A.D. THE SOURCE OF THIS SCENE IS THE CODEX GOMEZ DE OROZCO FROM THE COIXTLAHUACA REGION OF NORTHERN OAXACA, MEXICO.

first century A.D., many of the art symbols of the Classic and Postclassic horizons of Mesoamerica reflected death and resurrection themes—sometimes in beautiful symbols and sometimes in grotesque symbols tied to animal, bird, and human sacrifice.

The Prophet Abinadi Foresees the Redemption of the Messiah-Redeemer

An event from the Book of Mormon concerning a prophet and two kings appears to have a parallel in the discovery of Stela 10 at Kaminaljuyu, Guatemala. The episode and its archaeological parallel are now documented.

During the second century B.C., a Book of Mormon prophet by the name of Abinadi was distressed by the lack of understanding of his people concerning the Law of Moses and the redemption of God. Abinadi said, "Behold, did not Moses prophesy unto them concerning the coming of the Messiah, and that God should redeem his people? Yea, and even all the prophets who have prophesied ever since the world began—have they not spoken more or less concerning those things?" (Mosiah 13:33).

Recently, Munro S. Edmonson of Tulane University published an important book on Mesoamerican calendar systems, *The Book of the Year: Middle American Calendrical Systems*. Our immediate interest is his conclusions on the Kaminaljuyu, Guatemala, calendar system in general and Stela 10 in particular.

The Preclassic Calendar at Kaminaljuyu, Guatemala

Stela 10 at Kaminaljuyu (Figure 9–4) was found during the 1950s by Gustavo Espinosa in the archaeological context of the Miraflores phase (about 200 B.C. to about the time of Christ). Actually, "Stela 10" is a misnomer because this monument is really a royal throne. In 1977, Edwin Shook, former archaeologist of the Carnegie Institution of Washington, D.C., showed Warren that the bottom side of this heavy monument contains the stubs of three legs.

This Kaminaljuyu "throne" has carved on its surface part of the bodies of two individuals and also an Olmec style at the right side of the "throne." Preclassic hieroglyphs are located at the top on the left side, and about three dozen glyphs are located under the arms of the human figure at the bottom. The upper-left-hand date is the year 7 Wind in the Kaminaljuyu calendar. The Olmec style date on the right side is the year 1 Lord in the Olmec calendar. Down at the base of the "throne" is the year 8 Wind in the Teotihuacan calendar. Edmonson points out that the

FIGURE 9–4: LATE PRECLASSIC STELA 10 AT KAMINALJUYU, GUATEMALA.

monument reflects a correlation of three different calendar systems for the same date. This date is 6 November 147 B.C. in the Gregorian calendar. The Tikal Long Count calendar would record the date as 7.10.10.8.2 8 Wind 0 Zotz. The upper-left-hand human figure is depicted as dead, with an inverted trident sign over his eye. This particular sign could be interpreted as death by fire (see Parsons 1964, 82ff and Norman 1976, 116–17). The hieroglyphs above this person's head are poorly preserved but at this point of time would be nondecipherable in any event. The human figure at the bottom of the "throne" would apparently represent royalty because this is a throne. The larger number of hieroglyphs are well preserved but unreadable. The right-hand Olmec-style head represents the Olmec year of 1 Lord, as indicated above.

This Kaminaljuyu "throne" (Stela 10 in the literature) has a few parallels to an interesting episode recorded in the book of Mosiah in the Book of Mormon. First, the date that is recorded in three different Mesoamerican calendars is 147 B.C. In Mosiah 17, we are told that a king Noah in the land of Nephi had a prophet by the name of Abinadi put to death by fire. In the words of Mormon, "And now, when Abinadi had said these words, he fell having suffered death by fire; yea, having been put to death because he would not deny the commandments of God, having sealed the truth of his words by his death" (Mosiah 17:20). At the bottom of the page containing this verse is a date recorded as "About 148 B.C." In fact, the date refers to Abinadi's death as described in verse 20.

A second parallel in this episode mentions a King Noah who was offended by the prophet Abinadi's words to the point of having him condemned to death by fire. However, King Noah himself also died by fire; and because the trident sign on the upper-left-hand figure (which has the meaning of "Ahau" or "divine kingship") is upside down, it signifies the king is dead. (Schele and Freidel 1990, 54, 115, 411, 419, 436) This figure is probably King Noah rather than the prophet Abinadi. It is significant that the lower human figure on this "throne" probably represents another member of royalty, perhaps King Limhi.

It may be important that the dead king is associated by a date from the local Kaminaljuyu calendar and that the living king is associated with a new calendar that originated just eighteen years earlier—that is, 8 November 165 B.C. (7.9.12.3.10 1 Ok 18 Sip) in the Gregorian calendar (Edmonson 1988, 121). Certainly, the date on the "throne" from the O1mec calendar indicates cultural influences from survivors of the earlier Olmec civilization.

Discovery of the True Length of the Tropical Year

Modern astronomy calculates the true length of the tropical year as having been 365.24220309 days when the LDS Church was organized in 1830 and at the birth of the Messiah-Redeemer as having been 365.24231545 days. (Lefgren 1980, Table 4) These measurements are based on the movements of the sun between the Tropic of Cancer (twenty-three degrees and twenty-seven minutes north of the equator) and the Tropic of Capricorn (twenty-three degrees and twenty-seven minutes south of the equator).

In ancient Mesoamerica, the priest-astronomers did not calculate the leap year into their elite calendar systems. The consequence of that practice is that these elite calendar systems had a year of 365 days. As noted above, these priest-astronomers also used a "calendar round" composed of 52 years of 365 days and a ritual calendar made up of 73 cycles of 260 days. In fifty-two years, both the year and the ritual calendars added up to exactly 18,980 days. After many centuries of careful record keeping, the priest-astronomers of Mesoamerica realized that if a calendar system's new year began on the spring equinox, as an example, the new year would not fall on the spring equinox with the passing of the years. These calendar specialists discovered that twenty-nine calendar rounds equaled 1,508 years of 365 days and that a new year that had begun on the spring equinox would once again fall on the spring equinox. It so happens that 1,508 years of 365 days equal 550,420 days and that 1,507 years of 365.2422 days equal 550,420 days (Edmonson 1988, 112).

Munro Edmonson's calendrical research has discovered that the true length of the tropical year was first determined in Mesoamerica at Kaminaljuyu, Guatemala. He dates this event as 21 March 433 B.C. in the Gregorian calendar (Edmonson 1985, 118). However, in spite of this discovery, the Mesoamerican elite priest-astronomers did not calculate the leap year into the year calendars. From the perspective of the Book of Mormon, that inauguration of the Kaminaljuyu calendar would have occurred a few years before the death of the prophet Enos. (Enos 1:25)

Conclusions

Stela 10, or the "throne" from Kaminaljuyu, Guatemala (located on the western edge of modern Guatemala City), has taken on great importance with the publication of Edmonson's new book *The Book of the Year: Middle American Calendrical Systems*. Edmonson has shown that the true length of the tropical year was discovered at Kaminaljuyu and that its leaders began this calendar on 21 March 433 B.C. However, the Stela 10 "throne" at Kaminaljuyu has the date of 6 November 147 B.C. in three different calendars. This monument shows one king in death caused possibly by fire and a second royal figure present, probably ascending to the throne. This ascension is important enough to have been recorded in three different calendar systems.

The date and events indicated on the Stela 10 "throne" parallel the episode in the book of Mosiah involving the death of the prophet Abinadi at the direction of king Noah.

However, the first century B.C. Nephite calendar is slightly different from the basic Mesoamerican elite calendars in several features.

Finally, the hypothesis that the ancient city of Nephi was probably Kaminaljuyu because Kaminaljuyu was the largest and most important site in highland Guatemala during Book of Mormon times is reinforced by the content and calendrical dates recorded on the Stela 10 "throne."

Siguenza

Siguenza's biographer, Irving Albert Leonard, says of this great scholar:

> He was unfortunate enough to live in a time and environment when chiefly those writings which glorified the Church and its servants were thought worthy of the press. The rigorous censorship imposed by the Inquisition too often precluded the publication of other works of a more secular nature.
>
> In 1668, at the age of 23, Siguenza began his studies of the ancient glories of the aborigines of New Spain. . . . While this was not the first time that this had been done in New Spain, Don Carlos undoubtedly brought together,

hampered as he was by his many other duties and limited resources, the most complete aggregation of original books, manuscripts, maps, and paintings related to native life before the arrival of the Spaniards, that had ever been assembled before his time. He was aided in this laudable enterprise by his association with the De Alva Ixtlilxochitl family from whom, no doubt, he received much instruction in the Mexican languages which he mastered.

Some of the Indians, particularly those belonging to noble families, had hidden certain of them [ancient historical documents] and, through fear of their new masters, did not dare to reveal their knowledge of them. Thus, it was not only through the most painstaking efforts of Don Carlos and the wide cultivation of friendships with the natives that he was able to bring forth these manuscripts and paintings from their hiding-places and submit them to the scrutiny of his curious eye.

Siguenza suspected that his lifetime work—his *Phoenix of the West*—would be suppressed. It was. It mysteriously disappeared at the time of his death and has never been found. This was the book that its author, the great Siguenza, believed would throw further light on the work of God. Siguenza's biographer, Irving Albert Leonard, reports as follows concerning Siguenza's attitude toward the book and his fears concerning it:

It was his happy belief that in his *Phoenix of the West* he was throwing further light on the work of God. Thus, it was that he devoted the full measure of his intellectual resources to so noble a task. And this gratifying conviction moved him to be especially concerned regarding the ultimate fate of his work. Remarking somewhat dolefully that many of his works would probably die with him, Don Carlos exclaims: "May God our Lord grant that this may not be true of what I have ascertained about the preaching of the Apostle Saint Thomas in this land.". . . But his devout prayer, seemingly, remained unanswered, for investigators, from shortly after the death of Siguenza up to the present, have sought diligently but vainly for it. (Leonard 1929, 98)

At his [Don Carlos'] death, it seems as if a "surprise attack" upon his papers had been sounded and everyone got possession of what he could. Siguenza's abiding interest in all matters pertaining to the Indians, together with his intimacy with the De Alva Ixtlilxochitl family, drew him like a magnet to the nearby pyramids of Teotihuacan, of which region this illustrious Indian family were the overlords. These structures claimed his close attention and afforded him much food for cogitation.

If it cannot be said that he extended human knowledge in the field of mathematics, astronomy, and kindred sciences, he showed far more understanding and enlightenment on these subjects than did the vast majority of his contemporaries on either side of the Atlantic. What can be stated with confidence is that the diversity of his interests, and the high degree of attainment reached in all of them, and his prolific literary activity mark him as one of the greatest scholars of the seventeenth century in the Western Hemisphere—including the English colonies—and a figure whom no true historian of the early cultural history of the New World can properly neglect.

> He was a poet, a philosopher, a mathematician, an astronomer, an antiquarian, and a historian . . . and [in] nearly all of them he excelled. . . . Don Carlos was a thinker. . . . With tireless zeal, despite limited financial resources, he collected a museum of Mexican antiquities and other material pertaining to the early history of New Spain—a collection which excited the admiration of later scholars though they had access to but a small part of it. Becoming proficient in the languages of the aborigines through his studies and his daily contacts with the Indians, he was able to decipher many of the early monuments and interpret Indian events in terms of the Christian calendar. (Leonard 1929, 1–2)

Chapter 10
ARCHAEOLOGICAL AND DOCUMENTARY EVIDENCES: THE TREE OF LIFE

The tree of life is one of the oldest and most prevalent religious symbols in the Near East and in Mesoamerica. This correlation indicates to many students and scholars that widespread religious and cultural ties exist between Mesoamerica and the Near East (Mesopotamia, Palestine, and Egypt) and tends to confirm the migration of at least some Mesoamerican populations from the Near East to America. As Willets has noted:

> The notion of a Tree of Life, growing in a paradise inaccessible to ordinary mortals, and bearing fruit capable of rejuvenating, reanimating, or prolonging life when eaten, is part of the stock of world myth. Sometimes associated with a Well or Fountain of Life-giving water, and varying in species according to its geographical setting, it crops up in Egyptian, Sumerian, Babylonian, Phoenician, Norse, and Gaelic Folk-lore, and no doubt in that of many other cultures as well. . . .
>
> The *motif* traveled widely. Like the myth behind it, it is known in almost every ancient culture of the Old World, including Assyria and Babylonia, Palestine, Egypt, Mycenae, and India. The Arabs carried it to Spain, Sicily, and western Europe, while under Byzantine auspices it reached Russia and Italy.
>
> All versions have the same heraldic air—a highly stylized, geometrical tree flanked by two figures. At Mohenjo-daro, these are bulls; at Suza, lions; on Sumerian seals, mountains; on Sassanian silks, duck or the Holy Ibis; from Assyria, figures with eagles' heads; from Cyprus, goats eating; from Crete, snakes. (Willetts 1965, 159–60)

Count Goblet D'Alviella's classic work *The Migration of Symbols* which, after more than eighty years, is still one of the best sources on symbols, notes that the first type—the tree between facing animals—first appears in southern Mesopotamia at the time of Sargon I, "some four [*sic* two] thousand years before our era." He traces its route to the Phoenicians, who abstracted it into "an interlacing of spirals and strap-like curves," some of which bear winged sphinxes. They transmitted it to "the whole of Western Asia," but its introduction in Greece may have predated even the Phoenician influence. Moving in the other direction, the Persians adopted it after the fall of Babylon and transmitted it eastward into India immediately before Alexander's invasion. Thus, it appears among Buddhist sculptures at Bharhut (D'Alviella 1956, 122–24).

A second variation, according to D'Alviella, is the image of the tree between two human or semihuman personages facing each other. As might be expected with two variants so closely related, many combinations of beast-headed humans and human-headed animals exist. This variant followed the same route and appears in China as well as India. He continues:

> From the Indian Archipelago—or from Eastern Asia—it may have even reached the New World, if we are to judge from the resemblance of the scene depicted on the Javanese medals to certain images found in manuscripts connected with the ancient civilization of Central America.
>
> We have seen that the Cross was used, in the symbolism of the ancient inhabitants of America, to represent the winds which bring the rain. These crosses sometimes assume a tree-like form, and are then composed of a stem bearing two horizontal branches, with a bird perched on the fork, as in the famous panel of Palenque. Moreover, this tree is sometimes placed between two personages facing one another, with a sort of wreath of feathers on their heads, who cannot but recall the monstrous aspect of the beings depicted on both sides of the Tree upon the medals of Javanese temples. . . . We have here certainly fresh evidence in favor of the theory which already relies upon so many symbolical and ornamental similarities in order to discover, in the pre-Columbia civilization of America, the traces of intercourse

with Japan, China, or the Indian Archipelago. (D'Alviella 1956, 12)

Other characteristics of the great mythic trees are that they emit a fluid or substance that bestows or sustains life; they may be the home of a deity or a manifestation of a deity; and they may also, through their stems, flowers, and fruits, represent symbols of fertility.

For those in the more modern Judeo-Christian tradition, the mention of the tree of life and associated fountains begins with the description of "the tree of life also in the midst of the [Garden of Eden]. . . . And a river went out of Eden to water the garden; and from thence it was parted, and became into four heads" (Genesis 2:9–10). In the Slavonic version of the apocryphal book of Enoch II, "the tree is the source of the four rivers which flow to the earthly Eden," and, as such, "they [the rivers] had the power of the tree of life" (Goodenough 1958, 7:126, 128).

Thanks to the biblical record, there is a literary tradition of the tree of life; but although "many other elements of symbolism were clearly connected with the tree cults of the ancient world, the oldest and most persistent is the mystic notion that the tree represents, symbolizes, the deity and is, or represents the source of life" (Goodenough 1958, 7:91).

The most direct connection of the tree of life and the fountain of water appears in the New Testament, where John wrote: "And he shewed me a pure river of water of life, clear as crystal, proceeding out of the throne of God and of the Lamb. In the midst of the street of it, and on either side of the river, was there the tree of life, which bare twelve manner of fruits, and yielded her fruit every month: and the leaves of the tree were for the healing of the nations" (Revelation 22:1–2).

Thus, we see a vivid manifestation of the Old World tradition linking tree and fountain in the first century A.D.— long after the New World inhabitants had established their own forms of the symbols. (See also Genesis 3:22, 24; Proverbs 3:18, 11:30, 13:12, 15:4; and Revelation 2:7.)

From the Book of Mormon

One particular Book of Mormon description of the tree of life is given by Lehi, an Old World/Mesoamerican prophet. He saw the tree in a dream, and said to his family:

> I beheld a tree, whose fruit was desirable to make one happy. . . .
>
> I knew that it was desirable above all other fruit.
>
> And as I cast my eyes round about, that perhaps I might discover my family also, I beheld a river of water; and it ran along, and it was near the tree of which I was partaking the fruit. . . .
>
> And I beheld a straight and narrow path, which came along by the rod of iron, even to the tree by which I stood; and it also led by the head of the fountain. (1 Nephi 8:10, 12–13, 20)

Lehi's son, the prophet Nephi, who saw the same vision as his father, only with added details, states: "I beheld that the rod of iron, which my father had seen, was the word of God, which led to the fountain of living waters, or to the tree of life; which waters are a representation of the love of God; and I also beheld that the tree of life was a representation of the love of God" (1 Nephi 11:25).

Izapa Stela 5

In 1943, the Smithsonian Institution of the Bureau of American Ethnology published its Bulletin 138, entitled *Stone Monuments of Southern Mexico*, by Matthew W. Sterling. Plate 52 in Bulletin 138 is a photograph of a cast of a large ancient stone monument discovered at the ancient ruin of Izapa near the present town of Tapachula in the state of Chiapas, Mexico. Izapa is near the border of Guatemala and not far from the Pacific Ocean.

Izapa Stela 5, shown in Figure 10–1, is possibly one of the most important graphic depictions of the tree of life. It is a stone carving that weighs fifteen tons and is 255 centimeters high. Dated to the late Preclassic Guillen phase, about 300–50 B.C., it is the earliest Mesoamerican depiction of the tree of life discovered so far.

FIGURE 10–1: IZAPA STELA 5 TREE OF LIFE DATING FROM 300 TO 1 B.C. IZAPA IS
LOCATED IN SOUTHWESTERN CHIAPAS, MEXICO, NEAR THE PACIFIC OCEAN AND A
FEW MILES FROM THE GUATEMALAN BORDER. (COURTESY OF V. GARTH NORMAN.)

The most recent study of this stela is by V. Garth Norman,
who has summarized the significance of Stela 5:

> What makes the monument so interesting . . . is its
> possible connection to the Book of Mormon. In the 1950s
> and early 1960s, studies by Dr. M. Wells Jakeman of the
> Brigham Young University Department of Archaeology
> indicated that certain features of the monument seem to
> correspond to features of Lehi's vision of the Tree of Life.
> [See also 1 Nephi 8 and 11.] The most obvious of the
> parallels is a fruit-bearing tree in the center with a stream
> running by. A pathway extends from the river's head to the
> tree, and a broad grooved line paralleling the path lines
> suggests the rod of iron. Two cherubim-like beings attend

the tree, and seated around it are six people who, it was suggested, could represent Lehi's family in the attitudes they assume in Lehi's vision. Attaching their names to the figures, we see Lehi on the left and attended by Sariah, facing Laman, and on the right Nephi, attended by Sam, facing Lemuel. In fact, Dr. Jakeman deciphered possible name hieroglyphs above the heads of two of these figures as "Lehi" and "Nephi". . .

The years of research since Dr. Jakeman's first study have neither proved nor disproved his thesis. As yet, published data have been inconclusive, and will continue to be until we have a more complete picture of Izapan culture. In the 1970s I published an interpretive study of Izapa monuments, including Stela 5, in a large work entitled "Izapa Sculpture." The study shows that Stela 5 occupies a central position, conceptually speaking, in relation to the other carvings discovered in Izapa, which display, among other concepts, the following: (1) There is an anthropomorphic god whose prime symbol is the sun and who dwells in the heavens and on mountains. (2) He is god of the Tree of Life, which relates to life after death. (3) At death, the human spirit rises into heaven from the body. (4) A physical resurrection is implied. (5) Worship involves sacrifice and divine sacrificial atonement. And (6) the spirit of an unborn child originates in the heavens.

New Details and Information Concerning Izapa Stela 5

Norman continues:

Some of the new details (of my research) do more than support previous interpretations; they strengthen those interpretations in deeper and more meaningful ways. For example, there is a glyph beyond the head of the river where the path line originates, decipherable as "dark mists," in its relationship to Maya hieroglyphics. In the Lehi vision context this glyph could express the duality of the spiritual journey from darkness into the full gospel light achieved at the Tree of Life. (See 1 Nephi 8:4–8, 22–24.) It is located at the far right center of the carving, where the creation life-cycle begins in which rain bands or "mists" cover the eyes and ears of a human head. Other concepts now recognizable are that immortality is connected with eating the fruit of the tree, and that the two cherubim mentioned earlier are male and female, as was the case in the ancient Israelitish temple, and function together in behalf of man in bringing him to the Tree of Life.

My current research involves astronomical orientations and calendar significance of the monuments at Izapa. This study could provide a key to help unlock the meaning of the monuments as a whole, integrated unit supporting the Izapa temple center function. Also, Old World comparative studies are under way to help trace the roots of Izapan culture and evaluate its role in the rise of Mesoamerican civilization. (Norman 1980, 54–55)

The tree (1), the river (2), the path (3), and the rod of iron (4) are clearly portrayed on the stone. Cherubim typical of Mesopotamian and Egyptian scenes are shown on each side of the tree. They face the tree and are in human form but have bird heads. Bird heads, and sometimes only wings on the human form, characterize the guardians in Assyrian and Egyptian art.

Because the Book of Mormon gives such a clear meaning and interpretation of the symbols carved on the stone, it seems likely that Lehi's and Nephi's words were used by those who carved the Izapa Stela 5 tree-of-life stone. Remember, the river represents the barrier of evil between people and true happiness. The rod of iron represents the word of God, which, if followed, leads one to the tree of eternal life and happiness. The tree symbolizes the love of God; and if a person loves God, he or she will keep God's commandments, and this obedience leads to the fruits of the tree— happiness and eternal life. It is an entire philosophy of life, set out succinctly on fifteen tons of stone.

The Cross: Symbol of Life Rather Than Death

The cross representing the tree of life was one of the ancient symbols of the Messiah-Redeemer of Mexico. Figure 10–2, from an ancient Aztec codex, shows the cross on the cloak of Quetzalcoatl. Ixtlilxochitl wrote that Quetzalcoatl was "the first who worshipped and placed the cross [among them] which some called *Quiahuiteotlchicahualizteotl,* . . . which means: god of rains and of health and tree of sustenance or life" (Hunter and Ferguson 1950, 211). The cross and the tree of life, both related to the highest god—the God of Life—were regarded in ancient Mesoamerica as identical symbols.

In early Christian tradition, the tree of life was considered the prototype and the equivalent of the cross of the crucifixion. Alan W. Watts makes this point clear in his book *Myth and Ritual in Christianity:* "The clear identity of the Cross with this central tree of Eden is shown, not only in the legends of the Holy Rood which assert that the Cross of Christ was made from the wood of that Tree, but also in the famous Great Cross of the Lateran, a mosaic dating, perhaps, from the time of Constantine" (Watts 1954, 159).

Watts describes crucifixion scenes in early Christian art in which the various elements of the ancient tree-of-life symbol (as shown in Figures 10–2, 10–3, and 10–4), including the bird above the cross-tree and the skull (monster) beneath, are "contrasting figures of life and death."

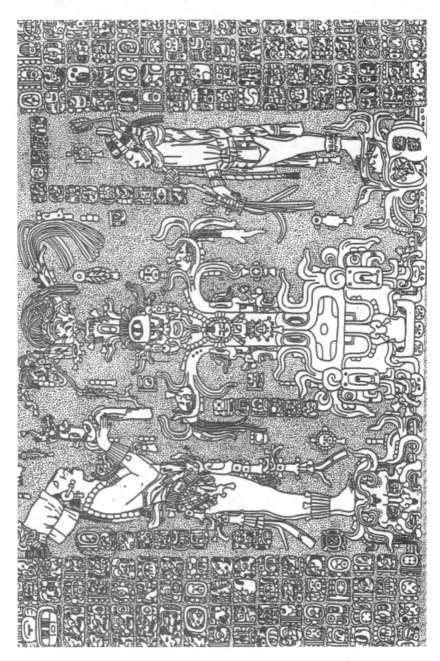

FIGURE 10–2: TABLET OF THE FOLIATED CROSS FROM PALENQUE, CHIAPAS, MEXICO. THE CARVING DATES FROM A.D. 692. NOTE THE HUMAN HEADS IN THE LEAVES OF THE MAIZE TREE REPRESENTING BIRTH. (COURTESY OF LINDA SCHELE.)

FIGURE 10–3: ASSYRIAN TREE-OF-LIFE SCENE FROM NINEVEH IN THE EIGHTH CENTURY B.C.

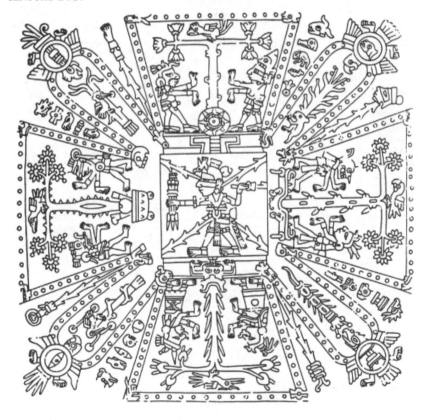

FIGURE 10–4: DIRECTIONAL TREES FROM PAGE 1 OF THE FOURTEENTH CENTURY A.D. CODEX FEJERVARY-MAYER FROM CENTRAL MEXICO.

The tree of life from the Temple of the Cross at Palenque, Mexico, which dates from A.D. 692, is in the form of a cross and includes all the other elements—the bird above, the monster beneath, and the guardians on each side of the tree-cross. The cross tree of life is shown with the quetzal bird on top in Figure 10–5 (Items 6 and 7). Thus, Ixtlilxochitl's claim that the biblical tree of life was known in ancient Mesoamerica has been confirmed in stone by surviving physical evidence.

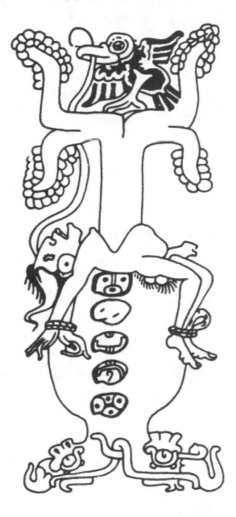

FIGURE 10–5: TREE OF LIFE GROWING FROM A HUMAN HEART (THE MAYA CODEX DRESDEN, PAGE 3, DATING FROM BETWEEN THE FOURTEENTH TO THE EARLY SIXTEENTH CENTURY A.D.).

Peter Martyr D'Anghera, an Italian geographer and historian who wrote in 1516 on the discovery of the Yucatan and the Maya, observed:

> They worship idols, and some of them, but not all, are circumcised. They have laws, and are extremely honest in trading, which they carry on without money. Crosses have been seen amongst them; and when they were asked, through interpreters, the meaning of that emblem, some of them answered that a very beautiful man had once lived amongst them, who had left them this symbol as a remembrance of him; others said that a man more radiant than the sun had died upon the cross. (MacNutt 1912, 7–8)

J. Eric S. Thompson, Maya scholar of the Carnegie Institution, wrote in *The Rise and Fall of the Maya Civilization* that at the time of the Spanish conquest, the Maya people associated the Christian cross with their own ancient tree of life, "conventionalized in art as a cross, decked with vegetation, on which the Quetzal bird perched" (Thompson 1954, 142). Thus, we see that the quetzal bird, itself a symbol of the Mesoamerican Christ, or highest god, was associated with the ancient American cross.

Figure 10–6 is a photograph taken by Rafael Girard of Guatemala City. Girard has worked many years among the present-day Maya and particularly among the Chortis, a subdivision of the Mayan people, in Guatemala. The Chortis have held tenaciously to the religion and general way of life of their ancient ancestors. The ancients, for many centuries before the coming of the Spaniards, used the cross in their religious ceremonies, covering it with green vegetation as they continue to do today—as illustrated in Figure 10–6.

FIGURE 10–6: CROSS, PHOTOGRAPHED IN THE NATIVE PRESENT-DAY CHORTI MAYA TEMPLE OF CAYUR, GUATEMALA, BY RAFAEL GIRARD IN 1962.

The New World Christians of old emphasized the resurrection and the hope of eternal life—of life after death—instead of emphasizing the agony of Calvary. In keeping with their symbolism of the cross, "The Maya believed in the immortality of the soul and a life hereafter which the soul enjoyed when it left its earthly body" (Morley 1946, 221).

In his discussion of Mexico's Messiah, Morley points out that *Itzamna* stood at the head of the Maya pantheon with the father, *Hunab-Ku*, the Creator, "who does not appear to have played an important part in the life of the common people" (Morley 1946, 222–25). In Christianity, it is the Son who deals directly with man. Morley tells us that the glyph or day-sign for *Itzamna* was a benevolent deity, always the friend of man. He was the God of Life—the Light and the Life of the World—the Resurrection and the Life.

From Yucatan comes direct confirmation of the claim of Ixtlilxochitl that the cross was associated with the tree of life in ancient Mesoamerica. Chilam Balam, who lived in the town of Mani in northern Yucatan during the closing decades of the fifteenth century and the early part of the sixteenth century, was revered by the Maya of Yucatan as a prophet. His people, the Itza, were the followers of *Itzamna*—that is, they may have been Christians of ancient Yucatan and Chiapas, Mexico.

Chilam Balam's book is described by Ralph L. Roys as having been "written in the Maya language but in the European script which the early missionaries [from Spain] adapted to express such sounds as were not found in Spanish. . . . Many passages were no doubt originally transcribed from older hieroglyphic manuscripts, some of which were still in existence in northern Yucatan as late as the close of the seventeenth century" (Roys 1933, 3).

Roys continues:

> Shortly before the arrival of the Spaniards in the New World, Chilam prophesied the return of *Itzamna-Quetzalcoatl,* the bearded, white-robed, white-skinned Messiah of his ancient ancestry. When the Spaniards arrived, the Mayas of Yucatan believed at first, as did Moctezuma's people of central Mexico, that the "Fair God" had finally returned as promised. (Roys 1933, 187)

His people thereafter regarded Chilam Balam as a great prophet. Actually, he had merely repeated the prophecy of the Fair God himself who had announced anciently that someday he would return. The prophet Chilam said a number of interesting and important things about *Itzamna,* the ancient prophecy of *Itzamna's* return , and *Hunab-ku,* father of *Itzamna.* For instance: "There is the sign of *Hunab-ku* on high. The raised wooden standard [the cross] shall come. You see the mutbird surmounting the raised wooden standard. Good indeed is the word of God that comes to us. The day of our regeneration comes. You do not fear the world, Lord, you are the only God who created us. It is sufficient, then, that the word of God is good, Lord. [He is] the guardian of our souls. He who receives him, who has truly believed, he will go to heaven with him. Let us exalt his sign on high. . . . The First Tree of the World [the tree of life] is restored; it is displayed to the world. This is the sign of *Hunab-ku* on high. You shall be converted to the word *of Hunab-ku,* Lord; it came from heaven. Oh it is he who speaks to you! (Roys 1933, 167–69)

The raised wooden standard surmounted by the bird is an obvious reference to the tree of life, illustrated in Figures 10–3, 10–5, and 10–7. The tree of life is also referred to by Roy as the "First Tree of the World."

Remembering that the Jaredites brought with them records detailing the creation of the world and the creation of Adam and Eve in the Garden of Eden and remembering as well that the Brass Plates that Lehi's colony brought with them contained much of what we call the Old Testament, this reference may show the direct influence of the book of Genesis upon the Maya many centuries before the time of Columbus. The tree of life found in 1952 by Alberto Ruz on the sarcophagus lid of the pyramid tomb at Palenque, Mexico, dates about eight hundred years before Columbus. Therefore, Chilam Balam's reference to the tree of life as a thing known to his own people has been verified in stone. Archaeologists have also found representations of it in the Near East and in Mexico (Parrot 1961, 359).

FIGURE 10–7: TREE-OF-LIFE SCENES IN THE FORM OF CROSSES FROM CODEX BORGIA, AFTER KINGSBOROUGH.

The God of Maize

The ancient Maya prayed to the Messiah for good crops of corn. Their society depended upon corn for its very existence. The Messiah thus became associated with maize and was sometimes referred to as the "God of Maize." A good example of the tree of life from Mesoamerica, as shown earlier in Figure 10–2, is from the Tablet of the Temple of the Foliated Cross at Palenque, which illustrates the tree of life as a corn or maize plant and depicts the resurrection or rebirth of plants as well as humans. Related to this scene of the tree of life as a corn plant among the Classic Maya of ancient Mesoamerica is a similar idea used by the Hopi Indians of the southwestern United States. The sacred corn plant symbolizes life to the Hopi.

When the Spaniards came with their medieval European version of Christianity, the Maya immediately recognized this Messiah in the Spanish doctrines and identified "Jesus, as the Bread of Life, with the maize God" (Thompson 1954, 237). The Maya knew that the Christ of Cortes was identical to the "God of Light and Life" of their own New World ancestors and that they themselves were a branch of the Old World fold of the Messiah-Redeemer.

Jade: Green Stone of Life

As Dr. Ackerman has pointed out in connection with the concept of vitalism of the ancients of Palestine, the evergreen tree was a manifestation of the vital life force. Also, the deciduous plants, "dead" in the winter but "revivified" in the spring by bursting into green foliage, were manifestations of life and the resurrection. Rain came from the Creator Sky-God, and from rain the green plants developed (Ackerman 1950, 3–24). The ancient Mesopotamians, and after them others throughout Palestine, believed that the green grass, grains, and plants were given birth each year through divine power (see Frankfort 1946, 143).

The same idea prevailed in ancient Mesoamerica. There, jade, native to the region, green and precious, was likewise a symbol of the Messiah-Redeemer, God of Life—Quetzalcoatl. Covarrubias tells us that jade was linked to rain, vegetation, life, godliness, water, maize, and the sky (Covarrubias 1947, 109). These are aspects or symbolisms of the ancient Jehovah-Creator-God of Palestine manifest in the Milky Way serpent symbolism of Mesopotamia, Palestine, and Egypt. J. Eric S. Thompson adds that according to the ancient Maya, the symbol for water was a jade bead, because water and jade were both precious and green (Thompson 1954, 166). It is interesting and consistent that the serpent, jade, and the Milky Way each represents water, the source of life. The basis for the symbolism is in the oldest religious tradition of the world's oldest civilization.

Jade has been found in connection with the highly sophisticated Preclassic culture of the Valley of Mexico, which culture has been radiocarbon dated to 1700 B.C. Mexican and Central American jades are pure and native. In 1952, Robert Leslie found a boulder of jade measuring eleven inches in diameter in a freshly plowed field on the north bank of the Motagua River of Guatemala. Alfred Kidder, Jessie Jennings, and Edwin Shook found a jade boulder at Kaminaljuyu near Guatemala City in 1946 during archaeological efforts conducted for the Carnegie Institution.

The Stone of Israel

In Genesis 49:24, the Messiah-Redeemer of Israel is referred to as "the shepherd, the *stone* of Israel." The same comparison was made in ancient Mesoamerica. The sixteenth-century Maya prophet Chilam Balam refers to jade as a symbol of the Messiah-Redeemer, calling it "the first precious stone of grace." He puts it into an allegory of the birth, crucifixion, and resurrection, or "coming forth," of Jesus. His allegorical reference to Christ is so apparent in this connection that J. Eric S. Thompson, distinguished Carnegie Maya scholar, asserts, with reference to it, "Christian ideas have led to the identification of Jesus, as the bread of life, with the maize god" (Thompson 1954, 237). The ancient book of Chilam Balam of Chumayel has been translated from the Maya tongue into English by Ralph Roys:

> Three, seven, eight thousand was the creation of the world, when he who was hidden within the stone, hidden within the night was born, and occurred the birth of the first precious stone of grace, the first infinite grace. . . . Not yet had he received his divine rank. Then he remained alone within the grace. Then it was pulverized [crushing of green jade stone = crucifixion]. There were his long locks of hair. . . . [H]is divinity was assumed when he came forth [the resurrection].

Thompson explains the allegory:

> The precious stone of grace is jade, which in the Mexican allegorical writing is the ear of corn, before it ripens. The passage states that the green corn, like precious jade, is hidden within the rock. Then the rock is smashed asunder, and the maize is born and becomes divine. The maize god always has long hair, perhaps derived from the beard of the maize in its husk. Hence the reference to the long locks. (Thompson 1954, 237)

Chilam Balam believed that the Messiah-Redeemer of early Mexico was Jesus of Nazareth. The first Spanish padres to arrive in Mesoamerica held the same opinions; and they, too, were careful in how they put their views on paper. The native nobles of Guatemala also held to the view that Naxcit-Gucumatz, their Messiah, was identical with the Messiah-Redeemer of Israel.

The Quetzal Bird: Symbol of the God of Life

As was pointed out above, a bird reposing on top of the tree of life was a symbol of the God of Life. This was true in both Assyria and Mesoamerica, as is illustrated in Figures 10–3 and 10–4 (Ferguson 1958, 85). The bird, like the serpent, was a symbol of the highest god, the God of Life. In Egypt, the sun disc was given wings. The winged disc—the solar bird—represented the highest god, the God of Life. Respecting the Egyptian symbol,

Count Goblet D'Alviella tells us "that the Winged Globe is the Egyptian symbol *par excellence*. According to the inscription at Edfu, it was Thoth himself who caused it to be placed above the entrances to all the temples in order to commemorate the victory won by Horus over Seth, i.e., by the principle of light and good over that of darkness and evil" (D'Alviella 1956, 205).

It symbolized the God of Light, the Egyptian hope of life after death. Goblet D'Alviella goes on to say:

> The Winged Globe of the Phoenicians is found wherever their art was introduced, in Carthage, Cyprus, Sardinia, Sicily, and among different peoples of Palestine. It has even been pointed out on Israelitish seals of the oldest epoch, and nothing prevents us from supposing that—like the serpent, the golden bull or calf, and the idolatrous images denounced by the prophets—it *served, perhaps, to furnish a figured representation of Yahweh.* (Ferguson 1958, 127, emphasis added). (See Figure 10–3.)

In ancient Israel, then, the bird (or Winged Globe) placed above the tree of life symbolized Yahweh, or Jehovah, the Messiah-Redeemer.

In Mesoamerica, the bird was also used in conjunction with the serpent and with the tree-of-life symbol. The bird most often used in Guatemala and southern Mexico was the lovely quetzal bird. As has been said, one of the primary symbolic names of the Messiah-Redeemer of ancient Mexico was *Quetzalcoatl.* In the name itself, we have a bird symbol and the serpent associated together, as in Palestine.

Gucumatz (Maya equivalent of Quetzalcoatl) was described as a serpent covered with green feathers, the name having been derived from the Quiche word *guc* (*kuk* in Yucatan Maya), "green feathers" (particularly those of the quetzal), and *Cumatz,* "serpent." In the *Popol Vuh,* the Messiah is referred to in Maya as *Ah Raxa Lac,* meaning "Lord of the Green Plate or the earth," *Ah Taxa Tzel,* meaning "Lord of the Green Gourd, or the blue bowl—the sky" (Goetz and Morley 1950, 78).

In a book devoted exclusively to the serpent-bird symbolism of ancient Mexico, *La Serpiente Emplumada,* Jose Diaz-Bolio makes it clear that Quetzalcoatl, God of Life, was symbolized by jade in his role as God of Water and Life. The author refers to the Messiah-Redeemer of Mexico as the God "Man-bird" (Diaz-Bolio 1952, 81). The beautiful green quetzal bird was one of the major symbols of this anthropomorphic god. In the same paragraph, Diaz-Bolio refers to the solar-serpent symbolism of Quetzalcoatl.

A look at Figure 10–8, a representation of the quetzal bird, will be helpful. The long, undulating tail feathers of the quetzal bird call to mind the undulating serpent—most ancient of the Milky Way, Life-God symbols. That the ancients of Mesoamerica used the quetzal feathers as an emblem of the ancient Mesopotamian Milky Way symbolism is clear. In the June 1937 issue of the Mexican archaeological journal *El Mexico Antiguo,* the then editor of that journal, Dr. B. P. Reko, wrote: "The quetzal-bird . . . because of its long tail-feathers symbolized the bifurcated galaxy [the Milky Way]." Further, the tail feathers of the quetzal bird are green—the color green itself being symbolic of life and the Creator Life God.

FIGURE 10–8: LACANDON MAYA HOLDING THE SACRED QUETZAL BIRD. PHOTO BY THOMAS STUART FERGUSON OF A STAINED-GLASS WINDOW IN HOTEL LOS LAGOS, COMITAN, CHIAPAS, MEXICO, MAY 1956.

We have seen that the personal and anthropomorphic Quetzalcoatl possessed all the attributes of Christ as the Light and the Life of the World. In view of the Milky Way serpent symbolism, it is not difficult to understand why the quetzal bird was chosen in southern Mexico and Guatemala as the sacred bird of that region, where it lived and is still to be found.

Thus, it is demonstrated that the quetzal bird—with its long, green, serpent-like, undulating tail feathers in association with the serpent and as the primary symbol of life and vitalism—was a common aspect of the tree of life, as well as a representation of the Messiah-Redeemer, in ancient Mesoamerica.

The Stepped Fret: A Stylized Tree of Life

The art and culture of Mesoamerica were primarily religious. One great characteristic of a religion is its tendency to preserve forms with the meaning accumulating around them. Of all the motifs and symbols of Mesoamerica, possibly none is more important than the stepped fret (a line depicting a series of rising or descending steps, as viewed from the side), which absolutely dominates its art. Hermann Beyer documented approximately 250 variations in his study cited in Paul Westheim's *The Art of Ancient Mexico*. Despite its prevalence and its importance, scholars express no consensus on what the stepped fret means.

The meaning of the stepped fret has puzzled scholars for years. Herman Beyer, whose documentation of the form Westheim cites, found it a purely decorative formal element. Westheim disagrees. Even while he acknowledges that the lack of written sources and the antiquity of the form may prevent a final interpretation, he argues:

> The art of ancient Mexico is markedly religious art, an art of supra sensible contents of knowledge. What determines the creative will is not the esthetic experience but the religious. . . . It is difficult for us to believe that one of the essential ornaments of the world of ancient Mexico was no more than a decorative element. In the first place, the great frequency of the stepped fret and the fact that it was used for centuries oppose this thesis. As we can observe from some of the "dying" European styles, any exclusively ornamental form would have spent itself in the course of time, lost its attraction, and been superseded by new formal creations with new fascination and suggestive force. The stepped fret was not replaced by new ornaments because the Nahua people saw in it a psychic or magic value beyond that of the esthetic. The stepped fret is no more a purely decorative form than is the cross. (Westheim 1965, 100–1)

Westheim, noting that the symbol is never associated with death, suggests that "it constitutes a sign of magic protection against death" and agrees with other Mexicanists that it is a stylized representation of the serpent and the water—both of which are closely associated. He himself argues more specifically that the stepped fret may be derived from the zigzag form of lightning, an attribute of the rain god Tlaloc. "It proves nothing that our eyes cannot at first glance distinguish in the stepped fret the serpentine form from which it probably is derived. Rather, it shows that since time immemorial the Nahua people were so familiar with this sign that the stylization could be limited to a mnemotechnical [memory aid] insinuation" (Westheim 1965, 105).

Observing that the stepped fret is "totally asymmetrical," Westheim argues that it represents a religious world view of "tension":

> The dynamic rhythm of the stepped fret springs from the clash of antagonistic formal elements and from the violent interruptions that are produced again and again in its drawing. The stairway is a vehement ascent; the hook breaks this movement, twists it, destroys it with identical vehemence. It is as though a demoniacal force had committed itself to annihilating all the energy inherent in the stairway. In the next figure we see the same ascent, the same interruption. Each time that the stairway breaks away, it is prevented from achieving a free, unhampered development; its destiny is always to come upon the counter force that destroys it, pushes it back down to the level it started from. There is a near harmonious flow. There is a struggle of elements, an interruption of the course of the movement, a brusque change of direction, a new advance, a new defeat, birth, and death. A rhythm that rests in the constant repetition of the motif and in an energetic contrast among the different elements. (Westheim 1965, 108)

This exciting aesthetic definition provides an alternative reading to the symmetrical shapes of such typical Old World forms as the lotus, the palmette, the rosette, and the Greek meander:

> The spiral form exists in all cultures. It has one almost identical basic form with many variations, but the value of the essence is, in each case, entirely different. The Celtic spiral is ecstatic longing for redemption; the Greek meander is neutrality, euphony, esthetic harmony; the oriental tapestry of ornaments is a passive submersal in the consciousness of the infinite. And the stepped fret expresses the vital tension of forces subject to a rhythm. (Westheim 1965, 112–13)

It remained for Darrell J. Stoddard, an appreciator of Mesoamerican art and a former Brigham Young University student of archaeology, to connect this potent Mesoamerican symbol to the most widespread symbol of the Old World—the tree of life. Much of what follows is based on his research.

In Greece, one of the most interesting aspects of the tree of life develops through a process of representation and abstraction that strips it to its essential form. As D'Alviella notes:

> A representation . . . does not aim at being a reproduction. A reproduction implies if not identity with at least similitude to, the original; but a symbol only requires that it shall have certain features in common with the object represented, so that, by its presence alone, it may evoke the conception of the latter, as is the case with a missile weapon and lightning, a sickle and harvest-time, a ring and marriage, a pair of scales and the idea of justice, kneeling and the sentiment of submission, and so forth. (D'Alviella 1956, 1)

Stoddard comments:

> It is, I believe, a universal trait of human nature to create artistic symbols just as it is to create words which are in themselves symbols; but with pictorial symbols as with words, we cannot understand those of a foreign civilization without some common ground from which to view the symbol or understand the word. . . . The process through which a work of art is reduced to an abstract symbol is something which may take several hundred years, or as I have observed in the art of children (who readily create and interpret their visual world through symbols much the same as primitive peoples) may take just a few minutes. It is a process which may be compared to the origin of folk poetry which evolves through being passed by word of mouth through numerous generations with each generation eliminating that which is insignificant. . . . In the graphic or visual arts, the end product may be unintelligible—and usually is—to those who do not know of the process through which it evolved and the portentous meanings which it may hold, but to those who comprehend its significance it is all

the more meaningful because the imagination is set free. (Stoddard 1968, 8–9)

Greek Ionic Columns

In the case of the tree of life, Greek architecture was heavily influenced by Egypt and "the territories of other nations with which she maintained commercial relations, the Canaanites and Hittites, so that we have to take into account the remains in Palestine, Phoenicia, Cyprus, and Anatolia" (Dinsmoor 1950, 58). In all these regions, a "sacred tree" design was popular. It has been traced back from the thirteenth- or fourteenth-century Anatolian cylinder seals to the throne room of Nebuchadnezzar in the sixth century. In all cases, we see some form of the spiral or volute—a stone carved to look like the two ends of a rolled-up scroll. Since Greeks actually served in these latter courts, the influence could have been direct as well as indirect in creating the Ionic column that has become the hallmark of Greek architecture the world over.

Dinsmoor observes clear "arboreal" or tree elements in the Proto-Ionic capitals, but by the sixth century B.C., the column had evolved into its classic form. Gone are the leaves, to be replaced by the "egg-and-dart ovolo, which thereupon becomes the characteristic lower member and likewise, because of its Oriental origins, the most typical Ionic moulding" (Dinsmoor 1950, 62). Frequently accompanying the Ionic column is a decorative frieze or capital motif—the palmette. Dinsmoor calls it "a floral decoration of Mesopotamian origin related to the sacred tree, at first imitated faithfully by the Greeks and later varied with pointed or even flame-shaped petals" (Dinsmoor 1950, 393). The palmette is also a stylized tree of life.

The spiral volutes or scrolls that so distinctively mark the Ionic capital are, Stoddard argues, a representation of the fountain of living water. Some examples show the column rising between paired volutes, which puzzles scholars, who know that leaves should be on the top of the trees. In Mesopotamian art, however, "whorls symbolize water. . . . These are traditional motifs and the artist makes no attempt to free himself from them" (Moscati 1962, 97–98). These whorls are simple spirals, just as parallel zigzags represent water in Egyptian mural art and the letter *M* in Greek is drawn from the symbol for "sea." The association of life-giving liquid with the tree and the placement of volutes at the base of the tree become clear.

Nor is it confusing when the volutes are moved to the top of the tree. As Stoddard explains, "They were originally at the bottom of the tree and then were moved to the top as an architectural necessity to reduce the length of the lintel required to span the distance between columns" (Stoddard 1968, 12). Another insight Stoddard contributes that no other scholar has noticed is that the

> Greek fret which consists of a running band of spirals in various forms as a decorative motif is almost certainly a variation of the tree-of-life volute. It is often in an interlocking pattern and is used on the interior as well as the exterior and may be either circular or rectangular. . . . I have observed that in nearly every culture which uses the spiral as a design, the modification of the spiral into a rectilinear form also is used with the same meaning. (Stoddard 1968, 13)

The Image in Mesoamerica

The pre-Columbian depiction of the stepped fret, as with the tree of life, is found in archaeological ornamentations and elsewhere. If Stoddard's perception is correct and if the tree-of-life symbol with an associated fountain of water has shaped the distinctive forms of Greek architecture, then the possible links between this powerful Old World image and the universally prevalent but mysterious stepped fret of ancient Mesoamerica become very intriguing. (See photo of stepped fret at the bottom of the title page.)

In Paul Westheim's chapter on the stepped fret, he points out the following:

> Together with the plumed serpent, the stepped fret (Xicalcoliuhqui) is the most typical ornamental form of the Valley of Mexico, territory of the Nahua tribes. It is as characteristic of Nahua culture as the stylized lotus flower of Egyptian art, the rosette of Assyrian art, the palmette and meander of Greek art, and the ornament of lacery or plaits, an ornament steeped in exaltation of the Celto-Irish. We find the stepped fret as far north as Arizona (Pueblo

Indians, Casas Grandes), passing through Yucatan, to as far south as Peru, where it is of predominant importance in ornaments. (Westheim 1965, 92–93)

Westheim agrees with Beyer that the typical forms of the stepped fret are the stairsteps, the spiral, and the hook. Sometimes the spiral will be on the inside of the steps and sometimes on the outside. It can be curved or rectangular. In appraising photographs of hundreds of manifestations of the stepped fret, Stoddard felt an insight emerging as he studied a temple portrayed in one of the pre-Hispanic codices that had two volutes on top of a stepped temple. The parallelism matched that of the volutes on an Ionic column, and the bisected temple, complete with volute, formed a stepped fret.

The association of the tree of life, the water of life, and the feathered serpent—the Mesoamerican deity most closely associated with the Christ figure—makes a rich and powerful combination of symbols with obvious links to their counterparts in the Old World. Placing the fret atop a temple where the altar is located and where a priest would go to commune with deity is also appropriate, particularly since the stepped temples have traditionally been thought to represent sacred mountains—or places of communication with deity.

The Stepped Fret Among the Hopi

The stepped fret in Mesoamerica today is found primarily in ornamental objects (Kubler 1962, 173–75). The stepped fret, however, is found as a living cultural element among the Hopis of the American Southwest and probably constitutes the single most popular design element in Hopi jewelry, pottery, and weavings. Darrell Stoddard, who made many trips to the Hopi reservation, interviewed dozens of Hopis at First Mesa, Second Mesa, and Third Mesa, Arizona. Initially reluctant to discuss the stepped fret with him, they eventually divulged that the spiral of the stepped fret was a symbol of eternal life, sacred water, and the serpent. They did not mention the tree of life, would not tell him any meaning attached to the stepped portion of the figure, and remained clearly reluctant to talk about it at all, saying that oral information from Hopi informants about the meaning of the stepped fret was too sacred to discuss with Stoddard.

Figure 10–9 shows a stalk of corn topped by a stepped fret, an appropriate conjunction because corn is the most important food crop among the Hopis, as it also was among the Indians of Mesoamerica.

FIGURE **10–9:** HOPI SILVER JEWELRY SHOWING A CORN STALK CAPPED BY A STEPPED FRET.

Another typical variation, as seen in Figure 10–10, is the stepped fret with an attached curve that the Hopis claim represents a water bird. This representation is extremely interesting for two reasons. In both Mesopotamian art, as we have seen, as well as in depictions of Mesoamerican art, a bird nearly always appears above the tree. The *Codex Fejervary-Mayer* alone has four tree-of-life forms, each with the spiral symbol, life symbol, a bird at the top, and figures facing the tree (Westheim 1965, cover, 13). The fact that it is a water bird is particularly significant for a desert people and makes the link stronger between the "fountain" and the tree.

FIGURE **10–10:** HOPI SILVER JEWELRY DEPICTING THE STEPPED FRET AND A DETACHED CURVE THAT REPRESENTS A WATER BIRD.

The Rio Grande Pueblo Indians also use the stepped fret, a combination of the serpent symbol and the stepped temple. The two symbols are always associated to form the stepped fret. The Zuni Indians, whose territory is adjacent to that of both the Rio Grande Pueblos and the Hopis, also use the stepped fret. The area of cultural influence of this symbol is further evidence of its power in Mesoamerica. The stepped fret is never seen among northern Indians or eastern Indians. The Navajos, who arrived in Hopi territory in the seventeenth century, use the fret a great deal in their rugs, but they never put their rug designs together in the stepped-fret form.

The fleur-de-lis, a stylized form that appears often in Mesoamerican art, also has elements that suggest the flowing use. Its outside curves represent the two streams flowing from the center, while the inverted V in the middle represents a plant budding from the life-giving waters. Thus, it may represent an artistic experiment that is an alternative to the stepped-fret representation of the tree of life.

Wind-Jewel: Symbol of Quetzalcoatl

One version of what may be a stepped fret is the wind-jewel symbol (Figure 10–11) used to identify Quetzalcoatl. The only form of the stepped fret found in nature, it is derived from making a transverse cut of a voluted brachiopod or conch shell. Such a cut produced a stepped effect around the outside of a spiral, a unique combination of shapes. Furthermore, the wind-jewel symbol, like the stepped fret, is never found in association with the god or the cult of the dead in Mesoamerica but instead is related to water, wind, and fire—also symbols of Quetzalcoatl.

FIGURE 10–11: WIND JEWEL ON THE CHEST OF QUETZALCOATL FROM THE CODEX MAGLIABECCHIANO (LATE POSTCLASSIC PERIOD OF CENTRAL MEXICO).

In yet another interesting parallel, the wind jewel is also associated with birth. Another birth symbol is the snail or the sea shell. Many Mesoamerican deities are depicted as being born out of sea shells, and human reproductive organs are frequently portrayed in the form of snails or sea shells (Westheim 1965, 115–19). Not unexpectedly, representations of Quetzalcoatl often depict him wearing a necklace of snails.

Before the meridian of time, the stepped fret symbolically represented the stepped temple and tree of life or fountain of living waters. After the visit of Jesus Christ to the western hemisphere, it became his symbol. Interestingly, the same symbols (temple, tree of life, and fountain of living water) are also identified with Christ in Christian (eastern hemisphere) art and theology.

The Spirit of the Lord asked the prophet Nephi: "Knowest thou the meaning of the tree which thy father saw? And I answered him, saying: Yea, it is the love of God, which sheddeth itself abroad in the hearts of the children of men; wherefore, it is the most desirable above all things. . . . Yea, and the most joyous to the soul" (1 Nephi 11:21–23).

Notes to Chapter 10
The Eternal Conflict: Opposition in All Things

The concept of a conflict between two great forces, good and evil, dominated the religious thinking of the ancients of Mexico. Miguel Covarrubias describes the Mexican idea concisely:

> The legends of the struggle between Quetzalcoatl and Tezcatlipoca [the devil] are probably a Toltec rationalization to correlate historical events with an older myth, the eternal war between good and evil, black and white, war and peace, darkness and light, which is the basic undercurrent in Mexican religious philosophy. An old Indian legend claims that the feud dated back to the beginning of the world, when Tezcatlipoca ruled over the earth as the sun that lit and fed an incipient world. (Covarrubias 1947, 136)

The tree-of-life symbol illustrates this concept. Men and women are given intelligence to make choices. If there were no opposites, humans would have no choices to make, for there would be nothing upon which to exercise their intelligence and choice. The joy of living is in making selections. To interfere with the freedom of exercising preferences is to interfere with the plan of God. For humans to exercise freedom, the things to be acted upon must not be all of one kind. There must be an opposition, or there is no freedom. If there were no opposition, life would be homogeneous, like gelatin—uniform, simple, and of no consequence.

To know life, we must know death. To appreciate harmony, we must know discord. To know good, we must understand evil.

God provided us with a world that was not prefabricated and predetermined for us. Were it not so, there would be no growth, no progress, and no maturing. With opposites and opposition in all things, we have infinite possibilities for eternal progress, everlasting growth, and endless maturing. Men and women can go on from achievement to achievement, in eternal progression.

The key to real success and happiness, according to the tree-of-life symbolism, is to make those choices in harmony with the word of God. God reveals the way but does not compel men and women to follow it. The opposite way, which leads to death and sorrow, is permitted for good reason.

The Tree of Knowledge: Opposed to the Tree of Life

Besides the tree of life, a second sacred tree played a role in the lives of ancient Mesoamericans—the tree of enlightenment or truth. In Old Testament terminology, this latter would be the tree of knowledge of good and evil. The illustrations from the Near East for the tree of knowledge of good and evil are represented by the two serpents intertwined to form a caduceus (in modern times, the symbol of the medical profession). This tree of knowledge of good and evil and the tree of life in the ancient mythologies are cosmic trees and have their setting in the nighttime sky. They also have connections with the Milky Way, particularly the tree of life. Several examples of clay cylinder seals from the ancient Near East show different examples of both the tree of life and the tree of knowledge of good and evil.

These two sacred trees are related to the concept of Hamlet's Mill and the movements of the planets and constellations. (Hamlet's Mill, which is discussed further in the appendix, is a northern European concept of the universe in the shape of an hour glass. The earth is in the middle, and all the planets, stars, and constellations revolve around a spindle that passes from the top of the universe, north, to its bottom, south.)

In India and the Far East, as well as in parts of Europe, often the symbolism of the two trees is combined in the same tree so that the symbolism of the tree of enlightenment, or the symbols of the tree of knowledge of good and evil as well as the tree of life, is shared in the same scenes. In the Near East and in ancient Mesoamerica, we see illustrations of the two trees separately.

The surest placement of this Messiah-Redeemer symbolism in pre-Columbian time is in the archaeological representation of the tree of life. Here, as shown in Figure 10–12, we have a Classic Maya illustration equivalent to the tree of knowledge and enlightenment at Palenque in the Tablet from the Temple of the Cross. Here, the tree in the form of a cross is coming out of the head of a monster at its base. (Might this have reference to the Garden of Eden scene, when Satan usurps the right of Christ to give all revelation by himself giving light and knowledge to Adam and Eve?) The head of the monster has a band of seven planetary signs representing the sun, moon, Mercury, Venus, Mars, Jupiter, and Saturn.

Figure 10–12: Tablet of the Cross from the Temple of the Cross at Palenque, Chiapas, about A.D. 692. This tablet gives much mythological and legendary ancestry from the Maya rulers Pacal and Kan-Bahlum, who lived in the seventh century A.D. However, the earliest mythological ancestry dates back into the third millennium B.C. (Courtesy of Linda Schele)

Obviously, this is a cosmic tree. The other tree, the tree of life, in the Near East was depicted by the ancient Sumerians as a god by the name of *Dumuzi*. He is considered the son of the Abyss, referring to the waters of the underworld and lord of the tree of life, the ever-dying, ever-resurrected Sumerian god (Campbell 1976, 14). Dumuzi, known to the Hebrews as *Tammuz*, is referred to in the Old Testament in Ezekiel 8:14.

In Mesoamerica, the early Spanish historian of the sixteenth century, Diego de Landa, says this of the tree of life: "The Tree of Life was a symbol of good as opposed to evil, since it is said to have been created with great virtue against the evil spirit" (Tozzer 1941, 43).

A good example of the tree of life from Mesoamerica, as shown earlier in Figure 10–2, is from the Tablet of the Temple of the Foliated Cross at Palenque, which illustrates the tree of life as a corn plant and depicts the resurrection or rebirth of plants as well as humans. It is associated with the daytime sky, whereas the tree of knowledge of good and evil, or the world tree, is shown associated with the nighttime sky and the planets and not in the context of rebirth or resurrection.

In Mesoamerica, we can associate the two trees with two different concepts of paradise. One is the Paradise of Tamoanchan, which refers to the thirteenth or highest heaven. It was the connecting link between mankind and the gods in the heavens until a fall took place in which the trunk of the tree was split and broken. The second tree is associated with the earthly Paradise of Tlalocan and the Rain God Tlaloc. It is located in the east in the land of rain and is generally considered to be the Gulf Coast area of Mesoamerica. Tlaloc is also considered the god of rain and the god of mountains. An important Tlaloc ceremony in Mesoamerica involved a large tree that was erected in the ceremonial center for rituals. Surrounding this large central tree were four smaller trees representing the four directions associated with the tlaloques, who were helpers of the rain god. As mentioned earlier, the rain god Tlaloc in Mesoamerica is associated with the planet Saturn. In the Near East, the god of this tree of knowledge, or the world tree, is also associated with the planet Saturn.

What we have, then, is a mythology involving Hamlet's Mill and the structure of the universe, with the movements of the constellations and the planets all being part of this mythology, and particularly seven planets: the moon and the sun plus the five planets visible to the unaided eye—Mercury, Venus, Mars, Jupiter, and Saturn. But we find in this mythology that two other positions often represent eclipses. These eclipse dragons have two heads. The seven planets and these two eclipse phenomena bring the total number of positions in this model to nine (Table 10–1). The nine positions represent the nine Lords of the Night or underworld. Sometimes the eclipse positions are considered as divisions of Saturn.

Table 10–1

Preliminary Deity Parallels to the Nine Lords of the Night

Mesoamerica	India	Mesopotamia	Syria	Egypt	Greece
Xiuhtechutli Constell: Pleiades Planet: Sun	Agni Constell: Pleiades Planet: Sun	Utu/Shamash Planet: Sun	Sipish Planet: Sun	Re/Atum, Af Planet: Sun	Helius Planet: Sun
Itztli Planet: Moon	Vyana Planet: Moon	Enkidu/Nannar Planet: Moon	Tanit- phanebalos Planet: Moon	Thoth Planet: Moon	Geryon/Selene Planet: Moon
Piltzintecuhtli, Itzam-Yeh Constell: Ursa Major Planet: Mars	Kalmasha Planet: Mars	Nergal Constell: Ursa Major Planet: Mars	Resheph/Mot Planet: Mars	Seth Constell: Ursa Major Planet: Mars	Aries/Typhon Planet: Mars
Cinteotl Constell: Orion Planet: Mercury	Vishnu Planet: Mercury	Gilgamesh/ Dumuzi Constell: Orion Planet: Mercury	Assur* Planet: Mercury * s r Osiris Asura (epithet of Marduk)	Osiris Constell: Orion Planet: Mercury	Dionysus/ Hermes Constell: Sirius Planet: Mercury
Mictlantechutli Planet: Jupiter	Suka Planet: Jupiter	Enlil/Marduk Planet: Jupiter	Dagan/Teshub Planet: Jupiter	Anubis Planet: Jupiter	Zeus/Jove Planet: Jupiter
Chalchiuhtlicue Planet: Venus	Guari Planet: Venus	Inanna/Ishtar/ Nidaba/Nisaba Constell: Virgo Planet: Venus	Astarte/Kamish Constell: Virgo Planet: Venus	Hathor/Isis Planet: Venus	Aphrodite/Hera Planet: Venus
Tlazolteotl Planet: Saturn-1	Prajapati Planet: Saturn-1	Ninhursag Planet: Saturn-1	Ashertu/Beltis Planet: Saturn-1	Tefnut Planet: Saturn-1	Rhea Planet: Saturn-1
Tepeyollotl Yax Balam/ Xbalanque Planet: Saturn-2/front head of cosmic monster	Ganesa Planet: Saturn-2/head of eclipse dragon, ascending node	Enki/Ea/Apsu Planet: Saturn-2	Baal/Leviathan/ Shalim Planet: Saturn-2	Geb/Ptah/Shu/ Khonsu Planet: Saturn-2	Kronos Planet: Saturn-2
Tlaloc/Hun Ahaw/ Hunahpu Planet: Saturn-3/rear head of cosmic monster	Visvakarma Planet: Saturn-3/tail of eclipse dragon, descending node	Anu, Sky Planet: Saturn-3	Kumarbi/ Koshar/Baal Hadad/Dagon/ Shahar Planet: Saturn-3	Min/Khem/ Horus Planet: Saturn-3	Uranus Planet: Saturn-3

In the table opposite, we have charted the nine positions for Mesoamerica, India, Mesopotamia, Syria, Egypt, and Greece. What is very intriguing is the possibility that these nine astronomical positions may be in the Old Testament. This possibility will now be dealt with.

The two eclipse phenomena that are emphasized in the Ennead refer to powers in mythology that are greater or higher than the planets, even the sun, because the two trees were above and beyond the sun. They could even darken the earth or eclipse the sun. But they were not visible (just a section is visible to the observer here on earth); therefore, they are represented in mythology as dragons with double heads—a creature that no one has ever seen on earth. Associated with these two-headed dragons are the stars or constellations known as Polaris, or the North Star, and Sirius, representing the equivalent of the South Polar region of the universe. In Egypt, Mesopotamia, India, and Mesoamerica, we find a good deal of mythological information and a certain amount of artwork depicting these two-headed eclipse demons. But in ancient Israel, we have an artifact that represents seven of these deities correlated with planets and constellations. This is the Menorah, the golden seven-lamp candlestick described by Moses when he came down from Mt. Sinai (Exodus 25:31–40 and 37:12–24).

Carol L. Meyers explains:

> In Hebraic tradition the Tree of Life represented scripturally goes back to Adam and Eve in the Garden of Eden wherein two trees played a symbolic role, the Tree of Knowledge of Good and Evil and the Tree of Life. The Tree of Life ritualistically symbolizes this tradition as found throughout other parts of the Near East or the ancient Hebrews, but the Hebrews expanded the cosmic symbolism by transferring the plant motif from god to the people of Israel, resulting in a perpetual point of contact with the Divine sphere, [so that the] conception of Israel as the Tree on God's mountain can be seen as the ultimate challenge to the pagan fertility and immortality themes. . . . [Thus,] the people of Israel . . . achieve collective immortality existing forever on

their inherited land, and in this sense share the eternal attributes of the tree deity. (Meyers 1976, 156)

Bonnie E. Percival writes: "The most well known ritualistic symbol of the stylized Tree of Life in Hebraic traditions is the seven- branch lampstand called the Menorah. The Menorah, like the Tree of Life in the cella [inner part] of Mesopotamian temples, has been an integral part of the Jewish temples since the Tabernacle of Moses in the wilderness" (Percival 1984, 8).

Meyers suggests that the Menorah is "a symbol of the cosmic tree within the tabernacle precinct to contribute toward securing the reality of God's presence" (Meyers 1976, 180). Meyers also points out that the "ornamentation [of the Menorah] is the combination of three elements, cup, knob, and flower, repeated three times on each of the branches and four times on the main stem stand" (Meyers 1976, 22). The Menorah represents the almond tree in full bloom. Indeed, the word *Menorah* means "made like almonds" or "almond blossoms."

However, the Menorah deals with only seven of the nine elements of our model. All nine elements are brought together in the Old Testament in Zechariah 4. In this chapter, an angel of the Lord appears to the Prophet Zechariah (about 537 B.C.) as the Jewish people are coming out of captivity in Babylon and going back to Jerusalem. The angel shows the Prophet Zechariah a candlestick of gold with a bowl on top of it. The candlestick has seven lamps, and there are two olive trees, one upon the right side of the bowl and the other on the left side.

The angel asks Zechariah if he knows what all of this means, and when he says he does not, the angel explains, referring to the seven candlestick lamps:

They are the eyes of the Lord, which run to and fro through the whole earth.

Then answered I, and said unto him, What are these two olive trees upon the right side of the candlestick and upon the left side thereof?

And I answered again, and said unto him, What be these two olive branches which through the two golden pipes empty the golden oil out of themselves?

And he answered me and said, Knowest thou not what these be? And I said, No, my Lord.

Then said he, These are the two anointed ones, that stand by the Lord of the whole earth. (Zechariah 4:10–14)

These two anointed ones are the two witnesses of the book of Revelation who in the last days prophesy in the streets of Jerusalem, are killed, and then three days later are taken up into the heavens before the eyes of all the people of Jerusalem. (A more complete discussion of the two witnesses is found in Revelation 11.) In our Ennead model, the two anointed ones take the position of the two heads of the eclipse dragon.

Zechariah 4 and related biblical scriptures indicate that we may have the equivalent of nine astronomical elements (the seven planets and the two witnesses or eclipse events) in the Old Testament story that we find in Near Eastern mythology and the mythology of other parts of the world.

Chapter 11
ARCHAEOLOGICAL AND DOCUMENTARY EVIDENCES: DESTRUCTIONS IN MESOAMERICA AT THE TIME OF THE CRUCIFIXION

Particularly clear and abundant archaeological evidence exists of widespread destruction in Mesoamerica dating from the period of Christ's crucifixion. The New Testament relates that at the moment of Christ's death, "the veil of the temple was rent in twain from the top to the bottom; and the earth did quake, and the rocks rent; And the graves were opened; and many bodies of the saints which slept arose, And came out of the graves . . . and went into the holy city, and appeared unto many" (Matthew 27:51–53).

The record known as the Book of Mormon is more extensive and detailed:

And now it came to pass that according to our record . . . the thirty and third year had passed away;

And the people began to look with great earnestness for the sign which had been given by the prophet Samuel, the Lamanite, yea, for the time that there should be darkness for the space of three days over the face of the land. . . .

And it came to pass in the thirty and fourth year, in the first month, on the fourth day of the month, there arose a great storm, such an one as never had been known in all the land.

And there was also a great and terrible tempest; and there was terrible thunder, insomuch that it did shake the whole earth as if it was about to divide asunder.

And there were exceedingly sharp lightnings, such as never had been known in all the land.

And the city of Zarahemla did take fire.

And the city of Moroni did sink into the depths of the sea, and the inhabitants thereof were drowned.

And the earth was carried up upon the city of Moronihah, that in the place of the city there became a great mountain.

And there was a great and terrible destruction in the land southward.

But behold, there was a more great and terrible destruction in the land northward; for behold, the whole face of the land was changed, because of the tempest and the whirlwinds, and the thunderings and lightnings, and the exceedingly great quaking of the whole earth;

And the highways were broken up, and the level roads were spoiled, and many smooth places became rough.

And many great and notable cities were sunk, and many were burned, and many were shaken till the buildings thereof had fallen to the earth, and the inhabitants thereof were slain, and the places were left desolate.

And there were some cities which remained; but the damage thereof was exceedingly great, and there were many of them who were slain.

And there were some who were carried away in the whirlwind; and whither they went no man knoweth, save they know that they were carried away.

And thus the face of the whole earth became deformed, because of the tempests, and the thunderings, and the lightnings, and the quaking of the earth.

And behold, the rocks were rent in twain; they were broken up upon the face of the whole earth, insomuch that they were found in broken fragments, and in seams and in cracks, upon all the face of the land.

And it came to pass that when the thunderings, and the lightnings, and the storm, and the tempest, and the quakings of the earth did cease—for behold, they did last for about the space of three hours; and it was said by some that the time was greater; nevertheless, all these great and terrible things were done in about the space of three hours—and then behold, there was darkness upon the face of the land.

And it came to pass that there was thick darkness upon all the face of the land, insomuch that the inhabitants thereof who had not fallen could feel the vapor of darkness;

And there could be no light, because of the darkness, neither candles, neither torches; neither could there be fire kindled with their fine and exceedingly dry wood, so that there could not be any light at all;

And there was not any light seen, neither fire, nor glimmer, neither the sun, nor the moon, nor the stars, for so great were the mists of darkness which were upon the face of the land.

And it came to pass that it did last for the space of three days that there was no light seen; and there was great mourning and howling and weeping among all the people continually; yea, great were the groanings of the people, because of the darkness and the great destruction which had come upon them.

And in one place they were heard to cry, saying: O that we had repented before this great and terrible day, and then would our brethren have been spared, and they would not have been burned in that great city Zarahemla.

And in another place they were heard to cry and mourn, saying: O that we had repented before this great and terrible day, and had not killed and stoned the prophets, and cast them out; then would our mothers and our fair daughters, and our children have been spared, and not have been buried up in that great city Moronihah. And thus were the howlings of the people great and terrible. (3 Nephi 8)

Earthquakes and Volcanoes

The very nature of earthquake and volcanic activity typical of the Mesoamerican area is consistent with this whole set of phenomena as the Book of Mormon described it. Also, the range of nineteenth and twentieth-century activities gives us helpful analogues that we can project backward to reconstruct the seismic activity of the past.

Although earthquakes and volcanoes are certainly not unknown in either North or South America, we think it is significant, for example, that there is no historical record of volcanoes or earthquakes in the Andes from the time of the European arrivals until quite recently in our own century; and it was not until 1983 that an archaeologist discovered an archaeological site north of the general Andean region that had been covered by volcanic material. However, since this eruption occurred about 600 B.C., it is not of great interest to this study.

Mesoamerica, on the other hand, is known for its seismic activity. One text on the archaeology of Mesoamerica is called *The Sons of the Shaking Earth,* taking its title from a common characteristic of the whole area. (Wolf 1959)

Volcanoes at the Time of Christ

An interesting and quite typical site is Tres Zapotes in southern Veracruz, in the Tuxtla Mountains just south of the mouth of the River Papaloapan where it empties into the Gulf of Mexico. In the late 1930s, Matthew W. Sterling and Philip Drucker did exploration and testing at this site, discovering at a certain level a cap of volcanic ash that covered the archaeological materials. Then, later, evidence surfaced that the site had been reinhabited. They published their findings, including profiles showing the excavations, ash layers, and pottery examples. Because pottery dating over half a century ago was less exact than it is now, we know from more recent work that the volcanic layer occurred at the time of Christ and covered materials that dated back several centuries before the time of Christ.

No one had reported any recent work in southern Veracruz except John E. Clark, a Brigham Young University professor and director of the New World Archaeological Foundation. As a graduate student, he wrote on 12 February 1983 of Matacapan, a site about twenty miles from Tres Zapotes and midway between San Andres Tuxtla and Lake Catemaco. He reported that Robert Santley had discovered a Middle Preclassic (1500 B.C.–600 B.C.) site there (letter written to John L. Sorenson). Santley, an archaeologist from the University of New Mexico, worked earlier on the Teotihuacan project in the Valley of Mexico. Clark says, "These deposits were capped with 10 cm or more [about four inches] of volcanic ash from the Volcano San Martin"—the same volcano whose eruptions covered Tres Zapotes. The site was apparently abandoned at this time and reoccupied in the Classic period (A.D. 250–A.D. 900) when the visible mounds were built containing the Teotihuacan architecture. What nobody knew was that below these mounds was this long sequence of Late, Middle, and Early Preclassic materials capped with a volcanic ash layer.

In the Spring of the Year

Santley believes that the 1982 test pits were in an ancient corn field and that the eruption, by inference from the size of corn plants in the ash, took place in the spring of the year.

Although we have known for over fifty years that the same volcano we mentioned above put a layer of ash over the site of Tres Zapotes, we have only recently discovered the extent of the area it covered. At Tres Zapotes, the ash layer varied between forty and seventy-one centimeters thick (between fifteen and twenty-seven inches). San Martin, the volcano in question, is northeast of both sites but is much closer to Tres Zapotes. Meteorologists tell us that by April or May, the wind would be blowing west-southwest. Thus, Tres Zapotes would receive more ash than Matacapan.

Additional insight comes from a graduate paper prepared in 1981 by James E. Chase of the University of Colorado about the San Martin volcanic eruption and its effect on the Olmec at Tres Zapotes, Veracruz. He found that the archaeological site of Cerro de las Mesas, which is west-northwest from San Martin—the opposite direction from Tres Zapotes—has no ash layer. Thus, only Tres Zapotes and Matacapan, which are much closer to San Martin and within the path of the prevailing spring wind, show an ash layer. These findings suggest that sites south and west of this volcano would probably show evidence of ash, a hypothesis that could be easily tested by excavating a series of test pits to see how large an area is affected by that eruption. Of course, the blackening of the sky from airborne ash would be much larger than the ground area that received it. A useful field project would be an intensive survey of the fifty square miles around San Martin. Practically every site tested would likely show a similar ash layer, with some very exciting prospects for Preclassic occupation below the ash layer.

Effects of a Volcanic Eruption

Chase's paper catalogs some interesting effects of a volcanic eruption. When the ash begins to fall back toward the earth, it is accompanied by many gases, including hydrochloric acid, hydrofluoric acid, carbonic acid, carbon dioxide, and ammonia. If the ash fall is heavy, people will naturally suffocate, not only from the ash content itself but also from these gases, which are lethal in large quantities. Animal, plant, and aquatic life would also succumb.

At Tres Zapotes, the ash fall was so thick that unquestionably nothing could have survived. It would have taken about eighty or ninety years for the soil to rebuild itself enough so that crops could profitably be grown. Survivors from nearby areas would have had to leave the area. All drinking water would have been contaminated.

As an interesting parallel, a 1964 volcanic eruption in Nicaragua created such huge quantities of ash that the area experienced ninety mud flows in a single year. Because mud flows are deep deposits of ash, they are highly unstable. The impact of any significant amount of rain makes the ash flow down slopes, seeking a lower resting bed. Speeds of these mud flows can vary from twenty to thirty miles an hour, and one flow was clocked at fifty-nine miles an hour. According to the records, the distances a single mud flow has moved can range from five miles (the average is between five and ten miles) up to the recordholder—ninety-nine miles. Chase notes the presence of about six feet of soil just above the ash layer that seems to have come suddenly at Tres Zapotes, thus paralleling the mud flows described for Nicaragua.

Even though much of Mesoamerica receives heavy seasonal rains, the situation would be further complicated by the volcano itself. The heat it injects locally into the atmosphere would trigger torrential rains as a side effect as this heated material contacted the stratosphere's colder, wet air. Furthermore, if there is any weakness in the underlying rock strata, earthquakes would be triggered by volcanic action. Near the coast, this seismic activity would create tidal waves of huge heights and immense power. A common Mesoamerican pattern is for an erupting volcano to trigger an earthquake. In some cases, an earthquake can also cause a volcano. The noise, needless to say, would be deafening— lightning, thunder, great cracks where rock strata are giving way, and the noises of the eruption itself.

Many Massive Eruptions About A.D. 30

El Salvador has been an excellent place to study the archaeological effects of volcanoes. Payson Sheets, an archaeologist from the University of Colorado at Boulder, investigated the volcano Ilopango, which had produced a layer of ash between seventeen and thirty-five inches thick. Again, because of the young corn plants in the ash, he was able to determine that the volcano had erupted in the spring. The layer he investigated was dated at approximately A.D. 250 and included excellent preservation, including homes where dishes were still on the tables—highly reminiscent of Pompeii.

Interestingly, he found evidence of at least four different volcanic eruptions. He dated the particular layer he was working on at A.D. 250, but test pits show that volcanic activity can be dated as early as the time of Christ. Not far away near the border of Guatemala is the site of Chalchuapa, a large Preclassic site that was occupied into times. A layer of volcanic ash between the archaeological strata has been dated by radiocarbon processes to A.D. 30, a date that provides a correlation with the crucifixion of Christ. It might be hypothesized that these active volcanoes over much of the Mesoamerican area would have erupted periodically, with perhaps a mega-event occurring near the time of Christ. (Sheets 1983)

Another area in El Salvador near San Salvador has archaeological sites buried under thick ash layers about the time of Christ. A 1955 article by Muriel Porter, written while she was attending the University of California at Berkeley, reports her study of a site covered by ash ranging from thirty to sixty-five feet deep. Clearly, nothing could survive that kind of density (Porter 1955).

Cummings studied the site of Cuicuilco, near the National University in Mexico City. Another site about five miles away, Copilco, has a lava flow thirty feet thick, covering architecture, burials, and pottery vessels, as shown in Figure 11–1. This layer of lava dates from the time of Christ. Further confirmation of the dating is that Cuicuilco and Copilco are on the west side of the Valley of Mexico where the volcano Xitle is located; and about thirty miles northeast is the huge site of Teotihuacan. Between two architecture levels at Teotihuacan appears a layer of volcanic ash probably blown in from that eruption. By radiocarbon dating, that eruption dates to A.D. 30.

FIGURE 11–1: A STRIKING EXAMPLE OF CIRCUMSTANTIAL EVIDENCE SUPPORTING THE BOOK OF MORMON IS THE THIRTY-FOOT-THICK LAYER OF VOLCANIC LAVA COVERING THE ARCHAEOLOGICAL SITE OF COPILCO IN SOUTHWESTERN MEXICO CITY. THIS LAVA LAYER DATES BY RADIOCARBON TO A.D. 30, ± 60 YEARS—CLOSE TO THE YEAR OF THE DEVASTATING DESTRUCTIONS THAT TOOK PLACE AT THE TIME OF THE CRUCIFIXION OF THE MESSIAH-REDEEMER, AS DESCRIBED IN 3 NEPHI 8 IN THE BOOK OF MORMON.

In short, then, from the Valley of Mexico on the north to El Salvador on the south, we have a pattern of major volcanic eruptions. The north saw lava flows over thirty feet thick; the south saw ash layers of up to sixty-five feet deep. Between these points is the volcano San Martin in the Tuxtla Mountains, which covered at least two sites at the same time. This new information will probably reinforce, not modify, this pattern of distribution of volcanic eruptions throughout Mesoamerica.

Sunken Cities

We have mentioned to this point only volcanic activity and mud flows. In highland Guatemala to the west of Guatemala City lies a large inland lake, Lake Atitlan (probably the Waters of Mormon). During a period of low water in the 1930s, ruins were detected in the water; and Samuel Lothrop, then with Harvard, was able to recover some ceramics that had the same style and pattern as the Miraflores ceramics from nearby Kaminaljuyu and dated from about the time of Christ, as did the ash layer immediately beneath the Ilopango volcano in El Salvador. It is reasonable to hypothesize that this city in the lake was Preclassic, was occupied near the time of Christ, and was covered subsequently by the lake waters. There are, interestingly, several volcanoes in the mountains surrounding the lake.

In a 1973 report of the New World Archaeological Foundation, Gareth Lowe, then field director, mentioned discovering an Olmec monument on the coast of Chiapas that had been broken and displaced by a shift in the earth at some point **after** it was carved, about 500 B.C. Of course, many other evidences of earthquakes are found as well.

Another event, which can be regarded only as a footnote, is Mound 5 in Chiapa de Corzo in the Mexican state of Chiapas, which shows that the roof burned and fell in on a collection of 830 whole vessels sitting on the floors. Radiocarbon dating of the main roof beam supplies a date of about A.D. 30. However, there is no evidence of more widespread burning in the same site, and we cannot generalize that the city itself experienced a fire at the time.

Studies Incomplete

We think it is well to remember that our study of volcanic and seismic activity in Mesoamerica is far from complete and that modern studies continue to revise our picture of what volcanoes do and don't do. For example, the 1982 eruption of El Chichon in Chiapas, Mexico, turned the site of Palenque gray from the ash fallout, well over a hundred miles away. John L. Sorenson quotes the report of a 1793 eruption in the Tuxtla Mountains, which has some interesting parallels: "Don Joseph Mozino reports that it all started with a buildup of towering clouds over the mountains and great grand thunderclaps but underground, that sounded like all the artillery in Veracruz going off" (Sorenson 1985, 322). The account estimates the number of these thunderclaps at four hundred, says they could be heard hundreds of miles away, and concludes, "No doubt the thunder was of two kinds. One resulted from exceptionally violent storms caused by the heat and dust and the other from the fracturing of the strata underground" (Sorenson 1985, 322).

We think we must also be cautious about the size of the area we include in the destruction zone. John L. Sorenson has pointed out that in the centuries immediately following Christ, figurines seem to disappear from Teotihuacan and southeastern Mesoamerica in general (Sorenson 1955, 60). This is a general pattern, not a universal pattern; if we look in more distant areas, the figurines reappear. And, of course, in more recent layers, we also find them in widespread use.

However, the evidences uncovered thus far are striking of huge volcanic eruptions, mud slides, earthquakes, and destructions in several areas in Mesoamerica dating to about A.D. 30. These archaeological discoveries parallel remarkably the natural destruction described in the Book of Mormon at the time of the crucifixion of the Savior.

Chapter 12
SHAMANISM: TRADITIONS, FALSE DOCTRINES, AND THE PRIESTCRAFTS OF MEN

Throughout this work, we have considered divine revelation as being the only certain source of knowledge about Jesus Christ and his mission of infinite atonement. The patriarch-prophet Abraham is a good example of the sure word of prophecy and proper authority to speak for God. He says:

> I sought for mine appointment unto the Priesthood according to the appointment of God unto the fathers concerning the seed.
>
> My fathers, having turned from their righteousness, and from the holy commandments which the Lord their God had given unto them, unto the worshiping of the gods of the heathen, utterly refused to hearken to my voice;
>
> For their hearts were set to do evil, and were wholly turned to the god of Elkenah, and the god of Libnah, and the god of Mahmackrah, and the god of Korash, and the god of Pharaoh, king of Egypt;
>
> Therefore they turned their hearts to the sacrifice of the heathen in offering up their children unto these dumb idols, and hearkened not unto my voice, but endeavored to take away my life by the hand of the priest of Elkenah. The priest of Elkenah was also the priest of Pharaoh. (Abraham 1:4-7)

Further, we are told that "Abraham received all things, whatsoever he received, by revelation and commandment, by my word, saith the Lord, and hath entered into his exaltation and sitteth upon his throne" (D&C 132:29).

The Stars in Heaven

Through the ages, the stars in heaven have been associated with divine promises of fertility. From the basically rural vantage point of the ancient cultures, the ever-present heavens were a vivid reminder to people of their relationship with God. To Abraham's descendants, in particular, the stars, especially the Milky Way, may have been a visible reminder of God's covenant with the House of Israel. To the Nephites, the stars were a source for analogies and signs of the times (see 1 Nephi 1:10; 2 Nephi 24:13; Isaiah 14:13; Helaman 14:5, 20; 3 Nephi 1:21; and 3 Nephi 8:22).

In shamanism, the stars were also important—but for vastly different reasons. Instead of being reminders of God's love and power, turning the hearts of the people to God, the stars became sources of revealed knowledge in and of themselves. Shamans, the first astrologers (a pseudoscience, according to the *New World Dictionary*), studied the heavenly bodies constantly, claiming to foretell the future of human affairs, both macro and micro, through the supposed influence of the relative positions of the moon, sun, and stars.

We will not go into great detail about shamanism in this chapter. For a full treatment of the world wide development of shamanism, see the appendix.

God's Two Trees

According to Moses, "And I, the Lord God, planted the tree of life also in the midst of the garden, and also the tree of knowledge of good and evil" (Moses 3:9). "But of the tree of the knowledge of good and evil, thou shalt not eat of it, nevertheless, thou mayest choose for thyself, for it is given unto thee; but, remember that I forbid it, for in the day thou eatest thereof thou shalt surely die" (Moses 3:17).

> And now the serpent was more subtle than any beast of the field which I, the Lord God, had made.
>
> And Satan put it into the heart of the serpent, (for he had drawn away many after him,) and he sought also to beguile Eve, for he knew not the mind of God, wherefore he sought to destroy the world.
>
> And he said unto the woman: Yea, hath God said—Ye shall not eat of every tree of the garden? (And he spake by the mouth of the serpent.)
>
> And the woman said unto the serpent: We may eat of the fruit of the trees of the garden;
>
> But of the fruit of the tree which thou beholdest in the midst of the garden, God hath said—Ye shall not eat of it, neither shall ye touch it, lest ye die.

> And the serpent said unto the woman: Ye shall not surely die;
>
> For God doth know that in the day ye eat thereof, then your eyes shall be opened, and ye shall be as gods, knowing good and evil.
>
> And when the woman saw that the tree was good for food, and that it became pleasant to the eyes, and a tree to be desired to make her wise, she took of the fruit thereof, and did eat, and also gave unto her husband with her, and he did eat. (Moses 4:5–12)

As has been noted, the Lord spoke to Moses of two trees that were a part of the creation of man. In the prophetic view of creation, the tree of life represents the love of God and Jesus the Christ, the Messiah-Redeemer. It represents spiritual life or eternal life in the presence of God the Eternal Father. It represents the gift of free agency and the gift of immortality or eternal life.

On the other hand, the tree of the knowledge of good and evil is symbolic of the adversary, for it was Lucifer who enticed our first parents to partake of its fruit.

World Man and World Tree

In the shamanistic view of creation, rather than the tree of life, the main focus is on the World Tree of knowledge and the associated and very knowledgeable World Man. The World Tree is represented by the Milky Way, the planets, and the constellations and seems to parallel the tree of the knowledge of good and evil. The World Man is the First Father of the ancient Maya traditions. There is a stress of fatalism in the World Tree symbolism, for the movement of the stars is very predictable and cannot be altered. That was the value to the shamans of the "Long Count" calendar, the Sacred Almanac calendar, etc. Such calendars "proved" their knowledge of how things were going to turn out—and therefore of their great power. Included in that was the power to shape or twist religious beliefs to their own ends.

For instance, in shamanism, the hope of resurrection is proclaimed, but it is dependent on the individual's own efforts and blood sacrifice and human sacrifice. First Father, who identifies with the World Tree in death, becomes the Cosmic Corn Tree after his resurrection by his "Hero Twin" sons.

The Creation Story

The creation story of the shamans in both the Old World and the New World had a number of shared cultural traits. A large number of these cultural traits cluster into a basically similar creation story involving the stars in heaven. However, there developed two levels of this creation story, differing in details depending on whether the ancients were using a seven-day week or a nine-day week. The seven-day week had seven planetary deities and seven creative periods. The later nine-day week focused on nine planetary deities and five creative periods or ages. Most of our attention is on the Five World Age system with the nine-day week—the latter creation story having more information to clarify important details.

As was pointed out earlier, the Five World Age creation story occurs in ancient Mesoamerica on three different scales of time. One level was the Equinoctial level of nearly 26,000 years; the second Mythological level of 5,200 years; and a more historical account of around 2,600 years. The calendars of the ancient Near East in the third and second millennium B.C. included a 364-day calendar, a 360-day calendar, and a 365-day calendar. As we have also pointed out, these calendars are all present in ancient Mesoamerica.

Additionally, there is both a strong Mesopotamian (Sumero-Babylonian) and a strong Egyptian cultural influence on the shamans' creation story. The Mesopotamian creation story appears to be more important on the earliest level, and the Egyptian influence is greatest on the later. Nimrod and his son Gilgamesh in Mesopotamia and Osiris in Egypt have many astronomical and ritual connections with this creation story, the Maya god First Father or Hun-Nal-Ye, and the concept of "divine kingship" (Gruener 1987, chaps. 8–15). The Mesopotamian *Epic of Gilgamesh* supplies many planetary features of the shamanistic creation story that are present in ancient Mesoamerica.

The Great Goddess Religion

Basically, the shaman's creation story is derived from the Great Goddess religion that prevailed throughout the ancient Near East. This religion centered on the concept of Divine Kings, deification of planets and constellations, special calendars, a World Man who absorbs all the other planetary gods at the end of each year, the death of the World Man, and his subsequent magical resurrection on New Year's Day.

The *Epic of Gilgamesh* is considered by Gruener (1987, 96) as the bible of Divine Kingship in the Great Goddess religion (see also Heidel 1946).

In this epic, the shamanistic gods reflect a "shape-shifting" quality. In other words, they can absorb different forms in nature— a good example being the World Man who absorbs the planetary gods in the Underworld, including different animal or plant forms. Murray Hope describes this shamanistic ability as "the process by which a shaman, during an altered state of consciousness or out of the body experience (OOB), assumes the shape, appearance, or contours of his or her totem beast, . . . the ability of the practitioner to change shape at will during out of the body experiences, in dream state, or in outer time" (Hope 1996, 244). What a contrast to the revelatory process of ancient Hebrew prophets like Abraham mentioned above.

Many cultural parallels are discussed in the appendix and are too numerous to recount in this summary. However, we can see that the shamanistic creation story from both hemispheres has many similarities to the prophetic and scriptural creation story. Obviously, these similarities made the secret society/shamanistic creation story very appealing to those who sought more rewards from their society. They could gain economic and political power, which would probably be denied them unless they affiliated with the shamanistic secret combinations.

Secret Combinations

Beginning in the days of Cain and continuing through all generations, whenever there have been people on the earth who did not care to follow the counsel of the Lord or his Hebrew prophets, Satan has revealed to them his oaths, vows, and secret covenants or combinations. Murder, plunder, robbery, power, the destruction of freedom, and the persecution of God's true followers have been the objectives of these secret societies or combinations.

According to Moses:

> And it came to pass that Cain . . . loved Satan more than God.
>
> And Satan said unto Cain: Swear unto me by thy throat, and if thou tell it thou shalt die; and swear thy

brethren by their heads, and by the living God, that they tell it not; for if they tell it, they shall surely die; and this that thy father may not know it; and this day I will deliver thy brother Abel into thine hands.

And Satan sware unto Cain that he would do according to his commands. And all these things were done in secret.

And Cain said: Truly I am Mahan, the master of this great secret, that I may murder and get gain. Wherefore Cain was called Master Mahan, and he gloried in his wickedness. (Moses 5:28–31)

Cain, therefore, was the first shaman, and his secret covenant with Satan was the beginning of the secret shamanistic societies or combinations.

The Book of Mormon gives an explanation of how some of these ancient Near Eastern shamanistic beliefs and rituals arrived in ancient Mesoamerica. Note the following from the Book of Mormon:

Yea, that same being [Satan] who did plot with Cain, that if he would murder his brother Abel it should not be known unto the world. And he did plot with Cain and his followers from that time forth.

And also it is that same being who put it into the hearts of the people to build a tower sufficiently high that they might get to heaven. And it was that same being who led on the people who came from that tower into this land; who spread the works of darkness and abominations over all the face of the land, until he dragged the people down to an entire destruction, and to an everlasting hell. (Helaman 6:27-28)

Shamanism in Mesoamerica

In Chapter 2, as we discussed the Jaredite people who came from the tower on the plains of Shinar, we pointed out how Moroni describes the beginning of shamanism in their "choice land." He records:

Now the daughter of Jared being exceedingly expert, and seeing the sorrows of her father, thought to devise a plan whereby she could redeem the kingdom unto her father.

Now the daughter of Jared was exceedingly fair. And it came to pass that she did talk with her father, and said unto him: Whereby hath my father so much sorrow? Hath he not read the record which our fathers brought across the great deep? Behold, is there not an account concerning them of old, that they by their secret plans did obtain kingdoms and great glory?

And now, therefore, let my father send for Akish, the son of Kimnor; and behold, I am fair, and I will dance before him, and I will please him, that he will desire me to wife; wherefore if he shall desire of thee that ye shall give unto him me to wife, then shall ye say: I will give her if ye will bring unto me the head of my father, the king. . . .

And it came to pass that they all sware unto him [Akish], by the God of heaven, and also by the heavens, and also by the earth, and by their heads, that whoso should vary from the assistance which Akish desired should lose his head; and whoso should divulge whatsoever thing Akish made known unto them, the same should lose his life.

And it came to pass that thus they did agree with Akish. And Akish did administer unto them the oaths which were given by them of old who also sought power, which had been handed down even from Cain, who was a murderer from the beginning.

And they were kept up by the power of the devil to administer these oaths unto the people, to keep them in darkness, to help such as sought power to gain power, and to murder, and to plunder, and to lie, and to commit all manner of wickedness and whoredoms. (Ether 8:8-10, 14-16)

Core Cultural Elements

Many of the cultural elements of the Great Goddess religion and the cult of Divine Kingship appear to be the core of the secret societies or combinations described above. Note the emphasis on bringing records from the Old World with this type of information. When the secret combination is organized, it is in secrecy with oaths and covenants. The oaths and covenants involve the heavens above as well as the earth. The penalty for divulging the secrets is decapitation. Further note that these events took place among people related to the royal family.

A Prophetic Warning

Although we have been considering secret societies or combinations as they existed anciently, we should point out that Moroni issued a rather stern warning to those who would one day read his record:

And whatsoever nation shall uphold such secret combinations, to get power and gain, until they shall spread over the nation, behold, they shall be destroyed; for the Lord will not suffer that the blood of his saints, which shall be shed by them, shall always cry unto him from the ground for vengeance upon them and yet he avenge them not.

Wherefore, O ye [who read this], it is wisdom in God that these things should be shown unto you, that thereby ye may repent of your sins, and suffer not that these murderous combinations shall get above you, which are built up to get power and gain—and the work, yea, even the work of destruction come upon you, yea, even the sword of the justice of the Eternal God shall fall upon you, to your overthrow and destruction if ye shall suffer these things to be.

Wherefore, the Lord commandeth you, when ye shall see these things come among you that ye shall awake to a sense of your awful situation, because of this secret combination which shall be among you. . . .

For it cometh to pass that whoso buildeth it up seeketh to overthrow the freedom of all lands, nations, and countries; and it bringeth to pass the destruction of all people, for it is built up by the devil, who is the father of all lies. (Ether 8:22–25)

When speaking of secret combinations, Moroni uses the phrase "which shall be among you." In other words, this is not an "if" sort of prophecy. Despite the movement toward political peace, there *is* a secret combination among us today (perhaps many combinations) that will murder the righteous and seek "to overthrow the freedom of all lands, nations, and countries." Nephi the son of Lehi also prophesied that such a secret combination would be among us:

The Gentiles are lifted up in the pride of their eyes, and have stumbled, because of the greatness of their stumbling block, that they have built up many churches; nevertheless, they put down the power and miracles of God, and preach up unto themselves their own wisdom and their own learning, that they may get gain and grind upon the face of the poor.

And there are many churches built up which cause envyings, and strifes, and malice.

And there are also secret combinations, even as in times of old, according to the combinations of the devil, for he is the founder of all these things; yea, the founder of murder, and works of darkness; yea, and he leadeth them by the neck with a flaxen cord, until he bindeth them with his strong cords forever. (2 Nephi 26:20–22, emphasis added)

Alma prophesied that if such secret combinations exist, then the land has a curse upon it that will ensure destruction to all who participate in such combinations and who by their apathy or greed uphold them (see Alma 37:28–31). Finally, Moroni, in a thundering denunciation of prideful, uncommitted "followers" of Jesus Christ in our day, asks in conclusion:

O ye pollutions, ye hypocrites, ye teachers, who sell yourselves for that which will canker, why have ye polluted the holy church of God? Why are ye ashamed to take upon you the name of Christ? Why do ye not think that greater is the value of an endless happiness than that misery which never dies—because of the praise of the world?

Why do ye adorn yourselves with that which hath no life, and yet suffer the hungry, and the needy, and the naked, and the sick and the afflicted to pass by you, and notice them not?

Yea, *why do ye build up your secret abominations to get gain*, and cause that widows should mourn before the Lord. . . .

Behold, the sword of vengeance hangeth over you; and the time soon cometh that he avengeth the blood of the saints upon you, for he will not suffer their cries any longer. (Mormon 8:38–41, emphasis added)

The above comments clearly point out that secret combinations will exist in the last days, even among those who consider themselves to be righteous but who are filled with pride unto greediness, causing them to be deceived. (See Yorgason and Yorgason 1990, 131–33.)

Samuel's Law

Anciently, obsession with things of the world led to destruction, and it is certain that such obsessions will do the same thing today. Hugh Nibley calls this the operation of Samuel's Law. He says:

> The Prophet Samuel the Lamanite sets forth the interesting rule that when "the economy" becomes the main and engrossing concern of a society—or in the routine Book of Mormon phrase, when "they begin to set their hearts upon their riches"—the economy will self-destruct. This is how [Samuel] puts it: "Ye do always remember your riches; . . . your hearts are not drawn out unto the Lord, but they do swell with great pride, . . . envyings, strifes, malice, persecutions and murders, and all manner of iniquities" (Helaman 13:22). Note well the sequence of folly: first we are well pleased with ourselves because of our wealth, then comes the game of status and prestige [careerism becomes the order of the day in a business society of "many merchants . . . and also many lawyers, and many officers [and] the people . . . [are] distinguished by ranks, according to their riches and their chances for learning" (3 Nephi 6:11–12)], leading to competitive maneuvers, hatred, and dirty tricks, and finally the ultimate solution [of murder]. Where wealth guarantees respectability, principles melt away as the criminal element rises to the top [The Gadianton Protective Association soon became the biggest business in Mesoamerica "as the more part of the Nephites did unite with those bands of robbers" (Helaman 6:21)]: "For this cause hath the Lord God caused that a curse should come upon the land, and also upon your riches" (Helaman 13:23). "And behold, the time cometh that he curseth your riches, that they become slippery, that ye cannot hold them; and in the days of your poverty ye cannot retain them" (Helaman 13:31). [The situation] ends in utter frustration and total insecurity as morals and the market collapse together and the baffled [economic] experts surrender [to the criminal or shamanistic element that remains in power]. (Nibley, *The Prophetic Book of Mormon*, 1989, 349–50)

Self-Indulgence

In other words, modern society, being unwittingly guided and directed by Lucifer and his minions, the shamans, advocates self-indulgence. Today, individuals and families are being torn apart and destroyed by pervasive self-indulgence. Instead of developing self-control, many today spend their lives not seeking earnestly the riches of eternity but rather allowing their eyes to be full of greediness for the pleasures of the world (D&C 68:31). Pleasure and happiness are considered the main goals of life. Pleasure-seeking behavior and avoidance of pain are the very human instincts of the natural man; but, as we know, the natural man is an enemy to God (Mosiah 3:19). Such statements as "whatever turns you on" or "if it feels good, do it" are absolutely contrary to the temperate doctrines of Christ. Yet they are widely subscribed to even by many who consider themselves as modern followers of Christ—despite the fact that we know full well that acceptance of such immediate gratification is detrimental to our long-range, eternal goals.

On the national and global fronts, we live in what we call a dynamic society, a progressive, competitive, acquisitive, self-indulging mingling of cultures that, to survive, must always be expanding. However, in the long run, this will turn out to be a physical impossibility. But still we keep indulging ourselves. Nibley points out,

> We have contrived a way to keep things going by destroying our natural resources at an accelerating pace as long as there are any left, while assuring an expanding market by ever more extravagant excesses of Madison Avenue unreality, inventing outrageous needs for pernicious products. To keep producing what we do not need, not only high-powered advertising but deliberate obsolescence is necessary. (Nibley, *Approaching Zion*, 1989, 273)

We are reminded that when we were children, our mothers did their entire month's grocery shopping in a small store that would hardly fit in the cold cereals department of a modern "supermarket." And we had more than sufficient. But who is a modern supermarket super for—the self-indulging consumer who can never fully satisfy his or her wants or the gain-seeking supplier of pernicious products who has advertised his or her way into our pocketbooks? Doesn't it seem possible that this is part of the secret conspiracy the Lord reminded us of through Moroni and others?

The Plop-Plop, Fizz-Fizz Society

In today's permissive world, adults and children are taught to listen to and think about whatever they want, to do "whatever turns them on," and to open their mouths and find instant gratification and relief. For instance, one widely promoted, self-indulging philosophy is that sexual intimacy is a way of saying to an instantly vanishing partner, "I briefly noticed you; thank you for noticing me, but you owed me one anyway because I probably noticed you first." The act means a great deal more than this to most animals.

Also promoted in today's permissive world are prescription drugs for "minor aches and pains," "tension headache," "night cough," "tired blood," and a variety of other ailments and symptoms. For those who need even more help, "extra-strength" preparations are available. The message is clear: The answer to whatever ails a person can usually be found in capsule or syrup form. Is it any wonder that illicit drugs and the illicit use of prescription drugs have become so popular among *all* age groups in society today? (See Yorgason and Yorgason 1990, 131.)

Illicit Drugs: The product of a Secret Combination

Donald Ian MacDonald, associate clinical professor of pediatrics at the University of South Florida, writes:

> During the decades of the 1960s and 1970s, an unprecedented and tragic increase in the use and abuse of psychoactive drugs occurred in this country. Its most dangerous impact was on young people, particularly teenagers. In earlier decades, though many adolescents smoked cigarettes and often began to experiment with alcohol, they were essentially drug-free so far as illicit drugs were concerned. By 1982, however, the percent of high school seniors who had some experience with illicit drugs climbed from essentially zero to over 65%. (Macdonald 1984, v)

In a chapter titled "The Drug Epidemic," Macdonald traces the history of illicit drug abuse by American adolescents and their parents. He shows not only the effects of various drug substances but also the apparent causes behind the growth in their use. He says, referring to adults in the 1960s and 1970s:

> These people, also, were dealing with life chemically, but their chemicals were the legal tranquilizers and sedatives

prescribed by their physicians for stress and anxiety. It was a frequent occurrence in the early 1970s for pediatricians to see in their offices glassy-eyed and tranquilized mothers of young children. These were respectable middle-class housewives, women whose physicians had prescribed diazepam (Valium) or chlordiazepoxide (Librium) to help them cope with the stress of their daily lives. Along with these and other exciting and less legal new drugs, the acceptability and use of alcohol continued to escalate. The hope of better living through chemistry seemed to have arrived. (Macdonald 1984, 3)

Frightening Statistics

Macdonald further points out that this acceptance of drug use was shown by the Johnston-Bachman-O'Malley study, first commissioned by the National Institute on Drug Abuse in 1975. In that year, "the senior class had had only 17% of its members initiated [to marijuana] by the time they were freshmen. In startling contrast 34.1% of freshmen in 1975 had already tried pot. Of these, 16.2% had begun by the eighth grade" (Macdonald 1984, 4).

Macdonald continues by pointing out that in 1979, 52 percent of male high-school seniors admitted to consuming five or more alcoholic drinks at one sitting within the previous two weeks, with the percentage of females admitting to the same thing only slightly less (Macdonald 1984, 5). Cigarette smoking was a different matter. By 1977, girls took the lead in cigarette consumption in America, a lead they continue to hold according to the most recent studies. And this addiction, introduced into society for money, is deadly. "Over 200,000 Americans died in 1981 as a result of cigarette smoking, and the American Cancer Society estimates that by 1985 lung cancer will be the leading cause of death in American women" (Macdonald 1984, 6). One has to wonder at the cigarette ad that says, "You've come a long way, baby."

Another survey conclusion is the following:

In 1979, more than 50 million Americans had tried marijuana at least once. Young adults (18–25 years) were the most frequent users (68%), followed by youths aged 12–17 years (31%) and adults aged 26 years and older (20%). . . .

Within the youth group . . . females are more likely than males to be current cigarette smokers. . . . In 1980, the lifetime prevalence of marijuana, tobacco and alcohol outstripped those of all other drugs, at 60%, 71% and 93%, respectively. . . .

Those students who show less successful adaptation to the educational environment (by low grades and truancy) show above-average drug use. Also, those who spend many evenings out for recreation and those with heavy time commitments to a job and with relatively high income report higher-than-average drug use. *Lower-than-average drug use is reported by those with strong religious commitments and conservative political views.* (Litt 1983, 2–5, emphasis added)

Interesting findings, we feel. In a more recent study (1988) prepared by the American Academy of Pediatrics and the Center for Advanced Health Studies, the following statements are made:

More than 90% of adolescents in the United States will have used alcohol before graduating from high school, and two thirds of seniors report drinking within the past month. Fifty percent of seniors report having ever used marijuana, and one fourth of seniors report having used it in the last thirty days. Approximately 5% of seniors use either marijuana or alcohol daily. Alcohol and marijuana use began before entrance to high school for approximately 30% and 10%, respectively, of seniors. . . . Seventeen percent of high school seniors . . . [have used cocaine], with 5% reporting using it in the past month. (Schonberg 1988, preface)

Initial drug use is . . . now occurring at an earlier age. Ten times as many high school seniors report that they began drinking before leaving the sixth grade as did a decade ago. The percentage of students using drugs by the sixth grade has tripled since 1975. In the early 1960s, marijuana use was virtually nonexistent among 13-year-olds; at the present time, one in six 13-year-olds has used marijuana. "Crack," a highly addictive, inexpensive, smokable form of cocaine, is now widely available. Cocaine use among teenagers has increased: 17% of the senior class of 1985 reported that they had used cocaine in the past year. The 1986 National Household Survey of Drug Use reveals some potentially serious developments in patterns of drug abuse by 12-17-year-old youth, the youngest age group surveyed. Twenty-four percent of boys and 23% of girls in this age group had used an illicit drug within the last year. . . .

Patterns of alcohol, tobacco and marijuana use among youth are of special concern because these three substances are often considered "gateway" drugs. Most people who become seriously involved with illicit drugs have started with these substances. (Schonberg 1988, 2–3)

The pattern of use changes; risk remains a constant. For most young people, such risk arises through their own drug use; nonetheless, even that minority of youth who abstain from psychoactive drugs are not immune to the dangers created by their peers. (Schonberg 1988, preface)

Untimely Death—A National Disaster

These abuses, plus the use of illegal substances, have resulted in a tragic national disaster. Macdonald reports:

In the 15- to 24-year range, the leading causes of death are accidents, homicides, and suicides. All have a strong correlation with drug and alcohol use. Marvelous technical and medical advances in our society have produced declining death rates for all ages with each passing decade in this century, with one exception. Mortality rates in the 15- to 24-year age range have risen significantly in the last 20 years. (Macdonald 1984, 8)

And according to the American Academy of Pediatrics and the Center for Advanced Health Studies:

Of the 25,000 accidental deaths among youth annually, approximately 40%, or 10,000, are alcohol related. Homicide is the second leading cause of death among adolescents. Of the 5,500 adolescent homicide victims each year, 30% are intoxicated at the time they are killed. Drug use is a leading, if not the leading, cause of death among adolescents. (Schonberg 1988, preface)

Macdonald continues:

The effect of drugs on the non-using population cuts much deeper than the mortality figures. Perhaps more important is the weakening of our national fibre in a number of measurable and fairly obvious ways. Areas affected include scholastic performance, work performance, family relationships, military readiness, the cost of goods and services, the crime rate, and the filling of our mental health institutions. Scholastic aptitude test (SAT) scores in this country fell for eighteen straight years following 1964, when less than 2% of the population had ever tried pot. . . . Drug use is related to truancy, sleeping in school, change in short-term memory, and attention ability. (Macdonald, 1984, 10)

In 1980, a worldwide survey of United States military personnel on active duty revealed that 5% used marijuana daily and 26% had used it within the past 30 days. In 1980 the Pentagon spent $95 million on drug and alcohol programs aimed at prevention, treatment and rehabilitation. In that year 25,000 servicemen were referred for treatment. . . .

The National Institute on Alcohol Abuse and Alcoholism estimated that in 1980, alcohol-related industry losses were $30 billion. . . .

Pediatricians have become increasingly concerned about child abuse and its disastrous effects on young people and families. They should be aware that more and more of the abused young people have parents who are chemically dependent. . . .

A survey by an Oklahoma legislator revealed that 62% of all prisoners in that state were incarcerated for crimes directly related to alcohol and/or drug use. (Macdonald 1984, 10–11)

[And] women who used marijuana during pregnancy were five times more likely to deliver infants with features compatible with the Fetal Alcohol Syndrome [mental retardation, microcephaly—reduced or nonexistent brain, and irritability], [which] suggests that the effects of [alcohol and marijuana] on the fetus may be additive. (Macdonald 1984, 72; see also Yorgason and Yorgason 1990, 139–43)

The Role of "Getting Gain"

Can anyone possibly argue that the designs of the alcohol, tobacco, and illicit drug "industries" is financial gain with a capital G, no matter the harm that their products bring to consumers? Macdonald says the following about financial gains by the drug people:

Drugs, legal and otherwise, are big business. . . .The American tobacco and alcohol industries . . . gross . . . $27 billion a year. As impressive as those figures are, they are dwarfed by the profits from illegal drugs. It was estimated that "in 1980 the retail, street-level transaction value of the illegal drug trade in the United States was about $79 billion," which was up 22% from 1979, with escalation continuing. When compared with sales of the largest U.S. business corporations in 1980, only Exxon at $103 billion was greater. . . . The profit motive for traffickers has been powerful and compelling. (Macdonald 1984, 92)

Concerning just the tobacco industry alone, a recent news article declared, "Smoking costs U.S. $52 billion a year" (*Deseret News*, 20–21 February 1990, 3).

Truly this is a conspiracy, a secret combination, and a plague of the worst order. (See Yorgason and Yorgason 1990, 137–38.)

The above comments were made nearly a decade ago, and a good many of the "secrets" of at least one of the shamanistic combinations Moroni must have been prophesying of—the tobacco industry—have been brought to light. (See Yorgason and Yorgason.)

Alcohol, which we believe is the product of another secret combination, is widely promoted as a key part of all sorts of social and athletic activities. Fun is made to equate with drinking, and all great athletes look forward to retirement so they can spend their time in bars arguing over which beer is lightest. It was once a common belief in this country that weekends were for family, church, and relaxation. Now the message is clearly that "weekends were made for Michelob."

What shamanistic rubbish!

Self-Indulgence of the Mind

In another vein but still dealing with damaging and often damning self-indulgence, can anyone possibly doubt that those who promote self-indulgence of the mind can be any less a secret combination? Consider carefully the words of the prophet Alma to his son Corianton: "Forsake your sins, and go no more after the lusts of your eyes" (Alma 39:9). In our day, what does the expression "the lusts of your eyes" mean?

Probably no product is advertised with greater alacrity and determination in our world by Satan and his shamans today than illicit sex. Movies, videos, sitcoms, soap operas, magazines, newspapers, billboards, commercials, designer fashions, novels, radio and television talk-show hosts, nonfiction books, rock and country music, music videos, and even "good ol' boy" radio disc jockeys all promote illicit sex, vulgarity, and promiscuity. In our present world, there is literally no way to escape it. How we respond to this nefarious campaign of Lucifer's will, in great measure, determine whether we are independent of the worldly power of the secret combinations of which we have been speaking.

As Jesus Christ taught the Nephites, "The light of the body is the eye; if, therefore, thine eye be single, thy whole body shall be full of light. But if thine eye be evil, thy whole body shall be full of darkness" (3 Nephi 13:22–23). In our opinion, the resurrected Christ is saying that we become what we decide to look at, to watch, and to allow our eyes to feast upon. Every waking minute of every day we have a choice, and we will quite literally become what we choose.

Most of us are familiar with the notorious serial killer Ted Bundy and his last-minute admission about the deadly impact of pornography on his thinking and subsequent activities. In his last mortal interview, he made the following comments:

> This is the message that I want to get across, that as a young boy, and I mean a boy of 12 or 13 certainly, that I encountered . . . in the local grocery store, in a local drug store . . . soft-core pornography. . . . [In people's garbage,] we would come across pornographic books of a harder nature . . . [and] of a more graphic, explicit nature. . . .
>
> This kind of literature contributed and helped mold and shape the kinds of violent behavior [that I am accused of]. . . .
>
> My experience with pornography . . . is once you become addicted to it . . . I would keep looking for more potent, more explicit, more graphic kinds of material.
>
> Like an addiction, you keep craving something that is harder, harder, something which . . . gives you a greater sense of excitement. Until you reach a point where the pornography only goes so far, you reach that jumping off point where you begin to wonder if maybe actually doing it would give you [a thrill] which is beyond just reading it or looking at it ("Bundy Tells Broadcaster the Fatal Effects of Pornography," *Deseret News*, 26–27 January 1989, A4–A5).

Need we say more about the satanically inspired dangers of polluting the mind with such filth? By the same token there is the danger of polluting our minds with rock and heavy metal music:

> Rock music grew up in a time of youthful rebellion [in the 1960s and 1970s]. Interwoven with the music were messages of sex, drugs, and protest. More recently, homosexuality and Satanism have been added to these themes.
>
> Rock music has become the music of the young. . . . Many teenagers understandably enjoy the beat and the use of fascinating electronic effects. Much of the music, though, is definitely counterculture. Strong messages to "let it all hang out," "do drugs," and "have sex" abound. Pleasure is king. Popular rock star Eric Clapton sings, "Cocaine, cocaine, she's all right, she's OK." Adults who largely ignore these media messages are seen by children as passively accepting them. Outrage might be more appropriate. (Macdonald 1984, 92; see also Yorgason and Yorgason 1990, 145–46)

Astrologers and Technocrats

The interesting thing about shamanism is that it will teach for doctrine whatever it takes to convince people that they are in control and that there is no need for God—who must not, therefore, exist. Hugh Nibley says:

> Rather surprisingly, the age of Enoch is consistently described as the time of great intellectual as well as material sophistication. "[The fallen angel] Azael . . . taught [men] to make knives and breastplates and all kinds of military hardware; and to work the ores of the earth, and how gold was to be worked and made into ornaments for women; and he showed them polishing [eye-paint] and cosmetics and precious stones and dyes. . . . And the sons and daughters of men adopted all these things and led the saints astray. And there was great wickedness on the earth, and they became perverted and lost in all their ways. . . . Along with that their leader Semiazas taught them scientific formulas (*epaodas kata tou nous*), and the properties of roots and plants of the earth. The eleventh, Pharmakos, taught all manner of drugs, incantations, prescriptions, formulas. [Others] taught them stargazing, astrology, meteorology, geology, the signs of the sun and moon. All of these began

to reveal the mysteries to their wives and children" (Nibley, *Enoch the Prophet*, 1986, 184).

So it is in our day. Nibley addinA significant aspect of the Apocalyptic picture is the technological advancement of the doomed and wicked world, in which men defy God confident in their technical and scientific knowledge. . . . [Men] thought to emancipate themselves from dependence on God through technological know-how, in the manner of the doomed super-race of Peleus and Thetis. "This is not as foolish as it sounds," says the Zohar, "for they knew all the arts . . . and all the ruling chieftains in charge of the world, and on this knowledge they relied, until at length God disabused them by restoring the earth to its primitive state and covering it with water." In the days of Enoch, even the children were acquainted with the mysterious arts (what we would have called advanced science); R. Yesa asks: "With all that knowledge could they not foresee destruction?" To this R. Isaac replies: "They did know, but they thought they were safe because they had means of preventing [the angel in charge of fire and the angel in charge of water] from executing the judgment upon them. What they did not know was that God rules the world. [Cf. Moses 4:6.] . . . God gave them a respite all the time that the righteous men Jared, Methuselah, and Enoch were alive, but when they departed from the world, God let the punishment descend . . . and they were blotted out from the earth." "Alas," cries R. Simeon, "for the blindness of the sons of men, all unaware as they are how full the earth is of strange and invisible beings and hidden dangers, which could they but see they would marvel how they themselves can survive on the earth." In Enoch's time they had all sorts of engineering projects for controlling and taming nature (as did Abraham's Nimrod), but the Lord altered the order of creation so that their very mastery of nature as they understood it became their undoing. The same scientific hubris that led them to reject God led them to insult nature, and the upheavals that ensued demonstrate the very real ecological connection between the sins of men and the revolt of the elements that was formerly viewed as the fatal extravagance and irrationality of Apocalyptic. (Nibley, *Enoch the Prophet*, 1986, 78–79)

And so it goes today. We are so enamored of our own technological and scientific advances that we assume we are in control and that we have no need of God. Hence, we ignore him and his eternally vital commandments. Then, in our moments of uncertainty and fear (because we can obtain no lasting comfort or protection from such shamanistic sources), we, as the ancients, turn to astrologers and the stars (of heaven or Hollywood—the results are the same) and seek vainly for answers, for comfort, and for direction. But because such nondivine revelation has always been a sham (from shamanism) and a lie, both God and nature are insulted, and once again all the elements are revolting and exist in a state of continual upheaval—chaos that can only increase as wickedness grows.

Modern Calendars

We are even forced to consider the most recent "calendaring" systems, the incredibly proliferating daytimers and dayplanners of our own fast-paced society. As shamans sought to control the lives of the ancients by regulating their time, do not these modern systems tend to do the same?

But is time really ours to control? Who set the courses of the sun, moon, and stars? Who created the earth and placed it in its orbit or set it to spinning in twenty-four-hour revolutions? To Abraham, the Lord said:

> I am the Lord thy God; I dwell in heaven; the earth is my footstool; I stretch my hand over the sea, and it obeys my voice; I cause the wind and the fire to be my chariot; I say to the mountains—Depart hence—and behold, they are taken away by a whirlwind, in an instant, suddenly.
>
> My name is Jehovah, and I know the end from the beginning. (Abraham 2:7–8)

Concerning a knowledge of his establishment and control of time in our day, God adds:

> And also, if there be bounds set to the heavens or to the seas, or to the dry land, or to the sun, moon, or stars—
>
> All the times of their revolutions; all the appointed days, months, and years, and all the days of their days, months, and years, and all their glories, laws, and set times, shall be revealed in the days of the dispensation of the fulness of times. (D&C 121:30–31)

And who appointed unto man the length of his days? "For there is a time appointed for every man," God declares, "according as his works shall be" (D&C 121:25).

To every thing there is a season, and a time to every purpose under the heaven:

A time to be born, and a time to die; a time to plant, and a time to pluck up that which is planted;

A time to kill, and a time to heal; a time to break down, and a time to build up;

A time to weep, and a time to laugh; a time to mourn, and a time to dance;

A time to cast away stones, and a time to gather stones together; a time to embrace, and a time to refrain from embracing;

A time to get, and a time to lose; a time to keep, and a time to cast away;

A time to rend, and a time to sew; a time to keep silence, and a time to speak;

A time to love, and a time to hate; a time of war, and a time of peace. (Ecclesiastes 3:1–8)

But can any of this be changed? The writer of Ecclesiastes continues:

I said in mine heart, God shall judge the righteous and the wicked: for there is a time there for every purpose and for every work.

I said in mine heart concerning the estate of the sons of men, that God might manifest them, and that they might see that they themselves are beasts.

For that which befalleth the sons of men befalleth beasts; even one thing befalleth them: as the one dieth, so dieth the other; yea, they have all one breath; so that a man hath no preeminence above a beast: for all is vanity.

All go unto one place; all are of the dust, and all turn to dust again. (Ecclesiastes 3:17–20)

The message we get from all this is that our time, in fact, belongs to the Lord, who will determine how much of it we have and how it should be used. If we think to control time as our own, or to insist—through our daytimers and so forth—on being the only ones who can structure or regulate our time, then we are as duped as the ancients who submitted to the control of the shamans, and we lose the same sorts of divine blessings they lost.

Conclusion

The secret societies of the cultures of the people who lived in Mesoamerica during the time of the Book of Mormon parallel our day in what is occurring in governments, some corporations, time-control, gambling, sports, entertainment in movies, videos, novels, the Internet, etc. The goal of the shamans who direct secret combinations is to get gain and power regardless of moral issues, just as it has always been. "And it came to pass that there arose a rebellion among the people, because of that secret combination which was built up to get power and gain" (Ether 11:15). "And they did reject all the words of the prophets, because of their secret society and wicked abominations" (Ether 11:22).

According to Ezra Taft Benson, at one time President of The Church of Jesus Christ of Latter-day Saints, "You cannot escape this mass media environment which is controlled by financial censorship. . . . Radio, television, movies, magazines—all are monopolized by the money managers who are guided by one ethic, the words wealth and power" (Benson 1988, 326). "There has developed in this country, I am sorry to say, a species of so-called 'broadmindedness' which tolerates anything and everything. . . . I for one fail to see where this so-called 'tolerance' of evil has made society any better or individuals any happier. . . . We cannot build an enduring society except on principles of righteousness" (Benson 1988, 412).

Gordon B. Hinckley, current President of The Church of Jesus Christ of Latter-day Saints, continued in the April 1998 General Conference of the Church:

> I plead with you . . . to keep yourselves free from the stains of the world. . . . You must not fool around on the Internet to find pornographic material. . . . You must not rent videos with pornography of any kind. . . . Stay away from pornography as you would avoid a serious disease. It is destructive. It can become habitual, and those who indulge in it get so they cannot leave it alone. It is addictive. It is a five-billion-dollar business for those who produce it. They make it as titillating and attractive as they know how. It seduces and destroys its victims. It is everywhere. It is all about us. (Hinckley 1998, 49)

Finally, President Benson counseled: "The prophets, particularly of the Book of Mormon, saw our day. You will learn more from studying and reading the Book of Mormon [about our current problems] than you will by reading the daily paper or the slick magazines" (Benson 1988, 62).

Chapter 13
RELIGIOUS AND CULTURAL PARALLELS BETWEEN THE OLD WORLD AND THE NEW WORLD

A number of very substantial religious and other parallels suggest a significant probability of migrations of highly intelligent peoples from the Near East to America—with at least some individuals in their groups who were well schooled in the religious and cultural substance of their societies and who were intensely motivated toward the preservation and further development of their higher values.

In addition to what follows below, in the notes to this chapter, we will add an extensive list of religious and cultural traits common to both Mesoamerica and the Near East.

Plant Life Elements

George Carter, professor of geography at Johns Hopkins University, reported in February 1957:

> When we Europeans discovered them, . . . the Indian peoples of Mesoamerica were practicing agriculture, making pottery, raising some domesticated animals, practicing metallurgy, using practically all the known techniques of weaving, living in organized city states, even empires, and having great capitals that would rival Rome or Athens or Thebes or Babylon. . . . The work that was to reopen the Diffusionist controversy began with an attempt by a group of botanists to untangle the relationships of the cottons of the world. This group of botanists included Hutchinson, Silow, and Stevens who teamed up on this job, using the modern techniques of genetics. They soon found that they could divide the cottons of the world into three groups: (1) the wild and domestic cottons of the Old World, (2) the wild cottons of the New World, and (3) the domestic cottons of the New World. The New World domestic cottons particularly interested them. When they studied cells under

high-powered microscopes, they found that they contained
twice as many hereditary units (chromosomes) as did the
other cottons. Further, they could tell that there were two
sets of chromosomes there, one the Old World type and the
other the New World type. The most probable explanation
they could find was that man had brought a domestic cotton
from the Old World into the New, and that the two cottons
had crossed, combining the full sets of chromosomes from
both plants, and creating this new plant.

They then did a very interesting thing. They examined
the New World domestic cotton and carefully catalogued
all its characteristics. Next they searched the cottons of the
world to see just what two cottons, if combined, would give
them these characteristics. They found the answer in an
Asiatic domestic cotton and in a Peruvian wild cotton. They
succeeded in crossing these two plants and producing a near-
duplicate of the American domesticated cotton.

Cotton seeds are not particularly tough. Plant men do
not believe that they can float around the ocean and remain
alive. To have arrived in America, they must have been
carried by someone. (Carter 1957, 10)

Some scholars have told the world that there was an absolute
separation of Old World and New World plants   (Heiser 1973,
10–11).   Others have long believed that some New World plants
were imported in ancient times. But recent discoveries throw new
light on the question. In 1953, Carter wrote:

Some plants positively were pre-Columbian in the Old
World and the New World. . . . There is a formidable list of
plants, most of them related to the Middle American-
Southeast Asian areas, that range all the way from probable
to possible cultural transfers. The long-held doctrine of the
absolute separation of Old World and New World
agricultures is no longer tenable. The plant evidence should
be re-examined without bias. (Carter 1953, 71)

Carl O. Sauer, distinguished chairman, Department of
Geography, University of California (at Berkeley), wrote in 1952
in his book *Agricultural Origins and Dispersals,* "The transPacific
carriage of cotton, the true gourd, sweet potato, and coconut

appears proven, I should say, even for the coconut, as due to the deliberate action of man" (Ferguson 1958, 52).

Recently, a discovery of domesticated barley was reported from a Hohokam archaeological site near Phoenix, Arizona. The author mentions that "nearly half of the samples yielded barley" (Adams 1983, 32). The author goes on to suggest that the domesticated barley may have come from Mexico. This report represents the first discovery of barley in the New World. The Hohokam culture dates between 300 B.C.and A.D. 1400.

The Pentad

Among the astral-conscious Sumerians about 2700 B.C., the North Star figures prominently. These ancient astronomers considered it to be at the center of a great theoretical cross in the sky formed by the two major directions of the Milky Way. When it lay east-west, it was regarded as the equivalent of the equator. When it lay in a north-south direction, it was considered the equivalent of the meridian. (Ackerman 1950, 14).

A ring symbolized the rotating constellations among the Sumerians, and a transfixing ring represented the North Star. Figure 13–1, Danzante-carved slab elements from Monte Alban dating about 500 B.C., shows the classic pentad. According to Ackerman, "The main triad of Polaris and the twin terminal constellations is, therefore, sometimes supplemented by these secondary twins, inserted between the older and more important twins and the pole. This makes a pentad, and five is a sympathetic number to this system, since it refers also to the four quarters and the center" (Ackerman 1950, 17–18).

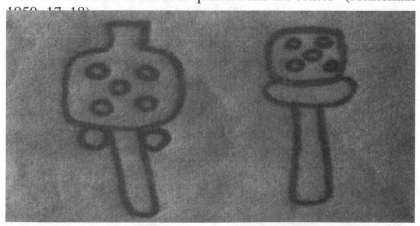

FIGURE 13–1: A PENTAD (5) TRANSFIXED BY A STICK FROM MONTE ALBAN, OAXACA, MEXICO, ABOUT 500 B.C.

The pentad glyph appears in the symbolism of Monte Alban dating to about 500 B.C. During the Classic and Postclassic periods in Mexico, the same glyph also represented five Venus years, according to Edward Seler and Raul Noriega (Noriega 1958, Tomo I, 265).

The Star of David

The Star of David, a six-pointed star formed of two often-interlaced equilateral triangles, is an ancient symbol of Judaism and is now the emblem of the state of Israel. Dating from at least the first millennium B.C., it is often referred to as *Solomon's Seal*.

Figure 13–2 is a remarkable representation of the Star of David within a circle with a feathered tail. It was found in Uxmal, a Maya site dating from about the tenth century A.D. D'Alviella comments on this identical carving and notes that the feathered tail "suggests in a striking manner the pennated tail of certain Assyrian, Phoenician, and Persian Globes" (D'Alviella 1956, 226). In Figure 13–3, an example from seventh-century Assyria shows a winged circle with a feathered tail.

FIGURE 13–2: A STAR OF DAVID SYMBOL FROM UXMAL, YUCATAN, MEXICO, ABOUT A.D. 1000.

FIGURE 13–3: WINGED CIRCLE WITH A FEATHERED TAIL FROM ASSYRIA ABOUT 800 B.C.

Altars and Incense Burners

Other interesting cultural parallels with religious significance are the altars and incense burners found on both hemispheres, each marked by four horns on the corners or sometimes by a profusion of horns in various patterns.

Bible readers are familiar with references to the horned altar: "And thou shalt take of the blood of the bullock; and put it upon the horns of the altar with thy finger" (Exodus 29:12). "Take of the blood of the bullock, and the blood of the goat, and put it upon the horns of the altar round about" (Leviticus 16:18). "And Adonijah feared because of Solomon, and arose, and went, and caught hold on the horns of the altar" (1 Kings 1:50).

Exodus 30:1 mentions the biblical altar of incense, in a sense a miniature or symbolic altar. What is the symbolism of the horns? The bull and cow, along with the serpent and felines, represented the life force of vitality and fruitfulness. In Egyptian art, the lower side of the horned cow is shown studded with stars, representing the Milky Way. It would be appropriate to apply such symbols of strength, power, and fertility to the altar used in approaching deity.

Sacred Mountains

An interesting passage from Isaiah reads:

> And it shall come to pass in the last days, that the mountain of the Lord's house shall be established in the top of the mountains, and shall be exalted above the hills; and all nations shall flow into it. And many people shall go and

say, Come ye, and let us go up to the mountain of the Lord,
to the house of the God of Jacob; and he will teach us of his
ways, and we will walk in his paths: for out of Zion shall
go forth the law, and the word of the Lord from Jerusalem.
(Isaiah 2:2–3)

When Abraham built his altar called *Bethel*, it was on top of
a mountain. Throughout southern Mexico and Guatemala, the
remains of ancient altars and shrines appear on mountain tops.

We have already mentioned the importance of the stepped
temple as a representation, both in the Old and the New Worlds,
of the sacred mountain. The Sumerians of the fourth millennium
before Christ used the terraced or staged temple tower. To this
the Zapotecs and Mixe of Yalalag in Oaxaca believe that the giver
of water and life is a water shepherd who lives in mountain springs.
Floods are, it is believed, caused by the water serpent, the great
river of the sky; and during storms, they claim to see the water
serpent emerging from the storm clouds.

Interestingly, in the Sumerian system, *Shakhura* ("waiting
room, antechamber") referred to the shrine or temple on top of
the temple tower, while the outer chamber before the "Holy of
Holies" on the ground-level temples at a later period in Sumer
were called by the same name.

These stepped temples have been documented as late as the
fifth century B.C. The Greek historian Herodotus tells of visiting
Babylon in the fifth century B.C., where he saw a temple tower
with seven stages, each painted a different color.

When comparisons are made between the temple towers
of Mesopotamia and those of Mesoamerica (Figure 13–4), some
striking similarities emerge. Both were usually laid out on the
points of the compass. Sun-dried adobe bricks were used in
both areas. For example, the temple at Ur (Figure 13–5), dating
from 2100 B.C. on the Euphrates, and the New World temple
towers at Cholula, Teotihuacan, Kaminaljuyu, and Chichen Itza
(Figure 13–6) are each a solid mass of sun-dried adobe
brickwork, all dating back to near the time of Christ. The
pyramid at Cholula is larger than any pyramid in Egypt,
measuring 1,132 feet at the base.

FIGURE 13–4: THE QUETZALCOATL PYRAMID OF CHOLULA, PUEBLA, MEXICO, IN
ALIGNMENT WITH MOUNT POPOCATEPETL. (PHOTO BY DANIEL BATES. COURTESY
DAVID A. PALMER AND THE SOCIETY FOR EARLY HISTORIC ARCHAEOLOGY.)

FIGURE 13–5: THE MOUNTAIN OF THE "HOUSE OF GOD" (OR ZIGGURAT) FROM
UR, SOUTHERN MESOPOTAMIA ABOUT 2100 B.C.

FIGURE 13–6: THE TEMPLE OF EL CASTILLO/KUKULCAN AT CHICHEN ITZA, YUCATAN, MEXICO, DATING FROM THE TENTH CENTURY A.D.

The Maya word for temple towers is *Ku*, the same word for God. *Hunab Ku* designated the Maya father-god of the universe. Thus, the concept of the temple as an artificial mountain made holy by the presence of God was also well known in the New World. Each of the four sides represents one of the cardinal directions. Sometimes each is painted a different color, representing the four directions (north, south, east, and west). A similar pattern of color-coding directions has been observed in pre-Christian Mesopotamia, Egypt, and China as well as in Mesoamerica (Kelley 1975, 7). Tozzer confirms that the linking of a color to each of the cardinal directions was customary for both Maya and Aztec (Tozzer 1941, 135). Alfonso Caso, noted for his important archaeological work at Monte Alban, confirms that the Aztecs assigned red to the east, black to the north, blue to the south, and white for the west (Caso 1958, 10).

Although these Mesoamerican structures are sometimes called pyramids, Joseph Lindon Smith, for one, observes that the Kaminaljuyu pyramid, which he made a special trip to see, had "not even a remote similarity" to the pyramids constructed by the Egyptian Pharaoh Cheops and his family. Instead, the Maya pyramid was "flat-topped and rectangular, only about sixty feet in height and made chiefly of adobe without a facing of stone." He found in it echoes of the Sumerian ziggurat (a stepped pyramid) (Smith 1956, 305). In 1949, Alberto Ruz of Merida, Yucatan, excavated the ruins of Palenque in Chiapas, discovering a secret stone stairway beneath the floor of the Temple of Inscriptions, which stands atop a pyramid. The stairway, blocked with stones, led into a secret burial chamber and tomb within the pyramid (Figure 13–7). In this burial chamber was a stone tomb vault. Hieroglyphics adorned the walls of this tomb, and a beautifully carved tree of life constituted the ornamentation on the tomb lid. In the tomb was a male (Pacal) wearing a wide collar of tubular beads in the form of a breastplate. The style is reminiscent of the typical Egyptian wide necklace. A full reconstruction of this pyramid tomb may now be seen in the National Museum in Mexico City. It seems persuasive to other observers, including us, that the ancient builders of this structure knew not only the ancient pyramid designs of Mesopotamia but also those of Egypt, for the stone stairway, the sealing of the passageway, the interior crypt, and the stone sarcophagus vault are a uniquely Egyptian combination.

FIGURE 13–7: CROSS-SECTION OF THE TEMPLE OF INSCRIPTIONS AT PALENQUE, CHIAPAS, MEXICO, SHOWING THE LOCATION OF PACAL'S TOMB.

We mention only seven temple towers dating back to Preclassic times that have been discovered: one at Teotihuacan near Mexico City, one at Cholula in Puebla, four more at Cuicuilco under a fall of volcanic lava on the southern outskirts of Mexico City that date to about the time of Christ by radiocarbon methods, and one at Uaxactun in Guatemala dating between 200 B.C. and A.D. 150 and ornamented with Olmec jaguar masks over white stucco. The temples on their summits have disappeared, and little is known of their design; but the Maya temples of the Classic era were designed with an interior corbeled vault consisting of stone slabs, each higher stone projecting farther into the room. This design originated in Mesopotamia (Frankfort 1955, 21) and was also used in Egypt, Syria, India, and Greece during the second and first millennia B.C.

The Cross

As we have mentioned elsewhere, another interesting artistic motif is the cross. The patee cross in Figure 13–8 shows an ancient solar symbol found among the Assyrians, Zapotecs, Teotihuacan, and Maya.

FIGURE 13–8: AN ASSYRIAN PATEE (MAYA KAN) CROSS FROM NINEVEH ABOUT 800 B.C.

This same distinctive shape is the glyph for the 260-day Tonalamatl in the calendar system dating to the first millennium B.C.

An interesting variation is the cross within a cross, a device that appears on a Babylonian seal of the first dynasty dated at about 2000 B.C. (Figure 13–9). It also appears in Hittite art dating to about 1500 B.C. (Ceram 1956, 86). Figure 13–10 appears on a vase in the Howard Leigh collection in the Frissel Museum at Mitla. A fourth example appears on a lintel in Cuilapan, Oaxaca, that dates from A.D. 400–950.

FIGURE 13–9: A CROSS WITHIN A CROSS FROM SOUTHERN MESOPOTAMIA ABOUT 2000 B.C.

FIGURE 13–10: A CROSS WITHIN A CROSS FROM MONTE ALBAN, OAXACA, MEXICO.

Ackerman, describing the cross of the Sumerians dating from the third millennium B.C., explains it as a cosmological and geographical symbol:

> Eventually in the *Enuma elish* . . . Tiamat [the Sumerian goddess associated with the Milky Way] in her turn is slain, and her hide is split in two and stretched across the heavens. The description is a bit confused, but a careful analysis indicates with reasonable probability that it was used to mark the celestial equator and meridian. The Milky Way is a rough equivalent of the equator and the meridian when it lies, respectively, East-West and North-South; hence the use of Tiamat's hide (or body) to define the imaginary lines. The equator-meridian cross (Four Quarters motif) is the most frequent seal-type in about the second quarter of the third millennium B.C." (Ackerman 1950, 14).

Calendars

The Mesoamerican calendars were extremely sophisticated. These people knew the exact time periods of the orbits of the five planets around the sun (visible to the eye) and how they aligned with each other at different times of the year as they interacted with the sun and the moon.

Calendars of high precision were based on many similar astronomical observations and calculations. In both the Near East and Mexico, the true solar year had been worked out to the sixth decimal point, 365.241987 days. In both lands, the exact time of the cycles around the sun of Mercury and Venus had been worked out—an achievement not accomplished in Europe until Kepler in the seventeenth century.

In May 1958, the Mexican scholar Raul Noriega, a man who was not afraid to examine carefully the relationships between the ancient Near East and Mesoamerica, was able to announce that he had deciphered numerous signs and glyphs of ancient Mexico hitherto imponderable and undeciphered. Noriega frankly states that he found the basic method of solving the riddle of Mesoamerican calendar and astronomical glyphs by studying the astronomy and mathematics of ancient Mesopotamia. His primary Near East source was *Tabletas Astronomicas Cuneiformes,* by O. Neugebauer.

Noriega shows that in both the Near East and in Mesoamerica, the ancients knew the time of the lunations of the moon, 29.53058857 days; of the cycles of Mercury, 115.8774 days; of Venus, 584 days; of Mars, 780 days; of Jupiter, 398.8846 days; and of Saturn, 378.0919 days. The ancients did not express the fractions of a day as accurately as we do today, but the ancients of both regions did use multiplication and division, working in high figures (Noriega 1958, 265–67).

The ancient Egyptians had a calendar with a year of 360 days plus five supplementary days, and the five supplementary days were regarded as unlucky. The ancient Maya had exactly the same system and also regarded the five supplementary days as unlucky.

Constellations representing the four directions and the solstices (the times of the year when the sun is farthest north and farthest south of the equator) and equinoxes (the two times of the year when the sun crosses the equator, making night and day of equal length in all parts of the earth, 21 March and 21 and 22 September) are identical to those of the early Israelites (Job 9:9). The ancients of Mexico and Guatemala (Figure 13–11) represented the four directions as follows: the Bear for the north, Orion for the south, Pleiades for the east, and Scorpion for the west (two of the four names having the same meaning).

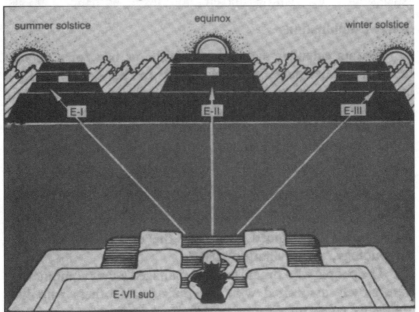

FIGURE 13–11: TEMPLE E-VII AT UAXACTUN, EL PETEN, GUATEMALA, DEPICTING THE OBSERVATION POINTS FOR THE SPRING AND AUTUMN EQUINOXES AND THE SUMMER AND WINTER SOLSTICES.

In ancient Egypt in the Middle Kingdom period, some references are made to the standard civil calendar. This calendar was twelve months of thirty days each. At the end of the twelfth month, the Egyptians added five more days, which brought the year to 365 days. That makes a striking parallel to a 360-day Mesoamerican calendar and also to the 365-day Mesoamerican calendar that lacks the leap-year accountability. The Maya called their 365-day calendar the *haab*. The Maya knew about the leap year, but ritually their system would not work the way they wanted it to work if they dealt with a leap year directly. These complex Maya calendars were studied and understood by the elite and the priests.

At the same time, the Maya used a lunar calendar that dealt with the agriculture cycle that had to use the leap year. The Maya knew that 1,508 years of 365 days is equivalent to 1,507 years of 365.2422 days with the leap year in it. The codices of Oaxaca illustrate the symbols of how the Maya account for this. An example is found in one codex from Coixtlahuaca, Oaxaca, where three of the solar leap-year cycles ended at A.D. 1412. This date takes one back to 3109 B.C., five years after the base data for the Maya Long Count calendar system. They started counting years forward from the base date year, 3114 B.C. So the Maya knew how to deal with the leap year when it was necessary; and it was, of course, necessary for agriculture.

The Maya appear to have received some information regarding the calendars from the Zapotecs (Moran and Kelley 1969, 163–64; Kaufman 1976, 112).

The Maya used this 360-day calendar year in the Long Count system right up to the arrival of the Spaniards in the 1500s.

The 360-day calendar year was prevalent in early Sumer/ Shinar of southern Mesopotamia. It appears that the 360-day calendar was also used by Noah:

> In the second month, the seventeenth day of the month, the same day were all the fountains of the great deep broken up, and the windows of heaven were opened.
>
> And the rain was upon the earth forty days and forty nights. . . .
>
> And the waters returned from off the earth continually: and after the end of the hundred and fifty days the waters were abated.

And the ark rested in the seventh month, on the seventeenth day of the month. (Genesis 7:11–12; 8:3–4)

These passages show that 150 days were exactly five months, which means that each month had thirty days. Twelve months of thirty days each is a 360-day calendar year.

The book of Numbers mentions that a day will be as a year in prophecy: "Even forty days, each day for a year, shall ye bear your iniquities, even forty years" (Numbers 14:34). Phrases like "seven times" or "three and a half times" occur in the Bible. In the book of Revelation, three and a half times turns out to be 1,260 days or 1,260 years. Thus, if 1,260 is divided by 3.5 (that is, three and a half times), the result is 360. So the length of one "time" is 360 days. In prophecy, these 360 days would equal 360 years.

Secret Combinations or Societies

Certain calendar days were fatalistic or bad for a person's birth date. The days were classified to be good, bad, or indifferent. If persons were born on a bad day, then no matter what they did, they could not overcome what they were destined to become.

The Long Count calendar was tied not only to astronomy but also with astrology and numerology. Lounsbury explains: "The power and use of Maya astronomy was to learn the habits of celestial powers so as to make predictable the hazards of living under their influence. . . . But in its interpretive edifice and its applications it pertained rather to the domain of astrology, demonology, and divination" (Lounsbury 1978, 804).

The people who organized and managed secret combinations were closely associated with the priests and others who were politically powerful. Secret combinations are made for gain and power. They were made by taking secret oaths and covenants and usually involved the murder of people who had something the secret combination wanted. Often, children who were not in line to inherit properties or political rule murdered their own family members to obtain power, properties, and wealth.

In many of the sophistications of the ancient calendars of Mesoamerica, the priests tried to find, through the mysteries of the planets, constellations, and their movements, the knowledge that allowed them to exercise predictive power over the people. These practices were all connected with astrology, demonology, and divination. Secret combinations used the calendars in devious ways. As more research is done with calendar systems, more evidence will probably be found showing that secret societies attempted to use the knowledge of astrology and demonology as a tool to exercise power over the local populations.

Comparable Locations

Harold Gladwin, an archaeologist from Santa Barbara, California, in his book *Men Out of Asia,* says of Old and New World parallels:

> If new faces turn up which refute your ideas, then you must obviously revise your hypothesis since you cannot change the facts, and, in this instance, we were soon confronted with the indisputable fact that many of the fundamental traits of high native American civilizations are not to be found in northeastern Asia, but are characteristic of southern Asia and the Near East. . . . The prototypes of culture traits in North America, north of Mexico, were almost exclusively confined [in the Old World] to China and northeastern Asia. The prototypes of those culture traits which are distinctive of Mexico, Central America, and the Andean region, can be traced exclusively to Polynesia, Melanesia, India, and the Near and Middle East. (Gladwin 1947, 178, 257–58)

Joseph Lindon Smith, who worked with art and archaeology for some of the world's great museums, spent time both in Egypt and in Mesoamerica. He observed:

> In Japan, China, and other Asiatic countries, there was nothing I saw that reminded me of the great Maya achievement in building in Yucatan, Honduras, and Guatemala. . . . Even in the temples of Angkor Wat and Angkor Thom, situated in the same kind of jungle surroundings, there were no similarities. It was in Egypt, of all countries, that I found striking features in common between the material cultures of the Maya and the Egyptians. In Egypt, the approach to a temple was through a series of great courts leading to enormous pylon gates. The idea of space in an approach to temples was carried out by the Maya with the same sense of majesty and space, and through similar great courts, but they used, instead of pylons, carved monoliths of incredible size. (Joseph Lindon Smith 1956, 300)

Nearly fifty years ago, Dr. Alfred Vincent Kidder, one of the foremost authorities on the archaeology of Mesoamerica, and Colonel Charles A. Lindberg made the first reconnaissance flights over Yucatan and Guatemala in search of ancient cities. Thereafter, as chief of Carnegie Institution's field program in Mesoamerica, Kidder spent the greater part of twenty years in directing excavations in the Maya area of southern Mexico, Guatemala, and Honduras.

Concerning the remains he helped uncover near the outskirts of Guatemala City, Kidder wrote in his 1946 Carnegie report that the culture is "on the level with, and extraordinarily like, those of our own cultural ancestors of the ancient Near East or Palestine." And the remains date as far back as several centuries before Christ.

The script of an ancient people is usually considered to be the most complex part of their civilization. It is also one of the best ways to identify a specific culture. In October 1957, Eduardo Martinez, a staff member of the New World Archaeological Foundation, excavated a cylinder seal at Chiapa de Corzo, Chiapas,

FIGURE 13–12: A CYLINDER SEAL FROM CHIAPA DE CORZO.

On 22 May 1958, a photograph of the impression of this seal was sent to Dr. William F. Albright, then an international authority on biblical languages and archaeology. Albright observed that the seal contained "several clearly recognizable Egyptian hieroglyphs." When he examined photographs of the impression on the seal, he observed that they resembled the seals of 3000 B.C. Mesopotamia in certain respects. This clay seal immediately sparked controversy. Rudolph Anthes, Egyptologist at the

University Museum in Philadelphia, pointed out the resemblance of the triangular glyph to the Egyptian hieroglyph meaning "given." However, additional examples would need to be found and studied before firm conclusions could be reached.

In the early 1960s, Pierre Agrinier gathered a six-hundred-word vocabulary from a Zapotec village in Oaxaca, Mexico. Swadesh found that 18 percent of these six hundred words appeared to be cognate with Hebrew. Because of this high relationship, linguists suggested that more research be done. This research was done under the direction of Morris Swadesh, a professor of linguistics at the National University of Mexico, who, before his death, was considered one of the top linguists in the world. Dr. Swadesh pioneered research on language families to reconstruct protolanguage vocabulary in the distant past. He also developed a special technique of language analysis that dates the separation of two languages in the same family (for example, Canaanite and Hebrew in the Semite language family). Swadesh possessed large data bases for the world languages and used computers in his analysis.

Concerning the fact that the language of one people would one day be brought together with the language of another, the Lord told Nephi:

> For behold, I shall speak unto the Jews and they shall write it; and I shall also speak unto the Nephites and they shall write it; and I shall also speak unto the other tribes of the house of Israel, which I have led away, and they shall write it; and I shall also speak unto all nations of the earth and they shall write it.
>
> And it shall come to pass that the Jews shall have the words of the Nephites, and the Nephites shall have the words of the Jews; and the Nephites and the Jews shall have the words of the lost tribes of Israel; and the lost tribes of Israel shall have the words of the Nephites and the Jews. And it shall come to pass that my people, which are of the house of Israel, shall be gathered home unto the lands of their possessions; and my word also shall be gathered in one. And I will show unto them that fight against my word and against my people, who are of the house of Israel, that I am God, and that I covenanted with Abraham that I would remember his seed forever. (2 Nephi 29:12–14)

The Abrahamic Covenant

In 1554 the native leaders of the ancient Guatemalan town of Totonicapan, under direct Spanish influence, recorded that their ancestors were descendants of Israel and that they were the sons of Abraham and Jacob. If we are to understand the significance of this statement, as well as why Jesus came to these people in ancient Mesoamerica, it may be helpful to understand more about Abraham and the House of Israel.

Abraham was a central character in the Old Testament. He was born about 2050 B.C. in Ur of the Chaldees in northern Mesopotamia. His name means "father of many nations," and he is the founder of the covenant lineage through which the Twelve Tribes of Israel sprang. Abraham begat Isaac, and Isaac begat Jacob, whose name God changed to Israel, which means "One who prevails with God" or "Let God prevail." It was Jacob, or Israel, who had the twelve sons whose descendants became the Twelve Tribes. The Jews are descendants of the tribe of Judah, one of Jacob or Israel's sons.

What made this family special was the covenant God made with Abraham. God commanded Abraham to sacrifice his only son, Isaac, whom he dearly loved. Abraham obeyed and had lifted the knife to slay his son when an angel of the Lord called to him:

> Lay not thine hand upon the lad, neither do thou anything unto him: for now I know that thou fearest God, seeing thou hast not withheld thy son, thine only son from me. . . .
>
> I will bless thee, and in multiplying I will multiply thy seed as the stars of the heaven, and as the sand which is upon the sea shore. . . .
>
> And in thy seed shall all the nations of the earth be blessed; because thou hast obeyed my voice." (Genesis 22:12, 17–18).

Among the promises was that Abraham's descendants would be entitled to all the blessings of the gospel, that Christ would come through his lineage, and that Abraham's posterity would receive certain lands as an eternal inheritance (Genesis 17; 22:15–18). These promises taken together are called the Abrahamic covenant. It was renewed with Isaac (Genesis 26:1–4) and again with Jacob (Genesis 28; 35:9–13; 48:3–4).

Being an heir to the Abrahamic covenant does not make someone a "chosen person," but it does give a responsibility to carry the gospel to all the peoples of the earth (Matthew 3:9). The Jews, for example, have faithfully preserved the instructions from God as found in the Torah, which includes the five books of Moses in the Old Testament.

In approximately 945 B.C., the Twelve Tribes were divided into two groups. The tribes of Judah and Benjamin, called *Judah*, had their capital at Jerusalem. The larger group, composed of ten tribes, was called *Israel*. They had their capital at Samaria. When both these groups failed to keep their part of the covenant, the Lord chose to punish them: "And the Lord said, I will remove Judah also out of my sight, as I have removed Israel, and will cast off this city Jerusalem which I have chosen, and the house of which I said, My name shall be there" (2 Kings 23:27). "I will not utterly destroy the house of Jacob, saith the Lord. For, lo, I will command, and I will sift the house of Israel among all nations, like a corn is sifted in a sieve, yet shall not the least grain fall upon the earth." (Amos 9:8–9)

The larger group soon went into apostasy and was eventually captured by the Assyrians and carried away captive into Assyria. Today they are referred to as the "ten lost tribes." When they are ready to obey the gospel, they will be gathered again:

> And it shall come to pass in that day, that the Lord shall set his hand again the second time to recover the remnant of his people, which shall be left, from Assyria, and from Egypt, and from Pathros, and from Cush, and from Elam, and from Shinar, and from Hamath, and from the islands of the sea.
>
> And he shall set up an ensign for the nations and shall assemble the outcasts of Israel, and gather together the dispersed of Judah from the four corners of the earth. (Isaiah 11:11–12)

The ancient Mesoamericans, knowing that they had descended from Jacob or Israel through his son Joseph and his grandson Manassah, concluded that they would be privy to the same promises and blessings.

Religious Parallels

As we have repeatedly pointed out, the Mexican historians of the sixteenth and seventeenth centuries provided voluminous information of a Messiah who died for all mankind. These histories parallel the Bible and Book of Mormon accounts of Christ.

More than five centuries before Jesus' birth in Palestine, Nephi declared: "And we talk of Christ, we rejoice in Christ, we preach of Christ, we prophesy of Christ, and we write according to our prophecies, that our children may know to what source they may look for a remission of their sins" (2 Nephi 29:13).

And nearly a thousand years later, Moroni added:

And then shall ye know that I have seen Jesus, and that he hath talked with me face to face, and that he told me in plain humility, even as a man telleth another in mine own language, concerning these things. (Ether 12:39)

And again I would exhort you that ye would come unto Christ, and lay hold upon every good gift, and touch not the evil gift, nor the unclean thing. . . .

Yea, come unto Christ, and be perfected in him, and deny yourselves of all ungodliness; and if ye shall deny yourselves of all ungodliness and love God with all your might, mind and strength, then is his grace sufficient for you, that by his grace ye may be perfect in Christ; and if by the grace of God ye are perfect in Christ, ye can in nowise deny the power of God.

And again, if ye by the grace of God are perfect in Christ, and deny not his power, then are ye sanctified in Christ by the grace of God, through the shedding of the blood of Christ, which is in the covenant of the Father unto the remission of your sins, that ye become holy, without spot. (Moroni 10:30, 32–33)

Notes to Chapter 13
Introduction to Comparative Lists of Cultural Traits Between Mesoamerica and the Near East

Atomic energy dating by radiocarbon determinations, a postwar achievement of infinite importance to archaeology, places the very high ancient culture of Mesoamerica in the second millennium before Christ. It appeared full blown, with agriculture, cities, ceramics, and textiles. Nothing primitive underlyies this culture from which it developed step by step.

If there were Israelites in Mesoamerica centuries before Christ was born, they should have left things behind. A list of religious and cultural traits common to both Mesoamerica and the Near East has been prepared. Many of the elements are uniquely shared by only those two cultures, while other elements are common to other societies also. This list includes Palestine and surrounding lands. Dr. W. F. Albright says:

> Situated between the two principal foci of ancient Eastern civilization, Egypt and Mesopotamia, Palestine drew continuously from both. Nearly all important elements of ancient Oriental material culture originated in one or the other of these lands, and inevitably spread from them through Syria and Palestine. The culture of Palestine was more or less mixed in all periods, containing Egyptian and Mesopotamian components as well as elements from other minor sources. Substantially, the same is true of the literature, learning, and religion of Syria and Palestine. Thus the people of Palestine became acquainted with all significant developments of ancient Eastern civilization. (Albright 1949, 253)

The more complex the element in the list, the less likely the chance of its being invented independently in Mesoamerica. The fewer elements found in Siberia, Alaska, Canada, and the United States, the less likely the probability of transfer by land.

Authorities cited can be identified by means of the bibliography at the end of this book.

Belief and Ritual Elements
A. Shared and significant

1. Books, with long strips of paper folded like a screen,

six inches wide (Thompson 1954, 169; Funk and Wagnalls
1936, 112)

2. Colors representing four quarters of the world

3. Creation story very similar among Genesis, Babylonians,
and the Maya (Kramer 1945, 12)

4. Cross as symbol of god of life (Ferguson 1958, 175ff.)

5. The game of Parcheesi (Sorenson 1971, 228, n. 3)

6. Pyramid burial of dignitaries (as at Palenque, Mexico)

7. Truncated pyramids ("mountains of God") (Sorenson
1971, 229)

8. Mythological monsters of sky and earth, including
celestial dragon (Sorenson 1971, 235)

9. Religious traditions of creation by God, first parents, great
flood, great tower and confusion of tongues, darkness
before creation (see Ferguson 1958, chap. 3)

10. Underworlds, one below the other (Thompson 1954,
226–27; Funk and Wagnalls 1936, 222)

11. Duality concept: good versus evil, an eternal struggle
(Morley 1946, 215; Thompson 1954, 227, 223, 250)

12. Astral worship (Funk and Wagnalls 1936, 83; Ferguson
1958, chap. 5)

13. Astrology (Thompson 1954, 138, 140, 249)

14. Astrology almanacs (Thompson 1954, 138)

15. Astronomy (Thompson 1954, 55, 70, 79; Funk and
Wagnalls 1936, 83)

16. Calendars of high precision based on similar
astronomical observations and calculations

17. Constellations representing the four directions, solstices,
and equinoxes

18. Zodiacal sequence (twelve symbols in the Old World,
thirteen in Mesoamerica—the scorpion and serpent being
common in both) (Morley 1946, 311; Aveni 1980, 199–204)

19. Venus cycles (Thompson 1954, 144)

20. Lime sizing of paper writing surfaces (Thompson 1954,
169; Funk and Wagnalls 1936, 716)

21. Lunar time count (Morley 1946, 306)

22. New Year renewal ceremonies (Vaillant 1944, 200; Frankfort 1948, 322)

23. Sacred "books of God" (Ferguson 1958, chap. 10)

24. Seven-day time cycle or week (Jakeman 1947, 4, 24; Thompson 1954, 144)

25. Signs for numerals and of relative value according to position (Thompson 1954, 155)

26. Poetic religious literature with typical Old Testament type antiphons (Thompson 1954, 170)

27. Incense burners and altars with horns projecting at the top or from four corners (Sorenson 1971, 231)

28. Incense burners, cone-shaped, with triangular windows (as seen in the Louvre and in Guatemala museums)

29. Circumcision, with stone knife used in the operation (Tozzer 1941, 114)

30. Flint blades with entwined serpent handle used in human sacrifice (Breasted 1948, Figure 9; Morley 1946, Figure 14)

31. Baptism, the ancient Maya term for it being *caput sihil,* meaning "to be born again," a biblical term for the same rite (Ferguson 1958, 156)

32. Serpent of seven heads—a symbol (Ahuucchhapat in Maya) (Ferguson 1958, 95)

33. Feline (leopard, jaguar, cat, etc.) thrones (as in Egypt and at Chichen Itza in Mexico)

34. Feline-skin garb for important priests in ceremonials (Ferguson 1958, 111)

35. Feline symbols (Ferguson 1958, 110)

36. Bearded men and gods (as found at La Venta, Mexico; Von Wuthenau, 1975 and Magleby 1979, 1–51)

37. Pot held by a deity with flowing streams coming out from it in opposite directions (Ferguson 1958, 180–81)

38. "S" glyph representing clouds and water in early Babylonia and in early art in Mexico (Ferguson 1958, 92)

39. Sacred bird, symbol of highest God, directly above sacred tree, in elaborate and identical ancient tree-of-life symbol (Ferguson 1958, 85)

40. Tree-of-life symbol, with sacred bird representing God, a priest on each of two sides of tree and facing tree, one with scepter, and the earth monster beneath the tree (Ferguson 1958, 175–82)

41. Belief that God would ultimately destroy the world by fire in the final age (Ferguson 1958, 41)

42. Double-headed eagle (or condor) (Ferguson 1958, 128)

43. Art style showing head in profile view, but the eye and upper torso of human body in full frontal position, in conventionalized, unrealistic Egyptian and Maya form (Ferguson 1958, 112)

44. "Bes" as a phallic symbol (Ferguson 1958, 77)

45. Earth monster, symbol of opposition and death (Thompson 1954, 220)

46. Eternity-of-time idea (Thompson 1954, 140; Isaiah 60:15; Deuteronomy 33.27)

47. Eye symbol—all-seeing eye of God, or eye of the sky (Morley 1946, 223)

48. Red, symbolic color: the color of Bee Crown in Egypt, the "Red Crown" (Deseret Crown); red the color of the Maya bee god of Mexico (Thompson 1954, 225)

49. Suffering for sin—concept that an individual suffers for his or her sins and society suffers for the general transgressions of its members (Tozzer 1941, 106; Bible)

50. Supreme being—creator God—and his Son (Thompson 1954, 232)

51. Totemism (symbols representing clans or lineages)

B. Shared and possibly significant

52. Blocking (with stones) of staircases leading to tombs within pyramids (as in Egypt and Palenque, Mexico)

53. Four corners of the earth, or four quarters of the world recognized (Ferguson 1958, 102)

54. Priesthood with temple rituals

55. Temples and religious structures dominant in architecture

56. Sky divided into a plurality of heavens in horizontal layers, one above the other (Thompson 1954, 225; Funk and Wagnalls 1936, 152) (part of No. 10 above)

57. Decimal system (indicated but not established beyond question in Mexico; Jakeman 1947, 3–4)

58. Hieroglyphs (Ferguson 1958, 22–24, 224)

59. Historical annals (Ferguson 1958, 136)

60. Mathematics (addition, subtraction, multiplication into high figures)

61. Paper or writing surface made from fiber of a tree, and also from plants, fiber pounded to cloth-like consistency and covered with thin lime sizing (Thompson 1954, 169; Funk and Wagnalls 1936, 716)

62. Parchment (Tozzer 1941, 78)

63. Sundials (Morley 1946, 144–46)

64. Sun worship and symbolism (Thompson 1954, 227; and as in Egypt)

65. Venus as Morning Star and Evening Star (Thompson 1954, 145)

66. Zero date of one aspect of Maya calendar as 3114 B.C. (GMT correlation); and dynastic dating in Egypt begins about 3100 B.C. (Regarding the zero concept, see Thompson 1954, 155, 158.)

67. Burials beneath floors of houses and urn or jar burials of infants (as found by New World Archaeological Foundation near Tehuantepec and as in Israel; Tozzer 1941, 131)

68. Burial of sacrificial victims beneath foundation of building upon its erection

69. Embalming, including removal of viscera (Mason 1957, 76, 221; Hayes 1958, 303, 320)

70. Shaft burial chambers (Ferguson 1958, 106; Peterson 1959, 292)

71. Burial of attendants with deceased dignitary, to accompany master to next world (Thompson 1954, 218; Funk and Wagnalls 1936, 118)

72. Red ocher, a mixture of hydrated oxide of iron with clay, used to cover body of deceased (Peterson 1959, 223; Frankfort 1955, 116; Mason 1957, 48, 58)

73. Ceramic incense burners covered with a white wash (exhibits from Iran in Louvre)

74. Feline decoration on incense-burning stands

75. Offerings of incense, food, blood, and flesh

76. Carved stelae (as found at Tikal, Guatemala, by Edwin Shook 1960, 29–35)

77. Fertility figurines (Ferguson 1958, 114)

78. Figurines of ceramic, of pregnant women and figurines with the eye pupils punctuated, also with small punched holes at corners of the mouth (Ferguson 1958, 56, 321)

79. Blood-letting (Thompson 1954, 60, 187, 189, 195, 248; Funk and Wagnalls 1936, 110)

80. Blood sacrifice (blood from sacrificial victim sprinkled over ritual area) (Leviticus 1:5; Thompson 1954, 249)

81. Flaying of sacrificial victim (Morley 1946, 237)

82. Sacrifice of doves and quail (Ferguson l958, 164)

83. Self-mutilation (Thompson 1954, 60; Funk and Wagnalls 1936, 118)

84. Slaying of sacrificial victims by pushing them from a height.

85. Holy water used in purification rite (Ferguson 1958, 108)

86. Libations (pouring wine or liquid on the ground or on a sacrifice), including use of wine in ceremony (Ferguson 1958, 108)

87. Aspergillum (a brush for sprinkling water) in sprinkling (Tozzer 1941, 323; Funk and Wagnalls 1936, 755)

88. Rain-inducing ritual

89. Crescent moon glyph

90. Eagle symbolism (Peterson 1954, 290)

91. Foreshortening in art (reducing or distorting a represented object to create a three-dimensional effect) (Thompson 1954, 173)

92. Fresco mural painting of life scenes (as at Chichen Itza, Bonampak, Teotihuacan)

93. Painting on stucco (as at Bonampak, Chichen Itza, Teotihuacan)

94. Morning star as a symbol of deity

95. Bird masks worn by priests (Ferguson 1958, 228)

96. Confession (Thompson 1954, 256)

97. Cylindrical altars (Ferguson 1958, 164)

98. Fasting, individual and community, including fasting for the dead (Thompson 1954, 60, 135–36, 189, 253)

99. Fleur-de-lis (Ferguson 1958, 83)

100. High headdresses designed to convey identification of the deity portrayed (as in Egypt and among the Maya)

101. Large fans in ceremonies (as at Bonampak, Mexico)

102. Phallic symbols (as at Chichen Itza, Mexico)

103. Rubber in Central America and frankincense in Arabia called "the blood" of the trees producing them

104. Sacred seer stones (Ferguson 1958, 235–36)

105. Sacred things uncontaminated by human touch.

106. Salt not eaten during periods of fasting (Thompson 1954, 60)

107. Scapegoat idea (Ferguson 1958, 162)

108. Small sweat rooms with steam apparatus

109. Transubstantiation (a change into another substance) concept.

110. Linguistic borrowing by Zapotec speakers located in Oaxaca, Mexico, from Semitic speakers (Agrinier 1969, 4–5; R. F. Smith ms.)

111. Compass-point orientation of buildings (as at Teotihuacan; Thompson 1954, 76)

112. Festivals at the end of certain periods of time (Ferguson 1958, 154)

113. Sarcophagus of stone used for royal burials (as at Palenque, Mexico)

114. Figurine cults (Peterson 1959, 262)

115. Human sacrifice (Ferguson 1958, 108)

116. Black magic (Tozzer 1941, 314; Ferguson 1958, 309)

117. Burnt offerings of all or parts of animals (Tozzer 1941, 114; Ferguson 1958, 164)

118. Divinations and black magic (Tozzer 1941, 314)

119. Omen days of good and bad luck (Thompson 1954, 139)

120. Gods in image of man (Ferguson 1958, chap. 7; Thompson 1954 264)

121. Perspective in art

122. Swastika or gama cross (Keleman 1956, Plate 193)

123. Childless women considered shameful

124. Continence or self-restraint in connection with certain occasions, particularly by priests (Thompson 1954, 60, 135, 238, 253)

125. Dancing, essentially in religious ritual (Thompson 1954, 257; Funk and Wagnalls 1936, 165)

126. Idolatry (Ferguson 1958, 45)

127. Marks worn to impersonate gods

128. Pottery vessels with life scenes painted on them (Thompson 1954, 177)

129. Religious pilgrimages (Thompson 1954, 114)

Special Elements

A. Shared and significant

1. Armies of ten thousand men per unit (Bible mentions such armies, as does the Book of Mormon and Bernal Diaz for Mexico)

2. Names of persons chosen according to day of birth or some special circumstance at birth (Funk and Wagnalls 1936, 605; Morley 1946, 464)

3. Parasol (umbrella) as token of rank

B. Shared and possibly significant

4. Civic centers (Ferguson 1958, 76; Teotihuacan, La Venta, and Chiapa de Corzo are examples)

5. Crested war helmets (Tozzer 1941, 122, 172)

6. Cupbearers.

7. Dowry payments by groom (Morley 1946, 188)

8. High priest elected from a certain lineage (Thompson 1954, 249; Funk and Wagnalls 1936, re "Priesthood")

9. Litters for carrying prestigious persons (Morley 1946, Plate 88; Thompson 1954, 218; Mason 1957, 74; Hayes 1953, 92, 122)

10. Moats, artificial—surrounding cities for defensive purposes, supplemented by walls (Ferguson 1958, 285)

11. Nose rings (Isaiah 3:21; Keleman 1956, Plate 215)

12. Palisades (to enclose with poles)

13. Quilted armor (Landa 121; Hunter and Ferguson 1950, 273–76)

14. Slings (Peterson 1959, 163)

15. Intentional deformation of the skull (Ferguson 1958, 273)

16. Modification of head shape of infants (Thompson 1954, 40)

17. Trepanation (highly technical surgical procedure on skull) Mason 1957, 223; Louvre Museum)

18. Tattooing and scarification (Mason 1957, 81; Tozzer 1941, 293)

19. Hornets used in warfare (Exodus 23:28; Deuteronomy 7:20; Peterson 1959, 163)

C. Shared but common to many societies

20. Genealogy records (Thompson 1954, 249)

21. Helmets for warriors (Ferguson 1958, 326, Exhibit 137; Vaillant 1941, 51)

22. Shields, including woven material (Peterson 1959, 163)

23. Short skirts for warriors

24. Slavery (Thompson 1954, 126,193, 221)

25. Spears (Ferguson 1958, 265)

26. Spouses selected by parents with consideration for preference of candidate for marriage (Thompson 1954, 211; Funk and Wagnalls 1936, 553)

27. Stabbing instruments (Ferguson 1958, 108, 265)

28. Walled or fenced fortified cities, with city gates (Ferguson 1958, 85; Peterson 1959, 293)

Political Elements

B. Shared and possibly significant

1. Finger rings of gold (Isaiah 3:1; Keleman 1956, Plate 228)

2. Crown of gold (Keleman 1956, Plates 220, 229)

C. Shared but common to many societies

3. Theocracy (Morley 1946, 163, 210; Mason 1957, 74)

4. Thrones (Thompson 1954, 58, 60, 70, 77, 89, 111)

Economic and Subsistence Elements

A. Shared and significant

1. Beekeeping and stingless bees. The word in early Egypt for bee DSRT (Deseret) was apparently known in Mesoamerica—and with the same meaning (Ferguson 1958, 250)

B. Shared and possibly significant

2. Beeswax (Thompson 1954, 262)

3. Bottle gourds, dried fruit shells used as bottles (any of a family of climbing plants bearing fleshy, many-seeded fruit) (Thompson 1954, 239; Ferguson 1958, 52)

4. Chickens

5. Coconuts (Ferguson 1958, 52)

6. Common beans (in Maya *bul,* Hebrew *pul)*

7. Cotton, of thirteen-chromosome variety (Ferguson 1958, 20–21)

8. Grain amaranths (any of several plants such as cockscomb and prince's feather)

9. Irrigation (Ferguson 1958, 273; F. Peterson, *Ancient Mexico* 45)

10. Lima beans (excavated by Edwin Shook, see Ferguson 1958, 263)

11. Pottery spindle whorls (Thompson 1954, 77, 88; Peterson 1959, 268; Proverbs 31:19)

12. Red dye (cochineal) obtained from the dried bodies of small plant lice (Thompson 1954, 159; Funk and Wagnalls 1936, 142)

13. Sweet potatoes (Ferguson 1958, 52)

14. Wild bees (Thompson 1954, 262; Funk and Wagnalls 1936, 273; Deuteronomy 32:13)

C. Shared but common to many societies

15. Agriculture, with cultivation (Thompson 1954, 160)

16. Fish catching by poisoning water with plant juices that stupefy fish—including the use, apparently, of poisons derived from plants from a common ancestor (in America, the plant was *Tephrosia toxicaria;* in southern Asia, it was *Tephrosia candida*)

17. Fishhooks (Thompson 1954, 185)

18. Maize (existence in the Old World is controversial)

19. Markets, including specialized markets.

20. Metates (hollowed out stone used to grind seeds and grain) (saddle querns)

21. Net fishing (Thompson 1954, 181)

22. Pearls (Thompson 1954, 69)

23. Eagles (Peterson 1959, 290)

Technological Elements

A. Shared and significant

1. Bottle-shaped, underground cisterns. A unique and striking cultural parallel between ancient Israel and Yucatan-Guatemala-Mexico is the peculiar bottle-shaped underground cistern for the storage of water during dry seasons. In 1934, Bible archaeologist

Nelson Glueck discovered seven such cisterns at the ruins of Sela, an ancient Bible community in Eastern Palestine. His diary reports the discovery as follows: "Difficult of approach, and commanding a wonderful view over Petra, the position . . . corroborates the biblical passages which refer to Seta as an inaccessible nest. On the flat top of the acropolis are seven pear-shaped cisterns filled with debris. The rainwater was led to them by channels cut in the rock surface" (Glueck 1935, 32).

In June 1955, Seta was again visited by an expedition of the American School of Oriental Research. William H. Morton reports on the cisterns as follows: "These cisterns are plastered throughout and bottle-shaped in outline, each having a small mouth about two feet in diameter, but rapidly expanding to a diameter of 8 to 10 feet. . . . Rockcut channels angling across the natural slope of the incline serve to divert surface rainwater into the cistern mouths" (Morton 1956, 32).

Reporting on the discovery of many of the underground bottle-shaped pits in Guatemala and Yucatan, Carnegie archaeologist A. Ledyard Smith says: "There is no doubt that in northern Yucatan, where paving and gutters have been found around the entrances and the walls were covered with plaster, in some cases bearing designs of water symbols, chultuns (bottle-shaped pits) served as cisterns." He describes one of the Central American pits as follows: "Cut out of living rock, it had a circular shaftlike entrance just large enough to admit a man. The neck of the entrance extended about 40 cm. above the natural rock and was built of small stones and marl with a collar at the top to receive a capstone. The entrance, cut through the hard limestone crust, led down to a small bottle-shaped chamber with a foothold cut in the east and west sides" (Smith 1950, 17, 48, 84–85)

O. G. Ricketson Jr. gives the diameter of the circular rooms as measuring up to 2.28 meters—that is, up to about 8 1/2 feet (Ricketson 1937, 123).

Edwin Shook and Michael D. Coe have each observed that these bottle-shaped cisterns were in use over a wide area of Mesoamerica during Preclassic times—i.e., before A.D. 250. Thus, we have a parallel with the Near East involving a highly technical thing—a bottle-shaped cistern for the storage of water, about eight feet in diameter, plastered, cut into living rock, with a small aperture, and with channels on the surface above to direct rainwater into the cistern. The experts say the chultuns may have also had other uses in the New World.

2. Breastplates worn by high priests, divided into twelve segments (Thompson 1954, Plate 19; Funk and Wagnalls 1936, 867)

3. Casting by lost wax process (Vaillant 1941, 147)

4. Cement, the principal ingredient being limestone raised to a temperature sufficiently hot to burn out the carbon, used for plaster, stucco and mortar in Egypt, the Near East, and Mesoamerica (as at Chiapa de Corzo and Teotihuacan, Mexico) (Peterson 1959, 282–83)

5. The cubit as unit of measurement from the elbow to the tip of the finger (demonstrated at Yagul by David Vincent 1958)

6. Dyeing designs on cloth and pottery by coating with removable wax on the parts not to be dyed, the batik method (Peterson 1959, 50, 255)

7. Purple dye obtained from shell ash by technical process (Morley 1946, 209; Thompson 1954, 159; Funk and Wagnalls 1936, 142)

8. Wheeled toys of pottery (Ferguson 1958, 103)

B. Shared and possibly significant

9. Turquoise mosaics (Hayes 1953, 307, Ferguson 1958:159)

10. Panpipes (syrinx) (Ferguson 1958, 288, Exhibit 133; Gladwin 1947, 273)

11. Battle trumpets, including conch-shells (Thompson 1954, 185)

12. Trumpets and carved trumpets or twisted trumpets and conch-shell trumpet (Thompson 1954, 185, 195, 200, 257, and Plate 17; Funk and Wagnalls 1936, 599)

13. Cylinder seals with identical designs (Ferguson 1958, 51)

14. Stamp seals (Ferguson 1958, 25)

15. Altars of unworked stones (as in Israel and at Cuicuilco, Mexico)

16. Alabaster or onyx vases (as in the National Museums of Mexico and Egypt)

17. Aqueducts (as at Palenque, Mexico) (Thompson 1954, 64)

18. Arch, both corbeled (a stepped arch) and true (one true arch has been found in Maya architecture)

19. Asphalt-surfaced walls

20. Avoiding the use of glaze, though known, in ceramic art.

21. Bas relief in stucco (as at Palenque, Mexico)

22. Beaten sheets of gold and silver and copper (as in Museum at Oaxaca, Mexico)

23. Bells of copper and bronze worn on ankles and wrists (Thompson 1954, 184)

24. Blast furnaces (Vaillant 1941, 148)

25. Blowgun (Thompson 1954, 124)

26. Boats with sails (Heyerdahl 1952, 514–620)

27. Bone carving and bone awls (Ferguson 1958, 205)

28. Boots or shoes with upturned toes (as at La Venta, Mexico) (Albright 1949, 211)

29. Brocade textiles (Thompson 1954, 180 and Figure 84)

30. Bronze (Thompson 1954, 184)

31. Caps peaked or pointed like nightcaps (Hunter and Ferguson 1950, 318)

32. Celts of copper (Thompson 1954, 184)

33. Ceramics decorated with groups of four or five wavy lines in red paint produced with multiple-brush applicator (as found at Chiapa de Corzo and other Preclassic sites)

34. Copper tubing (Thompson 1954, 21, 69; Peterson 1959, 27)

35. Damask (silk or linen material woven into elaborate patterns) (Morley 1946, 405–409)

36. Drain pipes of ceramic (Thompson 1954, 179)

37. Ear plugs (Ferguson 1958, 51, upper right)

38. Fez (Gladwin 1947, 270)

39. Filigree (ornamental work in gold or silver wire) work in metals

40. Games of chance with counting board (Vaillant 1941, 204)

41. Gauze weaving (Gladwin 1947, 12)

42. Iron-age processes (blast furnaces, smelting, and casting)

43. Iron pyrite mirrors and hematite (Thompson 1954, 21)

44. Jade carving *(Lapidary Journal* 14.4:296ff.)

45. Jewel boxes of shell (Thompson 1954, 185)

46. Kiln-fired bricks and kiln-made lime *(Southwestern Journal of Anthropology* 16:428–41)

47. Kilts (short, plaited petticoats worn by men) (Lloyd 1961, 237)

48. Lapis lazuli and jade, as symbolic sacred stones

49. Large double canoe with planks and superstructure and sails and rudder-oar (Heyerdahl 1952, 513ff.)

50. Lime plaster (as at Chiapa de Corzo, Mexico)

51. Maces (Morley 1946, l64; Mason 1957, 74; Hayes 1953, 12, 19, 24)

52. Masonry construction (all over Mesoamerica)

53. Mechanical stone thrower for use in war (Thompson 1954, 160)

54. Mirrors (Thompson 1954, 21, 183, 218)

55. Carved mother of pearl (Keleman 1956, 282)

56. Obsidian blades (see Mesopotamian exhibit, University of Pennsylvania Museum)

57. Oil lamps.

58. Pattern-burnishing decoration in ceramic art

59. Reservoirs lined with stone or cement (Thompson 1954, 25, 76)

60. Resist painting (a protective coating that resists the paint) of ceramics (Peterson 1959, 45)

61. Rubbing paint of a contrasting color into the incised or engraved patterns in ceramic art

62. Rudder-oar on boats (Heyerdahl 1952, 513ff.)

63. Sculptured sphinx images

64. Stone-lined water drains (as at Teotihuacan, Mexico)

65. Umbrella (Ferguson 1958, 228, lower right of Exhibit 109)

66. Unleavened bread (tortilla) (Funk and Wagnalls 1936, 272)

67. Wire or threads of gold in textiles (Exodus 39:3; Peterson 1959, 219)

68. Headrests (typical Egyptian-type headrests have been found in Mesoamerica)

69. Honey-wine (Funk and Wagnalls 1936, 274; Thompson 1954, 254; Tozzer 1941, 92)

70. Flint-edged swords (Gladwin 1947, 272)

C. Shared but common to many societies

71. Adobe bricks (as in truncated pyramids at Cholula, Mexico, and at Ur, Iraq)

72. Application of a coating or slip, usually of a contrasting color, to pottery surfaces (such as pottery found all over Mesoamerica)

73. Appliqué technique in ceramics (as seen in museums)

74. Arrowheads of metal

75. Awls (a pointed tool for making small holes in leather or wood) of bone (as in museums of Mexico)

76. Baked-clay tiles.

77. Bark cloth (Thompson 1954, 181, 191, 259)

78. Bichrome (two colors) painting of ceramics (Ferguson 1958, 50)

79. Bow, arrow, and quiver (Thompson 1954, 88, 124, 185)

80. Carved or sculptured clay vessels with human and animal heads and bodies (Ferguson 1958, 52)

81. Ceramic dishes, bowls, ollas, etc., of plain black, white, red, brown wares (as excavated from any Preclassic site in Mesoamerica)

82. Ceramic pots with unsupported spouts (Ferguson 1958, 50)

83. Ceramic storage jars (as seen in museums of many areas and Thompson 1954, 215)

84. Collars, broad and beaded, worn by dignitaries (Ferguson 1958, 112)

85. Elaborate city gates (Thompson 1954, 105)

86. Embossed or raised designs on pottery surfaces (Gladwin 1947, 134)

87. Fine wood carving (as at Tikal, Guatemala)

88. Flint blades, thin and leaf-shaped, made by pressure flaking (Thompson 1954, 182)

89. Flutes (Ferguson 1958, 288)

90. Herring-bone, incised designs on dishes.

91. Human features on pottery surfaces (Ferguson 1958, 51)

92. Incised patterns on sun-dried ceramic surfaces before baking (Peterson 1959, 255; Gladwin 1947, 134)

93. Iron oxide pigment (Morley 1947, 350)

94. Jewelry of metal, including rings, bracelets, necklaces (Morley 1947, 350)

95. Knitting (Mason 1957, 254 and Plate 50B)

96. Lapidary art (Thompson 1954, 182)

97. Large jars with four vertical handles

98. Maps (Peterson 1959, 27)

99. Metallurgy (Ferguson 1958, 20, 273)

100. Needles of bone (Thompson 1954, 187)

101. Pigments of iron oxide (red) and carbon (Morley 1947, 413)

102. Plaster floors (as at Teotihuacan, Chiapa de Corzo, etc.)

103. Plating with precious metals (Thompson 1954, 184)

104. Potter's wheel (Kluckholm's statement 1956, 53)

105. Pottery vessels covered with a plaster-like stucco (Ferguson 1958, 50, vessel in lower left corner of page)

106. Razors of obsidian and flint (Tozzer 1941, 94; Mesopotamian Exhibit, University of Pennsylvania Museum, museums of Mexico)

107. Red and black pottery with painted designs (Gladwin 1947, 134)

108. Red pottery ware with polished surfaces and black interiors—at 300 B.C. not known in northeastern Asia, but known in Palestine and Mesoamerica (Ferguson 1958, 50)

109. Reed mats (Thompson 1954, 215, 221; Funk and Wagnalls 1936, 100)

110. Roads, well engineered, of a baserock, surfaced with cement or with stones (Thompson 1954, 160; Keleman 1956, Plate 300)

111. Robes, long and with short sleeves (Ferguson 1958, 37)

112. Rope (Thompson 1954, 181)

113. Sandals (Thompson 1954, 221)

114. Stone foundations for dwellings (as at Teotihuacan)

115. Stucco masks on walls (Ferguson 1958, 101)

116. Stucco walls and floors (as at Teotihuacan, Chiapa de Corzo)

117. Tapestry (Thompson 1954, 181; Gladwin 1947, 181)

118. Tetrapod (four-legged) trays (Gladwin 1947, 135)

119. Textiles (turbans, Ferguson 1958, 326, Exhibit 136)

120. Tripod vessels (as seen in museums of Bible lands and Mesoamerica)

121. Tripod ceramic trays (Gladwin 1947, 135)

122. Tunics (Thompson 1954, 78; Vaillant 1941, 51)

123. Turbans (Ferguson 1958, 326)

124. Tweezers of metal (Thompson 1954, 185)

125. Twisted-strand ceramic handles for vessels

126. Vertical loom with ten or more working parts (Gladwin 1947, 217)

127. Wheel and axle principle known (not in use at time of Columbus—having disappeared) (Ferguson 1958, 104)

128. White pottery with painted designs (Gladwin 1947, 134)

129. Repoussé (raised relief by pounding from the inside) technique (Morley 1946, 432)

130. Plumb bobs (a pointed weight attached to a line dropping straight down, used by surveyors, carpenters, etc.) (Peterson 1957, 281)

Chapter 14

Afterward: Where Do We Go from Here?

Believers have marveled and nonbelievers have scoffed at Joseph Smith's claim that at the tender age of fourteen, in a grove of trees in upstate New York, he saw and heard God the Father present to him, by way of introduction, his Son Jesus Christ. The same marveling and scoffing have been true regarding Joseph's additional claim that the Book of Mormon, which he professed to have translated from ancient metal plates inscribed with an unknown form of Egyptian/Hebraic characters, is a true record from ancient Hebrew prophets about a coming Messiah-Redeemer—this same Jesus Christ whom young Joseph Smith was introduced to and who was known in the Old World as well as in the Americas.

Despite the scoffing and outright persecution of nonbelievers, Joseph himself always asserted the truthfulness of his vision and the literal existence of the ancient record he claimed he translated. More significantly, he was ever eager to compare his translation with the actual remnants of those ancient civilizations his translation described.

As has been pointed out earlier, in 1841, just eleven years after the Book of Mormon was published, Joseph Smith spoke of the book and travels of John Lloyd Stephens in Central America, Chiapas, and the Yucatan. Joseph Smith declared, "It would not be a bad plan to compare Mr. Stephens' ruined cities with those in the Book of Mormon: light cleaves to light, and facts are supported by facts. The truth injures no one" (*Times and Seasons*, 3:927).

For those to whom the truthfulness of the Book of Mormon has been revealed, there appear to be two separate ways they may serve the Lord and assist in building up his earthly kingdom—that is, two separate attitudes they should develop.

The first was revealed to Joseph Smith in behalf of his father before The Church of Jesus Christ of Latter-day Saints was organized: "Now behold a marvelous work is about to come forth among the children of men. Therefore, O ye that embark in the service of God, see that ye serve him with all your heart, might, mind and strength, that ye may stand blameless before God at the last day" (D&C 4).

The second attitude, or way to serve, concerns service to God and to others that goes beyond Church callings:

> For behold it is not meet that I should command in all things; for he that is compelled in all things, the same is a slothful and not a wise servant; wherefore he receiveth no reward.
>
> Verily I say, men should be anxiously engaged in a good cause, and do many things of their own free will, and bring to pass much righteousness;
>
> For the power is in them, wherein they are agents unto themselves. And inasmuch as men do good, they shall in nowise lose their reward. (D&C 58:26–28)

In the 1940s and 1950s, some remarkable individuals who had read the Book of Mormon and had responded to the spirit and motivation of church service felt moved upon to engage additionally in relevant service, particularly as pertaining to the ancients of Mesoamerica and the messages they might have left for us. Two of these men were Milton R. Hunter, an LDS Church General Authority, and M. Wells Jakeman, a Brigham Young University archaeology professor. Their initiatives contributed to Jakeman publications in 1945, 1949, 1952, 1953, and 1954.

A highly motivated lawyer, Thomas Stuart Ferguson, joined Milton R. Hunter in the publication in 1950 of *Ancient America and the Book of Mormon*. An FBI agent during World War II, Tom Ferguson had subsequently involved himself in exciting and inspiring Book of Mormon and archaeological studies, writings, and research and organizational promotions. Tom's boundless energies resulted in his publication of *Cumorah Where?* (1947), *Joseph Smith and American Archaeology* (March 1953), *One Fold and One Shepherd* (1958 and 1962), and *The Messiah in Ancient America* (1987), as well as the writing of many personal papers.

An "appraisal" before a professional archaeology group at Brigham Young University by Fred W. Nelson Jr. in 1983 touched high points of Tom's contributions, which are of special interest here. This appraisal is crowned by Tom's own testimony of the Book of Mormon: "The greatest witness to the truthfulness of the Book of Mormon is the book itself. But many are the external evidences that support it" (Warren and Ferguson 1987, 283).

Now that Thomas Stuart Ferguson has emerged as one of the greatest movers toward an understanding and acceptance of Jesus Christ as the Messiah-Redeemer of Mesoamerica and because his historical and documentary findings have established themselves as important supportive evidences, we may well consider his objective for all these activities. In the foreword to *The Messiah in Ancient America*, Paul R. Cheesman says: "In 1958, Thomas Stuart Ferguson published his book *One Fold and One Shepherd*. In his introduction, he outlines the purpose of his book: 'To shed some light upon the mysterious origins of these once-great and glorious Mesoamerican civilizations.' Ferguson suggests that part of the answer lies in the migrations recorded in the Book of Mormon."

A formally and legally organized institution, scientifically directed and substantially financed, was needed to archaeologically, historically, and scientifically research and report those migrations. As amply reported in Appendix A of *The Messiah in Ancient America,* Thomas Ferguson researched, promoted, negotiated, initially financed, and formalized "a new institution to be incorporated under the laws of California as the New World Archaeological Foundation" (NWAF). In February 1946, Tom Ferguson made his first trip to Mexico in the company of his good friend, J. Willard Marriott, who assisted Tom in the funding of the NWAF.

On 20 October 1952, the state of California officially acknowledged the incorporated status of the NWAF as a nonprofit, scientific, fact-finding body with Thomas Stuart Ferguson as president; Alfred V. Kidder, one of the leading Mesoamerican archaeologists in the world at that time, as first vice president; LDS General Authority Milton R. Hunter, vice president; and Scott H. Dunham, secretary treasurer. In addition to Thomas Stuart

Ferguson and LDS Apostles John A. Widtsoe and LeGrand Richards, there were four distinguished directors of the New World Archaeological Foundation. By 1 January 1961, these directors had succeeded in having the NWAF attached to and administered through Brigham Young University. Elder Howard W. Hunter of the Quorum of the Twelve Apostles served as chairman of the board.

Under this new system, the BYU-New World Archaeological Foundation became the sole source of funding for all LDS Church-sponsored archaeological fieldwork in Mesoamerica. The emphasis on gaining scholarly credibility occurred during the years of 1961 to 1975. In December of 1961, a major find occurred when a fragment was discovered that contained the oldest Maya Long Count calendar date system found in Mesoamerica until that time. (This discovery is especially significant in the later dating achievements of archaeologist Bruce Warren, long a fieldman of NWAF, a principal coauthor of *The Messiah in Ancient America,* and now a principal coauthor of the present volume.)

The following comments under "New World Archaeological Foundation" from President Howard W. Hunter's biography may bring to life, for some readers, some of the early days of this organization:

> The opportunity to learn about an entirely different type of history came to Elder Hunter on January 26, 1961, when he was appointed chairman of the advisory board for the New World Archaeological Foundation (NWAF), a professional research organization based at Brigham Young University and involved in archaeological work on Mesoamerica (southern Mexico and northern Central America).

> In the late 1940s a group of (LDS) Church members interested in the Book of Mormon as it might relate to archaeology was conducting studies in Mesoamerica in an effort to establish possible ties with sites mentioned in the Book of Mormon. One of them, Thomas Ferguson, developed contacts with prominent archaeologists at the Carnegie Institution and Harvard University on the need

for expanded research on civilizations in ancient America, and their support resulted in the organization of the NWAF. It was incorporated as a nonprofit organization in October 1952, with financing through individual LDS donors, though much of the fieldwork was done by non-LDS scholars.

Exploratory work was begun in 1953; then, with Church financing, large-scale excavation commenced in 1955 at a major site at Chiapa de Corzo in southern Mexico. Investigations later expanded to other areas of Mexico and to Guatemala. In March 1959 the BYU board of trustees approved incorporating NWAF within BYU, and two years later the name of the foundation was changed to BYU-New World Archaeological Foundation.

Elder Hunter took an active interest in the foundation, meeting often with board members and personally inspecting the archaeological sites two or three times a year. He also took a strong fatherly interest in the staff workers and their families. His expeditions, often combined with Church assignments, took him into primitive—at times even dangerous—areas, and he immersed himself in learning as much as possible about the ancient civilizations and artifacts.

Many entries in his journals, such as the following, illustrate the sense of adventure he received from this assignment:

> Pierre came to the motel before daybreak with six saddle horses. . . . We left before six o'clock for a ride up the mountain to see the ancient ruins of Tonala. The trail was very steep and rocky and we traveled five or six miles to an elevation of over 2,000 feet. The ruins consist of many walls, terraces and large structures overlooking the coastal plain and the Pacific Ocean. . . . It was one o'clock when we got back to the motel. This was a long time in the saddle for one who doesn't get more exercise than an office chair (12 December 1964).

> We went to Chiapa de Corzo . . . an extensive site of about 140 mounds dating from approximately 1000 B.C. to the Classic period. The large structure which we have restored was in use at the time of Christ. We returned to

Tuxtla Gutierrez, went to the laboratory, and discussed plans for digging in the sites of Izapa, Mirador and Chiapa de Corzo this coming year (14 December 1964).

Elder Hunter served as chairman of the foundation for some twenty-four years, and in all those years, he never tired of visiting archaeological sites. John Gardner, a physicist who taught at Brigham Young University, accompanied Elder Hunter on several of these trips. On occasion, Harold Brown was privileged to drive Elder Hunter to some of the important sites that were visited in connection with Elder Hunter's NWAF activities. Referring to these experiences, Harold says, "I was Elder Hunter's chauffeur as well as his close companion. With him, I experienced numerous insights and discoveries as we visited archaeological sites in parts of Mesoamerica. I very much enjoyed his comments about the sites. The following material from Elder Hunter's biography reflects the flavor of some of Elder Hunter's comments as we drove to and from archaeological sites":

> I have been here several times, but this famous site never ceases to be interesting. (Hunter 1994, 198–201) The 22-kilometer trip [by jeep] is over the worst road I have ever been on. For an hour we climbed over rocks and hills, through bush and canyons before arriving at the ancient Mayan site of Xcalumkin. . . . We went with the crew into the Mayan Indian Village of Cumpich. An Indian woman cooks for them in her hut, and they wanted us to have Sunday dinner: eggs, beans and tortillas. The hut has a dirt floor, and while we ate, cats, dogs, turkeys and pigs wandered in and out. I didn't mind that too much, but I didn't appreciate having the chickens fly on the table while we were eating (14 April 1968).

At El Mirador in Guatemala:

> They took us to some of the excavations and to the top of El Tigre, one of the highest of the temple mounds. On the way back we watched hundreds of spider monkeys swinging through the tops of the trees. The parrots and tucans were screeching and the whole jungle seemed to be alive. We kept a lookout for snakes. The rains earlier in the

month have driven them into the trees and several workers
on archaeological sites have died from their bites. We saw
three snakes on the trail. One was the deadly bushmaster,
one a coral, and the other we couldn't identify. About four
o'clock the howler monkeys came, yelping and howling in
the trees. . . . We had dinner in the mess tent—rice and beans.
Brother Bradford [Elder William R. Bradford of the First
Quorum of the Seventy] and I slept on top of sleeping bags
in a tent with net siding to keep out the mosquitos and bugs
of the jungle (8 March 1980). (Hunter 1994, 201)

According to one noted archaeologist, by 1967, the BYU-
New World Archaeological Foundation was recognized both in
Mexico and abroad as the most active and most respected non-
Mexican institution working in Mesoamerica.

Others who have been influenced throughout the years with
the Foundation's research include Bruce Warren, Gareth W. Lowe,
Hugh Nibley, Darrell J. Stoddard, and Joseph L. Allen, who is the
author of the excellent book *Exploring the Lands of the Book of
Mormon*. These and a host of others have learned for themselves
that the historical, geological, geographical, cultural, and especially
theological information contained in the Book of Mormon is further
substantiated every time a new Mesoamerican discovery is made.

Darrell Stoddard, a former archaeology student at Brigham
Young University and ardent student of the Book of Mormon,
related the following enlightening story about the Book of Mormon
in connection with Mesoamerica:

In about 1970 in Espanola, New Mexico, I met Tony
Shearer (a Native American author and lecturer of ancient
Mesoamerican civilizations). At that point in his life, he
was involved in giving Hispanics and Indian people a sense
of self-esteem by revealing to them their glorious past, i.e.,
the high cultures of Mesoamerica from which they came.
When he learned I was a Latter-day Saint (he was not), he
went into his bedroom and brought out a Book of Mormon
that he kept on the night stand by his bed.

He then related a fascinating incident which occurred
while he was at an archaeology site in Mexico with one of

Mexico's foremost archaeologists. He explained they had just unearthed a doorway to a Mayan temple. They discovered on the lintel over the doorway a sculpted figure of an old man with a long beard (long beards are not typical of American Indians). The archaeologist then turned to Shearer and exclaimed, "What will the Mormons do when they see this?"

Shearer added, "Archaeologists make fun of the Book of Mormon, while nearly everything they uncover confirms it. I keep the Book of Mormon next to my bed and read it almost daily. I take it with me to Mexico while studying archaeology and history there."

As has been shown, *New Evidences of Christ in Ancient America* describes many new discoveries from a variety of well-documented sources that, as Shearer states, "confirm" the Book of Mormon. These new discoveries are startling. The overwhelming evidences known today regarding this volume of ancient scripture are striking. New discoveries by archaeologists and other scholars are occurring at an ever-increasing rate.

Joseph Smith wrote, "It will be seen that the proof of Nephites and Lamanites dwelling on this continent, according to the account in the Book of Mormon, is developing itself in a more satisfactory way than the most sanguine [optimistic] believer in that revelation could have anticipated" (*Times and Seasons*, 3:921).

And the ancient Mesoamerican prophet Nephi added, "God sendeth more witnesses, and he proveth all his words. Behold, my soul delighteth in proving unto my people the truth of the coming of Christ" (2 Nephi 11:3–4).

And so we ask, were the goals of Thomas S. Ferguson in safe harbor at the time of his death in 1983? Did anyone have an adequate vision of the goals, as well as the motivation and means necessary, to carry on should substantially more need to be done? Proverbially, "Where there is no vision, the people perish" (Proverbs 29:18).

How fortunate that Tom's son Larry has the potential to carry on the work of his father. Larry's vision has led to a conviction that both the spiritual or revelatory and the archaeological research in Mesoamerica, as well as the publication aspects of NWAF, need not only be maintained but also given renewed impetus.

Together with Bruce Warren, Larry prepared and published *The Messiah in Ancient America* as a concrete step toward continuing his father's and others' goals. Response to the publication was gratifying as well as enthusiastic, but it was not the end.

Larry also saw the need for a specific revelatory understanding of the Messiah-Redeemer by both believers and an interested public—as well as the need for greater visibility of archaeological, historical, and documentary evidence and articles related to Christ and his mission.

Larry's father had talked for years about his vision of a world-class Book of Mormon museum that should be built in Utah. As a youth, Larry listened keenly to his father's comments—to the point that Larry has continued his father's goal and is now working toward the completion of a museum that will teach the world about the cultures of the high civilizations that lived in Mesoamerica during the Book of Mormon era from 2600 B.C.–A.D. 421 as well as the Native American cultures of North and South America after A.D. 421.

At one point, Larry conferred with Harold Brown about the possibility of the museum's being located in Mexico City. Harold had served in prominent LDS Church leadership roles in Mexico and had helped Paul Cheesman with BYU archaeological promotions based on archaeological findings in Mexico. As part of his own interests in Mesoamerica, Paul Cheesman had been independently exploring archaeological sites in southern Mexico for Brigham Young University. Because of Harold Brown's familiarity with the Mesoamerican area, his contact with Mexican government authorities, and his long friendship with Paul, Harold had helped Paul obtain authorizations for his explorations. As a result of their work together, Harold became a significant contributor to a movie about Paul's explorations.

After meeting with Harold, Larry decided that the museum should not be built in Mexico City. Larry later searched in Salt

Lake and Provo for a suitable site for the museum. By that time, Harold had returned to his home in Provo, where he began working with Larry in determining a possible location for the museum in Salt Lake City or Provo. Eventually, Larry appealed to his good friend Dan Clark, and sought Dan's advice as to where the museum should be built. After heartfelt prayer, Dan said he thought the museum should be built in St. George, Utah, a location that had never previously been considered.

Larry then asked the advice of Linda Sappington, who lives in St. George, as to where such a museum might best be located. She immediately responded, "At Anasazi Valley," in which Shela Wilson had purchased eighty acres. Shela had worked along with her late husband in building the Polynesian Cultural Center in Laie, Hawaii, and her vision is to develop a large Native American cultural center to teach the world through drama, archaeology, and entertainment and, of course, through the museum, about Christ's visits to America as described in the ancient record known as the Book of Mormon.

At Anasazi Valley are found four Anasazi ruins dating from A.D. 800–1200. In 1988 and 1989, Asa Nielsen supervised BYU's archaeological work there. At the beginning of that archaeological work, on 23 January 1988, the late Paul Cheesman invited Elder Vaughn J. Featherstone to a meeting at the site.

Elder Featherstone, who was at the time the president of the Utah South Area for the LDS Church, told those who had gathered that the previous night, while he had been reading in Ezekiel about the dry bones coming forth out of the earth (see Ezekiel 37), he had been given a strong feeling that he should dedicate the eighty acres for a museum. He then proceeded to do so.

In that dedicatory prayer, Elder Featherstone stated:

Holy Father, this day a great work commences; one that will bless hundreds, thousands, millions and even tens of millions in the generations ahead. . . . [We ask thee to] bless the museum, which will house many things, that great means will be brought to contribute things that will be part of a culture for this time and season. And, Holy Father, move upon those who have means, and artifacts—and other things that they will have at the museum—that they might also find it in their hearts to contribute much of which they have to make this again a place of learning, spiritual experiences, and growth. . . .

Holy Father, we dedicate . . . that it might prove to be a blessing to this part of the community, and to the Lamanites, and the Indians and to the generations of this whole world—world wide; that from all parts of the world, people will come and be impressed with the heritage of the Lamanite people who dwelt upon this land.

New Evidences of Christ in Ancient America has been written to enlighten readers about the traditions, cultures, and history of the peoples who lived anciently in the Americas—particularly in Mesoamerica—and to show how their lives were affected by the life and mission of the Lord Jesus Christ. As such, the book becomes another witness that the Book of Mormon is an actual ancient record detailing the word of God. The museum that is now in the initial planning stages will be a visual, educational, and living witness to the world of these same truths.

We hope you will want to become involved!

Appendix
SHAMANISM: TRADITIONS, FALSE DOCTRINES, AND THE PRIESTCRAFTS OF MEN— A MORE COMPLETE REVIEW

In all dispensations of time, when revealed truth came directly to the Lord's prophets, counterfeits to truth from the adversary also flourished. We will discuss the development of these sources of Messiah-Redeemer knowledge—false traditions, false doctrines, and intentional changes made as peoples have moved both physically and spiritually away from the true God and the influence of his living prophets. In these cases, the tendency has been to allegorize and attenuate or dilute such vital doctrines as the atonement and redemption, transforming them into what the Apostle Paul refers to as "the traditions of men" (Colossians 2:8).

What we are about to show are the counterfeits that are inspired by the adversary and that are created by men we call shamans, who are not living the commandments of Christ and so can know nothing of him. Therefore, such shamans use counterfeit means to receive revelation, and the revelation they receive is counterfeit. Nevertheless, in many cases, scholars who make in-depth studies of such shamanistic traditions have ingeniously traced their origins, evolution, and relationships to original sources and meanings. These are important to consider, for they are evidences of a "universal memory" of originally revealed and scripturally preserved witnesses of Christ. We will review these parallels, symbolisms, allegories, and elaborate traditions.

But remember, what we will be seeing is an emphasis of worshiping and deifying the creator's products as well as the neglect of the creator himself.

Shamanism

As we noted elsewhere, "Shamanism—the powerful psychological and spiritual process for recreating the Cosmos and turning death into life in all the dimensions of Reality—was the driving force behind every aspect of ancient Maya life" (Gillette 1997, 117).

What are shamans? "Shamans are specialists in ecstasy, a state of grace that allows them to move freely beyond the ordinary world—beyond death itself—to deal directly with gods, demons, ancestors, and other unseen but potent beings" (Freidel, Schele, and Parker 1993, 33). Shamans are "inspired, ecstatic, and charismatic individuals, male and female, with the power to control spirits, often by incarnating them, and able to make journeys out of the body, both to 'heaven' and 'hell'" (Bowker, 1997, 884). In other words, shamans are false prophets!

How are ecstatic states achieved by shamans? "The enducing of ecstatic states is accomplished in many ways, including exclusion of general sensory stimuli through drumming, concentration on a mirror, etc., and through tobacco, alcohol, and hallucinogens" (see M. J. Harner, ed., *Hallucinogens and Shamanism*, 1973). The spirits involved are not regarded as inherently either good or evil—the outcome depends on context and whether they are controlled (Bowker 1997, 884). A state of ecstacy is achieved when a shaman privately fasts, intensely meditates, trance dances, blood-lets, or uses hallucinogenic drugs such as alcohol, morning glory seeds, nicotine, peyote, toxic mushrooms, etc.

Let us journey into the mythical and magical world of the shamans to expose their methods and motives—to show that the underlying motives of shamanistic priestcrafts are to enhance the powers of the "priests" and to use their powers for pecuniary or other selfish gains.

Shamanistic Calendars

As we have pointed out in Chapter 2, basic to understanding Mesoamerican civilization in pre-Columbian times is knowing about those peoples' dependence on controlling the flow of events by means of several different calendars. We will briefly concern ourselves with just three of the many calendars of ancient Mesoamerica.

The shamanistic priests of Mesoamerica used the "Long Count" calendar to control events fatalistically on an astronomical or equinoctial precession level and also on the mythological level of ritual. The same shamanistic priests then used the "Sacred Almanac" calendar to further control the fates of all individuals by their birthdays as recorded in the "Sacred year" phenomenon, to rigidly keep these and other Mesoamerican calendars in continuous harmony through time.

Remember that the very accurate "Long Count" calendar was based on a count of days from a beginning event in the distant past—this event being the start to reorganizing the world following the chaos following the flood. The base date used in this book is 10 August 3114 B.C.

The calendar is made up of several units composed of multiples of twenty (with one exception to this rule). Our needs require that we use only five of these calendrical units. These are from small to large as follows: (1) *kin*, 0–19 days; (2) *winal*, eighteen 20-day periods (this *winal* unit is the one exception to the multiples of 20 rule); (3) *tun*, 20 possible periods of 360 days; (4) *katun*, 20 possible periods of 7,200 days; and (5) *baktun*, 20 possible periods of 144,000 days. Thus, all dates in this "Long Count" calendar will be an accumulation of days in the five positions mentioned above from the base date or beginning date of the calendar to the event being dated.

A second calendar was the "Sacred Almanac" calendar, which is made up of a cycle of 260 days. This Sacred Almanac calendar has twenty day signs and thirteen numbers. The permutation of these twenty days signs and the thirteen numbers gives a matrix or chart with 260 slots. Every person's birthday was recorded in the Sacred Almanac calendar. The 260 days do not fit any planetary orbit but may represent the amount of time between a woman's missing her first menstrual period until the birth of her baby.

The third calendar we must consider is the 365-day "Vague" Solar calendar. It is labeled "Vague" because the calendar does not account for the "leap-year" phenomenon. This calendar is composed of eighteen "months" of twenty days, which adds up to 360 *life* days. The eighteen months are followed by a short period of five *dead* days, which makes the "Vague" Solar year one of 365 days.

Once again, allow us to give you an example of how a date in the Gregorian calendar looks in these three calendars. The date we will illustrate is Thursday, 6 April 1 B.C. This date would be recorded on a monument or other artifact as follows: 7.17.17.17.13 1 Ben 6 Mak. Table 1 below shows the breakdown of this date in the three calendars.

Table 1

Long Count calendar:

Baktun:	7	x	144,000	=	1,008,000 days
Katun:	17	x	7,200	=	122,400 days
Tun:	17	x	360	=	6,120 days
Winal:	17	x	20	=	340 days
Kin:	13	x	1	=	13 days

1,136,873 days

(from the base date of 10 August 3114 B.C. to 6 April 1 B.C.)

Sacred Almanac calendar: 1 Ben
Vague Solar calendar:6 Mak

Further details of the "Long Count" calendar included the use of a 360-day year, a nine-day week, and a tradition of Five World Ages. The "Long Count" calendar was an innovation in the Late Olmec period of ancient Mesoamerica and, according to several Mesoamerican legends, an introduction from foreigners who arrived by ships from the east. We believe these foreigners were included with the Mulekites mentioned in the Book of Mormon. (Mosiah 25:2 and Helaman 6:10, 8:21). Undoubtedly, shamanistic priests were in the company of these foreigners.

The Early Olmec had shamanistic priests, but they had a Four World Age system and a seven-day planetary week. Their year was a 364-day year with a mechanism to adjust periodically for the "leap year."

World Man and World Tree

Before discussing the shamanistic Five World Age system, we need to consider the cultural trait of the World Man and the World Tree. This Mesoamerican shamanistic version of the World

Man-World Tree needs to be compared with the Mosaic prophetic tree of life and tree of the knowledge of good and evil.

We will start with a quotation from the book *The Shaman's Secret: The Lost Resurrection Teachings of the Ancient Maya*:

> This wondrous Tree [World Tree] had its roots in the Underworld. On the earth plane it shaped all time and space. Its topmost branches spread into the Overworld where they organized the space-time of the heavens and set the star fields in motion. In the Maya imagination this miraculous Tree manifested on earth as the giant ceiba. In the Underworld it appeared as the calabash—or cacao-tree. . . . The World Tree manifested in the night sky as the Milky Way in various forms, including the Crocodile Tree and the Canoe of Life and Death. . . . It was the pathway by which shamans, shaman-kings, and the dead could travel between the Underworld, the earth plane, and the Overworld, and it was the Xibal Be—the "Road of Awe"— along which Pacal is falling into the Underworld in his sarcophagus portrait. The World Tree was also First Father's body—the Cosmic Corn Plant, which the Maya call "First-Tree-Precious." (Gillette 1997, 34–35) (See Figure 1.)

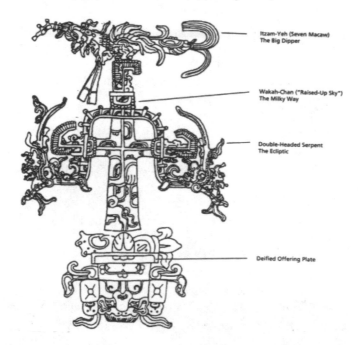

FIGURE 1: THE WORLD TREE FROM THE SARCOPHAGUS LID AT PALENQUE, CHIAPAS, MEXICO.

The reader will note that the World Tree shaped time and space on earth and in the heavens (including setting the star fields). This control of time was a function of the Long Count calendar with its dependence on a 360-day year and a nine-day week.

To better understand where this shamanistic World Tree fits best in the Mosaic creation tradition, we will consider the following scriptures:

> And I, the Lord God, planted the tree of life also in the midst of the garden, and also the tree of knowledge of good and evil. (Moses 3:9)

> But of the tree of the knowledge of good and evil, thou shalt not eat of it, nevertheless, thou mayest choose for thyself, for it is given unto thee; but, remember that I forbid it, for in the day thou eatest thereof thou shalt surely die. (Moses 3:17)

> And now the serpent was more subtle than any beast of the field which I, the Lord God, had made.

> And Satan put it into the heart of the serpent, (for he had drawn away many after him,) and he sought also to beguile Eve, for he knew not the mind of God, wherefore he sought to destroy the world.

> And he said unto the woman: Yea, hath God said—Ye shall not eat of every tree of the garden? (And he spake by the mouth of the serpent.)

> And the woman said unto the serpent: We may eat of the fruit of the trees of the garden;

> But of the fruit of the tree which thou beholdest in the midst of the garden, God hath said—Ye shall not eat of it, neither shall ye touch it, lest ye die.

> And the serpent said unto the woman: Ye shall not surely die;

> For God doth know that in the day ye eat thereof, then your eyes shall be opened, and ye shall be as gods, knowing good and evil.

> And when the woman saw that the tree was good for food, and that it became pleasant to the eyes, and a tree to be desired to make her wise, she took of the fruit thereof, and did eat, and also gave unto her husband with her, and he did eat. (Moses 4:5–12)

In the prophetic view of creation, the tree of life represents the love of God and Jesus the Christ, the Messiah-Redeemer. It represents spiritual life or eternal life in the presence of God the Eternal Father. It represents the gift of free agency and the gift of immortality or eternal life.

In the shamanistic view of creation, the main focus is on the World Tree of knowledge and the associated World Man. The World Tree represents the Milky Way, the planets, and the constellations. The World Man is the First Father of the ancient Maya traditions. The World Tree seems to parallel the tree of the knowledge of good and evil. There is a stress of fatalism in the World Tree symbolism, which is reinforced by the Long Count calendar, the Sacred Almanac calendar, etc. The hope of resurrection is proclaimed, but it is dependent on the individual's own efforts and blood sacrifice and human sacrifice. First Father, who identifies with the World Tree in death, becomes the Cosmic Corn Tree after his resurrection by his "Hero Twin" sons. The tree of the knowledge of good and evil is symbolic of the adversary.

Now we are ready to examine the Five World Age Model on its astronomical, mythological, and historical levels.

Shamanism and the Five World Age Model

The Five World Age Model consists of a belief system of organized knowledge about the world by way of a set of symbols and assumptions based on those symbols. The basic premise is that the spiritual force of every human experience encompasses the world and the cosmos and everything in them. The techniques of shamanism for this model are mind-altering drugs, trance dancing, sense observations, etc. The two ways of viewing the Divine Model of the Cosmos is first, a transcendent creator as revealed to prophets and seers by divine revelation; or second, a pervading creation everywhere present—for example, a mythical and magical world as perceived by shamans. Our manner of viewing this Divine Model of the Cosmos in this chapter is the second model of the mythical and magical world of the shamans.

Three Levels of the Five World Age Model

Table 2 shows how the three levels of the Five World Age model would be structured in the Olmec/Maya Long Count calendar system. These three levels as shown are the Equinoctial, Mythological, and Historical.

In the table is shown the probable date of the flood at the time of Noah, which was Monday, 6 October 3127 B.C.

The base date or day one of the Olmec/Maya Long Count calendar system is shown, which was Monday, 10 August 3114 B.C.

The probable date of the Jaredite destruction is shown as Sunday, 16 October 301 B.C. (Ether 15)

Also shown is the probable Nephite destruction date of Friday, 11 October A.D. 385 at the Hill Cumorah in the Book of Mormon. (Mormon 6)

Practical considerations imply that all three models were created no earlier than the fourth to third centuries B.C. The Long Count calendar is required for the Equinoctial and Mythological levels of the Five World Age Model. The third or Historical level relies on the typical Mesoamerican Vague solar year calendar (each year is 365 days in length) and the Calendar Round of fifty-two Vague solar years.

The best and most comprehensive study of Mesoamerican calendars is the recent publication of Munro Edmonson entitled *The Book of the Year: Middle American Calendrical Systems.* Edmonson places the beginning of the Long Count on 13 June 355 B.C. (Julian calendar) or 7 June 355 B.C. in the Gregorian calendar that is used today. (Edmonson 1988, 23, 118–20)

The first or Equinoctial Level is based on long-term observations of the constellation in view on the spring equinox. The observed constellation drifts westward because of the wobble in the earth's spinning on its axis. It usually takes over two thousand years for one constellation to pass by the spring equinox position and the next constellation to make its appearance at this observation point. The constellations make up the Solar Zodiac, and by the time all twelve constellations would have passed the spring equinox observation point, nearly twenty-six thousand years would have elapsed.

In the Long Count, this amount of time is twenty-six thousand *tun* years. Each *tun* or life year is 360 days in length. In terms of the tropical solar year of 365.2422 days, this Equinoctial Precession cycle would last 25,626.83 years.

Long count
Calendar System
Five Equinoctical Precessional Ages (each age lasts 5,200 tun years)

1.	Saturday	23 February	23615 B.C.	13.00.00.00.00	4 Ahaw 3 Kayab
	Wednesday	7 July	18490 B.C.	13.00.00.00.00	4 Ahaw 18 Keh
2.	Wednesday	7 July	18490 B.C.	13.00.00.00.00	4 Ahaw 18 Keh
	Sunday	16 November	13365 B.C.	13.00.00.00.00	4 Ahaw 13 Mol
3.	Sunday	16 November	13365 B.C.	13.00.00.00.00	4 Ahaw 13 Mol
	Thursday	29 March	8239 B.C.	13.00.00.00.00	4 Ahaw 8 Sotz
4.	Thursday	29 March	8239 B.C.	13.00.00.00.00	4 Ahaw 8 Sotz
	Monday	**6 October**	**3127 B.C.**	**12.19.06.17.09**	**6 Muluk 17 Wo (flood)**
	Monday	10 August	3114 B.C.	13.00.00.00.00	4 Ahaw 8 Kumku
5.	Monday	10 August	3114 B.C.	13.00.00.00.00	4 Ahaw 8 Kumku
	Friday	21 December	2012 A.D.	13.00.00.00.00	4 Ahaw 3 Kankin

Five Mythological Ages (each age lasts 1,040 tun years)

1.	Monday	10 August	3114 B.C.	13.00.00.00.00	4 Ahaw 8 Kumku—base dat
	Saturday	6 September	2089 B.C.	2.12.00.00.00	4 Ahaw 18 Mak
2.	Saturday	6 September	2089 B.C.	2.12.00.00.00	4 Ahaw 18 Mak
	Thursday	2 October	1064 B.C.	5.04.00.00.00	4 Ahaw 8 Chen
3.	Thursday	2 October	1064 B.C.	5.04.00.00.00	4 Ahaw 8 Chen
	Tuesd.	29 October	39 B.C.	7.16.00.00.00	4 Ahaw 18 Sotz
4.	Tuesday	29 October	39 B.C.	7.16.00.00.00	4 Ahaw 18 Sotz
	Monday	**31 May**	**973 A.D.**	**10.07.05.05.09**	**4 Muluk 12 Chen**
	(water destruction in the Aztec year 1 Calli)				
	Sunday	25 November	987 A.D.	10.08.00.00.00	4 Ahaw 13 Kumku
5.	Sunday	25 November	987 A.D.	10.08.00.00.00	4 Ahaw 13 Kumku
	Friday	21 December	2012 A.D.	13.00.00.00.00	4 Ahaw 3 Kankin

Five Historical Ages

Jaguar Stage:

Thursday	27 September	964 B.C.	5.09.01.07.19	6 Kawak 7 Yax
Sunday	**16 October**	**301 B.C.**	**7.02.14.02.14**	**4 Ix 2 Pop** (Jaguar

destruction in year 1 Acatl) (probably Jaredite final battle at Hill Ramah and Jaredite destruction)

Monday	16 April	288 B.C.	7.03.06.14.19	6 Kawak 7 Yax

Wind Stage:

Monday	16 April	288 B.C.	7.03.06.14.19	6 Kawak 7 Yax
Sunday	**5 July**	**76 A.D.**	**8.01.15.06.02**	**4 Ik 15 Kumku**

(wind destruction)

Monday	18 January	77 A.D.	8.01.15.15.19	6 Kawak 7 Yax

Rain (fiery) Stage:

Monday	18 January	77 A.D.	8.01.15.15.19	6 Kawak 7 Yax
Thursday	**24 June**	**385 A.D.**	**8.17.08.06.19**	**4 Kawak 7 Kankin** o
Friday	**11 October**	**385 A.D.**	**8.17.09.01.19**	**4 Kawak 2 Chen** (Fir

battle of Nephites at Hill Cumorah and Nephite destruction)

Friday	4 November	388 A.D.	8.17.12.03.19	6 Kawak 7 Yax

Water Stage:

Friday	4 November	388 A.D.	8.17.12.03.19	6 Kawak 7 Yax
Monday	**31 May**	**973 A.D.**	**10.07.05.05.09**	**4 Muluk 12 Chen**

(water destruction in year 1 Calli)

Wednesday	30 April	988 A.D.	10.08.00.07.17	5 Kaban 5 Mol

(origin of the Mixtec Tilantongo calendar)

Sunday	22 May	1064 A.D.	10.11.17.10.17	4 Kaban 5 Yax

(furnace ritual at Teotihuacan)

Tuesday	24 May	1064 A.D.	10.11.17.10.17	6 Kawak 7 Yax

Movement or Earthquake Stage:

Tuesday	24 May	1064 A.D.	10.11.17.10.17	6 Kawak 7 Yax
Sunday	1 June	1558 A.D.	11.16.18.14.16	3 Kib 14 Pax

(Fifth stage still underway)

The natural disaster connected with the ending of the fourth era was large-scale flooding. The combined information in the Maya codices *Paris* (pages 19–24) and *Dresden* (page 74) and the Maya colonial book from the town of Chumayel (Roys 1933, 118) would date this flooding to 6 October 3127 B.C. Immediately following this flooding, the darkness of chaos that lasted until the Maya "First Father" commenced to reorganize the Cosmos, and the base date of the Long Count calendar was put in place to keep an accurate account of succeeding happenings. (Freidel, Schele, and Parker 1993, 75–107) This Long Count base date is 10 August 3114 B.C.

The fifth and final era of the Equinoctial Precession model begins with the base date of the Long Count calendar—that is, 10 August 3114 B.C.—and will end 21 December A.D. 2012 on the winter solstice. Its main creative period is the *11 Ahaw Katun* of 20 *tun* years dating from 3074–3055 B.C. Forty years have passed from the beginning of the *Katun* of Creation.

The second Five World Age Model is the Mythological level. This model takes the last or fifth age of the Equinoctial Precession model of 5,200 *tun* years and creates this Mythological Model with each of its five ages lasting 1040 *tun* years or with all five ages the full 5200 *tun* years. The last or fifth age of this model apparently starts with a new calendar (Mixtec Tilantongo calendar in A.D. 988 [Edmonson 1988, 42, 131] and about forty years later is the creation *Katun 11 Ahaw* going from A.D. 1027–1047). Thus, both these Five Age models end their Fourth Era or Age with a new calendar that begins about forty years before the *Katun* of creation. This final age of this second model also ends on 21 December A.D. 2012.

The Historical level of the Five World Age model is based on the version as found in the *Leyenda de los Soles* (*Codice Chimalpopoca* 1975, 119–22). This account was written down in its present form on 22 May 1558 (Julian calendar). The dates are in the Aztec calendar. The figure of 2.513 years is projected back into the past and structured in the Historical Five Age model. The length of each age is stated in years equaling several calendar rounds of fifty-two years each—for example, 676, 364, 312, 676, etc.

The fourth age of this model ends with the same elements as the Second World Age model—that is, flooding, the same but more detailed ritual events with specific details centering on Teotihuacan, the huge archaeological site about thirty miles northeast of Mexico City. It is likely that the beginning of the Tilantongo calendar and the *11 Ahaw Katun* of 1027–1047 of creation match the previous Mythological World Age model for events ending the fourth age and beginning the fifth age. The fifth or final age was still in progress in A.D. 1558 when the *Leyenda de los Soles* account in the Codice *Chimalpopoca* was written.

The Shaman's View of Creation and the Beginning of the Fifth World Age

We now are ready to consider the Maya shaman's view of the events and processes for ending the fourth World Age and beginning the fifth and final World Age.

First Father (Hun Hunahpu, Highland Maya or Hun-Nal-Ye, Lowland Maya) was reborn 13 June 3122 B.C. (Schele and Freidel 1990, 246) He was born just after the "flood" and was considered as being of divine birth. He plays important roles in the creation story, which has many parallels with the Old World version based on the Great Goddess religion. (Gruener 1987, chaps. 8–21) This creation story is centered on planetary deities, decapitation rituals, divine kingship, and calendrical ties to a lunar zodiac (ancient Mesopotamia) and a solar zodiac in Egypt and later Mesopotamia also.

Nimrod and his son Gilgamesh in Mesopotamia and Osiris in Egypt have many astronomical and ritual connections with a creation story and the concept of "divine kingship" (Gruener 1987, chaps. 8–15).

The shaman's creation story begins with the dark chaos following the flood. The center spot of the Cosmos is made manifest with the appearance of a turtle in the constellation of Orion. Then, three hearth stones are located on the back of the turtle (Figures 2 and 3). Maya texts state that "On 4 Ahaw 8 Kumku [Monday 10 August 3114 B.C., 00.00.00.00.00, the base or beginning date of the Olmec-Maya Long Count calendar] was seen the first image of the turtle, the great god lord" (Freidel, Schele, and Parker 1993, 66).

ecliptic

sun

cords of heaven

three stones

turtle

FIGURE 2: THE THREE COSMIC HEARTH STONES FROM THE MAYA CODEX MADRID.

FIGURE 3: THE HERO TWINS' RESURRECTING OF THEIR FATHER, FIRST FATHER, AS THE MAIZE GOD.

Another Maya text from Stela C at Quirigua, Guatemala, adds the following information: "The Jaguar Paddler and the Stingray Paddler seated a stone. It happened at Na-Ho-Chan, the Jaguar throne-stone [Figure 4]. The Black-House-Red-God seated a stone. It happened at the Earth Partition, the Snake-throne-stone. Itzamna set the stone at the Waterlily-throne-stone" (Freidel, Schele, and Parker 1993, 66).

FIGURE 4: THE COSMIC JAGUAR THRONE AS ILLUSTRATED ON THE MAYA VASE OF THE SEVEN GODS.

Five hundred forty-two days later, the First Father entered the sky to set the World Tree/Milky Way upright or in a north-south direction in the sky. This action by First Father lifts the sky off the surface of the earth. He next sets up an eight-partitioned house in the northern sky (Thursday, 2 February 3112 B.C.).

The above introductory events of creation are only preliminary to the main focus of creation events in the Katun 11 Ahaw, the Katun of Creation (Tuesday, 13 January 3074 to Saturday, 30 September 3055 B.C.). Most of the events in this Katun are structured by the planet Venus.

As an introductory event to this Katun of Creation, First Father and his brother are playing the sacred ball game on the surface of the earth a few days before the appearance of Venus as the evening star (Saturday, 7 June 3075 B.C.). Their activity causes a disturbance for the Lords of Death in the Underworld of Xibalbe.

The Death Lords invite them to journey to the "Place of Freight" in the Underworld (Friday, 13 June 3075 B.C.) probably on the calendar date of 7 Kimi 19 Muwan. One of the main Lords of Death has the calendar name of 7 Kimi or Seven Death. The two visitors are tricked and put to death by the Lords of the Underworld. First Father is transported in a canoe to the place of creation after his death on Wednesday 21 March 3071 B.C. (Closs 1992, 140-42; *Codex Paris*, 4; Love 1994, between pp. 14–17; and Freidel, Schele, and Parker 1993, 89-90) Later, First Father's decapitated head is hung in a calabash tree in the Underworld ball-game court (Figure 5). The "head-in-the-tree" action is tied to the lunar tritos eclipse date (Kelley 1980, S32-S35) of Tuesday, 18 July 3061 B.C. (Figure 5).

FIGURE 5: FIRST FATHER'S (HUN HUNAHPU) HEAD HANGING IN A CALABASH TREE.

The head of Hun Hunahpu as an ear of mature maize, detail of a mural from Cacaxtla, Tlaxcala, Late Classic period. Although appearing in a Central Mexican mural, this is a clear representation of a Classic Maya god.

FIGURE 6: FIRST FATHER'S HEAD SHOWN AS AN EAR OF MAIZE.

While First Father's head was hanging in the calabash tree, a daughter of the Underworld Lord who was called Seven Death (Kelley 1980, S38) became impregnated with First Father's spittle. The "Hero Twins" were thus conceived in the constellation of Gemini or "Twins" (Freidel, Schele, and Parker 1993, 83). The Underworld Lord Seven Death is associated with the planet Jupiter. (Kelley 1980, S22-S23)

The woman (soon) flees to the surface of the earth to the house of First Father's mother. Here the "Hero Twins" were born and begin preparing themselves for vengeance against the Lords of Death in the Underworld. They become experts in playing the sacred ball game and eventually go to the Underworld to confront the Lords of Death (Gillette 1997, 86) and resurrect their father and uncle.

First Father is resurrected from the carapace of the turtle (constellation Orion) again at the center of the Cosmos. (Freidel, Schele, and Parker 1993, 66)

First Father's resurrection by his "Hero Twins" sons leads to his becoming the maize or corn god with the title of *Hun-Nal-Yeh*. In the highlands of Guatemala, the Quiche Maya in their sacred book, the *Popol Vuh*, call this deity *Jun junajpu* or One Hunahpu. (Tedlock 1996, 351)

One of the astronomical and astrological products of *Hun-Nal-Yeh's* creative efforts is the organization of the COSMOS. He creates a path (the ecliptic band) along which the sun, moon, planets, and many constellations travel on an annual basis. This ecliptic band was a lunar zodiac made up of 364 days—thirteen lunar months beginning with the new moon and containing twenty-eight days. Each lunar month had four weeks of seven days, and each day represented a planet. The ancient Maya considered the sun and moon as planets. Thus, the week of seven days was arranged with the planets Saturn, Sun, Moon, Mars, Mercury, Jupiter, and Venus in that order. Today, these days would be Saturday, Sunday, Monday, Tuesday, Wednesday, Thursday, and Friday.

This lunar zodiac was associated with a Four World Age system, which was later changed to a Five World Age system that added two more days to the week. These two new days represented First Father's "Hero Twin" sons—thus adding a nine-day week to the picture. Along with these changes was the development of a solar zodiac with only twelve signs or months. Both the lunar zodiac and the solar zodiac assumed the ecliptic path to be a circle of 360 degrees.

The ecliptic path was symbolized as a two-headed serpent or the Cosmic Monster with the heads of the "Hero Twins" on each end of the serpent or monster. (Gillette 1997, 40-42, 73, 98, 137-39, 195-96; Freidel, Schele, and Parker 1993, 73, 78, 100–1, 381) The Twin, Yax Balam, represented the front head, and the other Twin, Hun Ahaw, represented the rear head.

In the Maya area of Mesoamerica, the best evidence for the lunar zodiac is in the *Codex Paris* (pages 19-24). The best recent discussion of this lunar zodiac is the work of Bruce Love. (1994, 89-102; see also Freidel, Schele, and Parker 1993, 99-107)

The discussion of the shaman's version of creation in Mesoamerica should raise the question of similarities to this story in the Old World. A recent study by Helena Paterson of the *Celtic Lunar Zodiac* (1998) helps to clarify the operation of the lunar zodiac from one Old World region.

James C. Gruener's recent book, *The Olmec Riddle: An Inquiry into the Origin of Pre-Columbian Civilization*, throws new light on Old World cultural influences in ancient Mesoamerica. He concludes: "The peoples of Mesoamerica used a calendar to register the progress of creation and life. Its structure was the same as that of the Sumero-Babylonian calendar" (Gruener 1987, vii).

Sumero-Babylonian Tradition of Divine Kingship

The Epic of Gilgamesh (its earlier Sumerian version is from the third millennium B.C. and the more-complete, later Babylonian version is from the second millennium B.C.) is considered by Gruener (1987, 96) as the bible of Divine Kingship in the Great Goddess religion (see also Heidel 1946).

In the *Epic*, the creation story begins in chaos (the Sumerian version says the "Land of the Living," whereas the Babylonian version says the "World of Nonexistence"). The Deity Enkidu is the new moon and begins organizing seven units that represent seven planets—that is, Saturn, Sun, Moon, Mars, Mercury, Jupiter, and Venus. In doing so, he becomes a "World Man" by representing each planet as he journeys along a path in the solar system that becomes the lunar zodiac.

When Enkidu dies as the "World Man" of the World of nonexistence, then Gilgamesh is born as Mercury in the Underworld and carries both the moon and the sun through the lunar zodiac path. Gilgamesh also becomes the "World Man" representing each of the seven planets in the Underworld.

When Gilgamesh dies in the Underworld as the "World Man," then the world of the earth's surface gives birth to the seven deities and the lunar-solar calendar of seven-day weeks. The seven-day weeks combine into a month of four weeks or a twenty-eight-day lunar month. Each lunar month begins with the new moon. In the course of the lunar-solar year, there are thirteen new moons, which create a year of 364 days. However, each year is short one day for a Vague solar year. It is believed that this problem was solved when an additional week at the end of each seven years of time was added.

New evidence from the archaeological site of Ebla in northern Syria confirms the importance of the seven-year cycle. Each Eblaite king was allowed to rule for seven years. (Pettinato 1981, 4, 74) The Ebla kings recorded in the large find of written tablets from Ebla all date to the third millennium B.C.

In the third millennium B.C., the creation story was recounted in seven stages, but during the second millennium B.C., the Babylonians changed the creation story to five stages or a Five World Age system. This latter Five World Age system diffused throughout the area of Indo-European-speaking peoples—examples being the Hittites, the early second millennium Greeks, and the Indo-Aryans (for example., the Sanskrit script in the Indus Valley and northern India).

Two Time Levels

It is believed that there were two different time levels for the diffusion of the shamanistic creation story—a third millennium B.C. level with the seven-day week and seven stages in the creation story and a later diffusion of the Five World Age creation story with a 360-day life year that ended in five additional days wherein the planetary deities all die and are resurrected on New Year's Day. This Five World Age version of creation used a nine-day week by starting the week with the Sun and ending the week by having Saturn divide into three parts or days. (Gruener 1987, chap. 15)

We have a lot more information on the Five World Age version of creation with its nine-day week because in both the Old World and the New World, it was more recent and there are more written documents available for study. The discussion above has followed the Five World Age version because we have more information, but future research should separate the two different time levels of sociocultural diffusion. This separation of the two levels of diffusion will have to await a future book.

For the present, we suggest that the Sumerian deities of Enkidu, Gilgamesh, and Dumuzi have many parallels with the "triad of gods" recorded at the Maya site of Palenque and are reborn or resurrected in the year 2360 B.C. (Kelley 1965, 93-134)

Shared Cultural Traits

Several cultural traits are shared between the *Epic of Gilgamesh* and the Maya shamanistic creation story. Some examples are the creation following a flood that leaves everything in chaos or darkness, decapitation rituals that have human heads representing the sun, heart sacrifice that is ritualized, canoes and/or ferry men that transport the main creative deity to proper location in the cosmos, zodiac constellations that form a circuit in the underworld, and a "World Man" who represents the seven deities of the week. (Gruener 1987, 7)

Egyptian Influence on the Shamanistic Creation Story

In 1994, Robert Bauval and Adrian G. Gilbert published the book *The Orion Mystery* in which they demonstrated that the pyramids at Giza were aligned with the Orion constellation, Sirius, and Ursa Major. The Egyptian god Osiris was directly tied to the constellation Orion—specifically the star Alnitak of Orion's belt (Figures 7 and 8).

FIGURE 7: THE EGYPTIAN GREAT PYRAMID OF GIZA IN ALIGNMENT WITH THE STAR ALNITAK OF ORION'S BELT AND THE GOD OSIRIS.

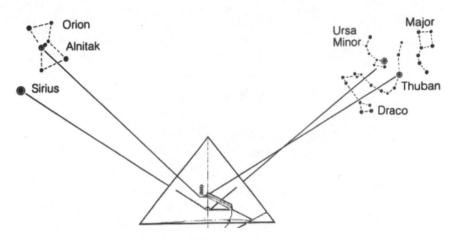

FIGURE 8: DETAILS OF THE GREAT PYRAMID'S SHAFT ALIGNMENT WITH THE STAR ALNITAK.

Diane E. Wirth wrote a paper in 1995 titled "Osiris and Hun Hunahpu" in which she discussed the detailed parallels between Osiris, the Egyptian god, and Hun Hunahpu, the Maya deity. Her Table I categorizes ten different complexes of cultural traits shared by Osiris and Hun Hunahpu and their associated companions and enemies. Wirth's paper makes a strong case for Egyptian cultural influence on the Maya and indeed on the Mesoamerican shamanistic creation story that resulted in the founding of the Fifth World Age discussed above.

Cultural Traits That Fit the Shaman's Model of Creation—the Serpent and the Milky Way

The serpent was a symbol of the Creator-God-of-Life at the very dawn of religion in Mesopotamia and Egypt. The ideas behind the symbol have been explained recently as a result of discoveries in Mesopotamian and Egyptian archaeology and inscriptions. The identical significance and meaning were attached to the serpent symbol in ancient Mesoamerica.

The body of a living serpent is never straight. It curves and undulates, as do all rivers and streams. The serpent was a logical likeness and symbol of the river. The river was the very basis of civilization in both Mesopotamia and Egypt—the very source of life. Water for the rivers came from the sky in the form of rain. And there was a great river in the sky (the source of rain) that could be seen at night—the wonderful and beautiful Milky Way. It was observed to curve and undulate across the sky as the Euphrates and the Nile curved through the river valleys. From the Milky Way came the source of life—rain water, for the rivers of the earth. The Milky Way came from the Creator-God, and the stars were regarded as the creative water or seed of God, the source of life.

The thinking of the ancients took them from the serpent back to the Creator in a series of logical, symbolic steps. The serpent = the river = the Milky Way = the source of water = source of life = Creator. Thus, the serpent equaled the Creator in the symbolism of the early Sumerians and Egyptians.

The serpent had been used as a life-creator symbol in Mesopotamia a thousand years before Abraham left his home at Ur. The serpent had been a life-creator symbol in Egypt for two thousand years before Moses lived there. It was one of the earliest symbols of deity used by civilized people and was a part of the sacred symbolism of earliest Israel and the entire Near East.

In Mesopotamia, the chief of all gods was *Apsu;* and his spouse, the mother goddess, was known as *Tiamat.* The latter was known as "Mother River," regarded as the "River of Heaven," the Milky Way. The serpent was regarded as a synonym for *Tiamat.* Exactly the same concepts existed in Egypt, having probably been transferred there from Mesopotamia. In Egypt, the sky goddess, *Nut,* is the same deity as *Tiamat.* She is symbolized by a band or river of stars representing the Milky Way. In one ancient Egyptian work of art, the band of stars representing the Sky Goddess is shown undulating across the underside of a milk cow (Milky Way), itself a symbol of life.

Serpents in the Sky

The top Babylonian creator deities, *Apsu* and his wife *Tiamat,* were the parents of twins, *Lahmu* and *Lahumu,* according to the traditions. Each of these twins was regarded as a god, and each was represented by a serpent. In the symbolism, a pair of serpents issued from the creator god and goddess. The Milky Way was deemed to issue from the creator god. There is a break or gap in the Milky Way, so it was regarded as twin rivers of the sky, going out from the Creator god. *Enki,* Babylonian "lord of the watery deep," is shown in the ancient art as holding a vase, out of which flows the Milky Way in the form of two undulating, serpent-like streams. This is shown in Figures 9 to 15. It is noted that the flowing vase is to be found in Mesoamerica.

FIGURE 9: FLOWING VASE IN THE HANDS OF A GODDESS FROM ANCIENT MESOPOTAMIA.

FIGURE 10: FLOWING VASES IN THE HANDS OF A KING FROM LAGASH, IRAQ.

FIGURE 11: FLOWING VASE IN THE HANDS OF A GODDESS ABOUT 2400 B.C. FROM ANCIENT MESOPOTAMIA.

FIGURE 12: FLOWING VASE FROM UR IN ANCIENT MESOPOTAMIA ABOUT 2000 B.C.

FIGURE 13: KING GUDEA HOLDING THE SYMBOLIC FLOWING VASE (ABOUT 2100 B.C.).

FIGURE 14: ZAPOTEC URN FROM ANCIENT OAXACA, MEXICO, WITH A PERSONAGE HOLDING A FLOWING VASE.

FIGURE 15: A PERSONAGE HOLDING A FLOWING VASE FROM A ZAPOTEC URN FROM ANCIENT OAXACA, MEXICO.

Figure 16 shows a beautiful serpent symbol found at La Venta, Mexico, in 1955. See also Figures 17 and 18 from La Venta, which have the earmarks of ancient Mesopotamia. In early Egyptian art, twin serpents undulate outwardly and down from the sun-disc (symbol of the creator god), just as the streams undulate downward from the flowing vases of Mexico and Mesopotamia.

FIGURE 16: LARGE FEATHERED SERPENT WITH PRIEST AND BUCKET CARVED ON MONUMENT 19 AT THE OLMEC SITE OF LA VENTA, TABASCO, MEXICO (SIXTH CENTURY B.C.). (PHOTO BY DANIEL BATES. COURTESY DAVID A. PALMER AND THE SOCIETY FOR EARLY HISTORIC ARCHAEOLOGY.)

FIGURE 17: ALTAR AT LA VENTA, TABASCO, MEXICO, SHOWING THE LIFE AND
BIRTH SYMBOL AT THE HEAD OF A SERPENT (ABOUT THE EIGHTH CENTURY B.C.).
NOTE THE PRESENCE OF THOMAS STUART FERGUSON.

FIGURE 18: CLOSEUP VIEW OF THE LIFE-BIRTH SYMBOL ON ALTAR 4 AT LA VENTA,
TABASCO, MEXICO.

Serpents Adorn Egyptian Crowns

The sacred serpent appeared on the front and center of the headdress or crown of the ancient Egyptian rulers. It was a symbol of the God of Life—a representation of the idea of life force and immortality. A beautiful, tall Maya crown dates to the sixth century A.D.; on the front and center of it is the head of a serpent, in exactly the position of the Egyptian Uraeus. The crown was found by the Mexican archaeologist Alberto Ruz, at Palenque in the state of Chiapas, Mexico, in 1952. Thompson shows the crown in *The Rise and Fall of Maya Civilization* (1954, 252). In the same tomb was found the beautifully executed tree of life mentioned earlier (Figure 19).

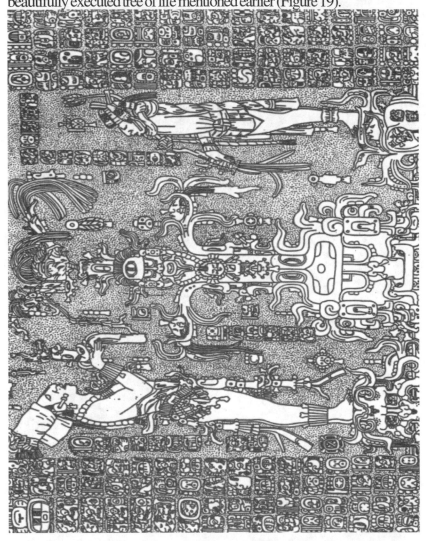

FIGURE 19: TABLET OF THE FOLIATED CROSS FROM PALENQUE, CHIAPAS, MEXICO. THE CARVING DATES FROM A.D. 692. NOTE THE HUMAN HEADS IN THE LEAVES OF THE MAIZE TREE REPRESENTING BIRTH. (COURTESY OF LINDA SCHELE.)

Moses' Fiery Serpent on a Pole

Moses chose wisely when he selected the serpent with which to illustrate a main point in his speech to the Israelites when he was trying to inspire them during the hard days in the wilderness:

> And the people spake against God, and against Moses, Wherefore have ye brought us up out of Egypt to die in the wilderness? for there is no bread, neither is there any water; and our soul loatheth this light bread.
>
> And the Lord sent fiery serpents among the people, and they bit the people; and much people of Israel died.
>
> Therefore the people came to Moses, and said, We have sinned, for we have spoken against the Lord, and against thee; pray unto the Lord, that he take away the serpents from us. And Moses prayed for the people.
>
> And the Lord said unto Moses, **Make thee a fiery serpent,** and set it upon a pole: and it shall come to pass, that every one that is bitten, when he looketh upon it, shall live.
>
> And Moses made a serpent of brass, and put it upon a pole, and it came to pass, that if a serpent had bitten any man, when he beheld the serpent of brass, he lived.
>
> And the children of Israel set forward, and pitched in Oboth. (Numbers 21:5–10, emphasis added)

Moses' point was simply that the serpent was a symbol of the Messiah-Redeemer who would come and be raised up on the cross so that eternal life might be given—if men and women would only believe. It is obvious that the brass serpent had no real intrinsic power. God was merely teaching Israel to look to him for life and protection and hope—hope for eternal life. The people had but to have faith in the word of Moses—the word of God—to live. They had but to believe him, as symbolized by the serpent, and cast their eyes on the brass serpent Moses raised up before them as a symbol of the Life Power of God. Doubtless many did not look because they did not believe they would be healed according to the promise of Moses. They perished.

John goes on to say: "And this is the condemnation, that light is come into the world, and men loved darkness rather than light, because their deeds were evil. For every one that doeth evil hateth the light, neither cometh to the light, lest his deeds should be reproved" (John 3:19–20).

That the serpent symbol of Moses represented the Creator-Messiah is borne out by curious language in the Babylonian *Enuma elish* of 2000 B.C.: "Gathered in council they [the Gods] plan the attack. Mother Huber [Tiamat-Mother River-Sky Serpent]—Creator of all forms—adds irresistible weapons, has borne monster serpents . . . so that whoever looks upon them [serpents] shall perish with fear, and they, with bodies raised, will not turn back their breast" (Jacobsen 1946, 175–76).

Thus, Moses, in 1422 B.C. (Long chronology), was not coming up with anything new when he raised up the serpent and told Israel to look upon it with faith and live and be raised up from the dead. The *Enuma elish* goes back at least six hundred years before Moses. The same serpent-life-God symbolism goes back to the dawn of civilization.

Jesus Compared Himself to the Serpent

Jesus also made reference to the serpent as the symbol of life and resurrection:

> And as Moses lifted up the serpent in the wilderness, even so must the Son of man be lifted up:
>
> That whosoever believeth in him should not perish, but have eternal life.
>
> For God so loved the world, that he gave his only begotten Son, that whosoever believeth in him should not perish, but have everlasting life.
>
> For God sent not his Son into the world to condemn the world; but that the world through him might be saved. (John 3:14–17)

A brass or bronze serpent on a pole or beam was maintained as a representation of the Messiah-Redeemer in the chief temple of Israel from the time of Moses until the temple of Solomon was destroyed in 586 B.C. (Farbridge 1923, 75; Smith 1955, 240)

The motif of the serpent on the cross as an emblem of Christ was often used in the early Christian art of the Mediterranean world. The serpent was a symbol of the Messiah in both the Old World and in Mesoamerica.

The Serpent in Mesoamerica

Since Jesus designated the serpent as a symbol of himself as God of Life in the days of Moses and again at the time of his earthly ministry, it is not surprising that we find it as one of the primary symbols in the New World. As a matter of fact, "serpent" is one of the symbolic names used in the New World in referring to the Creator-God. As has been stated earlier, *Coatl* means "serpent" or "twin" as it is found in *Quetzalcoatl*. The serpent symbol is found in Mexico and Central America in B.C. times. The serpent-life symbol runs rampant through the Classic Maya art and architecture after A.D. 300. It is found over central and southern Mexico and in Guatemala. It was perpetuated throughout central and southern Mexico to the coming of Cortes. It appears as early as 1200 B.C.–600 B.C. at La Venta, as shown in Figures 17 and 18.

People of the Serpent

There is powerful documentary evidence of an Atlantic crossing of a group of people from the Near East so intent on being identified with the serpent symbol that they called themselves *Chanes* or "serpent-men." Edward Herbert Thompson says of them in his book, *People of the Serpent*:

> It behooves us to be very open-minded in the matter of chronology and chronological estimates, and this may be taken here to apply especially to the strange happenings chronicled by the traditions of widely separate peoples concerning the mysterious appearance on the shores of the Gulf of Mexico of the *Chanes*—the people of the Serpent. These traditions tell us, and carvings on ancient walls and stone columns sustain them, that unknown ages ago there appeared strange craft at the mouth of what is now known as the Panuco River in the State of Vera Cruz. . . . In these craft were light-skinned beings, and some of the traditions have it that they were tall of stature and blue-eyed. They were clad in strange garments and wore about their foreheads emblems like entwined serpents. The leaders of the Ulmecas (Olmecs) were ever known as Chanes, or among the Mayas, as Canob—Serpents' Wise Men—or Ah Tzai—People of the Rattlesnake. . . . They built Chichen Itza—the City of the Sacred Well. (Thompson 1932, 77–79)

The Tzendal-Maya traditions come to us from the sixteenth- and seventeenth-century Tzendals, who lived in the Chiapas region in which the Chanes finally settled. These reports shed important light on the origin of the Serpent-Men of the Messiah. They were Chanes, "Serpents" of Quetzalcoatl—Itzamna. "At the head of their ancient [Mexican] calendar is placed *Nin*" (de la Vega). Howard Leigh (artist living in Mitla, Oaxaca, Mexico) notes that *Nan* means "lady" in the Zapotec tongue of Mexico. *Ninti* meant "lady of the rib" (Eve) in ancient Mesopotamia. Brasseur de Bourbourg, the French scholar of the last century, ties *Nin* closely to the Hebrew: "The Nin of the tzendales was the same as Cipactli of the Mexican traditions, a sea monster which figured allegorically as the father of the *Chan* [sky-serpent] race, as well as the tree [of life] with the serpent" (Brasseuer de Bourbourg 1851, 51–52).

Tan-nin is Hebrew meaning "sea-serpent" or "serpent" (Strong, *Hebrew and Chaldee Dictionary,* word 8577). Thus, some of the terminology from ancient Chiapas, Mexico, regarding the Serpent Men is identical with ancient Hebrew terminology.

One of the New World homelands and centers of the serpent people was *Nachan,* meaning "habitation of the serpent." The serpent center, *Tamoanchan* (believed to have been in the Tabasco-Chiapas region of southern Mexico) means literally "place of the bird-serpent." After providing his reader with this information, Rafael Girard, in *El Popol-Vuh Fuente Historica,* provides an illustration of the hieroglyph for the name *Tamoanchan.* Girard's illustration is reproduced here as Figure 20. It shows a bird above a serpent, and on the body of the serpent are stars. He states that, according to the concept of the present Maya Chorti priests, the bird is a representation of the God of the Sky. It is remembered that Tiamat (*Nut* in Egypt) is a sky goddess represented by the Milky Way and the serpent symbol in ancient Mesopotamia and Egypt. Here we have in the Tamoanchan hieroglyph the identical elements in Mexico in combination exactly as found in the Near East—stars and serpents. In the National Museum in Mexico City is a large mural from Teotihuacan, the great city of ancient Mexico dating to the days of Christ. Around the border of this huge mural is the body of a serpent, star-studded over its entire length—the Milky Way. Water falls from the hands of the deity portrayed in the mural.

FIGURE 20: BIRD AND SERPENT SYMBOL OF THE SKY GOD WITH STARS ON THE BODY OF THE SERPENT. SCENE FROM MAYA CODEX DRESDEN, PAGE 36.

J. Eric Thompson, Carnegie linguist, tells us that the term *Tamoanchan* "is pure Chiapan Maya: *Ta*, 'at,' *moan*, 'the *moan* bird,' *chan*, 'sky' or 'snake.' The complete word means 'at the moan bird sky' or 'at the moan bird and snake,' a clear reference to this celestial realm of Maya mythology" (Tax 1951, 36). The serpent was associated with the Milky Way of the sky in Mesoamerica just as it was in Mesopotamia and the ancient Near East.

In 1912, the National Museum of Mexico published a paper by Henning, Plancarte, Robelo, and Gonzalez entitled "Tamoanchan." In it the authors point out that *tamoanchan* was also one of several names used by the ancients in referring to their ancient, and now unidentified, lost capital.

Herman Beyer, linguist, identified the heavenly *Tamoanchan* with the Milky Way. (Henning et al. 1912, 43) Rafael Girard and others have pointed out that *tamoanchan* was the sky home of deity where there were water and rain in the center of the sky, the source of rain, the Milky Way. (Girard 1952, 25)

The late Sylvanus G. Morley, in his *The Ancient Maya*, describes an art object of ancient Mesoamerica that helps further in identifying the serpent with the Milky Way in that region, just as the two are associated in Bible lands:

> Across the sky stretches a serpent-like creature with symbols of constellations [including a patee cross representing the four world directions] presented on its side and signs for solar and lunar eclipses hanging from its belly. From its widely opened jaws, as well as from the two eclipse signs, pours a flood of water, falling down on the earth. Below the heavenly serpent, the Old Woman Goddess [Tiamat or Nut] with long talon-like fingernails and toenails, patroness of death and destruction, a writhing serpent on her head . . . holds an inverted bowl from which also gushes a destroying flood. Finally at the bottom stands *Ek Chuah*, the black God of War, the *Moan bird* of evil omen on his head; he holds in his right hand two javelins and in his left a long staff, all three pointing downward. (Morley 1946, 214)

There is some confusion of two Maya deities in Morley's description. Ek Chuah, the black God of War, is now known as the God M of the Maya pantheon with the calendar name 7 Death

(Figure 21) and is associated with the planet Jupiter. The deity with the Moan bird and destroying flood is the Maya God L with the calendar name 13 Death and is associated with the planet Saturn.

FIGURE 21: MISCELLANEOUS MONUMENT 60 FROM IZAPA, CHIAPAS, WITH THE GLYPH FOR "7 DEATH" (CA. 47 A.D.). (COURTESY OF V. GARTH NORMAN.)

The Dew from Heaven

Rain—the dew from heaven—came from the sky river. One of the names for the Messiah in Mesoamerica was *Itzamna,* which means "the dew from heaven." The primary symbol of *Itzamna,* as for Jehovah, was the serpent, the emblem raised up by Moses in similitude of the Messiah, who was raised up in Israel twelve hundred years after the time of Moses.

In Sumerian myths dating to the third millennium B.C., Enki lived at the source of the Two Deeps, or center of the Milky Way (near Kolob), see William Lee Stokes, 1991, 199), which flowed away from him in opposite directions and was regarded as his seed or life power. The Milky Way was also thought of by Phyllis Ackerman as the river of heaven, symbolized by the undulating serpent. Thus, the serpent representing water and life force is one of the oldest symbols of deity known to humanity and is related directly to the undulating streams from the flowing vase shown in Figure 22.

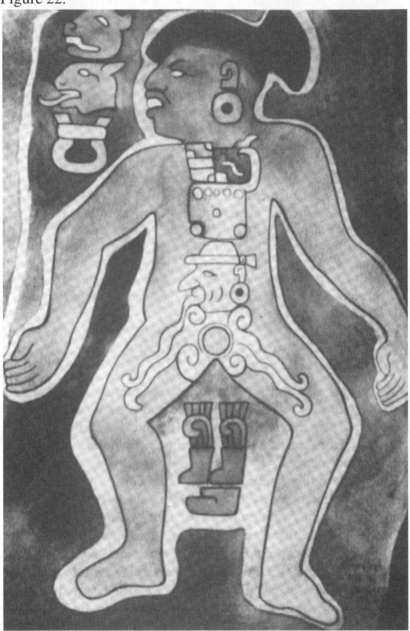

FIGURE 22: THE "LITTLE MAN" SYMBOL FROM DANZANTE 55 MONUMENT FROM MONTE ALBAN, OAXACA, MEXICO, ABOUT 500 B.C.

We have followed our "Stars in Heaven" representations of a Messiah-Redeemer through the Milky Way, rivers, serpents, self-denominated "serpent men," and "flowing vases" extensively represented in the Near East and in Mesoamerica, and we now continue on with the Flowing Vase and other figures known as The "Little Man," the Sacred Bucket, the Serpent and S Glyph (a seven-headed serpent), all bearing the serpent representation with apparent ties to the use of that symbolism by Moses and others of the Hebrew prophets who bore their prophetic witness of a coming redeemer from Adam to Malachi in the Old Testament and from Lehi to Samuel the Lamanite in the Book of Mormon.

The Flowing Vase: Milky Way

The Flowing Vase, which represents this creative utterance, has been identified in Sumerian art on cylinder seals, in full-round sculptured works, and in ceramics. (Van Buren 1933)

Mesoamerican figures holding flowing vases have been discovered in Oaxaca at Monte Alban, dating to the sixth century B.C. A particularly fine example is a large, hollow, clay figure unearthed ca. A.D.1300 in Mayapan. It is the god Chac holding a flowing vase in each hand (photograph in Covarrubias, plate 50).

The Little Man

During the 1930s, Alfonso Caso, a Mexican archaeologist, discovered just above bedrock at Monte Alban in Oaxaca a remarkable stone monument about five feet tall (Figure 22). It is carved to represent a bow-legged figure with its head in profile to the right. The face is of a "little man." Between the large figure's legs are more glyphs of unknown meaning.

The larger figure represents the ancient Sumerian astral god Apsu and the Egyptian god Khephri, and the small person on their abdomens is Mummu, above the flowing vase that represents the energy of the life force. Ackerman's description of the Sumerian figure could apply equally well to the Mesoamerican one:

> The phallic "Little Man" or Bes type [Bes was a lion-headed dwarf that kept evil spirits at bay], is commonly drawn with legs bowed in such wise as to create a void pattern of a glans; and Dr. [A Leo] Oppenheim suggests that one of the undeciphered lines [from the Sumerian epic

Enuma elish] concerning Mummu speaks of his legs as "too short to run." . . .

Mummu was a dwarf of the Bes type. But an extensive study of the Bes type indicates that the figure originated as a phallus-personation, corresponding to the widespread notion, and designation of the phallus as the "Little Man"; and the phallus is so depicted, for example, on some of the Maori gods, the "Little Man" being an exact miniature replica of the god himself. This identification of the Mummu as a phallus personation explains the old "Enuma elish" [Babylonian epic of creation].

"Mummu" is interpreted by later Babylonians as meaning "Creative Utterance" or "Life-Force" and this . . . "Utterance" with "Life-Force" would, therefore, be the semen. . . . All this means that in one branch of this astral cosmogony, the Milky Way was regarded as the creative semen of the Sky-god. (Oppenheim 1950, 10–11)

The Sacred Bucket

Another art motif of considerable interest is the sacred bucket, with parallels in both the Old and New Worlds. In *One Fold and One Shepherd*, Figures 16 and 24 show Assyrian examples from about 700 B.C. being held in the hand of a religious personage.

An interesting parallel is a bas-relief from La Venta in the state of Tabasco, Mexico, which was uncovered in a 1955 expedition jointly undertaken by the National Geographic Society, the Smithsonian Institution, and the University of California. Radiocarbon dating of the site establishes occupation at 1200 B.C. to 400 B.C., and this particular artifact seems to have been made in 500 B.C. It shows a being seated upon a serpent whose head is raised above the man's. He holds the bucket toward the rattles at the end of the serpent's tail. (Warren and Ferguson 1987, Figure 5, p. 9)

Serpent and S Glyph

Some of the ancient connections made between the serpent and the sky have already been discussed. In Sumerian mythology, rain came from the Milky Way, nourishing young plants as milk nourishes young animals and, as the stream of seed from the god, partaking directly of his generative powers. (Ackerman 1950, 9) An echo of this same belief appears in Job 26:13: "By his spirit he hath garnished the heavens; his hand hath formed the crooked [undulating] serpent." Miguel Covarrubias cites the belief that the "White-Cloud-Serpent" or Milky Way gave birth to the original creative couple, the Lord and Lady Sustenance.

As Figures 23 and 24 show, the high civilizations in both the Old and the New World demonstrate a fascination with the serpent motif and incorporated it into their art. On a Sumerian cylinder seal are two felines with snakelike necks intertwined in a graceful symmetrical design dating from about 3300 B.C. Frankfort comments that the symbol represents the god of the bringer of the fertilizing rain and is sometimes accompanied by the Imdugud bird, "which represents the dark clouds of the storm" (Frankfort 1956, 33–34).

FIGURE 23: JEMDET NASR DRAWING OF THE SERPENT-NECKED FELINES (ABOUT 3300 B.C. SUMERIAN CULTURE OF SOUTHERN MESOPOTAMIA).

FIGURE 24: STYLIZED SERPENT-NECKED DESIGN FROM THE MIXTEC CODEX NUTTALL, PAGE 26.

The Mesoamerican design appears in the Mixtec *Codex Vienna* dating from about A.D.1350, which is located in Vienna, Austria. It is much more stylized; but even so, the feet and curved tail of the animals suggest feline shapes.

The association of serpents and the simple or double S-shape with fertilizing rains and clouds is part of the mythological structure of both the Old and the New Worlds. The undulating shape of the S, reminiscent of the serpent, is a logical pictorial depiction of a river (or the Milky Way-sky-river and source of rain).

Bedrich Hrozny, professor of oriental languages in Prague, described S-shapes on the oldest cylinder seals discovered to date. They come from Uruk (biblical Erech) in Mesopotamia and date from about 3600–3100 B.C.:

> Some of the designs on these seals depicting animals with their long necks interwoven, appeared—under Sumero-Akkadian influence—early in Egypt. . . . Indeed, the cylinder seal itself appeared temporarily in Egypt during her earliest dynastic period, where it was used in the same way as in Sumer, viz. in the sealing up of clay vessels. But in the Nile Valley the cylinder seal was soon replaced by the native scarab. (Hrozney 1953, 36)

In Old World archaeology, this design is sometimes referred to as the guilloche pattern and seems to have first been created in metal, possibly gold wire, as ornamental work. "In the earlier forms the helix or S curve, seems to have prevailed probably brought from Egypt, and then in Syria contracted or consolidated, into the rope pattern" (William Hayes Ward).

An excellent example of the double-S glyph is a fresco from the Temple of the Tepantitla at Teotihuacan, not far from Mexico City, and dating from about A.D. 500 (Figure 25). It depicts a jaguar from whose mouth arises a "spiral scroll, signifying speech or song." Directly beneath his jaws is a design made of three interlocked S's "symbolizing water," from which droplets of rain emerge" (Groth-Kimball 1955). The double S-glyph is also a symbol of the jaguar paw. (Brotherston 1979, 256)

FIGURE 25: DOUBLE "S" GLYPH FROM TEOTIHUACAN NEAR MEXICO CITY ABOUT A.D. 500.

The Seven-Headed Serpent

A variation of the S-glyph is that of the seven-headed serpent, a symbol of the Sumerian storm god Ningishzida of the city of Lagash. In Figure 26, a Sumerian mace head dating to the third millennium before Christ the seven heads are seen in the center with two lion-headed eagles—in Mesopotamian art a representation of rain clouds. (Frankfort 1956, 32) It is noteworthy that the jaguar of southern Mexico symbolized the god of rain— Tlaloc, to the Aztecs. Cocijo, the Zapotec god of rain, symbolized by a jaguar mask, controlled the earth's fertility as a result. (Covarrubias 1957, 182–83) The book of Chilam Balam of Tizimin, a product of sixteenth-century Yucatan, includes the following statement: "We invoke *ah vuc dhapat,* the seven-headed serpent" (Makenson 1951, 48). A 1949 dictionary of Spanish-Maya refers to a traditional "fabulous serpent of seven heads" (Solis Alcala 1949). Budge notes that the seven-headed serpent was the emblem of Ea, god of the River of the Great Serpent (Milky Way). (Budge 1886, 132)

FIGURE 26: SEVEN-HEADED SERPENT AND LION-HEADED IMDUGUD EAGLE FROM SOUTHERN MESOPOTAMIA ABOUT 3000 B.C.

A marvelous example, Figure 27, found in El Tajin near Papantla in the state of Veracruz on the Gulf of Mexico, was called to our attention by retired Professor Floyd Carnaby of Utah State University. It shows a seated human figure with seven serpent heads emerging from the neck. Jose Garcia Payon, a Mexican archaeologist, calls it a representation of the deity Chicomecoatl, an important vegetation goddess. Her name, which means "Seven

Serpents," is referred to as "Seven Ears of Corn." He further observes that the seven serpents "radiate in the form of the Jewish ritual candelabrum" (Garcia Payon 1958, 49, 122; Covarrubias 1957, 184). This particular carving dates to the Classic era, about A.D. 250–900

FIGURE 27: LATE CLASSIC MONUMENT FROM EL TAJIN, VERACRUZ, MEXICO, ILLUSTRATING SEVEN SERPENTS IN PLACE OF A DECAPITATED HUMAN HEAD.

The Life-birth Symbol

A more remote symbol of the resurrection or redemption is that of the Life-Birth Symbol. This symbol appearing in the Middle Empire Babylonian period (Ward 1920, 414, 416) was related to the Flowing Vase. Ninhursag, the main female figure in the Babylonian pantheon (also called Ishtar) was the goddess and symbol of childbirth, new life, rebirth, and resurrection. As "the Lady of the Rib," Ninhursag can also be associated with the Eve figure of the Old Testament. Another remote symbol, cosmic in its scope, is treated in the notes to this chapter under the title of "Hamlet's Mill."

One of the oldest religious symbols in the world is the curving, upside-down U or omega-shaped sign that represents birth. It appears on many of the boundary stones used in Babylonia to mark dividing lines between private plots dating from 1350–650 B.C. It also appears on many early cylinder seals. (Ferguson 1958, 119–20)

This symbol was associated with the Sumerian "earth mother" goddess Ki, or Ninhursag, who was regarded as "the mother of the land," the midwife of heaven and earth.

It also appears as a symbol of fertility and childbirth in Sumerian, Babylonian (Figures 28 and 29), Assyrian, Egyptian, Palestinian, and Hittite art. It is found in identical form and with identical associated symbols in Mesoamerica as well. It appears at Monte Alban (Figure 30), at La Venta, Cerro de las Mesas, and in the state of Chiapas. It appears many times in the Mixtec *Codex Nuttall* (Figure 31) and in the Mixtec *Codex Vienna.* (Vaillant 1935, 54) In both the Near East and Mesoamerica, the symbol occurs with many variations (Figure 32).

FIGURE 28: WINGED CIRCLE WITH A FEATHERED TAIL FROM ASSYRIA ABOUT 800 B.C.

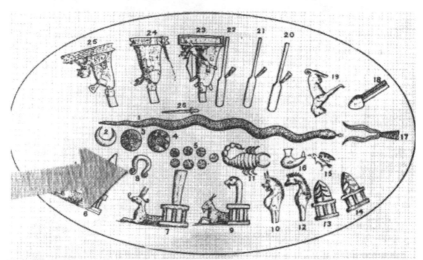

FIGURE 29: A BABYLONIAN ZODIAC WITH THE LIFE OR BIRTH SYMBOL, ABOUT THE SIXTH CENTURY B.C.

FIGURE 30: A SYMBOL OF LIFE OR BIRTH ON A ZAPOTEC URN FROM ANCIENT OAXACA, MEXICO.

FIGURE 31: A SYMBOL OF LIFE OR BIRTH FROM THE MIXTEC CODEX NUTTALL, PAGE 75, IN THE ELEVENTH CENTURY A.D.

FIGURE 32: THE LIFE, CHILDBIRTH, AND FERTILITY SYMBOL RENDERED IN SEVERAL VARIATIONS FROM BOTH THE NEAR EAST AND MESOAMERICA.

It can take a variety of forms, from a shape so flattened that it is barely curved, upside-down with the opening pointing upwards and with a variety of ornaments, but the general shape with the terminal curls is consistent.

On the boundary stones and cylinder seals of ancient Babylonia, this life symbol appears frequently with other astral symbols, including the serpent (Milky Way), the crescent moon, two stars, and seven dots, possibly representing a constellation. Moon, stars, and dots appear in Figure 33, a Zapotec artifact dating from the A.D. 100–400. Ward states, "The seven dots are among the most common emblems of the late period, but are not found in the first or middle Babylonian empire" (Ferguson 1958, 123). He also adds that some of the dots have stars within them.

FIGURE 33: A ZAPOTEC SYMBOL OF LIFE OR BIRTH WITH CELESTIAL SYMBOLS FROM ANCIENT OAXACA, MEXICO.

Hinke explains the reason for the presence of astral deity symbols on the boundary stones:

> It seems . . . that most public monuments were placed . . . under the protection of the Gods, to guard them against destruction by ill-disposed persons. A conspicuous example is furnished by the famous stela of Hammurabi, containing his code of laws, in which twelve of the great Gods are invoked to punish anyone who abolishes his judgments, over-rules his words, alters his statues, defaces his name, and writes his own name in its place. (Ferguson 1958, 123)

The life-birth symbol is found on the headdresses of Figure 32 from Mexico, in Figure 34 in connection with the feathered globe from Assyria, on two gold breastplates from Monte Alban, and on the ends of scepters or staffs in Middle Empire Babylonian cylinder seals (see Ward 1920, Figures 414, 416), where it is related to the Flowing Vase. Ward documents that it is sometimes formed by serpents (1920, 408)

FIGURE 34: WINGED CIRCLE WITH A FEATHERED TAIL FROM ASSYRIA ABOUT 800 B.C.

In one of several examples (Figure 35), the symbol appears as part of the headdress or coiffure of Mesoamerican figures, paralleling the same use in Babylonian, Egyptian, and Palestinian art (Figures 36 and 37). Jade had particular associations with life in Mesoamerica. The fact that the Ninhursag symbols in Figure 35 are carved from jade strengthens the view that the symbol retained its original Old World meaning in Mesoamerica. (See Figure 32, which shows the life symbol as a woman's headdress from ancient Mesoamerica.)

FIGURE 35: A SYMBOL OF LIFE OR BIRTH ON A PIECE OF JADE FROM ANCIENT GUATEMALA.

FIGURE 36: THE LIFE OR BIRTH SYMBOLS ASSOCIATED WITH THE GODDESS NINHURSAG OF ANCIENT MESOPOTAMIA AND THE GODDESS HATHOR FROM ANCIENT EGYPT.

FIGURE 37: THE SYMBOL OF LIFE OR BIRTH FROM ANCIENT PALESTINE.

The parallels are particularly compelling when we examine Ninhursag in greater detail. According to Oppenheim, she was known as "the mother of the land" and as the "great-grandmother" and "the Lady of Heaven." She was the main female figure in the Babylonian pantheon, where she was also known as Ishtar. She was the goddess and symbol of childbirth, new life, rebirth, and resurrection. "Present in human and animal reproduction, . . . she manifests herself wherever and whenever man or animal creates new life. . . . [She also] is linked to the cyclic phenomena of vegetal life, . . . the annual disappearance and rebirth of vegetation" (Oppenheim 1950, 70–71).

A female goddess of birth and rebirth with the same symbol appears in the *Codex Dresden* and the *Codex Madrid*, two of the three hieroglyphic books that have survived from the pre-Conquest Maya of southern Mexico and Guatemala. Maya scholar J. Eric Thompson identifies her as: "Ixchel [pronounced *Ish-chel*, an interesting sound-alike for the Babylonian *Ishtar*], the moon goddess, . . . patroness of childbirth, procreation, . . . and growing crops, . . . 'our mother,' 'lady,' . . . 'mistress.' . . . We have an explanation of the fact that the curl of hair, the symbol of the moon goddess is also the symbol of the earth sign. . . . Ixchel was the patroness of childbirth, sexual relations, disease, the earth and its crops, water, and the art of weaving" (Thompson 1950, 297–308).

Thompson points out that the hair-curl symbol of Ixchel is closely associated with the sign of the planet Venus in these codices. Oppenheim tells us that Ishtar, goddess of childbirth in Mesopotamia, was "worshiped as Evening and Morning Star [Venus]" (Oppenheim 1950, 71).

An interesting interpretation comes from Samuel Noah Kramer, curator of the tablet collections from Mesopotamia at the University Museum, University of Pennsylvania. His translation of a Sumerian cuneiform tablet that dates from about 2000 B.C. identifies Ninhursag/ Ninti as "the Lady of the Rib." Kramer suggests that Ninhursag can be associated with the Eve figure of the Old Testament. (Kramer 1945, 145, 149)

Pisces: The Zodiac Sign of the Fish

The zodiac sign of Pisces the Fish is connected not only with prophecies in the Old Testament but also with other major

Near Eastern religions like Zoroastrianism. In the Near East, it was a sign for the prophecy of a coming prince or Messiah. Connections are made herein between symbolisms of Hamlet's Mill in Mesopotamia and Mesoamerica as well as with some of the nine deities of the table found in the notes to Chapter 10.

Hamlet's Mill

The concept of Hamlet's Mill in mythology throughout the Old World and in the New World focuses on a view of the cosmos or the universe as being a large grinding mill. The universe is pictured with the earth at the center, with an imaginary line going straight up to the North Pole at the top of the sky and another imaginary line going down to the South Pole underneath the earth. As the earth revolves on its axis, it tilts and creates an imaginary circle up around the North Pole in the upper sky and a similar imaginary circle around the South Pole. That same circle would form an imaginary band around the earth called the ecliptic path. This ecliptic path is traveled by the sun, which completes the full circle once a year, every 365 1/4 days. (A model of this concept of Hamlet's Mill is seen in Figure 38.)

These three circles in the model are referred to as the Circle of the Equinoctial Precession. To briefly explain the Equinoctial Precession, we must imagine the earth again, surrounded by a 360-degree circle in a band whose width is between 23 1/2 degrees south latitude to 23 1/2 degrees north latitude. Within this band travel the visible planets and the visible constellations. This imaginary 360-degree circular band has been divided into twelve segments known as the solar zodiac. Each of the twelve signs of the zodiac occupies approximately thirty degrees of the 360-degree circle; thus, thirty times twelve equals 360 degrees. Once a year, each of these twelve signs occupies approximately one of our calendar months, so once every year each sign of the zodiac will have had its thirty days in our life.

The Equinoctial Precession phenomenon is a concept that visualizes the rising of a constellation on the east horizon on the 21st of March. This is the spring equinox. There is a gradual slippage westward of the nighttime constellations. Modern-day astronomers indicate that this slippage is approximately fifty seconds per year and therefore would not be noticeable except with the passage of many years. However, in Mesopotamia, the priests were beginning

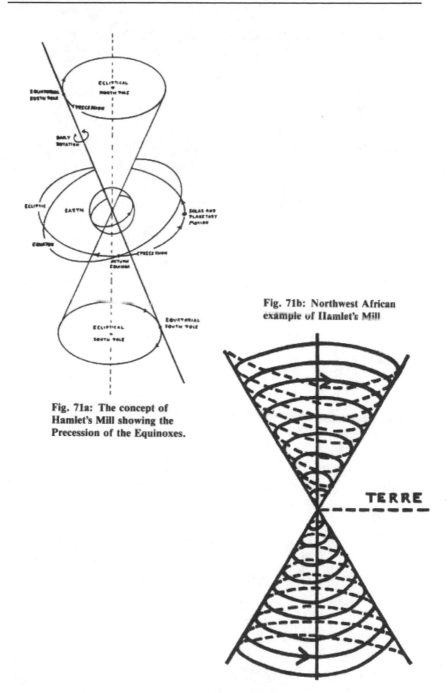

Fig. 71b: Northwest African example of Hamlet's Mill

Fig. 71a: The concept of Hamlet's Mill showing the Precession of the Equinoxes.

FIGURE 38: THE CONCEPT OF HAMLET'S MILL SHOWING THE PRECESSION OF THE EQUINOXES.

to observe this phenomenon by the fourth millennium B.C. From ancient Mesopotamia, the concept diffused throughout the Old World and into the New World as well.

In about 4320 B.C., the spring equinox would have fallen in the constellation of Taurus the Bull. At the rate of fifty seconds of movement of the nighttime sky per year, it would take approximately seventy-two years before one degree of the 360-degree imaginary circle could be recorded. If one degree takes seventy-two years, then the thirty degrees that make up the sign of Taurus would last 2,160 years (30 x 72). The spring equinox would begin in the zodiac sign of Aries the Ram in 2160 B.C. Aries the Ram then would be the spring equinox of the zodiac sign for the next 2,160 years, or down to 1 B.C. The next zodiac sign would be Pisces the Fish. This is significant because the zodiac sign Pisces is connected not only with prophecies in the Old Testament but also with other major Near Eastern religions like Zoroastrianism. In the Near East, it was a sign for the prophecy of a coming prince or Messiah. Pisces is also associated with the House of the Hebrews in Near Eastern mythology. It is possible that this date of 1 B.C., near the spring equinox, would be near the time of the birth of the Savior.

Another phenomenon associated with the equinoctial precession is the concept that the constellations and the planets travel in this zodiac path around the earth. These constellations and planets can be seen from the earth as it turns on its axis while circling the sun. This whole idea of rotating planets, constellations, etc., is the basis of the concept of Hamlet's Mill and its grinding motion.

In Egypt, we see the center line of the universe with the North Star at the top and two deities turning the mill (Figure 39). One deity is Seth; the other deity is Horus. In the Hindu material from India, we see the mill set upon a tortoise, a long snake representing the Milky Way; several heads on the snake are pulled back and forth in churning fashion. The deity Vishnu sits at the top at the North Star (Figure 40). In Mesoamerica, we see the same concept in the Maya *Codex Madrid*, in the form of the churn and a long path. A sun symbol on the path represents the sun traveling through the heavens and several individuals and pulling or churning along the sun's path (Figure 41).

FIGURE 39: EGYPTIAN GODS HORUS AND SETH ROTATING THE CHURN.

FIGURE 40: A HINDU EXAMPLE OF CHURNING THE MILKY OCEAN.
CHURNING OF THE MILKY WAY.

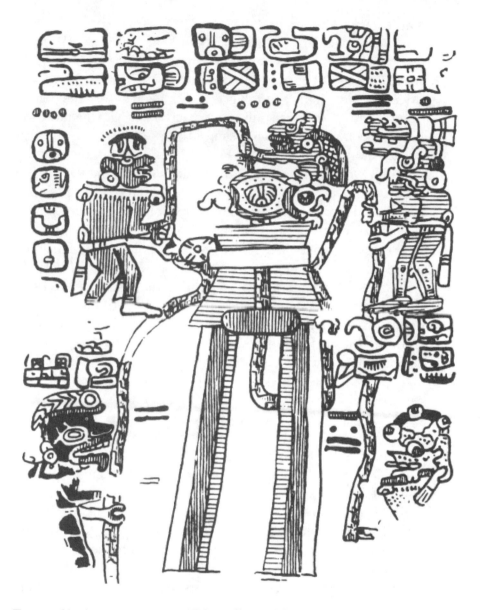

FIGURE 41: A SCENE FROM THE MAYA CODEX MADRID ILLUSTRATING THE

The Volador Ceremony

A spectacular ritual from ancient Mesoamerica needs to be researched more intensively and compared with the Old World scenes of the "churning Milky Ocean" (Figures 39 to 41) (Mesoamerica, India and Egypt). This ritual parallels the pentad design in the "Volador" ritual from Mesoamerica. One man, the center, shouts, dances, and plays music on top of a rotating platform located atop a very high pole. Four "flyers" leap off the rotating platform with the ropes tied around their waists and descend to the ground like "falling rain." The ritual is connected to petitions for rain and fertility. In India, the "churning Milky Ocean foam" is related to sperm. Further symbolism involves the center figure on top of the churn or pole as representing the polar star and the pole or column the spindle of the universe (see *Hamlet's Mill* 1969, 162). The Mesoamerican "Volador" ritual is widespread in Mesoamerica (Dahlgren de Jordan 1954, 280–86) but needs in-depth ethnographic documentation before the ritual disappears from the Mesoamerican scene. It is probable that the rain god Tlaloc and the four Tlaloques are the actors in the "Volador" ritual.

The section on the life-birth symbols connected with the Sumerian Goddess Ninhursag is associated with the eighth row in the chart, and the Goddess is represented by the planet Venus. These life symbols are associated with the planet Venus in the Near East and in Mesoamerica.

The sixth row, connected with the planet Mercury, involves some of the themes in this chapter (the theme of the serpent and the S-glyphs and particularly the seven-headed serpent, which would be associated with the Mesopotamian god Ningishzida; this same theme occurs in Mesoamerica on monuments from the Mexican states of Veracruz and Yucatan with an individual who has been decapitated. Seven serpents are shown in place of his head).

Also, the serpent and the S-glyph are connected with the planet Mercury in ancient Mesoamerica, just as the serpent deity Ningishzida was connected with the planet Mercury in Mesopotamia and in other parts of the Near East.

Likewise connected with the planet Mercury is the concept of purification, particularly in the form of a God of Healing. In Egypt, this was the God Thoth, who also, besides being the God of Healing, was the God of Writing. In Mesoamerica, it was Ixtlilton, the little black God of Healing. The "Volador" ceremony described above adds another theme to the sixth row.

For the third row, which represents the planet sun, we have the theme of the wing globe or the winged sun disc, but this symbol is not common in the Near East or in Mesoamerica. The wing bird is the eagle in both areas.

For the second row, connected with the front head of the eclipse demon, we have the concept of the tree of life, as mentioned earlier.

The pentad correlates with the first row. The pentad of four dots with a center dot represents the North Star. The center dot and the twin constellations forming five dots are a symbol that would correlate with the concept of the god Tlaloc. Tlaloc represents the center big tree or the tree of knowledge of good and evil, and the four surrounding trees of the four directions represent the Tlaloques in Mesoamerica. On an astronomical level, Tlaloc represents the direction of the Milky Way at two different times of the year, one at summer solstice and one at the winter solstice. In the winter, the Milky Way runs across the sky in an east-west direction; in the summer it runs in the north-south direction. If one places the east-west and north-south Milky Way patterns in the same location, they form a cross in the nighttime sky. In the Mayan area of Mesoamerica, the name of the underworld is the name of the Milky Way at the winter solstice, or Xibalbey. We have a name for the Milky Way at the summer solstice called Sacbey, which is also the name of a causeway between Chichen Itza and the archaeological site of Coba in the Yucatan Peninsula. Finally, each row of the table in the Chapter 10 notes is represented in Mesoamerica by one of the nine lords of the night (Figures 42 to 44).

FIGURE 42: THE NINE LORDS OF THE NIGHT: XIUHTECUTLI, ITZTLI, PILTZINTECHTLI, CINTEOTL, MICTLANTECUHTLI, CHALCHIHUITLICUE, TLAZOLTEOTL, TEPEYOLLOTL, AND TLALOC (AZTEC VERSION).

Figure 43: The Aztec symbols for the nine lords of the night.

Figure 44: The Maya symbols for the nine lords of the night.

"And behold, there shall a new star arise, such an one as ye never have beheld; and this also shall be a sign unto you. And behold this is not all, there shall be many signs and wonders in heaven" (Helaman 14:5–6).

POSTSCRIPT

In 1987, the Book of Mormon Research Foundation published *The Messiah in Ancient America*, a manuscript that Thomas Stuart Ferguson and I coauthored. Some of my contributions to that book have helped me in the writing of *New Evidences of Christ in Ancient America*. Although both books deal with Jesus the Christ as the Messiah-Redeemer of the Americas, *New Evidences* definitively pinpoints Mesoamerica as the likely location of New World events as recorded in the Book of Mormon.

Readers might wonder why we have restricted our evidences to a cultural area known to scholars as Mesoamerica. Readers might also wonder why we examine the claim of some scholars that the Mexican deity Quetzalcoatl has many parallels to Jehovah of the Old Testament and Jesus the Christ in the New Testament.

Our reasons are straightforward and are based on the evidences available at this time. For our purposes, any New World evidences of a Messiah-Redeemer among the ancient peoples who lived in the Americas other than in Mesoamerica lack adequate documentation and are extremely difficult to place in a specific time frame. However, evidences of the Messiah-Redeemer in Mesoamerica are pervasive and have been thoroughly documented and quite precisely dated.

We anticipate that many of our readers may not yet have associated the label *Mesoamerica* with Jesus the Christ, even though such associations have been routine occurrences by the scholarly world for over fifty years. The name *Mesoamerica* refers to the area of high culture or civilization that is confined to central and southern Mexico and northern Central America. In the Mesoamerican cultural area, we find extensive evidences from archaeology, languages, native writings, Spanish colonial writings, pre-Hispanic painted screen books, specific topographical features, and a large volume of anthropological and historical writings that can all be interwoven into a body of coherent knowledge about the Messiah-Redeemer.

For example, various writers in the past have suggested that the Central Mexican deity Quetzalcoatl has several parallels to the Jewish deity Jehovah and the Christian deity Jesus the Christ. However, in looking at such evidences of the Messiah-Redeemer, we must realize that several variants of this deity are found in Mesoamerican culture and that only one has close parallels with Jesus. At the same time, the calendars of both ancient biblical lands and ancient Mesoamerica combine to confirm these cultural parallels. In *New Evidences*, we show that the following calendars all dovetail for specific dated events: Gregorian, Judean, Olmec/ Maya Long Count, Mesoamerican ritual 260-day, and the vague solar calendar of 365 days. We anticipate that readers will be singularly impressed with such evidences as well as with numerous other evidences of Christ in Mesoamerica.

I am especially indebted to professional colleagues and organizations that have influenced my contributions to *New Evidences of Christ in Ancient America*. In 1938, Max Wells Jakeman received his Ph.D. in archaeology and ancient history at the University of California at Berkeley. The following year, he and some friends—Thomas Stuart Ferguson, Franklin S. Harris Jr., and a few others—founded the *Itzan Society*. This society was relocated on the Brigham Young University campus in April 1949 as the *University Archaeological Society* (UAS). I was privileged to be one of the original six who were part of the April 1949 event. In 1965, the UAS had another name change when it became the *Society for Early Historic Archaeology* (SEHA). In the years between 1949 and 1988, the UAS/SEHA published 164 newsletters and several bulletins and held over forty annual symposia of the scriptures.

In May 1985, a new archaeological research group, the Ancient America Foundation, was registered with the state of Utah and was given Internal Revenue Service clearance in 1988 as a nonprofit educational and scientific organization. During the years between 1989 and 1993, the SEHA and AAF merged to combine their research efforts. SEHA has focused on the scriptural interpretation of scholarly research data: AAF has focused on the scientific presentation of research in a format similar tothat of other scholarly institutions. During the 1990s, AAF/SEHA published a new series of newsletters that now number fourteen. I am grateful for my activities associated with AAF/SEHA, especially at this time because they have so greatly influenced my contributions to *New Evidences of Christ in Ancient America*.

Finally, I am pleased to recognize the influence of the Foundation for Ancient Research and Mormon Studies (FARMS) on my professional life and writing. When FARMS and Deseret Book jointly published John Sorenson's manuscript, *An Ancient American Setting for the Book of Mormon*, I observed the beginnings of true credibility in associating the events of the Book of Mormon with the geographic area known as Mesoamerica. That development served as a catalyst to increase my efforts to make others aware of my archaeological research on evidences of the Book of Mormon as reflected in Mesoamerica. *New Evidences of Christ in Ancient America* is one outcome of my belief that the Book of Mormon is indeed a translation of an ancient record about New World people who lived in Mesoamerica, and I appreciate the efforts of FARMS in fostering research that supports the role of Mesoamerica as the setting for the Book of Mormon.

Bruce W. Warren

Editor's Notes

When Larry Ferguson initially contacted me and asked me to edit the manuscript for *New Evidences of Christ in Ancient America*, I declined because of other commitments. After several additional pleas for help from Larry, I agreed to reorder my commitments and give first priority to the task of editing the manuscript.

As a professor of Management Communication at Brigham Young University, I like to think I know something about good writing. At times, however, I discover the need to bring myself back to reality lest I become too enamored with my presumed expertise. For example, a student will occasionally ask me a grammar question that I cannot definitively answer with absolute certainty. On such occasions, I remind my students that while I think I'm good at what I do, "I know just about enough to be dangerous."

Larry wanted me to edit *New Evidences* because he has confidence in my expertise to edit manuscripts and because he thinks I understand the Book of Mormon and its connections with Mesoamerica. Although I have read hundreds of articles and books about archaeological findings in Mesoamerica and although I have spent countless hours trying to assimilate my reading with the content of the Book of Mormon, I of course do not have all the answers about Mesoamerica as it applies to the Book of Mormon. Thus, if someone were to ask me about my depth of knowledge of Mesoamerica in connection with the Book of Mormon, my answer would be, "I know just about enough to be dangerous."

I do have several beliefs and feelings about the Book of Mormon that dominate my thinking and that help me edit such manuscripts as *New Evidences of Christ in Ancient America*. These beliefs and feelings are based, in most instances, on my reading of archaeological reports and books about Mesoamerica. I also consider my beliefs and feelings to be a gift given to me as a gift of the Spirit. Specifically:

• I believe the Book of Mormon is a translation of an ancient record about a small segment of the peoples who lived in ancient America.

• I believe Joseph Smith translated the Book of Mormon as he claimed—"by the gift and power of God."

• I believe, therefore, that the Book of Mormon is a **real** account about **real** people who "lived somewhere." I'm convinced that the "somewhere" is the geographic area in ancient America known today as _Mesoamerica_.

• I do not believe that the Book of Mormon geographical model I was taught for the first forty years of my life is correct. Specifically, I do not believe that the Isthmus of Panama is the narrow neck of land, that South America is the land southward, and that North America is the land northward. And I do not believe that the Hill Cumorah in upstate New York is the Hill Ramah/Hill Cumorah of the Book of Mormon.

• I believe the Hill Ramah/Hill Cumorah of the Book of Mormon is located somewhere in the vicinity of the Isthmus of Tehuantepec in Mesoamerica. I further believe that the Isthmus of Tehuantepec is the narrow neck of land.

I consider the above beliefs to be critical requirements for anyone who edits a latter-day manuscript such as _New Evidences of Christ in Ancient America_. My beliefs undoubtedly influenced Larry Ferguson in asking me to edit this new book about the Messiah-Redeemer in Mesoamerica.

I'm pleased that the authors and publisher have titled this book _New Evidences of Christ in Ancient America_. A large proportion the Americas' archaeological ruins that date to Book of Mormon times are found in Mesoamerica. To me, the "somewhere" of the Book of Mormon, therefore, is clearly Mesoamerica. When the peoples of the Book of Mormon reached the New World, they landed in and lived in Mesoamerica. I believe that all New World things I read in the Book of Mormon took place in **Mesoamerica**.

I agreed to edit this book because I realized it will make significant contributions to any reader's knowledge, appreciation, and testimony of the Book of Mormon as an ancient record that took place in Mesoamerica. I also agreed to edit the book because I was committed to Bruce Warren and Larry Ferguson for their desire to disseminate information about the Book of Mormon in relation to Mesoamerica. I became even more committed to the project as I became acquainted with the contributions of Harold Brown and Blaine Yorgason.

As you read *New Evidences of Christ in Ancient America*, I invite you to do so from the perspectives that the Book of Mormon is a **real** account about **real** people who lived in **Mesoamerica** and that *New Evidences* will increase your knowledge, appreciation, and testimony of the Book of Mormon.

In the final analysis, the Book of Mormon is either true or false. Either Joseph Smith translated an ancient manuscript by the gift and power of God, as he claimed, or he was "a sly charlatan with a very creative imagination" who invented the whole thing. I think your reading of this book help you believe as I do—that Joseph did translate an ancient Mesoamerican record and that the consequences of that belief are far-reaching indeed.

Ted D. Stoddard
Freelance Editor and Professor of
Management Communication
The Marriott School,
Brigham Young University

Bibliography

Ackerman, Phyllis. "The Dawn of Religions." *Ancient Religions: A Symposium*. Vergilius Ferm, ed. New York: Philosophical Library, 1950, 3–24.

Adams, Daniel B. "Last Ditch Archaeology." *Science* 4 (1983): 28–37.

Agrinier, Pierre. "Linguistic Evidence for the Presence of Israelites in Mexico." *Newsletter and Proceedings of the Society of Early Historic Archaeology*. No. 112, February 1969. Provo, Utah: Society for Early Historic Archaeology, 4–5.

Albright, William Foxwell. *The Archaeology of Palestine*. Baltimore: Penguin, 1949.

Allen, Joseph L. *Exploring the Lands of the Book of Mormon*. Provo: S. A. Publishers, 1989.

Bancroft, Hubert H. *The Native Races of the Pacific States*. 5 vols. San Francisco: The History Company, 1883–86.

Bauval, Robert, and Adrian Gilbert. *The Orion Mystery: A Revolutionary New Interpretation of the Ancient Enigma*. New York: Crown Trade Paperbacks, 1994.

Benson, Ezra Taft. "The Power of the World." *Ensign* 16 (May 1986): 81.

———. "The Gift of Modern Revelation." *Ensign* 11 (November 1986): 80.

———. *Teachings of Ezra Taft Benson*. Salt Lake City: Bookcraft, 1988.

Blom, Frans. *Conquest of Yucatan*. Boston: Houghton Mifflin, 1936.

Bowker, John, ed. *The Oxford Dictionary of World Religions*. Oxford: Oxford University Press, 1997.

Brasseur de Bourburg, Charles Etienne. *Lettres Pour Servir D'Introduction a L'Histoire Primitive des Nations Civilisees de L'Amerique Septentrionale*. Mexico: M. Murguia, 1851, 51–52.

Breasted, James Henry. *A History of Egypt*. New York: Scribner's,
        1948.

Bricker, Harvey M., and Victoria R. Bricker. "Zodiacal References
        in the Maya Codices." *The Sky in Mayan Literature*. Edited
        by Anthony F. Aveni. New York and Oxford: Oxford
        University Press, 1992, 148–81.

Brinton, Daniel G. "The Abbe Brasseur and His Labors."
        Lippincott's Magazine 1 (January 1868): 79–86.

———. *The Myths of the New World: A Treatise of the Symbolism
        and Mythology of the Red Race of America*. 3rd ed. rev.
        Philadelphia: David McKay, 1896.

Bruce, Robert. "The Popul Vuh and the Book of Chan K'in."
        Estudios de Cultura Maya. Vol. 10. Mexico: Seminario de
        Estudios Maya, Universidad Nacional Autonoma de
        Mexico, 1976–1977, 173–208.

Budge, Sir Ernest Alfred Wallis. *Babylonian Life and History*.
        London: Religious Tract Society, 1886.

Campbell, Joseph. *Oriental Mythology*. Vol. 2, *The Masks of God*.
        New York: Viking, 1976.

Carmack, Robert M. "New Quichean Chronicles from Highland
        Guatemala." *Estudios de Cultura Maya*. Vol. 12. Mexico:
        Seminario de Estudios Maya, Universidad Nacional
        Autonoma de Mexico, 1981, 83–103.

Carmack, Robert M., and James L. Mondlach. *El Título de
        Totonicapan: Texto, Traduccion y Comentario*. Fuente Para
        El Estudio de la Cultura. Vol. 3. Mexico: Universidad
        Nacional Autonoma de Mexico, 1983.

Carter, George F. "Plants across the Pacific." *Memoirs*. No. 9,
        Society for American Archaeology (1953): 62–71.

———. "Civilization Puzzle." *John Hopkins Magazine*, February
        1957.

Ceram, C. W. *Gods, Graves, and Scholars*. New York: Alfred A.
        Knopf, 1967.

Chadwick, Robert L. "Ezekiel 17: An Apparent Transatlantic
        Expedition around 500 B.C." Paper presented at the
        Twenty-Fourth Annual Symposium on the Archaeology of
        the Scriptures held at Brigham Young University on 26
        October 1974.

Chase, James E. "The Sky Is Falling: The San Martin Tuxtla
       Volcanic Eruption and Its Effects on the Olmec at Tres
       Zapotes, Veracruz." *Vínculos* 7 (1981): 53–69.
Clark, John E. Letter to John L. Sorenson, 12 February 1973.
Clawson, Dennis O. Letter to Bruce W. Warren, 18 December 1989.
Closs, Michael P. "Some Parallels in the Astronomical Events
       Recorded in the Maya Codices and Inscriptions. *The Sky in
       Mayan Literature*. Edited by Anthony F. Aveni. New York
       and Oxford: Oxford University Press, 1992, 133–47.
*Codice Chimalpopoca: Anales de Cuauhtitlan y Leyenda de los
       Soles*. Translated by Primo Feliciano Velazquez. Universidad
       Nacional Autonoma de Mexico. Publicacion de las Instituto
       de Investigaciones Historicas. Series 1, No. 1. Mexico:
       1945.
Coe, Michael D. and Richard Diehl. *In the Land of the Olmec*.
       Austin: University of Texas Press, 1990.
Coe, Michael D. et al. *The Olmec World: Ritual and Rulership*.
       Princeton: The Art Museum, Princeton University, 1995.
Covarrubias, Miguel. *Mexico South: The Isthmus of Tehuantepec*.
       New York: Alfred A. Knopf, 1947.
————. *Indian Art of Mexico and Central America*. New York:
       Alfred A. Knopf, 1957.
Dahlgren de Jordan, Barbra. *La Mixteca*. Cultura E Historia
       Prehispanicas. Mexico: Imprenta Universitaria, 1954.
D'Alviella, Count Goblet, Eugene Felicien Albert. *The Migration of
       Symbols*. New York: University Books, 1956. A
       reproduction of the original work published at Westminister
       in London, 1894.
Davies, Nigel. *Voyagers to the New World*. New York: William
       Morrow, 1979.
DeCharencey, H. *Les Cites Votanides*. Paris: Ch. Peeters, 1885.
Diaz-Boliu, Josc. *Le Serpiente Emplumada*. Merida: Registrade
       Cultura Yucatan, 1952.
Dinsmoor, William Bell. "An Account of Its Historic Development."
       In *The Architecture of Ancient Greece*. 3rd ed. rev. London:
       Unwin Brothers Ltd., 1950.
Doran, Edwin Jr. "The Sailing Raft as a Great Tradition." *Man
       Across the Sea: Problems of Pre-Columbian Contacts*.
       ditors Riley et al. Austin: University of Texas Press, 1974.

Edmonson, Munro. *The Book of the Year: Middle American Calendrical Systems*. Salt Lake City: University of Utah Press, 1988.

Farbridge, Maurice H. *Studies in Biblical and Semitic Symbolism*. Hartford, England: Stephen Austin and Sons, 1923.

Ferguson, Thomas Stuart. *One Fold and One Shepherd*. San Francisco: Books of California, 1958/1962.

Finkelstein, Louis, ed. *The Jews: Their History, Culture and Religion*. New York: Harper and Row, 1949.

Flannery, Kent V., and Joyce Marcus, eds. *The Cloud People: Divergent Evolution of the Zapotec and Mixtec Civilizations*. New York: Academic Press, 1983.

Frankfort, Henri. *Kingship and the Gods: A Study of Ancient Near Eastern Religion as the Integration of Society and Nature*. Chicago: University of Chicago Press, 1948.

———. *The Birth of Civilization in the Near East*. New York: Doubleday, 1956; Bloomington: Indiana University Press, 1959.

Frankfort, Henri, et al. *The Intellectual Adventure of Ancient Man*. Chicago: University of Chicago Press, 1946.

Freidel, David, Linda Schele, and Joyce Parker. *Maya Cosmos: Three Thousand Years on the Shaman's Path*. New York: William Morrow, 1993.

Furst, Jill Leslie. "The Tree Birth Tradition in the Mixteca, Mexico." *Journal of Latin American Lore* 3 (1977): 183–126.

Funk and Wagnalls. *New Standard Bible Dictionary*. 1936.

Garcia Payon, Jose. "Una Palma *en Situ*." *Revista Mexicana de Estudios Antropológicos*, Vol. 10. Sociedad Mexicana de Antropología, 1948–49.

Gibson, Charles, and John B. Glass. "A Census of Middle American Prose Manuscripts in Native Historical Tradition." *Handbook of Middle American Indians*. Vol. 15. Edited by Howard F. Cline et al. Austin: University of Texas Press, 1975, 322–400.

Gillette, Douglas. *The Shaman's Secret: The Lost Resurrection Teachings of the Ancient Maya*. New York: Bantam Books, 1997.

Girard, Raphael. *El Popol Vuh Fuente Historica*. Guatemala: Ministero de Educacion Publica, 1952.

———. *Los Mayas Eternos*. Mexico: Antigua Libreria Robredo, 1962.

Gladwin, Harold Sterling. *Men Out of Asia*. New York: Whittlesey House, 1947.

Glueck, Nelson. "Exploration in Eastern Palestine II." *Annual of the American School of Oriental Research*. Vol. 15 (1935), 1–202.

Goetz, Delia, and Sylvanus G. Morley, trans. *Popul Vuh: The Sacred Book of the Ancient Quiche Maya*. Norman: University of Oklahoma Press, 1950.

Goodenough, Erwin R. *Jewish Symbols in the Greco-Roman Period*. Vol. 7. Toronto: McClelland and Stewart, 1958.

Graves, Robert. *The Greek Myths*. Vol. 1. New York: George Braziller, 1957.

Groth-Kimball, Irmgard. *The Art of Ancient Mexico*. London: Thames and Hudson, 1955.

Gruener, James C. *The Olmec Riddle: An Inquiry into the Origin of Pre-Columbian Civilization*. Rancho Santa Fe: Vengreen Publications, 1987.

Hammond, Norman, and Gordon R. Willey, eds. *Maya Archaeology and Ethnohistory*. Austin: University of Texas Press, 1979.

Harner, Michael J. *Hallucinogens and Shamanism*. New York: Oxford University Press, 1973.

Hayes, William C. *The Scepter of Egypt*. New York: Metropolitan Museum of Art, 1953.

Heidel, Alexander. *The Gilgamesh Epic and Old Testament Parallels*. 2nd ed. Chicago: University of Chicago Press, 1949.

Heiser, Charles B. *Seed to Civilization: The Story of Man's Food*. San Francisco: W. H. Freeman and Company.

Henning, et al. *Tamoanchan, Estudio Arqueológico E Histórico*. Anales del Museo Nacional de Arqueologia, Historia y Etnologia. Vol. 4. Mexico: 1912, 433–62.

Herodotus. *The Persian Wars*. George Rawlinson, trans. New York: The Modern Library, 1942.

Heyerdahl, Thor. *American Indians in the Pacific*. London: G. Allen and Univin, 1952.

Hinke, William J. *A New Boundary Stone of Nebuchadnezzar I from Nippur*. Philadelphia: University of Pennsylvania, 1907.

Hrozny, Bedrich. *Ancient History of Western Asia, India and Crete*. Prague: Artia, 1953.

Huber, Jay M. "Lehi's 600 Year Prophecy and the Birth of Christ."
    Foundation for Ancient Research and Mormon Studies,
    Preliminary Report, HUB-82. Provo: Foundation for
    Ancient Research and Mormon Studies, 1982.
Hunter, Milton R., and Thomas Stuart Ferguson. *Ancient America
    and the Book of Mormon*. Oakland: Kolob Book, 1950.
Ixtlilxochitl, Don Fernando de Alva. *Obras Históricas*. 2 vols.
    Edmundo O'Gorman, ed. Mexico: Universidad Nacional de
    México, 1975.
Jacobsen, Thorkild. "Mesopotamia." *The Intellectual Adventure of
    Ancient Man*. Chicago: University of Chicago Press, 1946, 125–219.
Jakeman, M. Wells. "The Ancient Middle-American Calendar
    System: Its Origin and Development." Provo: Brigham
    Young University Publications in Archaeology and Early
    History, 1, 1949.
————, ed. and trans. "The Historical Recollections of Gaspar
    Antonio Chi: An Early Source Account of Ancient
    Yucatan." Provo: Brigham Young University Publications in
    Archaeology and Early History, 3, 1952.
Jett, Stephen C. "Diffusion Versus Independent Development: The
    Bases of Controversy." *Man Across the Sea: Problems of
    Pre-Columbian Contacts*. Edited by Carroll L. Riley et al.
    Austin: University of Texas Press, 1971, 5–53.
Jimenez Moreno, Wigberto. "Síntesis de la Historia Pretolteca de
    Mesoamérica." *Esplendor del México Antiguo*. Vol 1.
    Edited by Raul Noriega, Carmen Cook de Leonard, nd Julio
    Rodolfo Moctezuma. Mexico: Centro de Investigacions
    Antropologies, 1959, 1019–1108.
Kaufman, Terrence. "Archaeological and Linguistic Correlations in
    Maya Land and Associated Areas of Mesoamerica." *World
    Archaeology* 8 (1976): 101–18.
Kelemen, Paul. *Medieval American Art*. New York: The Macmillan
    Co., 1956.
Kelley, David H. "The Birth of the Gods at Palenque." *Sobriento de
    Estudios de Cultura Maya*. Vol. 5. Mexico: Universidad
    Nacional Automonado Mexico, 1965.
————. "American Parallels." *The Alphabet and the Ancient
    Calendar Signs*. By Moran and Kelley, Part II. Palo Alto:
    Daily Press, 1969.

————. "Eurasian Evidence and the Mayan Calendar Correlation Problem." *Mesoamerican Archaeology: New Approaches.* Edited by Norman Hammond. Austin: University of Texas Press, 1974.

————. "The World Ages in India and Mesoamerica." *Newsletter and Proceedings of the Society for Early Historic Archaeology.* No. 137. Provo, Utah, March 1975.

————. "Astronomical Identities of Mesoamerican Gods." *Archaeastronomy Supplement to the Journal for the History of Astronomy.* Part 2, Vol. 11, 1980, s1–s54.

Kidder, Alfred V., Jesse D. Jennings, and Edwin M. Shook. *Excavations at Kaminaljuyu, Guatemala.* Carnegie Institution of Washington, Publication No. 561, 1946.

Kingsborough, Edward King (Lord). *Antiquities of Mexico.* 9 vols. London: Henry G. Bohn Publisher, 1841–48.

Kramer, Samuel Noah. "Enki and Ninhursag." *Bulletin of American Schools of Oriental Research.* Supplementary Studies No. 1. New Haven, 1945.

Kubler, George. *The Art and Architecture of Ancient America: The Mexican, Maya, and Andean Peoples.* Baltimore: Pelican History of Art, 1962.

Las Casas, Fray Bartolome de. *Apologética Historia de las Indias.* 2 vol. Madrid: Biblioteca de Autores Españoles.

Laughlin, Robert M. *The Great Tzotzil Dictionary of San Lorenzo Zinacatan.* Smithsonian Contributions to Anthropology No. 19. Washington, D.C.: Smithsonian Institution Press, 1975.

Lafaye, Jacques. *Quetzalcoatl and Guadalupe: The Formation of Mexican National Consciousness, 1631–1813.* Chicago: The University of Chicago Press, 1976. Translated by Benjamin Keen. Originally published as *Quetzalcoatl et Guadalupe.* Paris: Editions Gallimard, 1974.

Lefgren, John C. *April Sixth.* Salt Lake City: Deseret Book, 1980.

Leonard, Irving Albert. *Don Carlos de Siguenza y Gongora.* Berkeley: University of California Press, 1929.

Lindemann, Hannes. "Alone at Sea for 72 Days." *Life* 43 (22 July 1957): 92–108.

Litt, Iris F., ed. *Adolescent Substance Abuse*: Report of the Fourteenth Ross Roundtable on Critical Approaches to Common Pediatric Problems. Columbus, Ohio: Ross Laboratories, 1983.

Lloyd, Seton. *The Art of the Ancient Near East*. New York:
    Frederick A. Praeger, 1961.

Lounsbury, Floyd G. "Maya Numeration, Computation, and
    Calendrical Astronomy." *Dictionary of Scientific
    Biography*. Vol. 15. Supplement on Ancient Science. Edited
    by Charles Gillespie, 1978.

Love, Bruce. *The Paris Codex: Handbook for a Maya Priest*.
    1 Austin: University of Texas Press, 1994.

Kuckert, Karl W. *Olmec Religion: A Key to Middle America and
    Beyond*. Norman: University of Oklahoma Press, 1976.

Macdonald, Donald Ian. *Drugs, Drinking, and Adolescents*.
    Chicago: Year Book Medical Publishers, 1984.

MacNutt, Francis Augustus. *De Orbe Novo, the Eight Decades of
    Peter Martyr d'Anghiera*. Translated from Latin with notes
    and introduction. 2 vols. New York and London: 1912.

Makenson, Maude. *The Book of the Jaguar Priest*. New York: 1951.

Mason, J. Alden. *The Ancient Civilizations of Peru*. Baltimore:
    Penguin, 1957.

McConkie, Bruce R. *A New Witness for the Articles of Faith*. Salt
    Lake City: Deseret Book Company, 1985.

Meggers, Betty J. "Transpacific Origin of Mesoamerican Civilization: A
    Preliminary Review of the Evidence and Its Theoretical
    Implications." *American Anthropologist*. No. 77 (1975): 1–27.

Meservy, Keith H. "Discoveries at Nimrud and the 'Sticks' of
    Ezekiel 37." *Newsletter and Proceedings of the Society for
    Early Historic Archaeology*. No. 142 (1978): 1–10.

Meyers, Carol L. *The Tabernacle Menorah: A Systematic Study of a
    Symbol from the Biblical Cult*. Missoula: Scholars, 1976.

Miller, Mary, and Karl Taube. *The Gods and Symbols of Ancient
    Mexico and the Maya*. London: Thames and Hudson, 1993.

Moran, Hugh A., and David H. Kelley. *The Alphabet and the Ancient
    Calendar Signs*. 2nd ed. Palo Alto: Daily Press, 1969.

Morley, Sylvanus G. *The Ancient Maya*. Palo Alto: Stanford
    University Press, 1946.

Morton, William H. "Umm el-Biyara." *Biblical Archaeologist*. 19
    (1956): 26–36.

Moscati, Sabatino. *The Face of the Ancient Orient: A Panorama of
    Near Eastern Civilization in Pre-Classic Times*. Garden
    City: Doubleday, 1962.

Neugebaurer, Otto. *The Exact Sciences in Antiquity*. New York: Harper Toreh Books, 1962.

Nibley, Hugh. *An Approach to the Book of Mormon*. 3rd ed. Salt Lake City and Provo: Deseret Book Company and Foundation for Ancient Research and Mormon Studies, 1988.

————. *Approaching Zion*. Salt Lake City and Provo: Deseret Book Company and Foundation for Ancient Research and Mormon Studies, 1989.

————. *Enoch the Prophet*. Salt Lake City and Provo: Deseret Book Company and Foundation for Ancient Research and Mormon Studies, 1986.

————. *The Prophetic Book of Mormon*. Salt Lake City and Provo: Deseret Book Company and Foundation for Ancient Research and Mormon Studies, 1989.

————. *The World of the Prophets*. Salt Lake City: Deseret Book, 1954.

Noriega, Raul. *Desciframientos de Inscripciones Ciclográficas del México Antiguo*. Mexico: Conferencia de la Asocición Mexicana de Periodistas, 1958.

Norman, V. Garth. *Izapa Sculpture: Text*. Part 2. Papers of the New World Archaeological Foundation, No. 30. Provo, 1976.

————. "Astronomical Orientations of Izapa Sculptures." M.A. thesis, Brigham Young University, 1980.

Oppenheim, A. Leo. "Assyro-Babylonian Religion." *Ancient Religions: A Symposium*. Edited by Vergilius Ferm. New York: Philosophical Library, 1950, 63–79.

Parrot, Andre. *The Arts of Assyria*. New York: Golden Press, 1961.

————. *Sumer: The Dawn of Art*. New York: Golden Press, 1961.

Parsons, Lee Allen. "The Middle American Co-Tradition." Doctoral dissertation. Widener and Peabody Museum Libraries, Harvard University, 1964.

Paterson, Helena. *The Celtic Lunar Zodiac: How to Interpret Your Moon Sign*. St. Paul: Llewellyn Publications, 1998.

Paxton, Merideth. "The Books of Chilam Balam: Astronomical Content and the Paris Codex." *The Sky in Mayan Literature*. Edited by Anthony F. Aveni. New York and Oxford: Oxford University Press, 1992, 216–46.

Percival, Bonnie E. "Tree of Life Symbolism: A Selected Diachronic Analysis." Unpublished ms., Provo, 1984.

Peterson, Frederick. *Ancient Mexico: An Introduction to the Pre-Hispanic Cultures*. New York and London: Putnam's Sons and George Allen and Unwin, 1959.

Pettinato, Giovanni. *The Archives of Ebla: An Empire Inscribed in Clay*. Garden City: Doubleday and Company, 1981.

Porter, Muriel Noe. "Material Preclásico de San Salvador." *Communicaciones del Instituto Tropical de Investigaciones Científicas*. Nos. 3–4, 1955, 105–12.

Pratt, John. "The Restoration of Priesthood Keys on Easter 1836." Parts 1 and 2. *Ensign* (June and July 1985): 59–68; 55–64.

Recinos, Adrian. *Popul Vuh: The Sacred Book of the Ancient Quiche Maya*. English version by Sylvanus G. Morley and Delia Goetz. Norman: University of Oklahoma Press, 1950.

Recinos, Adrian, and Delia Goetz. *The Annals of the Cakchiquels*. Norman: University of Oklahoma Press, 1953.

Reilly, F. Kent III. "Enclosed Ritual Space and the Watery Underworld in Formative Period Architecture: New Observations on the Function of La Venta Complex A." A paper presented at the Séptima Mesa Redonda, Palenque, Chiapas, June 1989.

Reko, Blas P. "The Royal Stars of the Hebrews, Aztecs and Quiches." *El Mexico Antiguo*. Vol. 3, Nos. 3–4: 49–56. Mexico: Sociedad Alemana de Mexicanistas, 1934.

————. "Star-Names of the Chilam Balam of Chumayel." *El Mexico Antiguo*. Vol. 3, Nos. 9–10: 1–52; Nos. 11–12: 13–84; Vol. 4: 21–67, 95–129, 163–78, and 255–83. Mexico: Sociedad Alemana de Mexicanistas, October 1935-May 1939.

Rouse, Irving. *Migrations in Prehistory: Inferring Population Movement from Cultural Remains*. New Haven: Yale University Press, 1986.

Roys, Ralph L. *The Book of Chilam Balam of Chumayel*. Carnegie Institution of Washington. Publication 436. Washington, D.C.: Carnegie Institution of Washington, 1933.

Sahagun, Bernardino de. *Florentine Codex: General History of the Things of New Spain*. Translated from Aztec and Spanish into English by Arthur J. O. Anderson and Charles E. Dibble. Book 1, *The Gods*. Santa Fe: School of American Research and the University of Utah, 1950.

————. Book 6, *Rhetoric and Moral Philosophy*. Santa Fe: School
     of American Research and the University of Utah, 1969.
————. Book 8, *Kings and Lords*. Santa Fe: School of American
     Research and the University of Utah, 1954.
————. Book 10, *The People*. Santa Fe: School of American
     Research and the University of Utah, 1961.
Santillana, Georgio, and Hertha von Deschand. *Hamlet's Mill.*
     Boston: David R. Godine, 1969.
Sauer, Carl O. *Agricultural Origins and Dispersals*. Bowman
     Memorial Series 2. New York: American Geographical
     Society, 1952.
Schele, Linda. *Maya Glyphs: The Verbs*. Austin: University of Texas
     Press, 1982.
Schele, Linda, and David A. Freidel. *A Forest of Kings: The Untold
     Story of the Ancient Maya*. New York: William Morrow, 1990.
Schonberg, S. Kenneth, ed. *Substance Abuse: A Guide for Health
     Professionals*. Elk Grove Village, Illinois: American
     Academy of Pediatrics, 1988.
Shao, Paul. *Chinese Influence in Pre-Columbia American Art*.
     Ames: Iowa State University Press, 1978.
————. *The Origin of Ancient American Cultures*. Ames: Iowa
     State University Press, 1983.
Shearer, Tony. *Beneath the Moon and under the Sun*. Albuquerque:
     Sun Publishing Company, 1975.
Sheets, Payson D. *Archaeology and Volcanism in Central America:
     The Zapotitlan Valley of El Salvador*. Austin: University of
     Texas Press, 1983.
Shook, Edwin M. "Tikal Stela 29." *Expedition* 2 (1960): 29–35.
Smith, Joseph Lindon. *Tombs, Temples, and Ancient Art*. Morman:
     University of Oklahoma Press, 1956.
Smith, Robert F. "Sawi-Zaa Word Comparisons." Unpublished ms.
     September 1977, 1–9.
Solis Alcala, Ermilo. *Diccionario Espanol-Maya*. Merida: Editorial
     Yihal Maya Thon, 1949.
Sorenson, John L. "A Chronological Ordering of the Mesoamerican
     Preclassic." Middle American Research Institute. Vol. 2, No.
     3. New Orleans: Tulane University Press, 1955, 43–68.

————. "The Significance of an Apparent Relationship Between the Ancient Near East and Mesoamerica." *Man Across the Sea: Problems of Pre-Columbian Contacts.* Edited by Carroll L. et al. Austin: University of Texas Press, 1971, 219–41.

————. *An Ancient American Setting for the Book of Mormon.* Salt Lake City: Foundation for Ancient Research and Mormon Studies and Deseret Book, 1985.

Spencer, J. E. and William L. Thomas Jr. *Cultural Geography: An Evolutionary Introduction to Our Humanized Earth.* New York: John Wiley and Sons, 1969.

Sterling, Matthew, ed. *Stone Monuments of Southern Mexico.* Bureau of American Ethnology. Bulletin 138, 1943.

Stoddard, Darrell J. "The Tree of Life Symbol as a Fountain of Living Water." Unpublished ms. Provo, 1968.

Stokes, William Lee. *Joseph Smith and the Creation.* Salt Lake City: Starstone Publishers and Cedar-Fort Incorporated, 1991.

Strong, James. *Hebrew and Chaldee Dictionary.*

Stross, Brian. E-mail correspondence with Bruce Warren, June 1998.

Talmage, James E. *The Vitality of Mormonism: Brief Essays on Distinctive Doctrines of The Church of Jesus Christ of Latter-day Saints.* Boston: R. G. Badger, 1919.

Tax, Sol, ed. *The Civilizations of Ancient America.* Chicago: University of Chicago Press, 1951.

Tedlock, Dennis, trans. *Popol Vuh: The Definitive Edition of the Maya Book of the Dawn of Life and the Glories of Gods and Kings.* New York: Simon and Schuster, 1985.

————. "Myth, Math, and the Problem of Correlation in Maya Books." *The Sky in Mayan Literature.* Edited by Anthony F. Aveni. New York and Oxford: Oxford University Press, 1992.

Thompson, Edward Herbert. *People of the Serpent.* Boston: Houghton Mifflin, 1932.

Thompson, J. Eric S. *Maya Hieroglyphic Writing.* Carnegie Institution of Washington. No. 589. 1950.

————. *The Rise and Fall of Maya Civilization.* Norman: University of Oklahoma Press, 1954.

Torquemada, Juan de. *Monarquia Indígena.* 3 vols. Mexico: Editorial Salvador Chavez Hayhoe (1723), 1943.

Tozzer, Alfred M., trans. *Landa's Relación de las Cosas de Yucatan*. Peabody Museum, Harvard University. Anthropological Ethnological Papers, Vol. 18.

Vaillant, George C. *Artists and Craftsmen in Ancient Central America*. Museum of Natural History, Guide Leaflet Series 88, 1935.

———. *Aztecs of Mexico*. New York: The American Museum of Natural History, 1944.

Ward, William Hayes. *The Seal Cylinders of Western Asia*. Washington, D.C.: The Carnegie Institution of Washington, 1920.

Warren, Bruce W. *BYU Studies*, 30. Summer 1990.

———. "Have Some Maya Scholars Recently Discovered Some Hieroglyphs That Mean 'And It Came to Pass'?" *Newsletter and Proceedings of the Society for Early Historic Archaeology*. No. 164.6, June 1988.

Warren, Bruce W., and Thomas Stuart Ferguson. *The Messiah in Ancient America*. Provo: The Book of Mormon Research Foundation, 1987.

Warren, Bruce W., and John A. Tvedtnes. "In Search of the Historic Nimrod." *Newsletter and Proceedings of the Society for Early Historic Archaeology*. No. 155.0, November 1983.

Warren, Bruce W. and V. Garth Norman. "Christ in Ancient America: Dating History and Tradition." Unpublished ms., 1995.

Watts, Alan Wilson. *Myth and Ritual in Christianity*. London: Thames and Hudson, 1954.

Willetts, William. *Foundations of Chinese Art*. New York: McGraw Hill, 1965.

Wirth, Diane E. *A Challenge to the Critics: Scholarly Evidences of the Book of Mormon*. Bountiful: Horizon Publishers and Distributors, 1986.

———. "Osiris and Hun Hunahpu." *Near Eastern Traditions in Ancient America*. Chapter 2. Unpublished, 1995.

Wolf, Eric R. *The Sons of the Shaking Earth*. Chicago: University of Chicago Press, 1959.

Yorgason, Blaine and Brenton Yorgason. *Spiritual Survival in the Last Days*. Salt Lake City: Deseret Book Company, 1990.

INDEX

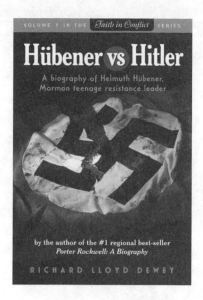

Hübener vs. Hitler
A Biography of Helmuth Hübener,
Mormon Teenage Resistance Leader

by Richard Lloyd Dewey

Nobel laureate author Günther Grass said Hübener's life should be held up as a role model to every teen in the world. Regional best-selling author Richard Lloyd Dewey (*Porter Rockwell: A Biography*) holds up Hübener's life as a light not only to all teens, but to adults as well.

As an active Latter-day Saint, young Hübener recruited his best friends from church and work and established a sophisticated resistance group that baffled the Gestapo, infuriated the Nazi leadership, frustrated the highest judges in the land, and convinced the SS hierarchy that hundreds of adults—not just a handful of determined teens—were involved!

While other books have told the story of the group of freedom fighters Hübener founded, this is the first biography of Hübener himself—the astounding young man who led and animated the group. The inspiring, spell-binding, true story of the youngest resistance leader in Nazi Germany.

Hardcover, $23.95   ISBN: 0-929753-13-5

Look for it in your favorite bookstore,
or to obtain autographed copies, see last page.

Porter Rockwell: A Biography

by Richard Lloyd Dewey

T he epic biography that traces Porter Rockwell from turbulent
Eastern beginnings to battles with Midwestern mobs to extra-
ordinary gunfights on the American frontier. Quotes hundreds of
journals, letters, and court records. Illustrated by western artist, Clark
Kelley Price.

Hardcover, $22.95   ISBN: 0-9616024-0-6

Look for it in your favorite bookstore,
or to obtain autographed copies, see last page.

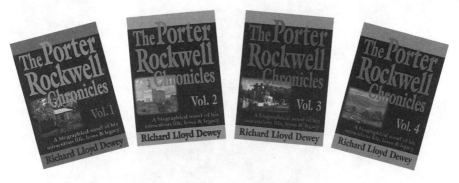

The Porter Rockwell Chronicles

by Richard Lloyd Dewey

This best-selling, historically accurate biographical novel series renders Porter's life in riveting story form, bringing it alive for adults and teens alike.

Volume 1 begins with his childhood years in New York where he becomes best friends with the future Mormon prophet Joseph Smith. The story continues through Porter's settlement with the Mormons in Missouri, where he fights against mobs and falls in love with and marries Luana Beebe.

Volume 2 covers the turbulent first four years in Nauvoo, where he continues to fight mobs and becomes Joseph Smith's bodyguard.

The Nauvoo period of his life draws to a close in Volume 3 as his best friend Joseph is murdered and his wife Luana leaves him and remarries, taking his beloved daughter Emily with her. Porter must bid a heartbroken farewell as he and the Mormons are driven from Nauvoo and flee west.

Volume 4 continues with his first ten years in Utah, where he is joyously reunited with his daughter Emily, takes on the U.S. Army in a guerilla war, and enters a new phase of adventures as U.S. Deputy Marshal.

Volume 1 (ISBN: 0-9616024-6-5)   Hardcover, $23.88
Volume 2 (ISBN: 0-9616024-7-3)   Hardcover, $23.88
Volume 3 (ISBN: 0-9616024-8-1)   Hardcover, $23.88
Volume 4 (ISBN: 0-9616024-9-X)   Hardcover, $24.88

Look for them in your favorite bookstore,
or to obtain autographed copies, see last page.

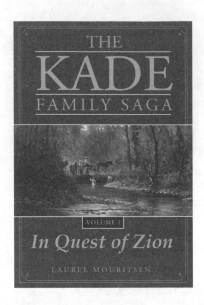

The Kade Family Saga, Volume 1:
In Quest of Zion

by Laurel Mouritsen

Sure to delight *The Work and the Glory* fans, the *Kade Family Saga* series of historical novels is steeped in likeable, life-like characters in the fictional story of the Kade family and their adventures spanning from Missouri to the Great Salt Lake basin.

In Volume 1, *In Quest of Zion*, we are introduced to the much-travailed Lydia Dawson, who meets the intriguing Mr. Kade, who writes for *The Evening and the Morning Star*—controversial newspaper for the Mormons, who have recently arrived in Missouri. The reader is pulled into their lives as they endure persecution, physical confrontations with enemies, and eventually deadly battles. The external threats are only half the story, though, as they struggle simultaneously with the emotional conflicts in their relationships.

Told with the skill of a masterful storyteller against a historically accurate backdrop, this story is at once exciting, heart-wrenching, and very satisfying.

Hardcover, $19.95   ISBN: 0-929753-07-0

*Look for it in your favorite bookstore,
or for ordering info, see last page.*

Jacob Hamblin:
His Life in His Own Words

Foreword by Richard Lloyd Dewey

Far from the gun-toting reputation of super-lawman Porter Rockwell, Jacob Hamblin was known in early Western history as the supreme peacemaker.

No less exciting than Porter's account, Jacob's adventures encountered apparent Divine intervention at every turn, a reward seemingly bestowed to certain souls given to absolute faith. And in his faith, like Porter, Jacob Hamblin was one of those incredibly rare warriors who are *absolutely fearless.*

His migrations from Ohio to Utah with life-and-death adventures at every turn keep the reader spellbound in this unabridged, autobiographical account of the Old West's most unusual adventurer among Native Americans.

In his own words, Jacob Hamblin bares his soul with no pretense, unveiling an eye-witness journal of pioneer attempts to co-exist peacefully with Native brothers, among whom he traveled unarmed, showing his faith in God that he would not be harmed.

Easily considered the most successful — and bravest — diplomat to venture into hostile territory single-handedly, Hamblin takes the reader into hearts of darkness and hearts of light.

Softcover, $10.95   ISBN: 0-9616024-5-7

Look for it in your favorite bookstore,
or to obtain autographed copies, see last page.

ORDERING INFORMATION

New Evidences of Christ in Ancient America   **$24.95**
by Blaine M. Yorgason, Bruce W. Warren, and Harold Brown.
Hardcover, 430 pp.
ISBN: 0-929753-01-1

Hübener vs Hitler   **$23.95**
A biography of Helmuth Hübener, Mormon teenage resistance leader,
by Richard Lloyd Dewey. Hardcover 606 pp.
ISBN: 0-929753-08-9

Porter Rockwell: A Biography   **$22.95**
by Richard Lloyd Dewey. Hardcover, 612 pp.
ISBN: 0-9616024-0-6

The Porter Rockwell Chronicles, Vol. 1   (Reg. $27.50) **$23.88**
by Richard Lloyd Dewey. Hardcover, 490 pp.
ISBN: 0-9616024-6-5

The Porter Rockwell Chronicles, Vol. 2   (Reg. $27.50) **$23.88**
by Richard Lloyd Dewey. Hardcover, 452 pp.
ISBN: 0-9616024-7-3

The Porter Rockwell Chronicles, Vol. 3   (Reg. $27.95) **$23.88**
by Richard Lloyd Dewey. Hardcover, 527 pp.
ISBN: 0-9616024-8-1

The Porter Rockwell Chronicles, Vol. 4   (Reg. $27.95) **$24.88**
by Richard Lloyd Dewey. Hardcover, 568 pp.
ISBN: 0-9616024-9-X

Porter Rockwell Returns Art Print   **$30.00**
by Clark Kelley Price. 36"w × 24"h, unsigned.
ISBN: 0-929753-0-6

The Kade Family Saga, Volume 1: In Quest of Zion   **$19.95**
by Laurel Mouritsen. Hardcover, 402 pp.
ISBN: 0-929753-07-0

Jacob Hamblin: His Life in His Own Words   **$10.95**
Foreword by Richard Lloyd Dewey. Softcover, 128 pp.
ISBN: 0-9616024-5-7

FREE SHIPPING!
Utah residents, add 6.25% sales tax.

Send check or money order to:
Stratford Books
P.O. Box 1371, Provo, Utah 84603-1371

Prices subject to change.